THE
FILM YEARBOOK

VOLUME 9

THE
FILM YEARBOOK

VOLUME 9

EDITED BY
JAMES PARK

PAN BOOKS
London, Sydney and Auckland

ACKNOWLEDGEMENTS

Thanks to the distributors, publicity companies, publications and individuals who supplied assistance in the preparation of this book:

Artificial Eye, Blue Dolphin, the British Film Institute, Columbia/Tri-Star, Dennis Davidson Associates, Electric Pictures, Enterprise, Entertainment, Guild, ICA Projects, JAC, Mainline, Oasis, Pathé, Rank, Twentieth Century-Fox, Variety, Vestron, Virgin, Warner Bros, Zakiya and Associates

Design by
JERRY GOLDIE

Cover by
JIM STANTON

Published in 1990
by Pan Books
Cavaye Place
London SW10 9PG

8 7 6 5 4 3 2 1

Copyright © James Park 1990

ISBN 0 330 318314 4

Printed and bound in Great Britain by
BPCC Hazel Books
Aylesbury, Bucks
Member of BPCC Ltd

Typeset by AKM Associates (UK) Ltd, Southall

CONTENTS

EDITOR

JAMES PARK is the author of *British Cinema: The Lights That Failed*, and the editor of *Cultural Icons*, a handbook of modern culture, politics, science and everything else. He is currently developing a feature film and researching a book about psychotherapists. This is the fourth time he has edited *The Film Yearbook*.

CONTRIBUTORS

SIMON BANNER is a freelance writer contributing articles to *The Times, 7 Days, You* magazine and the *Independent on Sunday*.

ANNE BILLSON is the film critic of the *Sunday Correspondent*. She has contributed to numerous publications, including *City Limits, Tatler* and *The Times*, and is currently completing her third book – a novel about upwardly-mobile vampires. Her interests include opera, skin diseases and bird-watching.

TONY CRAWLEY is the author of *The Films of Sophia Loren, Bébé: The Films of Brigitte Bardot, Screen Dreams: The Hollywood Pin-Up* and *The Steven Spielberg Story*. He has written on films for publication throughout the world and now lives in France, where he has a franglais rock radio show and has co-authored *Entre Deux Censures*.

STEPHEN DARK is a journalist who writes about the media, property and finance.

RAYMOND DURGNAT is a writer and lecturer on films and cultural history. Co-author of *King Vidor, American*, his next book will be *Michael Powell and the British Genius*. He has been a visiting professor at UCLA, Columbia, Dartmouth College, Oklahoma and elsewhere, as well as a staff writer at Elstree Studios in the good old days of Pathe News.

GRAHAM FULLER is senior editor at *Interview* magazine in New York. He also writes on film for the *Listener* and has contributed to the *Independent*, the *Guardian, Village Voice, American Film, Film Comment, Premiere* and *Sight and Sound*.

TIMOTHY GEE became enthusiastic about movies after seeing *Mrs Wiggs of the Cabbage Patch*. In 1960 he started working in the British film industry. He has edited films for Ken Russell (*Salomé's Last Dance*), Bryan Forbes (*The Raging Moon, The Stepford Wives, The Slipper and the Rose*) and Desmond Davis (*Clash of the Titans, The Country Girls* and *Ordeal by Innocence*).

PHIL HARDY is a cultural historian who is currently working on a major book on Crime in the Movies. His most recent publication was the *Faber Companion to Popular Music of the Twentieth Century*. A warm and wonderful human being, he lives amongst the rolling hills of North London.

JOHN HARKNESS is the film critic of Toronto's *NOW* magazine, and has been since the magazine's inception in 1981. His articles have appeared in *Sight and Sound, CineFile* and *Cinema Canada. The Word, The Flesh and David Cronenberg* was anthologized in *The Shape of Rage: The Films of David Cronenberg*. He is not working on a screenplay.

ANDREW KELLY is a film historian. His book on the anti-war cinema of World War 1 will be published next year. He is currently finalizing another book, on the making of *All Quiet on the Western Front*.

HARLAN KENNEDY is the European editor of *Film Comment*. He is a member of the Critics' Circle and of FIPRESCI, the international federation of film critics. For four years he was the London contributing editor of *American Film*, and he now writes frequently for *Emmy* magazine, *American Cinematographer* and the *New York Times*.

GREGG KILDAY, a senior writer for *Entertainment Weekly*, is based in Los Angeles where he reports on the film industry.

KIM NEWMAN is the author of *Nightmare Movies* and *Wild West Movies*. His second novel, *Bad Dreams*, was published recently. Writing as Jack Yeovil, he is the author of *Demon Download, Bloody Students, Krokodil Tears, Comeback Tour* and *Best in Velvet*, among others. He also writes regularly for the *Monthly Film Bulletin* and has a early-morning TV slot on Channel Four.

TIM PULLEINE is deputy film editor of the *Guardian*. He contributes reviews and articles to various publications, including *Sight and Sound* and *Monthly Film Bulletir*

DAVID THOMPSON is an arts producer for BBC TV, and produced the *Film Club* series. He is also a freelance journalist, writing for *Time Out*, the *Correspondent* and the *Independent*. A former programmer of the Electric Cinema, he co-edited *Scorsese on Scorsese*.

TREVOR WILLSMER started his career as an ice-cream salesman at the Kingston Granada. Following the publication and subsequent pulping of his first novel, *Jessie*, he formed Lone Wolf Productions, through which he has produced and directed a series of short films. He also runs an 8mm film distribution company.

SHATTERED MOVIES

'**G**et ready for the ride of your life,' reads the British poster for *Total Recall*, echoing the ambition of most movies today. Their aim is to put audiences on a rollercoaster for two hours, whizzing them rapidly through movie pyrotechnics and leaving them no opportunity to reflect on what's passing before their eyes. And when it's all over they'll emerge dazed, stunned and – all too often – feeling a little empty.

If movies go at such a pace nowadays it may be because their makers want to cover up the fact that the bits no longer fit together. Great performances, wizard art direction, stunning costumes, impressive special effects – but it's not enough to make a great movie. Too rarely is there a theme to knit the pieces into a whole, or even much of a story to get the audience involved with what's happening on the screen.

The 'big' idea of today's movies is that America's inner cities are tumbling into decay, taken over by criminal hoodlums dispensing death and drugs. That's the background to *Batman* and *Dick Tracy*, *Total Recall* and *RoboCop II*, in each of which a superhero comes to clean up the mess created by big business, of the conglomerate or criminal variety. But you won't find the sort of deep resonances in these movies that would make them touch people's real fears and anxieties.

Every element on these pictures is honed to expensive perfection, but there's an underlying assumption that it doesn't matter if the elements don't hang together, as long as they stun the audience, and provide promotable trailers, commercials and in-store merchandising.

Hollywood executives don't seem to care if their films have anything to say, as long as they've got what it takes to get people into the cinema. And what that involves is offering enough for audiences to talk about: people will talk about the budget, the sets, the performances and the opticals even though they hated the overall experience – indeed they'll talk about them even if they haven't seen the movie.

While it may be a great time for some screenwriters' bank balances, it's a terrible time for the craft of screenwriting. Because when the film is being primed for blockbusterdom, no-one worries about characterization or narrative consistency. There are scenes in every big movie made today whose only function is to keep the audience awake. And the most common dilemma in today's films is that which confronts Doug Quaid in *Total Recall*: which version of myself am I?;

or RoboCop: am I man or machine and, if I'm a machine, who wrote my programme?

When movies had some connection to what was happening in the world, filmmakers wanted audiences to care about the characters on the screen. But now that they're derived from comic strips and past movies, nobody can be bothered with the effort this entails. In *Dick Tracy*, for example, there's no attempt to paint in motivation for the lead character's desire to clean up the streets, nor is his shyness with girls turned into anything more than a sly in-joke. As a result, Warren Beatty stumbles through the movie in his wretched yellow coat looking more like a statue against a stunning backdrop than a character, even a cartoon character.

The explanation for these fragmented, disjointed movies is to be found in the studios' success in recovering control of the production process, so that the process of movie production increasingly approximates what happened when Hollywood made *The Wizard of Oz* or *Gone With the Wind*; the stakes are too high now to leave filmmaking in the hands of tetchy, erratic writers and directors. But while it's fair enough to write books about the Genius of the old System, the moguls of old had a concern for storytelling that seems completely lacking in today's cynical generation.

You could argue that these movies reflect the real state of the world today. How could films resemble anything other than a string of commercials when consumerism is the prevailing value, and it is advertising art that makes the strongest impact on our eyes and brains? How can movies be expected to expound a moral framework when there are no longer fixed value systems by which people can organize their lives. In such sick and schizophrenic times, what's the point of talking about authentic emotion?

After all, the studio head might observe, when serious, old-fashioned pictures do get made, of the sort exemplified by a film like *Clean and Sober*, it's tough getting audiences interested. To prevent the smaller pictures from looking too much like television, their makers are now forced to lay over them some sort of gimmick (*Look Who's Talking*), expensive high-gloss (*Revenge*), the kind of sentimentality that turns the touching and intimate into soggy goo (*Steel Magnolias, Dad*), or the easy endings of false sentiment that mar the third act of films such as *Dead Poets Society* or *Fat Man and Little Boy*.

But none of that is justification for the course being adopted by today's movie moguls. For if films are going to cost ever more in order to attract audience attention, then there's a danger that a handful of big flops will make the game no longer worth playing. And whether you blame the current state of cinema on the times or on television, if movies can no longer say anything significant about the culture in which they're made, then the medium must eventually succumb to its own irrelevance. And then again, if a sentimental, old-fashioned film like *Driving Miss Daisy* can gross over $100 million, who's to say that there aren't other approaches to cinema that could find an audience, even though they buck the contemporary trend. American cinema is certainly in need of some new ideas.

JAMES PARK

THE STARS DO SHTIK

J ack Nicholson sports a rictus grin and vaudeville cackle in *Batman*. Meryl Streep swathes herself in cod-romantic graces in *She-Devil*. Clint Eastwood does a feature-length John Huston imitation in *White Hunter, Black Heart*. Tom Cruise signs on for balding wig and wheelchair in *Born on the Fourth of July*. Mickey Rourke breaks out the Quasimodo make-up kit for *Johnny Handsome*. Paul Newman acts the Southern Buffoon as randy ol' Earl Long in *Blaze*. Al Pacino and Dustin Hoffman reach for the face putty and funny voices in *Dick Tracy*.

What ever is going on? Suddenly the stars are doing shtik, and vaudeville is the flavour of the acting season. If Jimmy Durante were alive today, there would be no room for him in Hollywood. The straight stars are doing all the music-hall material themselves.

The star system is a strange and wonderful thing. Many years ago, film-goers could look up into a night sky undimmed by the lights of oversize cities on earth (or the competing radiance of rival audiovisual entertainment systems) and see their stars brightly, steadfastly glow. Back then, film stars seldom changed. Bette Davis was Bette Davis, whatever the rôle. Humphrey Bogart was Humphrey Bogart, whatever the game or dame. And Gary Cooper, whether playing comedy for Capra, kitsch for Sternberg or cowboys for Mann and Zinnemann, was Gary Cooper.

. . . .

If Jimmy Durante were alive today, there would be no room for him in Hollywood. The straight stars are doing all the music-hall material themselves.

. . . .

The few stars back then who had special licences as character actors, like Charles Laughton, were the rule-proving exception. They were jesters in the court of stardom. They set off the fixed and jewelled perfection of the true royal family.

But stardom has gone through changes in recent years, and never more swiftly than in the last twelve months. To be a star today, you must climb aboard the Chameleon Express. Here, in special high-speed changing-rooms, you must be ready to step out at your next station almost totally unrecognizable. Oh Mr Hoffman, we were expecting an autistic savant, but my goodness you seem to be a heavily made-up comic-strip villain called Mumbles. And Mr Heston – it is Mr Heston, isn't it? I couldn't remember if you were wearing that parrot and wooden leg when you brought the tablets down from Mount Sinai. And what an interesting accent. Cornish?

Frightening times when a movie star, once a paragon of changeless luminosity, turns into the most stroboscopic creature under the sun.

Why is all this happening now? One precipitating factor – perhaps the main one – is that a cinema going through an identity crisis has communicated its anxiety to its players. Movie stars are putting on funny voices and funny walks, and enrolling for night classes in prosthetics, because time and fashion have knocked out many of the rôles in which an actor could once coast along on personal charisma.

. . . .

A cinema going through an identity crisis has communicated its anxiety to its players

. . . .

Time, fashion and television. Uncluttered humanist genres that were once the provinces of cinema, like romantic drama and realist comedy, are increasingly being requisitioned by soap opera and sitcom. It's the latest phase in the long-running, big-screen/small-screen war. When TV holds the monopoly on stars who never change, from Roseanne Barr to Don Johnson, what can the cinema do but develop a breed of stars who can change like crazy and still remain stars? (Just how diffferent the two worlds are becoming is shown by Miss Barr's own recent sortie into movies with *She-Devil*. The goddess of small-screen normalcy, transported to the kingdom of large-screen lunacy, looks as lost and out of place as a french fry in a wedding cake.)

Nor – worse news for the cinema – is television merely appropriating realism. With the super-soap era ushered in by *Dallas* and *Dynasty*, TV has shown it has imperialist designs on melodrama too. It has begun developing its own special line in baddies and goodies, in preposterous plots and Technicolor story twists.

It's this regular upping of the ante by TV that is sending the cinema, anxious to keep or create its own corner of the screen-entertainment market, spinning into ever higher stratospheres of desperate invention. When even melodrama is part-owned by the small screen, what can the large screen do but go one, or two, or three, better?

Enter shtik and super-shtik. Today, it's not enough for an adventure hero to be an adventure hero. Like Harrison Ford's Indiana Jones, he must wink and nod and wisecrack; he must behave as if the only thing lacking in his expressive equipment is speech balloons. And in a cinema where the hijacked calligraphy of the comic-strip has become one way to show how much brighter and more kinetic the large

A turtle?
You gotta be joking.

screen can be than the small, the screen must fill up with hyperbolic villains too.

In the old days, to have coated a star like Al Pacino, Dustin Hoffman or Jack Nicholson with feature-disguising make-up, and then made him scamper about with a funny voice, would have seemed like *lèse-majesté* at best, box-office madness at worst. (People buy tickets to see and hear their idols, don't they? They don't want to play hunt-the-star under a carapace of tics and mannerisms.) But today the star is a sport who will try anything. Indeed he *has* to try anything if he wants to stay at the top.

One suspected the onset of this *Zeitgeist* as long ago as the year of *Out of Africa*. In that movie Robert Redford refused to make any concession to disguise. Redford's determination to be Robert Redford, even though he was supposed to be playing a balding upper-crust Englishman, suddenly seemed like a performance from another aeon. While La Streep went into her state-of-the-art transports with accents and gestures and emotions, here was Redford as glamorous, impassive and obdurately changeless as ever. We might well have been watching Ronald Colman in *Lost Horizons*.

Another factor in the forced chameleonization of today's stars is that the public gets enough of the celebrity him or herself on TV chat shows and their ilk. Who wants to go to a movie to see Tom Cruise just being Tom Cruise, or Sally Field being Sally Field, or Mickey Rourke being Mickey Rourke, when they can see those things every day on *Entertainment USA* or the Johnny Carson show? To win new admirers and keep their old ones, Cruise must show willing when offered a wig-and-wheelchair rôle, Field must do a whole lot of Southern shtik in *Steel Magnolias* and Rourke must be gangsterdom's answer to the Elephant Man in *Johnny Handsome*.

No star today is proof against the mandate to 'be someone else'. If he resists the call, he is doomed. Burt Reynolds, never anything but amiable Burt Reynolds, has vanished from sight as a box-office contender. Jane Fonda, seldom anything but tautly idealistic Jane Fonda, has appeared in one box-office misfire after another. And Clint Eastwood, realizing he'd better look for an alternative vessel to the leaky lifeboat of the 'Dirty Harry' series, has leaped belatedly and unconvincingly towards the Good Ship Shtik. In *White Hunter, Black Heart* he plays John Huston as if he hated ever minute of it.

· ·

No star today is proof against the mandate to 'be someone else'.
If he resists the call, he is doomed.

· ·

Stars like this, who resist or resent the call to metamorphosis, are falling into Hollywood's out tray as surely as disguise-loving stars – or even stuntmen in animal suits (see *Teenage Mutant Ninja Turtles*) – win fans and influence movie trends. It is a strange time when an actor like William Hurt quits his Hamlet-like solemnity to play a ho-ho nutcase murderer in a Lawrence Kasdan black comedy (*I Love You to Death*); when Robert De Niro mugs and wumps as a convict in priest's garb in *We're No Angels*; or when Bruce Willis, insecure even after the he-man successes of *Die Hards 1 & 2*, decides to keep his career on the boil by playing a namby-pamby Englishman in *The Bonfire of the Vanities*.

The old verities about a star never changing his image have been put into spectacular reverse. Now the command is: 'Never be the same in two films running.' The increasing autonomy of the film stars, no longer the creatures of their contract studios, means that they run their own lives and careers; and in many instances they cultivate a public presence outside movies almost as prominent as their presence inside them. When we are not watching William Hurt expose his private life in a (yes, real!) televised court trial, we can tune in to Richard Gere talking about the Dalai Lama, Paul Newman selling mayonnaise or Rob Lowe in 'homevideos we never showed the children'. Last April we could even watch every star in the Hollywood firmament join hands on TV to radiate ecological messages in an Earth Day Telethon.

No wonder the stars try to be different when they appear on the movie screen. They probably realize we're up-to-here with them being themselves on the TV screen or cause-of-the-day platforms. The only stars today who can't or won't change from film to film are the ones who are walking embodiments of shtik already. We mean the comic-strip hulks and avengers whose whole *raison d'être* is to be impregnable and unchanging. Just as the character-actor star was the rule-proving exception in old Hollywood, so in the new Hollywood of 'All change, please', the Schwarzeneggers and Stallones are the stay-the-same aberrations proving a protean norm.

It's a strange time to be alive and movie-addicted. Perhaps the 1990s will continue the trend towards metamorphic megastars; perhaps the decade will put it in turnaround. Either way, the $64 million existential question is: how much monkeying around can a star do with his own persona and still remain, steadfastly and unassailably, a star? It is a question John Huston aired 30 years ago in *The List of Adrian Messenger*, when a galactic cast (Lancaster, Douglas, Sinatra, Mitchum, Curtis) ran around in impenetrable masks. It is also a new phrasing of that deathless philosophical conundrum: 'What is a horse?' Defined in the dictionary as as graminivorous quadruped, is a horse still a horse if it loses one of its legs and stops eating grass?

Keep watching the skies – or the Hollywood pastures.

HARLAN KENNEDY

FILMMAKERS' CHOICE

MICHAEL RADFORD *(White Mischief, 1984)*

Crimes and Misdemeanors – The first Woody Allen I've seen which attempted to deal with human nature beyond the level of a sophisticated gag.
Drugstore Cowboy – For William Burroughs' acting, and the refreshing lack of mechanistic plot.
Parenthood – Not great shakes but it did make me laugh.
Sweetie – An Australian *auteur* – no mean feat.
Time of the Gypsies – Effectively and beautifully played, thoughtful and poetic. Has remained with me longer than any other film this year.

COLIN VAINES (Enigma Productions)

I found it hard to get particularly enthusiastic about anything I saw in the past twelve months. My choice in a lean year:
Dead Poets Society – Slightly bland but Robin Williams is terrific.
Field of Dreams – I'm a real sucker for all those old, schmaltzy, slightly kitsch Hollywood fantasies about ghosts, second chances, etc.
Jesus of Montreal – For its cool wit and sophistication.
Life and Nothing But – A towering performance from Philippe Noiret.
My Left Foot – Not particularly cinematic, but boasting superb performances and a moving story.
sex, lies and videotape – The film that proves wit and style are more important than mega-bucks for a successful and engaging movie.
Sweetie – Mike Leigh meets David Lynch in a film that marks Jane Campion as one of the brightest young directing talents around.

After that, my choices are things of shreds and patches:
When Harry Met Sally – The fake orgasm scene.
The Fabulous Baker Boys – A slightly pedestrian movie, apart from the chemistry between Jeff and Beau Bridges, and Michelle Pfeiffer's incredible sexiness.
The Hunt for Red October – For Sean Connery's toupée.

CLIVE PARSONS (Film and General Productions)

. . . .

A disappointing year, and it wasn't difficult to narrow my choice down to ten:

The Bear
Born on the Fourth of July
Bull Durham
Cinema Paradiso
Crimes and Misdemeanors
Do the Right Thing
The Fabulous Baker Boys
Henry V
Jesus of Montreal
sex, lies and videotape

MARK SHIVAS (BBC Films)

. . . .

Cinema Paradiso
Crimes and Misdemeanors
Dead Poets Society
The Fabulous Baker Boys
Field of Dreams
Jesus of Montreal
sex, lies and videotape
Krzysztof Kieslowski's Decalogue
When Harry Met Sally

THE YEARBOOK CHECKLIST

FILMS OF THE YEAR
Cinema Paradiso
Crimes and Misdemeanors
Drugstore Cowboy
Enemies, A Love Story
Field of Dreams
Glory
Monkey Shines
Monsieur Hire
Road House
Sea of Love
sex, lies and videotape
Sweetie

HITS OF THE YEAR
Born on the Fourth of July
Driving Miss Daisy
Teenage Mutant Ninja Turtles
Total Recall
The War of the Roses

DISAPPOINTMENTS OF THE YEAR
Dead Poets Society
Dick Tracy
Fat Man and Little Boy
My Left Foot
Strapless

TURKEYS OF THE YEAR
The Abyss
Bert Rigby, You're a Fool
Chicago Joe and the Showgirl
Look Who's Talking
Old Gringo
Revenge
She-Devil
Valmont

👍 FILMS TO LOOK FOR
Batman
Blue Steel

A City of Sadness
Clean and Sober
The Cook the Thief his Wife and
  her Lover
Dead Calm
Encounter at Raven's Gate
The Fabulous Baker Boys
Fellow Traveller
Gremlins 2: The New Batch
Heathers
Henry V
Henry . . . Portrait of a Serial Killer
Honey, I Shrunk the Kids
Internal Affairs
Jesus of Montreal
The Kill-Off
The Krays
Last Exit to Brooklyn
Life and Nothing But
Melancholia
Miami Blues
Music Box
Mystery Train
Pathfinder
Pet Sematary
Piravi
The Plot Against Harry
Powwow Highway
Queen of Hearts
Reefer and the Model
Roger & Me
Rouge
Scenes from the Class Struggle in
  Beverley Hills
Shirley Valentine
A Short Film About Killing
A Short Film About Love
Sisters
Staying Together
Talk Radio
True Love
Uncle Buck
The Vanishing

When Harry Met Sally
The Witches
Yaaba

👎 FILMS TO AVOID

Another 48 Hours
Best of the Best
Bill and Ted's Excellent Adventure
Bird on a Wire
Black Rain
The Blood of Heroes
Chattahoochee
Checking Out
A Chorus of Disapproval
Conquest of the South Pole
Cookie
Coupe de Ville
Dad
Dealers
The Delinquents
Diamond Skulls
The Dream Team
El Dorado
Erik the Viking
Everybody Wins
Family Business
Far Out Man
The Fourth War
Fresh Horses
Friday the 13th VIII: Jason Takes
    Manhattan
Gleaming the Cube
Halloween 4: The Return of
    Michael Myers
The Handmaid's Tale

Harlem Nights
Homeboy
Ladder of Swords
Limit Up
Little Monsters
Loose Cannons
Mack the Knife
Millenium
My First Forty Years
Nightbread
Nuns on the Run
Opportunity Knocks
Phantom of the Opera
Rabid Grannies
The Rachel Papers
The Return of the Musketeers
The Return of the Swamp Thing
The Revolving Doors
Rude Awakening
See You in the Morning
A Shock to the System
Ski Patrol
Spaced Invaders
Star Trek V: The Final Frontier
Steel Magnolias
Stella
Tank Malling
To Kill a Priest
Two Moon Junction
Weekend at Bernie's
We're No Angels
When I Fall in Love
Where the Heart Is
Wild Orchid

THE FILMS
1 July 1989 – 30 June 1990

Short reviews by Kim Newman, Tim Pulleine, James Park,
John Harkness, Harlan Kennedy, Graham Fuller, Trevor Willsmer,
Cameron Bailey, David Thompson

THE ABYSS

TURKEY • TURKEY • TURKEY

Director James Cameron **producer** Gale Anne Hurd **camera** Mikael Salomon, Dennis Skotak **editor** Joel Goodman **design** Leslie Dilley **sfx** Laura Buff, Dream Quest Images, ILM, Fantasy II Film Effects **music** Alan Silvestri **cast** Ed Harris, Mary Elizabeth Mastrantonio, Michael Biehn, Leo Burmester, Todd Graff, John Bedford Lloyd, J. C. Quinn, Kimberly Scott, Captain Kidd Brewer Jr., George Robert Klek, Christopher Murphy, Adam Nelson
Running time: 139 mins
US release: Fox, Aug 9, 1989
UK release: Fox, Oct 13, 1989

ALL DOGS GO TO HEAVEN

Don Bluth's latest attempt at capturing the kiddie cartoon market is an improvement over the cuddly dinosaurs of *The Land Before Time*, but it still doesn't really click. An animal reworking of 1940s fantasy comedy dramas like *Angel on My Shoulder* or *Here Comes Mr Jordan*, the film has a German Shepherd called Charlie (voiced by Burt Reynolds) breaking out of the New Orleans dog pound in the 1930s and being rubbed out by his gangster partner 'Carface'. Charlie, like all dogs, goes to Heaven and meets a whippet angel at the Pearly Gates, but insists that he be allowed to return to life in order to finish some business. Following some strained plot contrivances, he is given another chance. Back on Earth, Charlie returns to his old ways but gradually discovers the appeal of goodness and icky stuff like that by associating with a large-eyed, very Disneyish orphan girl. The film seems to have been assembled by giving twenty different teams five minutes each to animate and then not letting them communicate with each other. The plot proceeds by fits and starts, and impressive bits are dropped in at random among the usual cutesy crudola. **KN**
Director Don Bluth **producers** Bluth, Gary Goldman, John Pomeroy **execs** George A. Walker, Morris F. Sullivan **script** David N. Weiss **camera**

Ciaran Morris, Jim Mann **editors** John K. Carr, Lisa Dorney **design** Bluth, Larry Leker **music** Ralph Burns **voices** Burt Reynolds, Vic Tayback, Judith Barsi, Dom De Luise, Loni Anderson, Melba Moore, Charles Nelson Reilly, Daryl Gilley, Candy Devine, Rob Fuller, Earleen Carey
Running time: 85 mins
US release: UA, Nov 17, 1989
UK release: Rank, Apr 6, 1990

ALWAYS

Even for Steven Spielberg, *Always* is an unfashionably lush and romantic movie, with heroically killed fire-fighting pilot Richard Dreyfuss returning from an after-life run by a still-elfin Audrey Hepburn to help handsome foul-up Brad Johnson become a real hero and incidentally get off with Holly Hunter. It's a pretty seamless piece of romantic entertainment, with the three principals deftly playing off the comedy and the smooching stuff in between the regulation aerial action scenes. Dreyfuss seizes the chance to play a complex light leading rôle, Hunter duly glows as the spunky air traffic controller who runs the show and John Goodman does some top-flight support as the hero's best buddy. An apparently effortless 'small' picture, indulging Spielberg's love for airplanes and whimsy, this failed to become a blockbuster, despite its huge budget, perhaps because the money was spent on effects so simple that they become invisible. **KN**
Director Steven Spielberg **producers** Spielberg, Frank Marshall, Kathleen Kennedy **script** Jerry Belson, Diane Thomas, from 1944 movie A Guy Named Joe by Dalton Trumbo **camera** Mikael Salomon **editor** Michael Kahn **design** James Bissell **sfx** Bruce Nicholson, ILM **music** John Williams **cast** Richard Dreyfuss, Holly Hunter, Brad Johnson, John Goodman, Audrey Hepburn, Roberts Blossom, Keith David, Ed Van Nuys, Marg Helgenberger, Doug McGrath, J. D. Souther
Running time: 123 mins
US release: Universal, Dec 22, 1989
UK release: UIP, Mar 23, 1990

AMERICAN STORIES
(Histoires d'Amérique: Food, Family and Philosophy)

It's no accident that Akerman directed the 'Sloth' segment in *The Seven Deadly Sins* – one feels on the evidence in this film that she's not above releasing audition tapes. Unedited! *American Stories* is a document of exile, based on the stories of Jews who arrived in New York during the nineteenth century and interspersed with amateurish Yiddish vaudeville routines, presented square on to the camera by actors who seem to have been requested to play dead. One can see the appeal of this material to the director (the Belgian child of Polish Jews), and there's a goofy charm on display, but Akerman's refusal to shape the material or the performances is an abdication of the artist's job. **JH**
Director/script *Chantal Akerman* **producer** *Bertrand van Effenterre* **execs** *Effenterre, Marilyn Watelet* **camera** *Luc Ben Hamou* **editor** *Patrick Mimouni* **design** *Marilyn Watelet* **cast** *Various*
Running time: 95 mins
UK release: Metro, Jan 12, 1990

AMSTERDAMNED

There's a psychopathic skindiver at large on the canals of Amsterdam, slaughtering at random and defying the police. Inspector Visser (Stapel), a cop with a neo-beard and a leather jacket, is put on the case, and divides his time between autopsies, cynical dialogue and romancing a museum attendant. Dick Maas, who made *The Lift*, was obviously charged by the Dutch tourist board with getting as much of Amsterdam on screen as possible. He doesn't manage to work in any tulips, but does offer a windmill scene, some Flemish old masters, lots of canals and discreet footage of the red-light district. The identity of the killer is a shade guessable, and some characters persist in doing silly things to keep the suspense up, but there is enough straight action to make up for those lapses. The powerboat chase alone is worth the price of admission, but there's also a car chase, some prowling in the sewers, a nasty trick with a speargun and a good bit of wino-drowning to keep up attention. **KN**
Director/script *Dick Maas* **producers** *Laurens Geels, Maas* **exec** *Geels* **camera** *Marc Felperlaan* **editor** *Hans Van Dongen* **design** *Dick Schillemans* **music** *Maas* **cast** *Huub Stapel, Monique van de Ven, Hidde Maas, Serge-Henri Valcke, Tannek Hartsuiker, Wim Zomer, Hidde Maas, Lou Landré*
Running time: 113 mins
US release: Vestron, Nov 23, 1988
UK release: Vestron, Jul 21, 1989

ANOTHER 48 HOURS

Violent, trashy and stupid, *Another 48 Hours* reunites the original cast and director to recreate the best sequences of the first film and milk the audience of cash. There is a chase/shootout involving a bus, a gunfight in a sleazy Chinatown hotel and a scene in a redneck bar . . . does this all sound familiar? A whore's movie at best, *Another 48 Hours* is Walter Hill's worst ever film. Yes, it's even worse than *Brewster's Millions*. **JH**
Director *Walter Hill* **producers** *Lawrence Gordon, Robert D. Wachs* **execs** *Mark Lipsky, Ralph S. Singleton* **script** *John Fasano, Jeb Stuart, Larry Gross* **camera** *Matthew F. Leonetti* **editors** *Freeman Davies, Carmel Davies* **design** *Joseph C. Nemec III* **music** *James Horner* **cast** *Eddie Murphy, Nick Nolte, Brion James, Kevin Tighe, Ed O'Ross, David Anthony Marshall, Andrew Divoff, Bernie Casey, Brent Jennings, Ted Markland, Tisha Campbell*
Running time: 95 mins
US release: Paramount, Jun 8, 1990

ANOTHER WOMAN

Woody Allen hits the psychodrama trail again. His third 'serious' film resembles a blind date between Ingmar Bergman and Anton Chekhov. An ageing university teacher Gena Rowlands has a mid-life crisis right there in front of us – her marriage is on the rocks, her belief in reason and the intellect likewise – an army of stars rally round to cluck or comfort, including Gene Hackman, Mia Farrow, Sandy Dennis and John Houseman. As with *Interiors* and *September*, the film is more like a sixth-form essay on Great Art than an example of it. But at least the cast ensure some flammable moments, and it's quite short. **HK**
Director/script *Woody Allen* **producer** *Robert Greenhut* **execs** *Jack Rollins, Charles H. Joffe* **camera** *Sven Nykvist* **editor** *Susan E. Morse* **design** *Santo Loquasto* **cast** *Gena Rowlands, Mia Farrow, Ian Holm, Blythe Danner, Gene Hackman, Betty Buckley, Martha Plimpton, John Houseman, Sandy Dennis, David Ogden Stiers, Philip Bosco, Harris Yulin, Frances Conroy*
Running time: 81 mins
US release: Orion, Oct 14, 1988
UK release: Rank, Jul 28, 1989

APARTMENT ZERO

In Buenos Aires, mother-dominated Anglo-Argentine Colin Firth, who manages a repertory cinema, takes in brash American Hart Bochner as a tenant, and then gradually realizes that the charming young man is in fact a mad killer, late of the military dictatorship's death squads. Firth, a repressed, spinsterish individual, becomes fascinated with Bochner, and eventually collaborates with him in the disposal of a corpse. He transforms himself, after Bochner's death, into another psychopath, preserving his dead friend's body for company in the flat, and dressing up in leathers to walk the night. *Apartment Zero* is an extended, fairly dreary psycho-thriller, caught somewhere between whimsy and meanness, in which the edgy performances don't make up for the attenuated storyline. Peculiarly, the film was subjected to an almost instant Hollywood remake, *Bad Influence*, with James Spader and Rob Lowe taking over from Firth and Bochner. **KN**

Director *Martin Donovan* **producers/script** *Donovan, David Koepp* **camera** *Miguel Rodriquez* **editor** *Conrad M. Gonzalez* **design** *Miguel Angel Lumaldo* **music** *Elia Cmiral* **cast** *Colin Firth, Hart Bochner, Dora Bryan, Liz Smith, Fabrizio Bentivoglio, James Telfer, Mirella D'Angelo*
Running time: 125 mins
US release: Skouras, Oct 18, 1989
UK release: Mainline, Sept 15, 1989

ARIEL

A curious mélange of road movie and predictable melodrama, coupled with intimations of anti-realism in the manner of early Godard, Kaurismäki's film has vigour and commendable economy. But the blackly comic series of accidents befalling a redundant worker and his girlfriend, caught up with crooks and vindictive officialdom, increasingly falls victim to contrivance, while the upbeat conclusion of their escape to a new life in South America (for all that it is fetchingly underscored by strains of 'Over the Rainbow' in Finnish) leaves an indeterminate impression. **TP**

Director/producer/script *Aki Kaurismäki* **camera** *Timo Salminen* **editor** *Raija Talvio* **design** *Risto Karhula* **cast** *Turo Pajala, Susanna Haavisto, Matti Pellonpää, Eetu Hilkamo, Erkki Pajala, Matti Jaaranen, Hannu Viholainen*
Running time: 72 mins
UK release: Electric, Oct 6, 1989

ASTERIX AND THE BIG FIGHT (Asterix et le Coup de menhir)

Goscinny and Uderzo books just don't work when padded out from 48 pages to feature length. This latest one is a big improvement on *Asterix in Britain* (largely thanks to better voice casting) but, deprived of the sly historical footnotes of the originals, only a few of the jokes hit home. The severely limited animation and emphasis on badly-timed shtick pare the characters' universal appeal down to primary-school level. Only for the very young and die-hard fans. **TW**

Director *Philippe Grimond* **producer/design** *Nicolas Pesques* **script** *George Roubicek, based on* *the series by René Goscinny, Alberto Uderzo* **camera** *Craig Simpson* **editor** *Jean Goudier* **music** *Michel Colombier* **voices** *Bill Oddie, Bernard Bresslaw, Ron Moody, Sheila Hancock, Peter Hawkins, Brian Blessed, Michael Elphick, Andrew Sachs, Tim Brooke-Taylor, Douglas Blackwell*
Running time: 81 mins
UK release: Palace, Oct 13, 1989

ASYA'S HAPPINESS (Istoriya Asi klyachinoi, kotoroya lyubila, da nie vshla zamuzh)

Hollywood really has transformed Andrei Konchalovsky. It's hard to credit this atmospheric account of life on a collective farm as the creation of the director who went on to make *Tango and Cash*. Asya (Savina) is lame, inarticulate, pregnant and wants to win back the affection of the man who knocked her up. Only slowly, against the carefully-painted backdrop of daily life, do emotions shift in the desired direction. Filmed in 1966 and banned for 20 years thereafter, *Asya's Happiness* is marked by striking, natural performances, evocative music, extraordinary landscape shots, precise attention to the details of daily life and evocative use of peasant music. It's a film that makes one hope other Soviet directors will stand their ground, rather than shifting in a Hollywood direction. **JP**

Director *Andrei Mikhalkov-Konchalovsky* **producer** *M. Zarhitskaya* **script** *Yury Klepikov* **camera** *Georgy Rerberg* **editor** *L. Pokrovskoi* **design** *Mikhail Romadin* **cast** *Alexander Surin, Iya Savvina, Lyubov Sokolova, Gennady Yegorychev, Ivan Petrov, M. Kislov*
Running time: 98 mins
UK release: Artificial Eye, Nov 10, 1989

THE ABYSS

James Cameron and John McTiernan were the archetypal action directors of the Reagan era. Their films of the mid-to-late 1980s constructed masculine myths of super-human endurance and vicious potency, that seemed to encapsulate the hawkish values of an administration actively developing the Star Wars defence initiative.

Cameron's *The Terminator* and McTiernan's *Predator*, both anchored by the almost inhuman musclature of Arnold Schwarzenegger, championed the superiority of American values and gut instinct over seemingly indestructible enemies (be they disco-hating robots or invisible alien warmongers).

Of the two, Cameron's fascination with lethal weaponry – underscored in *Aliens'* only romantic scene, when Michael Biehn and Sigourney Weaver flirt with each other as he shows her how to handle a machine-gun/grenade-launcher combo – positioned him closer to the Reaganite philosophy of strength through firepower. His metaphor of man as machine, defined in *The Terminator*, and reworked in *Aliens*, reflected America's fascination with its gun culture.

With the arrival of George Bush in the White House, 'a gentler, kinder America' was promised. How would these two directors adapt their filmmaking to a different cultural climate? Could Cameron and McTiernan wrap their dynamic camerawork around more liberal, perhaps humanistic, heroes?

McTiernan took the easier route. *The Hunt for Red October* welded hi-tech submarine technology and claustrophobic interiors to a relatively simple narrative of a Russian submarine commander's attempt to defect to the West.

Cameron's film for the end of the 1980s, *The Abyss*, was more ambitious, both thematically and visually. Yet its failings, on both levels, are striking.

A US nuclear submarine is lost and the army sequester a team on an underwater oil-drilling rig, headed up by Ed Harris, to investigate. Harris's estranged wife, Mary Elizabeth Mastrantonio, and a group of SAS-style naval experts led by Michael Biehn join the riggers. The sub is on the edge of a two-and-a-half mile abyss.

Mastrantonio encounters an aquatic alien. A hurricane cuts the platform off from its support ship and Biehn, increasingly psychotic because of underwater pressure sickness, arms a nuclear warhead in an attempt to blow up the aliens. Harris goes down into the abyss to disarm the warhead. The aliens save Harris, put him in the mother ship, which surfaces, carrying up with it the oil rig.

The film's title is a rather colourless metaphor for the emotional and psychological chasms that Harris and Mastrantonio (divorce) and Biehn (insanity) are teetering upon. Cameron perfunctorily signals Biehn's descent into madness from the moment he appears. He is a sulking, twitchy weirdo who scuttles bug-eyed around the oil rig. He succeeds in injecting some pace into the film, but his explosive exit two-thirds of the way through results in an already moribund narrative sinking, with Harris, slowly down into the abyss.

In failing to decide whether the narrative's focus is on the encounter with the aliens or on man's self-destructive impulses towards the environment (the aliens are explicitly linked to the sea), Cameron tries to plaster over his broken-backed script by stretching a torturous reconciliation between Harris and Mastrantonio across the narrative.

'I hate that bitch. I probably shouldn't have married her,' says Harris early on. Out of the redemption of their cynical marital discord, the film endeavours to carve testaments to spiritual renewal; the pair care not only for each other but also for the amorphous gelatine seahorses that represent the aliens.

This quasi-religious sentimentality with which Cameron soaks the riggers' encounters with the aliens seems painfully artificial and laboured, especially coming from a director who previously relied on the raw directness of his protagonists' propensity for mechanized violence to delineate their characters.

After being faced with an alien on the rig, whose form, composed of sea water, replicates the faces of those around it, Mastrantonio tells Harris, 'We all see what we want to see. Coffey [Biehn] looks and he sees hate. You have to look with better eyes than that.' That last statement might well be applied to Cameron.

Indeed there is little evidence of Cameron's directorial presence in the film. His fast-moving, fast-cutting camera style might well have been expected to lift the threadbare plot (which would have looked even more feeble if transposed to space) into a more challenging visual arena. But there is none of the claustrophobia-conveying camera movement one would expect in the cramped seabed oil-rig set. And the frenetic handling of several underwater sequences seems out of sync with the ponderous action on screen.

The much-hyped authenticity of the underwater sequences – the sets were built in disused nuclear tanks which were then flooded – fails to compensate for the banality of the storytelling. The special effects, notably the aliens (which are all too reminiscent of Carlo Rambaldi's creations for Spielberg's *Close Encounters of the Third Kind*), are too derivative and poorly executed to be impressive. The epic scale that the film aims fruitlessly for in the final moments, as the spacecraft surfaces with the oil rig and its support ship on top of its hull, is wasted by the graceless mixture of miniatures and gawping actors. The film unashamedly attempts to recreate the emotional awe evoked by the conclusion of *Close Encounters*, despite having skimped on the driven narrative structure which made that encounter so powerful.

Whatever else the abyss represents, it is difficult not to perceive it as a chasm into which Cameron's undoubted technical skills as a filmmaker sank without trace under the weight of *The Abyss*'s wholly misguided intention of locating emotional resonances for the 1990s in territory already claimed by Spielberg in the late 1970s.

STEPHEN DARK

BABAR, THE MOVIE

This does little more for the 'Babar' books than animate them. But in a climate of Ninja Turtles, it's a thankfully serene piece of work. The slight story – King Babar soothes his children with a tale of his exploits against the evil rhinoceroses – is tainted by stock Saturday morning villains, but it won't make nervous wrecks out of small children. **CB**
Director *Alan Bunce* **producers** *Patrick Loubert, Michael Hirsh, Clive A. Smith* **execs** *Loubert, Hirsh, Smith, Stephanie Sperry, Pierre Bertrand-Jaume, Yannick Bernard* **script** *Peter Sauder, J. D. Smith, John De Klein, Raymond Jaffelice, Bunce, from characters created by Jean and Laurent de Brunhoff* **editor** *Evan Landis* **design** *Ted Bastien* **music** *Milan Kymlicka* **voices** *Gordon Pinsent, Gavin Magrath, Elizabeth Hanna, Sarah Polley, Chris Wiggins, Stephen Ouimette, John Stocker, Charles Kerr*
Running time: 70 mins
US release: New Line, Aug 25, 1989
UK release: Winstone, 27 Jul, 1990

BACK TO THE FUTURE, PART II

Unlike most sequels, this really is like seeing the next episode of a serial. It opens with the last five minutes of the first film as Marty McFly (Fox), who is just back from 1955, is whisked off to 2015 by mad scientist Brown (Lloyd), in order to sort out some trouble with his as-yet unborn children. After a spell in a future of flying skateboards and 1980s nostalgia, the film whips back to an alternative 1985 caused by some tampering with the past, only to discover that the small-town setting has been converted into a violent hell-hole. The heroes are then forced to go back again to 1955 and the events of the first film in order to fill in some narrative gaps and set up for another bout of time-twisting in the next instalment. The film lacks the blend of nostalgic detail and bizarre family feeling that gave the first film heart as well as flash, but it replaces that with a plotline that never lets up, a wealth of interesting detail in all its time zones, and some mind-bending concepts. **KN**
Director *Robert Zemeckis* **producers** *Bob Gale, Neil Canton* **execs** *Steven Spielberg, Frank Marshall, Kathleen Kennedy* **script** *Gale* **camera** *Dean Cundey* **editors** *Arthur Schmidt, Harry Keramidas* **design** *Rick Carter* **sfx** *ILM* **music** *Alan Silvestri* **cast** *Michael J. Fox, Christopher Lloyd, Lea Thompson, Thomas F. Wilson, Harry Waters Jr., Charles Fleischer, Joe Flaherty, Elizabeth Shue, James Tolkan, Jeffrey Weissman, Casey Siemaszko, Billy Zane, J. J. Cohen, E. Casanova Evans, Jay Koch*
Running time: 108 mins
US release: Universal, Nov 22, 1989
UK release: UIP, Nov 24, 1989

BACK TO THE FUTURE, PART III

Back to the Old West for De Lorean time-rider Marty McFly, this time engaged in a race to prevent blacksmith Doc Brown from being despatched to Boot Hill by a surly, unwashed outlaw ancestor (Wilson) of the Biff dynasty. Lacking both the mind-boggling timeshift complexities and frenetic pace of *Back to the Future II*, this final instalment in the series shows little real empathy for its Western setting and runs out of steam altogether in a railroad finale blueprinted in the *Indiana Jones* chases. More subdued than in previous instalments, Michael J. Fox generously takes a back seat to Christopher Lloyd who makes the Doc more eccentric and bulgy-eyed than before under the romantic influence of Mary Steenburgen's winsome schoolmarm. **GF**
Director *Robert Zemeckis* **producers** *Bob Gale, Neil Canton* **execs** *Steven Spielberg, Frank Marshall, Kathleen Kennedy* **script** *Gale* **camera** *Dean Cundey* **editors** *Arthur Schmidt, Harry Keramidas* **design** *Rick Carter* **sfx** *ILM* **music** *Alan Silvestri* **cast** *Michael J. Fox, Christopher Lloyd, Mary Steenburgen, Thomas F. Wilson, Lea Thompson, Elisabeth Shue, Matt Clark, Richard Dysart, James Tolkan, ZZ Top*
Running time: 108 mins
US release: Universal, May 25, 1990
UK release: UIP, Jul 13, 1990

BAD INFLUENCE

This is a teeny-bopper version of *Internal Affairs*, or an American *Apartment Zero* (it shares a screenwriter with the latter film). Would-be corporate crawler James Spader meets the Devil, incarnated by Rob Lowe's manipulative sleaze, who makes his life a successful living hell. This tour of devious brutality and emotional treachery has its moments, but director Curtis Hanson (*The Bedroom Window*) overdoses on *film noir* mannerisms, and his stylistic twitches do not enhance the film, which never resolves its gay subtexts. **JH**
Director *Curtis Hanson* **producer** *Steve Tisch* **execs** *Richard Becker, Morrie Eisenman* **script** *David Koepp* **camera** *Robert Elswit* **editor** *Bonnie Koehler* **design** *Ron Foreman* **music** *Trevor Jones* **cast** *Rob Lowe, James Spader, Lisa Zane, Christian Clemenson, Kathleen Wilhoite, Tony Maggio*
Running time: 99 mins
US release: Triumph, Mar 9, 1990

BAD TASTE

An alien race have come to earth to test-market human flesh as a fast-food sensation sure to sweep the galaxy. If you don't find that idea funny, you might as well skip *Bad Taste* because

you won't be too pleased with the zero-budget technical qualities, indifferent action, repetitive machine-gun battles, ineffectually looped dialogue and crass verbal humour. However, if you're broad-minded (i.e. sick) enough to see the jokes, then this is a hoot. You won't easily forget the alien waving around the severed arm holding the sledge-hammer lodged in his head. It's gruesome fun for its incredible slapstick splatter, but it's no *Evil Dead* exercise in low-budget mastery. **KN**
Director/script/camera *Peter Jackson* **producer** *Peter Jackson* **editor** *Jackson, Jamie Selkirk* **design** *Caroline Girdlestone* **music** *Michelle Scullion* **cast** *Terry Potter, Pete O'Herne, Craig Smith, Mike Minett, Peter Jackson, Doug Wren, Peter Vere-Jones*
Running time: 91 mins
UK release: Blue Dolphin, Sep 15, 1989

🎬 BATMAN

Sheer bliss for the nasty-minded child in all of us, *Batman* is easily better even than such first-class superhero movies as *Superman* or *Raiders of the Lost Ark*, with a background as interesting as its hero and a *noir*-ish nightmare style far removed from the colourful camp of the 1960s TV show. Director Tim Burton reinvents Gotham City as a night-time hell of neon and garbage, overrun by vicious criminals. Although the ingredients are familiar from comics and TV, they've never been stirred together quite like this. Nicholson's Joker is a star turn, with more crazed twitches and one-liners to the minute than any previous super-villain and a penchant for such minor nastinesses as murdering his best friend on a whim, and Keaton acquits himself remarkably well as the slightly strange Bruce Wayne and the gruff-voiced monolith in Schwarzenegger-shaped body armour. The film is full of imaginative violence, clever rethinkings of the origins of its familiar characters, astonishing sets and witty lines. **KN**
Director *Tim Burton* **producers** *Jon Peters, Peter Guber* **execs** *Benjamin Melniker, Michael Uslan* **script** *Sam Hamm, Warren Skaaren, from story by Sam Hamm based on character created by Bob Kane* **camera** *Roger Pratt* **editor** *Ray Lovejoy* **design** *Anton Furst* **sfx** *Derek Meddings, John Evans* **music** *Danny Elfman* **cast** *Jack Nicholson, Michael Keaton, Kim Basinger, Robert Wuhl, Pat Hingle, Billy Dee Williams, Michael Gough, Jerry Hall, Jack Palance*
Running time: 126 mins
US release: Warner, Jun 23, 1989
UK release: Warner, Aug 11, 1989

THE BEAR

Jean-Jacques Annaud's outdoor epic is a slightly grittier version of the kind of animal story Uncle Walt used to make. An orphaned bear cub falls in with a wounded grizzly and they spend some time evading hunters, braving the rugged landscape and besting predators. While this doesn't really dwell on what bears proverbially do in the woods, it does feature plenty of ursine sex and violence, and even a pink-filtered magic mushroom trip. In the end, man and bear reach something of a mystical communion and decide not to kill each other, which I suppose should be a lesson to all of us. Sold as a state-of-the-art animal movie, it's a remarkable achievement for its pictorial beauties and Annaud's direction of the animals, but it still remains essentially uninvolving. The storyline is slimmer than is good for it, and the admirable eco-sentiments of the script are ridiculous in the context of the unpolluted 1880s. Barely bearable. **KN**
Director *Jean-Jacques Annaud* **producer** *Claude Berri* **script** *Gérard Brach, based on novel The Grizzly King by James Oliver Curwood* **camera** *Philippe Rousselot* **editor** *Noëlle Boisson* **design** *Toni Ludi* **music** *Philippe Sarde* **cast** *Tcheky Karyo, Jack Wallace, André Lacombe*
Running time: 98 mins
US release: Tri-Star, Oct 25, 1989
UK release: Columbia Tri-Star, Sep 22, 1989

BERT RIGBY, YOU'RE A FOOL

TURKEY • TURKEY • TURKEY

Director/script *Carl Reiner* **producer** *George Shapiro* **camera** *Jan de Bont* **editor** *Bud Molin* **design** *Terence Marsh* **music** *Ralph Burns* **cast** *Robert Lindsay, Cathryn Bradshaw, Robbie Coltrane, Anne Bancroft, Corbin Bernsen, Jackie Gayle, Liberty Mounten*
Running time: 94 mins
US release: Warner, Feb 24, 1989
UK release: Warner, Nov 10, 1989

⚑ BEST OF THE BEST

There are several Oscar nominees and winners in this mediocre martial arts movie – Eric Roberts, James Earl Jones, Louise Fletcher and Sally Kirkland – but none of them have anything to do. The story of a US karate team training for a big bout against the Koreans, the film has little to distinguish it but its cast, and the cast members do little on this occasion to distinguish themselves. **JH**
Director *Bob Radler* **producers** *Philip Rhee, Peter E. Strauss* **execs** *Michael Holzman, Frank Giustra* **script** *Paul Levine* **camera** *Doug Ryan* **editor** *William Hoy* **design** *Kim Rees* **music** *Paul Gilman* **cast** *Eric Roberts, James Earl Jones, Sally Kirkland, Phillip Rhee, Christopher Penn, John Dye, David Agresta*
Running time: 95 mins
US release: Taurus, Nov 10, 1989
UK release: Entertainment, Feb 9, 1990

THE BIG BANG

James Toback, not the most successful of American filmmakers (*Love and Money, The Pick-up Artist*) here turns to documentary. Abandoning sexual obsession for metaphysics, he gathers together a diverse group of people that includes basketball star Darryl Dawkins, violinist/drug addict Eugene Fodor, a gangster, a Holocaust survivor, and a fashion model, and gets them to talk about the big questions – the meaning of life, the universe and everything. It works. The film is an entertaining surprise, and Toback is better at drawing out these non-actors than he ever was at securing a performance from Nastassja Kinski. **JH**
Director *James Toback* **producers** *Joseph H. Kanter* **camera** *Barry Markowitz* **editor** *Stephanie Kempf*
Running time: 81 mins
US release: Triton, May 11, 1990

THE BIG PICTURE

Three quarters of the *Spinal Tap* team (writer-director Guest, co-writer McKean) take a conventional story of making it in Hollywood while keeping one's integrity, and turn it into an anatomy of local morals and manners. If some of the jokes are for insiders only, and Kevin Bacon's starring performance is a touch too familiar, there are great jokes on the unctuousness of award shows, insincerity as a form of honesty and various forms of betrayal. Jennifer Jason Leigh steals the picture as a film-school graduate who's now into 'ham radio performance art'. Dressed in black, her feet in out-size sneakers, her body in perpetual motion as if she couldn't express herself fast enough verbally, Leigh gives a performance that suggests pixies are dancing in her brain. **JH**
Director *Christopher Guest* **producer** *Michael Varhol* **execs** *William E. McEuen, Richard Gilbert Abramson* **script** *Michael McKean, Varhol, Guest* **camera** *Jeff Jur* **editor** *Marty Nicholson* **design** *Joseph Garrity* **music** *David Nichtern* **cast** *Kevin Bacon, Jennifer Jason Leigh, Emily Longstreth, J. T. Walsh, Martin Short, Michael McKean, Kim Miyori, Teri Hatcher, Dan Schneider, Jason Gould, Tracy Brooks Swope*
Running time: 99 mins
US release: Taurus, Sep 15, 1989

▼ BILL AND TED'S EXCELLENT ADVENTURE

Bill and Ted are not very smart students. They are flunking history but have enough smarts to use a phone booth as a time machine so they can shoot back to the past and get the real lowdown. And like, guess what? They join up with Joan of Arc's aerobics class and live it up with swingin' Abe Lincoln who advises them to 'Party on,

dudes!' Honest, I'm not making it up. Alex Winter behaves like a man in serious need of a lobotomy, Keanu Reeves like someone who's just had one, and the whole affair is so witlessly executed that it barely makes it as a bad movie. Nothing more than a brain-dead *Back to the Future* rip-off, the film sat on the distributor's shelf gathering dust until the writer's strike left a gap in the schedules. It promptly cleaned up at the box-office. I have seen the future of American cinema, and it's a downer, man. **TW**
Director *Stephen Herek* **producers** *Scott Kroopf, Michael S. Murphey, Joel Soisson* **execs** *Ted Field, Robert W. Cort* **script** *Chris Matheson, Ed Solomon* **camera** *Timothy Suhrstedt* **editors** *Larry Bock, Patrick Rand* **design** *Roy Forge Smith* **sfx** *Barry Nolan* **music** *David Newman* **cast** *Keanu Reeves, Alex Winter, George Carlin, Terry Camilleri, Dan Shor, Tony Steedman, Rod Loomis, Al Leong, Jane Wiedlin, Robert V. Barron, Clifford David, Hal London Jr., Bernie Casey*
Running time: 90 mins
US release: Orion, Feb 17, 1989
UK release: Premier, Apr 13, 1990

▼ BIRD ON A WIRE

Mel Gibson has been underground in the Witness Protection programme for fifteen years, and is now working at a Detroit gas station. Goldie Hawn, his ex-fiancée and now a yuppie lawyer, shows up with evil drug baddies David Carradine and Bill Duke in hot pursuit. There follows a comedy chase thriller that gives new meaning to the phrase 'brain dead'. *Bird on a Wire* really stars Mel's grin and Goldie's behind, or vice versa, and seems designed to draw people into air-conditioned theatres for a nice.nap. Unbelievably, it was directed by Roger Donaldson, who made *Smash Palace* and *No Way Out*. Or believably, since he also directed *Cocktail*. And how long is it since Hawn had her blonde shag cut? **JH**
Director *John Badham* **producer** *Rob Cohen* **execs** *Ted Field, Robert W. Cort* **script** *David Seltzer, Louis Venosta, Eric Lerner* **camera** *Robert Primes* **editors** *Frank Morriss, Dallas Puett* **design** *Philip Harrison* **music** *Hans Zimmer* **cast** *Mel Gibson, Goldie Hawn, David Carradine, Bill Duke, Stephen Tobolowsky, Joan Severance, Harry Caesar, Jeff Corey, Alex Bruhanski, John Pyper-Ferguson, Clyde Kusatsu*
Running time: 110 mins
US release: Universal, May 18,

BLACK RAIN (Kuroi Ame)

This is a deeply-felt, slow-moving, black-and-white account of the lives of three survivors of the black rain which fell on Hiroshima after the bomb had been dropped. Imamura audaciously recreates the abattoir horrors of the bombing

itself, and then takes on the problems confronting the survivors five years afterwards as they slowly die of radiation poisoning. This is a self-consciously important film, and the significance of the subject matter has somewhat intimidated Imamura, so that the result is somewhat impersonal and lacks the director's trademarkd dark humour. **JH**
Director *Shohei Imamura* **producer** *Hisa Iino* **script** *Toshiro Ishido, Imamura, from novel by Masuji Ibuse* **camera** *Takashi Kawamata* **editor** *Hajime Okayusu* **design** *Josep Omagalo* **music** *Toru Takemitsu* **cast** *Yoshiko Tanaka, Kazuo Kitamura, Etsuko Ichihara, Shoichi Ozawa, Norihei Miki, Kaisuke Ishide*
Running time: 123 mins
US release: Angelika, Feb 1, 1990
UK release: Artificial Eye, Jun 29, 1990

▼ BLACK RAIN

In stylistic terms Ridley Scott is a visionary, but he still seems obsessed with applying his overkill talents to the flimsiest pot-boiler scripts he can find. *Black Rain* is yet another re-run of the gun-toting fish-out-of-water scenario done masterfully 20 years ago in *Coogan's Bluff* and subsequently hammered into the ground by gimmicky TV shows like *McCloud* and imitative movies like *Brannigan, Red Heat* and *The Hidden*. Michael Douglas is the rebellious cop who's not above getting his hands dirty with a little charming corruption, burdened with a nice-guy sidekick (Garcia) who is only in the film to be killed. The villain is a smug young Japanese mobster (Matsuda) who wants to gain power in the traditionalist yakuza by stealing the plates which will enable the Eastern gangsters to make their own American money. Douglas busts Matsuda after the bad guy has slaughtered some rivals in a New York diner, and is given the job of taking the criminal back to Osaka for trial. Of course, Matsuda makes a cunning get-away, and the macho cop feels he has to bring his man to justice even if it means alienating everyone in Japan. Being a movie hero, Douglas picks up on some vital clues the entire Osaka police fail to spot, and takes to the unfamiliar streets for revenge, justice and honour. Even as an action movie, this is curiously unaffecting, and demonstrates that all the stunt-work in the world can't make up for a choppy storyline, bewildered actors and a serious lack of originality. In the many slow, dull spots, you find yourself wondering why it is that the only memorable characters in a Ridley Scott movie were robots? **KN**
Director *Ridley Scott* **producers** *Stanley R. Jaffe, Sherry Lansing* **execs** *Craig Bolotin, Julie Kirkham* **script** *Bolotin, Warren Lewis* **camera** *Jan De Bont* **editor** *Tom Rolf* **design** *Norris Spencer* **music** *Hans Zimmer* **cast** *Michael Douglas, Andy Garcia,*

Ken Takakura, Kate Capshaw, Yusaku Matsuda, Shigeru Koyama, John Spencer, Guts Ishimatsu, Yuya Uchida, Tomisaburo Wakayama
Running time: 125 mins
US release: Paramount, Sep 22, 1989
UK release: UIP, Jan 29, 1990

BLAZE

The title alludes to Blaze Starr, a showgirl who became the mistress of Earl (brother of Huey) Long, an eccentric populist governor of Louisiana, towards the end of his career some 30 years back. But Earl is very much the centre of the film: in Paul Newman's floridly practised performance, he comes alive to rumbustious effect, and the episodes of political machination, spiked with salty local idiom, are both pointed and amusing. The film is on less certain ground, however, in the lengthy expository scenes of Blaze's earlier life; and the closing passages, showing the veteran politico ascending to the great hustings in the sky with all the trimmings bar a heavenly choir, produce a dispiriting decline into sentimental calculation. **TP**
Director *Ron Shelton* **producers** *Gil Friesen, Dale Pollock* **execs** *David Lester, Don Miller* **script** *Shelton, based on the book* Blaze Starr: My Life *as told to Huey Perry* **camera** *Haskell Wexler* **editors** *Robert Leighton, Adam Weiss* **design** *Armin Ganz* **cast** *Paul Newman, Lolita Davidovich, Jerry Hardin, Gailard Sartain, Jeffrey DeMunn, Garland Bunting, Richard Jenkins, Brandon Smith*
Running time: 108 mins
US release: BV, Dec 13, 1989
UK release: Warner, Feb 4, 1990

BLIND FURY

Before the credits are over, GI Rutger Hauer has been blinded in an explosion in Vietnam, rescued from a swamp by some villagers, nursed back to health, grown a beard, mastered the art of swinging a samurai sword, shaved off the beard, returned to America, wandered around for 20 years without getting any older, and decided to look up his old buddy (O'Quinn), who is now a chemist under threat from a Las Vegas hood who wants him to manufacture designer drugs. Then the story starts – together with the film's problems. Hauer is given a rôle in which he can lop off limbs, be snidely amusing and do loony stunts like driving a car without the use of his eyes, but all the script asks him to do is to have a 'relationship' with O'Quinn's bratty son as they travel across country, with about 800 bad guys on their tail. You still get to see people chopped in half, but it's a shame that such a decent premise, so well cast, and with such a promising director (Phillip Noyce, fresh from *Dead Calm*) should wind up such a half-hearted movie. **KN**

Director *Phillip Noyce* producers *Daniel Grodnik,*
Tim Matheson execs *Robert W. Cort, David*
Madden script *Charles Robert Carner, from*
screenplay by Ryozo Kasahara camera *Don Burgess*
editor *David Simmons* design *Peter Murton* music
J. Peter Robinson cast *Rutger Hauer, Brandon Call,*
Terrance O'Quinn, Lisa Blount, Noble Willingham,
Meg Foster, Nick Cassavetes, Rick Overton,
Randall (Tex) Cobb, Charles Cooper, Sho Kosugi
Running time: 85 mins
US release: Tri-Star, Apr 13, 1989
UK release: Col/Tri-Star, Jul 13, 1989

🏴 THE BLOOD OF HEROES

In case you were wondering what Rutger Hauer
does between Guinness commercials or what Joan
Chen's been up to since *The Last Emperor*, here is
the answer – respectively breaking arms and
biting people's ears off in this post-apocalyptic re-
hash of *Rollerball* without the social commentary.
One might have hoped for something better than
pointless slow-motion gore from the reunion of
Hauer with *Blade Runner* writer David Webb
Peoples. Chen is outstanding, although she has
precious little to work with. **TW**
Director/script *David Webb Peoples* producer
Charles Roven exec *Brian Rosen* camera *David*
Eggby editor *Richard Francis-Bruce* design *John*
Stoddart music *Todd Boekelheide* cast *Rutger*
Hauer, Joan Chen, Vincent Phillip D'Onofrio,
Delroy Lindo, Anna Katarina, Gandhi Macintyre,
Justin Monju, Max Fairchild, Hugh Keays-Byrne,
Lia Francisa, Aaron Martin
Running time: 102 mins
US release: New Line, Feb 23, 1990

🎬 BLUE STEEL

This is a cop thriller with a very dodgy plot
that's transformed by Kathryn Bigelow's stylish
direction and Jamie Lee Curtis's performance as a
rookie cop who's not ashamed of her desire to kill
(scum). On her first day out on the streets she
guns down a supermarket raider while her
partner is on the john, and comes under
suspicion because no gun was found on the scene.
It's been picked up, in fact, by a psychotic
commodities broker (Silver) who makes Curtis
into his rôle model as he guns down strangers on
the street. The script could have made more of
the relationship that develops between the cop
and the psycho with a shared interest in guns,
and things do become a little preposterous when
repeated shootouts fail to bring down Silver's
unkillable golem. But Bigelow's camerawork
draws one right into the obsessions of the film's
characters, creating an experience of real
intensity. **JP**
Director *Kathryn Bigelow* producers *Edward R.*
Pressman, Oliver Stone exec *Lawrence Kasanoff*
script *Bigelow, Eric Red* camera *Amir Mokri*
editor *Lee Percy* design *Toby Corbett* music *Brad*
Feidel cast *Jamie Lee Curtis, Ron Silver, Clancy*
Brown, Elizabeth Peña, Louise Fletcher, Philip
Bosco
Running time: 102 mins
US release: MGM, Mar 16, 1990

BORN ON THE FOURTH OF JULY

HIT • HIT • HIT • HIT • HIT

Director *Oliver Stone* producers *A. Kitman Ho,*
Oliver Stone, Lope V. Juban Jr. script *Stone,*
Ron Kovic, from book by Kovic camera *Robert*
Richardson editor *David Brenner* design *Bruno*
Rubeo music *John Williams* cast *Tom Cruise,*
Bryan Larkin, Raymond J. Barry, Caroline Kava,
Josh Bryans, Seth Allen, Jamie Talisman, Sean
Stone, Anne Bobby, Samantha Larkin, Harvey
Morse, Kyra Sedgwick, Jessica Prunell, Frank
Whaley, Jason Klein, Jerry Levine, Lane R. Davis,
Tom Berenger, John Getz, David Warshofsky, Jason
Gedrick, Michael Compotaro, Willem Dafoe,
Corkey Ford, Rocky Carroll, Tony Frank, Jayne
Haynes
Running time: 144 mins
US release: Universal, Dec 20, 1989
UK release: UIP, Mar 3, 1990

BREAKING IN

For some reason John Sayles' comedy scripts are
rarely as funny as his horror outings, and if the
humour in the tale of old-timer Burt Reynolds
teaching young Casey Siemaszko the finer points
of burglary and con artistry is a little too gentle at
times, its originality in characterization more
than makes up for it. Reynolds in particular is
knockout as the ageing pro (complete with
greying anorexic toupé and less-than-perfect
teeth) in the kind of rôle that reminds you just
how interesting an actor he can be when he's not
smashing cars or shooting people. Bill Forsyth's
too-careful direction lets the piece down
somewhat, but never enough to stop it from
being a quietly enjoyable film that's well
worth keeping an eye out for. **TW**
Director *Bill Forsyth* producer *Harry Gittes*
execs *Andrew Meyer, Sarah Ryan Black* script
John Sayles camera *Michael Coulter* editor
Michael Ellis design *Adrienne Atkinson, John*
Willett music *Michael Gibbs* cast *Burt Reynolds,*
Casey Siemaszko, Sheila Kelley, Lorraine Toussant,
Albert Salmi, Harry Carey
Running time: 91 mins
US release: Goldwyn, Aug 25, 1989
UK release: Castle Premier, Aug 31, 1990

BULL DURHAM

Bull Durham differs from previous baseball movies in glorifying and sending up the game itself instead of turning it into a metaphor for success, American life or anything else. Kevin Costner is convincing as a career second-rater, the minor-league catcher who never made the majors but kept his pride. In his last year in the game, he imparts seasoning to self-centred but endearingly goofy Tim Robbins and challenges ageing ballpark groupie Susan Sarandon's assumption that the game is best played, and her bed is best occupied, by the immature. **BM**

Director/script *Ron Shelton* **producers** *Thom Mount, Mark Burk* **exec** *David V. Lester* **camera** *Bobby Byrne* **editors** *Robert Leighton, Adam Weiss* **design** *Armin Ganz* **music** *Michael Convertino* **cast** *Kevin Costner, Susan Sarandon, Tim Robbins, Trey Wilson, Robert Wuhl, Jenny Robertson, Max Patkin, William O'Leary*
Running time: 108 mins
US release: Orion, Jun 24, 1988
UK release: Rank, Aug 25, 1989

THE 'BURBS

Tom Hanks decides to spend his vacation at home in the suburbs, and starts to feel that something isn't right at the Klopek household, where mysterious holes are dug in the backyard at night during a thunderstorm and the furnace makes peculiar noises. In its twisted comic-horror approach to suburbia, *The 'burbs* is one of several films (*Parents, The Stepfather*) that sets out to counter the nostalgic, family-centred vision of Reagan-Bush Americana by finding madness and monstrosity in the heart of the nuclear family. For the most part, it follows *Explorers* in its unusual narrative strategy, presenting a situation filled with threat and mystery that then turns out to be entirely innocent. In his key speech, Hanks turns on his neighbours as the Klopek house burns with 'Don't you see, *we're* the ones who are acting suspiciously!' The film strings out its central situation perfectly for four-fifths of its running time, but fumbles at the last moment and can't quite make the final break with traditional menace-dominated storylines. **KN**

Director *Joe Dante* **producers** *Larry Brezner, Michael Finnell* **script** *Dana Olsen* **camera** *Robert Stevens* **editor** *Marshall Harvey* **design** *James Spencer* **music** *Jerry Goldsmith* **cast** *Tom Hanks, Bruce Dern, Carrie Fisher, Rick Ducommun, Corey Feldman, Wendy Schaal, Brother Theodore, Courtney Gains, Gale Gordon*
Running time: 103 mins
US release: Universal, Feb 17, 1989
UK release: UIP, Jul 28, 1990

BERT RIGBY, YOU'RE A FOOL

Is it a turkey, or a mixed-up swan? No! It's a flying chameleon that lost its sense of direction somewhere between the Yorkshire moors and the Hollywood Heights. The method in its madness might intrigue connoisseurs of the good bad movie, or the bad good movie. I still can't decide which.

The film's opening scene deliberately confuses us as to where it's at. In what looks like an English pub, an English barfly (Robert Lindsay) tells his hard-luck flashback to a gaudy gaggle of ghetto-Hispanics. Once he was a coalminer, back in Arthur Scargill country. But his crazy dreamy feet kept tap-dancing nostalgically, like the Kelly-and-Astaire musicals his old mum took him to. When there's trooble at t'pit, he slopes off with Sid Trampel's Original Travelling Amateur Show. He's spotted by a Hollywood director involved with soft-focus TV commercials for 'Crown Royal condoms – fit for a King'. And so to Tinseltown, where Bert's career droops forlornly. But is he downhearted? No! He survives by lowly jobs like dressing up as a gondola to deliver pizzas, and clipping hedges for the stars.

Glamour-queen Anne Bancroft, ageing gracefully but lustfully, overhears Bert up a tree doing an impersonation of Noël Coward. Older Woman melodrama looms. But hearing that his girl back home is preggers starts him thinking. And broad comedy breaks out. In that genyuwine English pub in LA, he does an impromptu turn and talent-spotters strike again. Soon he's rich and famous, and fulfils his dream; he reopens his home-town picture palace, and struts his song-and-dance-man stuff before a happy family audience. Yes folks, the good old days are here again. . .

Robert Lindsay, the star of the Cockney stage-musical *Me and My Gal*, is highly likeable, a big lolloping lad. Warners, not quite knowing what to do with him, put him in a genre that's still hot, though probably just peaked. It's one of those Comedies of Social Mobility, in which some resilient misfit gets bounced around the social snakes and ladders (*Trading Places, Down and Out in Beverly Hills, Working Girl*).

As a Brit-in-the-States comedy, this and *Stars and Bars* belong in the same pigeonhole. Whereas the Columbia film was corn-gobbling turkey, this patchwork quilt bristles with pieces and bits that are vivid, fresh and bright. Especially on its English side. True, working-class life lacks the grime, gloom and moral degradation assumed by the kitchen-sink school. Would you believe a mining-type family lovingly tending a blitz-era garden shelter, so that it makes a cosy nook? Yes I would. The Olde English Humour is right too. 'Why are you such a cheap bastard?' 'I dunno, I'll have to ask me mum.' That's right off the chestnut tree, a real folk joke, not corny, but classic.

Lindsay plays that interesting concept, a soft-hearted hard-hat. He combines the best of British (*nice* working class) and American (life is just a tap-dance, old son). Initially feckless, he settles down to, not yuppie, but Optimistic Young Fogey, values. The overall affection for happy-go-lucky eccentricity, nice-heartedness, and nostalgia, had me wondering, was it ever a David Puttnam project? At any rate, it's non-puritan niceness evokes *Mister Love*, Puttnam's bravely loony film about a kindly Casanova.

But the writer-director is Carl Reiner. Surprisingly, as he's best known for low-minded Steve Martin comedies like *The Jerk*, yock-horror comedies about disparate personalities coarsely cobbled together (*The Man With Two Brains*, *All of Me*) and *Dead Men Don't Wear Plaid*, another feat of shreds and patches. Reiner is the Dr Frankenstein of film comedy. His persistent interest in multiple-schizo states would explain Bert's mania for impersonating. Some moves in his routines are so well-finessed that they're slightly spooky.

All this looks like Reiner's attempt to move upmarket. Bert's affable-prole sexuality chimes in with other Brits well-loved Stateside, like Alfie and Shirley Valentine. His very name strikes a chord; it's Bertie like Alfie, and Rigby as in Eleanor. And the 'You're a Fool' bit half-echoes that moralistic song, 'Wot's it orl about, Alfie?' Box-office wise, Bert is Alfie's nicer brother, or rather, since *Alfie* appeared 24 years ago, his son.

Take a slice of Swinging Sixties realism, colour it rainbow, sprinkle with sweetened dilute of normal nearly-safe sex, throw in the American Dream, pour out mega-dollops of Nostalgia Syrup for the Good Old Days of *That's Entertainment* and you haven't missed a trick.

Only, concentrating on the trick takes your eye off the ball. Any which way you look at this movie, it's more like smart twists on *every* other movie worth remembering than it's like itself. It means well, it's not insincere, but it hasn't got any flow. Bert's fixation on Hollywood happy-happy lacks rhyme or reason, in his roots, in him. Okay, it's a change from the glum gumshoe fixations in some soulful Brit flicks; and anyway Reiner's done the gumshoe bit already, in 'Dead Men Only Act Corny'. But Bert is just too blank; the shuffle of impersonations and changes leaves Lindsay nothing definite to be.

Bert's stage-acts owe nothing to his life and mind; their audience seems to be watching some other show. When a moorland cinema-turned-bingo-hall triumphantly reverts to cine-variety for a family audience, 'tain't nowt t'do wi'England. It's Hollywood hooraying Hollywood.' Bert the Brit dreams the American dream, stands the heat of the American kitchen, and returns to coca-colonize his fellow-natives. It's a Cheer-Up America, the world loves you and you love yourself story.

And yet the English scenes are lovingly researched, the English actors bold and free. It's the American scenes which are writing-by-numbers. Where Reiner's extremely ingenious spirit is really at is hard to say – some place dark and zany, no doubt. But some place gentle and observant too. Will he ever get his two brains in synch?

RAYMOND DURGNAT

BORN ON THE FOURTH OF JULY

Questioning the American Way has always been the driving force behind Oliver Stone's pictures. In *Wall Street, Platoon* and *Salvador*, tarnished heroes do what they can to right the wrongs committed by US-backed guerrillas in El Salvador, the American army in Vietnam or greed-driven wheeler-dealers on Wall Street. You can tell how much political anger is driving these films from the way they occasionally lapse into preachiness.

The trouble with *Born on the Fourth of July*, Stone's latest, is that it's preachy through and through — suggesting that its success should be ascribed to America's need for an occasional sermon to assuage national guilt. Ron Kovic (Tom Cruise) is shown swallowing wholesale the patriotism of Fourth of July parades, the Catholicism espoused by his hysterical mother and the macho values battered into him on the wrestling floor. The fragile belief system thus constructed starts to totter one day in Vietnam, when his fellow soldiers fire upon women and children in the mistaken belief they're Viet Cong, and Kovic accidentally kills a colleague in the ensuing confusion. The boy who believed in 'being a man', fighting for his country *and* observing the sixth commandment has to come to terms with the possibility that the cause was never righteous in the first place.

And after a bullet severs his spine, he also has to learn to accept that he'll never walk again (Kovic tries so hard to do so he sustains a horrible fracture). The scenes in which he looks down at the shattered shards of his life lying around his useless legs carry a conviction that's lacking from the rest of the film. The hell inside his head is mirrored in the surroundings to which he has been consigned. At the camp hospital, so many men are dying around him that he gets palmed off with a priest and the last rites instead of the treatment he needs. Rats run around the floor of the Bronx hospital, where patients are hosed down as if they're already corpses, and unsympathetic black nurses play cards instead of attending to their duties. This horrific depiction of people abandoned by the country for which they fought (there's no money for medical equipment; it's all been allocated to planes and napalm) taps effectively into our sympathies.

But it becomes increasingly evident that Stone's only real interest in Ron Kovic is as a peg on which to hang his invective. The film keeps on making points — about how the glorification of war closes eyes to the suffering of its victims (the boy Kovic sees World War 2 veterans flinching from the Fourth of July firecrackers, as he will later do himself, but he doesn't seem to register the sight): about the link between macho values and killing ('I want you to kill' screams the instructor during Kovic's school training sessions) — and when the young Kovic regurgitates the values he's absorbed, he reveals no trace of adolescent savvy, adding no personal touch that would make the words coming from his mouth ring true.

This lack of interest in Ron's inner reality, in the way he's experiencing the values with which he's being force-fed, is all too evident in Stone's treatment of Kovic's relationship to his childhood sweetheart, Donna (Kyra Sedgwick). As kids, when she wants to kiss, he shows her instead how many push-ups he can manage. As an adolescent, he blows a chance to take her to the prom by boasting that he's going with a girl from out of town, but then runs through the rain (in a scene that seems plucked from another movie) for a final dance before he goes off to war. Nothing has happened to establish what sort of rapport exists between them. And so it's like starting afresh when they meet again, and he's in a wheelchair. Is her lack of interest in him anything more than the sort of distance that's bound to develop between old friends following different paths in life? Does it derive from his ongoing commitment to a war she no longer believes in? Or does it have to do with him being now a cripple? Nothing in the script, or in Cruise's performance, tells us how to read the scenes between them, or indicates how he feels watching students demonstrating against the war and police clubbing them down.

Throughout the film, Stone is torn between his desire to indict America for what happened to Ron Kovic, and the imperative to show how Kovic himself experienced what happened to him, slowly coming to terms with his own loss of manhood and his guilt about what he had done in Vietnam. When Kovic screams to his mother that he was sold a pack of lies, we're forced back to the question which Stone never really answered — why did this boy believe in those lies, and why, given that he volunteered for military service, should we feel as sorry for him as he does for himself? After the excursion to visit Donna, Ron takes to irritating everybody gathered around the bar-room pool table, including other ex-Marines. 'Quit the fucking pissing and moaning, you sorry son of a bitch,' one of them says to him, expressing sentiments shared with many members of the audience.

While Kovic's dilemma encourages sympathy, the way it's express-ed in Stone's film causes only irritation. Here's a guy who played soldiers in the wood, dreaming that 'someday we would become men.' He was a driven sportsman, in love with a girl he might one day have married. Suddenly all that is taken away from him. 'I'd give everything I believe in just to have my body again,' he says to his old schoolfriend. 'I want to be a man again. Who's ever going to love me?'

he later remarks to his parents. These are sentiments much more easily understood than all the arguments about politics, religion and family life ascribed by Stone to Kovic. The powerful sequence which shows him hanging out in Mexico and falling futilely in love with a whore was ruined for me by the anticipation of yet another big, bludgeoning statement.

Stone can't let up in his determination to turn *Born on the Fourth of July* into a tale of moral redemption. After killing the nineteen-year-old from Venus, Georgia on the battlefield, Kovic tries to confess to a senior officer, who rebuffs him; 'I don't need anybody to come in here and tell me this shit.' Back at home he tries to tell his mother the truth, but she too doesn't want to listen. It's only when he's stranded in the Mexican desert with another angry cripple, Charlie (Willem Dafoe), that he achieves some sort of catharsis through a screaming match in which each veteran claims to have killed more women and children than the other. 'Did you ever have to kill a little gook baby?' Charlie angrily demands.

Kovic then heads off to Georgia, where he confesses to the wife and parents of the man he accidentally killed. Their initial reluctance to listen is softened by their sensitivity to his pain and what it took to bring him there, and they end up giving him the pardon he needs. 'What's done is done, sir,' the mother says. 'I can't ever forgive you, but maybe the Lord can.' It is enough, seemingly, to turn Kovic from bland patriot to anti-war campaigner. He disrupts the 1972 Republican Party convention with two other crippled vets, and appears on television speaking against the war. Four years later he discards the scruffy style for a suit, and enters the national political arena.

Ron Kovic wrote the story of a paraplegic trying to come to terms with his disability, but Oliver Stone tried to turn it into another onslaught on the values around which American history has been built for the past three decades. The trick doesn't work. To accept the film's account of what happened to Ron Kovic as an indictment of America, one would have to start from a position of outright pacifism, which Stone never seems to be arguing for.

The courageous sequences in *Born on the Fourth of July* show what happens when the bottom falls out of somebody's world, but the movie seems more concerned to endorse anti-war radicalism. Stone is intent on substituting for the redundant certainties of pre-lapsarian America a set of values that are equally irrelevant to the realities of present-day America. Which forces one to locate the relative success of the film in a new nostalgia, no longer for 1950s suburbia but rather for a time when it was possible to believe that waving banners, burning flags and getting oneself arrested would be enough to change the world.

JAMES PARK

CADILLAC MAN

When Robin Williams plays straight, he becomes Kevin Kline. Here he's a philandering car salesman who is divorced, deep in debt and about to lose his job. Suddenly Tim Robbins, the offended husband of one of his work associates, shows up and takes everyone hostage. This has a superb cast (Pamela Reed and Fran Drescher in the same movie!) and some brilliant writing, especially in the long two-hander between Williams and Robbins during the hostage incident. But it starts very slow, continues very unevenly and features car salesman cross-talk that is second-hand Barry Levinson. JH
Director *Roger Donaldson* **producers** *Charles Roven, Donaldson* **script** *Ken Friedman* **camera** *David Gribble* **editor** *Richard Francis-Bruce* **design** *Gene Rudolf* **music** *J. Peter Robinson* **cast** *Robin Williams, Tim Robbins, Pamela Reed, Fran Drescher, Zack Norman, Annabella Sciorra, Lori Petty, Paul Guilfoyle*
Running time: 97 mins
US release: Orion, May 18, 1990

CAMILLE CLAUDEL

'I lived for your *Burghers of Calais*, now I'm going to live for myself!' cries Isabelle Adjani, hurtling off into the dark night of the soul after her fling with Rodin (Depardieu). Début director and ex-cameraman Bruno Nuytten gives us three hours of romantic agony as *l'art* and *l'amour* battle it out. If Camille Claudel, sculptress, madwoman and sister of Paul, had not existed, Adjani would have had to invent her. Indeed, for the most part, she does, coming on like *The Return of Adèle H.* as her shredded, beautiful heroine howls through the Paris streets, hell-bent on occupancy of the asylum Camille did indeed end up in. A substantial hit in its native France – where they like tormented artists – the film was a substantial miss everywhere else. HK
Director *Bruno Nuytten* **producer** *Christian Fechner* **script** *Nuytten, Marilyn Goldin, from book by Reine-Marie Paris* **camera** *Pierre Lhomme* **editor** *Joëlle Hache, Jeanne Kef* **design** *Bernard Vezat* **music** *Gabriel Yared* **cast** *Isabelle Adjani, Gérard Depardieu, Laurent Crevill, Alain Cuny, Madeleine Robinson, Philippe Clevenot, Katrine Boorman, Danièle Lebrun, Maxime Leroux, Jean-Pierre Sentier, Roger Planchon, Aurelle Doazan*
Running time: 174 mins
US release: Orion Classics, Dec 22, 1989
UK release: Cannon, Apr 7, 1989

CAMP THIAROYE
(Camp de Thiaroye)

Ousmane Sembéne can justly be regarded as the founding father of the African cinema which has emerged over the past couple of decades, and *Camp Thiaroye* amply confirms his status. Dramatizing an actual (if little publicized) event, the film is set in late 1944 at a bleak military transit camp in Senegal, where African *tirailleurs* are awaiting demob. French efforts to cheat them out of their severance pay provoke a mutiny, met in turn with an armed response amounting to a massacre. Didactic in method, and Brechtian in treatment, the film maintains a powerful, uncluttered thrust in dramatizing the processes of colonialism. TP
Directors/script *Ousmane Sembéne, Thierno Faty Sow* **producers** *Mamadou Mbengue, Mustapha Ben Jemia, Ouzid Dahmane* **camera** *Ismail Lakhdar Hamina* **editor** *Kahena Attia-Riveill* **design** *El hadj Abdoulaye Diouf* **music** *Ismaila Lo* **cast** *Ibrahima Sane, Sigiri Bakara, Hamed Camara, Ismaila Cissé, Ababacar Sy Cissé, Moussa Cissoko, Eloi Coly, Ismaila Lo, Pierre Londiche, Camara Med Dansogho*
Running time: 152 mins
UK release: Metro, Aug 25, 1990

CANDY MOUNTAIN

Wheeling and dealing his way from New York to Nova Scotia in search of missing master guitar-maker Elmore Silk (Yulin), callow Julius (O'Connor) loses his girl, his car and his money, and finds neither a hero nor a holy grail, but only a few bare truths about himself. Dandifying Tom Waits as Elmore's nouveau-riche brother-in-law and elegizing Bulle Ogier's romantic melancholy, this music-driven minimalist odyssey, co-directed by photographer Robert Frank and novelist/screenwriter Rudy Wurlitzer, is no throwback hippy lament, but a laconic, post-modern beat movie with not one superfluous moment. GF
Directors *Robert Frank, Rudy Wurlitzer* **producer** *Ruth Waldburger* **exec** *Gérald Dearing* **script** *Wurlitzer* **camera** *Pio Corradi* **editor** *Jennifer Auge* **design** *Brad Ricker, Keith Currie* **music** *Various* **cast** *Kevin J. O'Connor, Harris Yulin, Tom Waits, Bulle Ogier, Roberts Blossom, Leon Redbone, Dr John, Rita MacNeil, Joe Strummer, Laurie Metcalf, Jayne Eastwood, Kazuko Oshima, Eric Mitchell*
Running time: 92 mins
UK release: Oasis, Dec 29, 1989

CASUALTIES OF WAR

Having done telekinetic horror, Hitchcockian suspense and gore-spattered gangsterism, Brian De Palma here turns his prowling camera to Vietnam and comes up with one of those half-good films that are, in the end, more annoying than outright failures because the lousy things in them drag down the terrific stuff. Opening with an unexpected, eerie long shot on a train in 1973, as a chic Asian woman gets on and reminds

traumatized veteran Eriksson (Fox) of his time in the war, the film then cuts back to the combat zone and all the familiars of the Vietnam genre. Sergeant Meserve (Penn), upset by the death of his black buddy, orders his team to kidnap a Vietnamese girl. Although the others rape the girl and eventually help kill her, Eriksson stays out of it, racking up some heavy guilt points by failing to save her. Sean Penn does an admirable job as the psychotic sadist who is also a good soldier, and genuinely gets inside the attitudes that could have led his character to be so awful. But for a viewpoint character, we're stuck with Michael J. Fox who is not only too shallow a performer to bring it off but also playing a character for whom everything is made too easy. There are one or two moments that remind you this is a De Palma film, but quite a lot of it is so bombastic and pompous that it could almost have come from Richard Attenborough or David Puttnam. KN
Director Brian De Palma producer Art Linson script David Rabe, from book by Daniel Lang camera Stephen H. Burum editor Bill Pankow design Wolf Kroeger music Ennio Morricone cast Michael J. Fox, Sean Penn, Don Harvey, John C. Reilly, John Leguizamo, Thuy Thu Le, Erik King, Jack Gwaltney, Ving Rhames, Dan Martin, Dale Dye, Sam Robards, Darren E. Burrows
Running time: 113 mins
US release: Columbia, Aug 18, 1989
UK release: Col/Tri-Star, Jan 26, 1990

CAT CHASER

This film really ought to be dynamite, but instead it's just an ordinary fizzle. Elmore Leonard adapted his own novel for the screen, and there's a terrific supporting cast, with Frederic Forrest, Charles Durning and Juan Fernandez playing sleazy, scummy, doomed criminal characters as only they can. Part of the problem is that the characters come with too much back-story to be easily digested, so that the first half of the picture has to be a lumpy bore just to explain who they all are and how they fit together. Paul Weller is an ex-soldier who owns a run-down Florida beachfront hotel, and has a relationship going with Kelly McGillis, the wife of the ex-head of the Dominican secret police (Milian). Various plots are going on in Miami and Santo Domingo, and everyone would like to pick up a suitcase containing two million dollars, especially a crooked ex-cop (Durning) who works for Milian. The other big problem is that the lead actors don't fit into the film. Weller tries hard to catch the mix of Bogartian heroism and neurosis that characterizes a Leonard protagonist, but just flounders, and he doesn't really have that much effect on the plot until the last reel. McGillis is just absurd in a butch haircut, dropping her clothes quite often, and failing to get a grip on her performance. KN
Director Abel Ferrara producers Peter S. Davis, William Panzer execs Guy Collins, Josi Konski script James Borrelli, Elmore Leonard, Alan Sharp from the novel by Leonard camera Anthony B. Richmond editor Anthony Redman design Dan Leigh music Chick Corea cast Peter Weller, Kelly McGillis, Charles Durning, Frederic Forrest, Tomas Milian, Juan Fernandez
Running time: 90 mins
UK release: Entertainment, Dec 8, 1989

CELIA

A first feature by Ann Turner, Celia is a film of evident ambition. Set in the Australia of 1957, it attempts within the context of eccentric childhood anecdotage to analyze both the political stultification of the post-war era and the instinct towards non-conformity. The feeling it leaves, though, is increasingly one of over-ambition. The tone is stranded between comic realism and outright fantasy; the gothic trappings (the nine-year-old heroine contrives to murder a recalcitrant uncle) are unassimilated; and the symbolic implications of the myxomatosis campaign (of which Celia's pet rabbit, appealingly named Murgatroyd, is a victim) are belaboured to counter-productive effect. TP
Director/script Ann Turner producers Timothy White, Gordon Glenn exec Bruce Menzies camera Geoffrey Simpson editor Ken Sallows design Peta Lawson music Chris Neal cast Rebecca Smart, Nicholas Ede, Mary-Anne Fahey, Margaret Ricketts, Victoria Longley, Alexander Hutchinson
Running time: 103 mins
UK release: Electric, Mar 9, 1990
US release: Kim Lewis Marketing, Dec 22, 1989

CHATTAHOOCHEE

Chattahoochee hurls every cliché of the Southern prison movie/chain gang/mental hospital genre at the audience, to little effect. Featuring very bad performances (twitchy, overwrought, busy in the face) by Gary Oldman as a Korean War veteran who goes suicidal and winds up in the Chattahoochee prison, and by Frances McDormand as his wife, this is based on a true story but lacks authenticity. And it happened over three decades ago; so it's not exactly ripped from yesterday's headlines. JH
Director Mick Jackson producer Faye Schwab exec Aaron Schwab script James Hicks camera Andrew Dunn editor Don Fairservice design Patrick Tagliaferro music John Keane cast Gary Oldman, Dennis Hopper, Frances McDormand, Pamela Reed, Ned Beatty, M. Emmet Walsh
Running time: 103 mins
US release: Hemdale, Apr 20, 1990

C

CHECKING OUT

David Leland's first American film counts as a black comedy because it's about death and tries to lighten up with a few jokes, but it lacks the dementia necessary to turn out something like *The Loved One*. Jeff Daniels is a flabby aerospace executive who suffers a bout of hypochondria when his best friend drops prematurely dead from a heart attack over an outdoor grill, leaving tantalizingly unfinished a joke about why Italians don't have barbecues. Daniels becomes obsessed with his own health and consults a series of doctors, finally taking a dream-trip into an afterlife run by Howard Hughes, where damned souls sit around swimming pools forever. It's not just the presence of Melanie Mayron as Daniels' wife that makes this seem like an episode of *thirtysomething*, since this is one of a whole run of recent films – *Parenthood, sex, lies and videotape, See You in the Morning* – aimed at young affluents edging towards middle age with a lot of money and a need to indulge themselves in worrying about various side issues. As such it's quite sharp for about an hour, but it gets seriously strained during the farcical complications that lead up to the final dream-trip-to-heaven scene. Incidentally, Italians don't have barbecues 'because the spaghetti keeps falling through the grill.' It's not worth all the suffering to get to the punchline. KN
Director *David Leland* **producer** *Ben Myron* **execs** *George Harrison, Denis O'Brien* **script** *Joe Eszterhas* **camera** *Ian Wilson* **editor** *Lee Percy* **design** *Barbara Ling* **music** *Carter Burwell* **cast** *Jeff Daniels, Melanie Mayron, Michael Tucker, Kathleen York, Ann Magnuson, Jo Harvey Allen, Felton Perry, Ian Wolfe, John Durbin, Allan Havey*
Running time: 93 mins
US release: Warner, Apr 21, 1989
UK release: Virgin, Sep 29, 1989

CHICAGO JOE AND THE SHOWGIRL

TURKEY • TURKEY • TURKEY

Director *Bernard Rose* **producer** *Tim Bevan* **script** *David Yallop* **camera** *Mike Southon* **editor** *Dan Rae* **design** *Gemma Jackson* **music** *Hans Zimmer, Shirley Walker* **cast** *Kiefer Sutherland, Emily Lloyd, Patsy Kensit, Keith Allen, Liz Fraser, Alexandra Pigg, John Lahr, Harry Fowler, Angela Morant, John Surman, Janet Dale*
Running time: 103 mins
UK release: Palace, Apr 6, 1990

A CHORUS OF DISAPPROVAL

People tend to forget that Michael Winner used to make comedies. The reason is that they weren't very good. Unfortunately he's decided not to let sleeping dogs lie, turning in this spectacularly unsubtle comedy of manners revolving around an amateur production of *The Beggar's Opera*. Once again Winner shows that his true talent lies in soothing the disparate egos of a large cast without requiring them to act – Anthony Hopkins slices the ham so thick that the film could run into distribution problems in Israel – and only Irons as the bewildered innocent manages to hit the right note (bad accent notwithstanding). There's nothing even approaching humanity or comic timing, but the film clearly offered Winner a chance to do what he's best at – bringing in a turkey on time and on budget. TW
Director/producer *Michael Winner* **execs** *André Blay, Elliot Kastner* **script** *Alan Ayckbourn, Winner, from play by Ayckbourn* **camera** *Alan Jones* **editor** *Arnold Crust* **design** *Peter Young* **music** *John Du Prez* **cast** *Anthony Hopkins, Jeremy Irons, Richard Briers, Gareth Hunt, Patsy Kensit, Alexandra Pigg, Prunella Scales, Jenny Seagrove, Pete Lee-Wilson, Barbara Ferris, Lionel Jeffries, Sylvia Syms, David King*
Running time: 99 mins
US release: South Gate, Aug 18, 1989
UK release: Hobo/Curzon, Nov 3, 1989

CINEMA PARADISO (Nuovo Cinema Paradiso)

FILM • FILM • FILM • FILM

Director/script *Giuseppe Tornatore* **producer** *Franco Cristaldi* **camera** *Blasco Giurato* **editor** *Mario Morra* **design** *Andrea Crisanti* **music** *Ennio Morricone, Andrea Morricone* **cast** *Philippe Noiret, Jacques Perrin, Salvatore Cascio, Mario Leonardi, Agnese Nano, Pupella Maggio, Antonella Attili, Isa Danielli, Leopoldo Trieste, Enzo Cannavale, Leo Gullotta, Tana Cimarosa*
Running time: 122 mins (originally 155)
US release: Miramax, Feb 2, 1990
UK release: Palace, Feb 23, 1990

THE CITADEL (El Kalaa)

This Algerian film represents the sort of Third World enterprise that one wishes to admire and respond to: its attempt to create a portrait of a remote mountain village, ruled by superstition and strict Moslem law, gives every impression of coming from the heart and of seeking to illuminate a social situation at first hand. Yet while it may be inevitable that the cultural context poses difficulties to a western viewer, the confusion that the film engenders has deeper roots: the lack of narrative clarity and dramatic elucidation ends up by obfuscating the filmmaker's very attitude to his subject. Oddly, too, the fluency and polish of the visual surface contrive to exaggerate the problem by lending

the picture a touristic dimension which can hardly have been intended. **TP**
Director/script Mohammed Chouikh **producer/camera** Taha Harhoura **editor** Yamina Chouikh **design** Zerrouki Boukhari, Ahmed Kobbi **music** Djawad Fasla **cast** Khaled Barkat, Djillali Ain Tedelles, Fettouma Ousliha, Fatima Belhadj, Momo
Running time: 98 mins
UK release: Metro, Mar 30, 1990

◄ A CITY OF SADNESS (Beiqing Chengshi)

This is a bejewelled epic of family history from Taiwan's Hou Hsiao-Hsien. As communists and Chinese nationalists battle for control of the island after World War 2, we follow the lives and loves of three Taiwanese brothers: a shipping merchant, a drug dealer and a deaf-mute photographer. Despite a huge and proliferating cast – resulting in lines like 'Fourth uncle, they've arrested third uncle' – the film never loses its way nor its grasp on the counterpoint between private and public destiny. History blazes like gunfire outside, while inside tiny, resistant dramas of love or hope flame in the heart's hearths. Winner of the 1989 Venice Golden Lion. **HK**
Director Hou Hsiao-Hsien **producer** Qiu Fusheng **execs** H. T. Yan, Michael Yang **script** Wu Nianzhen, Zhu Tianwen **camera** Chen Huai'en **editor** Liao Qingsong **design** Liu Zhihua, Lin Chongwen **music** Naoki Tachikawa, Zhang Hongyi **cast** Li Tianlu, Chen Songyong, Gao Jie, Tony Leung, Wu Yifang, Xin Shufen, Chen Shufang, Ke Suyun, Lin Liqing, He Aiyun, Kenny Cheung
Running time: 160 mins
UK release: Artificial Eye, Mar 23, 1990

◄ CLEAN AND SOBER

Elements of 1930s-style social conscience melodrama co-exist here with a study in psychological dynamics, as a drug and drink-addicted junior executive sees his life fall apart and rebuilds it after a fashion with a fellow-unfortunate from lower down the social ladder. The casting of Michael Keaton, as the executive who initally checks into a detox programme only to escape creditors and police investigation into his involvement in a possible murder, is strikingly effective, not so much in its apparent contradiction of his earlier screen images as for the manner in which the hovering intimations of 'wise guy' comedy serve by default to intensify the darkness of dramatic texture. Directed in a deceptively plain fashion which encompasses a real command of tempo and nuance, this represents the kind of adult filmmaking for which there sadly seems to be no real audience anymore. **TP**

Director Glenn Gordon Caron **producers** Tony Ganz, Deborah Blum **exec** Ron Howard **script** Tod Carroll **camera** Jan Kiesser **editor** Richard Chew **design** Joel Schiller **music** Gabriel Yared **cast** Michael Keaton, Kathy Baker, Morgan Freeman, M. Emmet Walsh, Brian Benben, Luca Bercovici, Tate Donovan, Henry Judd Baker
Running time: 124 mins
US release: Warner, Aug 10, 1988
UK release: Warner, Jun 8, 1990

COMMUNION

Horror novelist Whitley Strieber (*The Hunger, Wolfen*) was abducted by extra-terrestrials and now wants to tell the world the truth. It would be more believable if someone with no imagination were abducted (say, James Michener), but that's Strieber's story and he's sticking to it. In *Communion*, Christopher Walken gives an intriguingly chilly performance as a self-absorbed writer, and there are cheap thrills to be had, but the film is more than a little conventional and the worshipful treatment of the story's 'truth' (Strieber wrote the script) makes everyone seem a little dull. **JH**
Director Philippe Mora **producers** Mora, Whitley Strieber, Dan Allingham **execs** Paul Redshaw, Gary Barber **script** Strieber, from his book **camera** Louis Irvin **editor** Lee Smith **design** Linda Pearl **music** Eric Clapton, Allan Zavod **cast** Christopher Walken, Lindsay Crouse, Joel Carlson, Frances Sternhagen, Andreas Katsulas, Terri Hanauer
Running time: 109 mins
US release: New Line, Nov 10, 1989

▼ CONQUEST OF THE SOUTH POLE

Amundsen, thou shouldst be living at this hour. With Leith, the port of Edinburgh, standing in for Antarctica, director Gillies MacKinnon translates to the screen Manfred Karge's symbol-heavy stage play about jobless youths fantasizing the conquest of the Pole. White sheets on a clothes-line play glaciers, coils of ship-chains are mountains and the dialogue yells its metaphors at us through the loud-hailed performances. Not so much a comment on a culture of society in crisis, more a product of love. Anti-Establishment hectoring in the guise of high art. **HK**
Director Gillies MacKinnon **producer** Gareth Wardell **exec** John Kelleher **script** Wardell, from play by Manfred Karge **camera** Sean Van Hales **editor** Stephen Singleton **design** Andy Harris **music** Guy Woolfenden **cast** Steven Rimkus, Ewen Bremner, Leonard O'Malley, Laura Girling, Gordon Cameron, Alastair Galbraith, John Mitchie, Julie-Kate Olivier
Running time: 95 mins
UK release: BFI, Mar 16, 1990

THE COOK THE THIEF HIS WIFE & HER LOVER

In a car park, gangster Albert Spica (Gambon) has his thugs strip naked a restaurateur who has incurred his displeasure and forces the victim to eat several loads of shit. After this appalling introduction, we learn more about the thief, none of it good. Recently, he's bought a restaurant run by the Cook (Bohringer), and every night he brings his entourage to gorge themselves on wonderfully cinematic meals while he abuses his delicate wife (Mirren), driving her into the embrace of a bookish diner (Howard), with whom she commits adultery in the ladies' toilet. Spica bullies and alienates his hired men, casually shoving a fork into the face of a girl who talks back, and plots a terrible revenge upon the lovers, which in turn leads to his own disgusting downfall. Beautifully art-directed, photographed, produced and acted, the film deals with the kind of subject-matter usually only found under the counter at your local video-nasty dealer. Guaranteed to offend everybody, it's compulsive and unforgettable, but you'd be hard-pressed to like the thing. KN
Director/script Peter Greenaway **producer** Kees Kasander **camera** Sacha Vierny **editor** John Wilson **design** Ben Van Os, Jan Roelfs **music** Michael Nyman **cast** Richard Bohringer, Michael Gambon, Helen Mirren, Alan Howard, Tim Roth, Ciaran Hinds, Gary Olsen, Ewan Stewart, Roger Ashton Griffiths, Ron Cook, Liz Smith, Emer Gillespie, Janet Henfrey, Arnie Breevelt
Running time: 124 mins
UK release: Palace, Oct 13, 1990

COOKIE

Since this doesn't have much in the way of a plot, one must assume that it's meant to be a character comedy about strained father-daughter relations. But then since there's not much characterization either (Emily Lloyd impersonates Madonna while Peter Falk impersonates himself), you have to find some other way of keeping awake through to the closing credits and the first screen funeral conducted to the accompaniment of Kylie singing 'I Should Be So Lucky'. On the plus side, Jerry Lewis gives a good understated performance, Brenda Vaccaro goes exuberantly over the top and provides a couple of laughs, and it's not as bad as She-Devil. TW
Director Susan Seidelman **producer** Laurence Mark **execs** Seidelman, Nora Ephron, Alice Arlen **script** Ephron, Arlen **camera** Oliver Stapleton **editor** Andrew Mondshein **design** Michael Haller **music** Thomas Newman **cast** Peter Falk, Dianne Wiest, Emily Lloyd, Michael V. Gazzo, Brenda Vaccaro, Adrian Pasdar, Lionel Stander, Jerry Lewis, Bob Gunton, Ben Rayson, Ricki Lake, Joe Mantello, Thomas Quinn, David Wohl, Joy Behar, Frank Gio

Running time: 93 mins
US release: Warner, Aug 23, 1989
UK release: Warner, Oct 6, 1989

COUPE DE VILLE

This is a story of family reconciliation, with a trio of incompatible brothers (Stern, Gross, Dempsey) forced by their father to drive the titular vehicle from Michigan to Florida without inflicting upon it a single scratch. The results are predictable and 'heartwarming', and the only reason for the early 1960s setting is to assemble a great soundtrack of pre-Beatles white pop. A TV movie, and not a good one. JH
Director Joe Roth **producers** Larry Brezner, Paul Schiff **exec** James G. Robinson **script** Mike Binder **camera** Reynaldo Villalobos **editor** Paul Hirsch **design** Angelo Graham **music** James Newton Howard **cast** Patrick Dempsey, Arye Gross, Daniel Stern, Annabeth Gish, Rita Taggart, Joseph Bologna, Alan Arkin
Running time: 99 mins
US release: Universal, Mar 9, 1990

COURAGE MOUNTAIN

Courage Mountain is yet another example of what some parents like to think their children should be seeing. As recent efforts go, it isn't too bad – the scenery is quite pretty, as is the period décor – but the result is very uninvolving. As Heidi, leading a group of orphans across the mountains to freedom through non-threatening explosions and avalanches during World War I, Juliette Caton is considerably less fun than when she was persuading Jesus it was okay to bonk Mary Magdalene, while saintly Leslie Caron just worries on the sidelines and nasty Yorgo Voyagis glowers and talks about killing them but unfortunately never gets round to it. On the plus side, we don't see much of Charlie Sheen. TW
Director Christopher Leitch **producer** Stephen Ujlaki **execs** Joel A. Douglas **script** Weaver Webb **camera** Jacques Steyn **editor** Martin Walsh **design** Robb Wilson King **music** Sylvester Levay **cast** Juliette Caton, Charlie Sheen, Leslie Caron, Yorgo Voyagis, Laura Betti, Jan Rubeš, Joanna Clarke, Jade Magri
Running time: 98 mins
US release: Triumph, Feb 16, 1990
UK release: Entertainment, Apr 6, 1990

COUSINS

Joel Schumacher ably remakes the 1975 French comedy of infidelity Cousin, Cousine, using North American ethnicity as a stand-in for Gallic spirit. Ted Danson and Isabella Rossellini meet when her mother marries his uncle. Their spouses' affair brings them together, and they satisfy their

honour by first attempting to be friends and then by remaining apart. Naturally, neither stratagem works and eventually they are lovers. Like *Moonstruck*, *Cousins* pays attention to the lives of the lovers' extended families, allowing Sean Young, Lloyd Bridges and others to pepper the film with funny moments. **BM**
Director *Joel Schumacher* **producer** *William Allyn* **exec** *George Goodman* **script** *Stephen Metcalfe, from film* Cousin, Cousine *by Jean-Charles Tacchella* **camera** *Ralf D. Bode* **editor** *Robert Brown* **design** *Mark S. Freeborn* **music** *Angelo Badalamenti* **cast** *Ted Danson, Isabella Rossellini, Sean Young, William Petersen, Lloyd Bridges, Norma Aleandro, Keith Coogan, Gina De Angelis*
Running time: 110 mins
US release: Paramount, Feb 10, 1989
UK release: UIP, Aug 25, 1989

CRAZY PEOPLE

Dudley Moore is the ageing *wunderkind* at the end of his tether who finally takes truth in advertising to its furthest limit ('Metamuesli – it helps you go to the toilet'; 'Volvo – they're boxy but they're good') and gets thrown into a mental institution for his troubles. He meets Darryl Hannah in there and, when his concept suddenly goes through the roof, they get together to form their own ad agency together with the inmates. It sounds dire, but it's mostly very funny, with Moore playing it straight to good effect. It's certainly head and shoulders above *How to Get Ahead in Advertising*. **TW**
Director *Tony Bill* **producer** *Tom Barad* **exec** *Robert K. Weiss* **script** *Mitch Markowitz* **camera** *Victor J. Kemper* **editor** *Mia Goldman* **design** *John J. Lloyd* **music** *Cliff Eidelman* **cast** *Dudley Moore, Daryl Hannah, Paul Reiser, Mercedes Ruehl, J. T. Walsh, Ben Hammer, Dick Cusack, Alan North, David Paymer, Danton Stone, Doug Yasuda, Bill Smitrovich, Paul Bates, Floyd Vivino, John Terlesky*
Running time: 90 mins
US release: Paramount, Apr 11, 1990

CRIMES AND MISDEMEANORS
FILM • FILM • FILM • FILM

Director/script *Woody Allen* **producer** *Robert Greenhut* **execs** *Jack Rollins, Charles H. Joffe* **camera** *Sven Nykvist* **editor** *Susan E. Morse* **design** *Santo Loquasto* **cast** *Martin Landau, Woody Allen, Mia Farrow, Alan Alda, Anjelica Huston, Sam Waterston, Joanna Gleason, Caroline Aaron, Jerry Orbach, Claire Bloom, Stephanie Roth, Jenny Nichols, David S. Howard, Anna Berger, Victor Argo, Martin Bergmann, Daryl Hannah*
Running time: 104 mins
US release: Orion, Oct 13, 1989
UK release: Rank, Jul 27, 1990

CRUSOE

This revisionist version of Defoe's classic centres on Crusoe's journey from slave trader to liberator through a *Hell in the Pacific*-style relationship with a cannibal warrior. Both Aidan Quinn and Ade Sapara turn in finely-rounded performances; the script is humorous and manages a few genuine surprises; the Scope photograpy captures some memorable images and highlights the best storm sequence in years, but ultimately the film's brevity counts against it. All the memorable set-pieces are there, but there is too little between them for us to become emotionally involved with Crusoe, no matter how much our liberal sympathies may approve of his final act of redemption. An honourable attempt nonetheless, and a vast improvement on Deschanel's first feature, *The Escape Artist*. **TW**
Director *Caleb Deschanel* **producer** *Andrew Braunsberg* **script** *Walon Green, Christopher Logue, from Daniel Defoe's novel* Robinson Crusoe **camera** *Tom Pinter* **design** *Velco Despotovic* **music** *Michael Kamen* **cast** *Aidan Quinn, Ade Sapara, Elvis Payne, Richard Sharp, Colin Bruce, William Hootkins, Shane Rimmer*
Running time: 91 mins
US release: Island, Mar 31, 1989
UK release: Virgin, Aug 11, 1989

CRY-BABY

The wicked promise of the title sequence – brash or trembling high-school kids lining up for vaccinations – is not fulfilled by the rest of *Cry-Baby*, a desperately disappointing comedy-musical from John Waters, who seems to be drifting inexorably towards mainstream respectability and appalling good taste. This clichéd story of star-crossed lovers – Johnny Depp as the tear-streaked rock 'n' roll biker Cry-Baby Walker, Amy Locane as the virginal prom princess – lacks the kind of social theme that gave *Hairspray* an edge, and consequently makes no more demands on the viewer than did *Grease*. It's fun spotting Waters' hommages – to *Rebel Without a Cause* and *Jailhouse Rock* among others – and the movie is buoyed up by Traci Lords, Willem Dafoe, Patti Hearst and Iggy Pop in small parts, but there's no mistaking the need for Divine inspiration. **GF**
Director/script *John Waters* **producer** *Rachael Talalay* **execs** *Jim Abrahams, Brian Grazer* **camera** *David Insley* **editor** *Janice Hampton* **design** *Vincent Peranio* **music** *Patrick Williams* **cast** *Johnny Depp, Amy Locane, Susan Tyrrell, Polly Bergen, Iggy Pop, Ricki Lake, Traci Lourds, Kim McGuire, Darren E. Burrows*
Running time: 85 mins
US release: Universal, Apr 6, 1990

CHICAGO JOE AND THE SHOWGIRL

The 1944 'Cleft Chin' murder (so called because of a facial oddity of the victim) was probably the most celebrated case of its kind on the home front during World War 2. Coverage of the subsequent trial, leading to the conviction of Welsh-born 'good time girl' Elizabeth Jones and US army deserter Karl Hulten for the killing of a taxi driver whom they robbed of £8, squeezed the war news off the front pages. Both were sentenced to hang, though in the event Jones's sentence was commuted, a decision apparently greeted with popular displeasure.

A few years later, via a novel with the quintessentially *noir* title, *Night Darkens the Streets*, a fictionalized account of Jones's life reached the screen in the pungent if hamfisted *Good Time Girl* from Gainsborough studios.

But if this erstwhile *cause célèbre* is much remembered now, it is probably due to its providing the peg for George Orwell's perverse and intriguing essay, *Decline of the English Murder*. This is effectively a companion piece to his earlier and longer article, *Raffles and Miss Blandish*, and as Orwell had there contrasted the supposed squalor of James Hadley Chase with the moral certainties of E. W. Hornung, so he laments the 'whole meaningless story' of the Cleft Chin case by comparison with the 'old poisoning dramas', products of a stable society where the all-prevailing hypocrisy did at least ensure that crimes as serious as murder would have strong emotions behind them. (Quite how ironical this conclusion is meant to be is none too easy to determine.)

With the intervening years, the balance has, in Orwell's terms, swung further and further from the old certainties, and now the Cleft Chin case itself, with (in his words) 'its atmosphere of dance halls, movie palaces, cheap perfume', might be thought to belong to something like an age of innocence. Anyway, the British cinema has seen fit to disinter it: after the headline-making episodes of the 1960s (*Scandal, Buster*) and the 1950s (*Dance With a Stranger*), it has been deemed time to reach back to the war years.

Strangely enough, the film begins on a note of outright fantasy, with Jones (Emily Lloyd) imagining herself as a Hollywood star arriving at a première. We are led to think that what follows will be filtered through her corrupted consciousness; but in the event this is only intermittently the case. Occasionally we see Jones, who lays fallacious claim to a show-business background, transformed into a movie-style gangster's moll, and Hulten (Kiefer Sutherland) into the acolyte of Al Capone that he passes himself off to be. There is even at one point the ill-advised incorporation of a snatch of *Double Indemnity*, with Hulten's image replacing that of Fred MacMurray in Jones's mind's eye.

Such gestures are for the most part, though, subordinated to an external recounting of events during the few days that elapsed between the couple's first meeting and the murder, which includes the near killing of an unfortunate young woman (Alexandra Pigg) to whom they duplicitously offer a lift in Hulten's stolen truck. This latter sequence is, oddly, the most sustained in the film; briefly, matters take on a savage independent life.

But in general the case history format creates a two-way bind. Dramatically speaking, such episodes as those involving Hulten's naïvely 'respectable' girlfriend (Patsy Kensit) and her parents seem largely unrevealing. And from a crypto-documentary viewpoint, there is, over and above the inevitably obtrusive 'costume drama' aspect of props and apparel, an undertow of the inauthentic about these strangely depopulated London streets; while surely even an audience born long after the war is liable to be puzzled by such incongruities as car headlights blazing in the black-out.

Orwell himself maintained that the episode 'belongs essentially to the war background'. Perhaps such a claim is tendentious; but in any case, the film, by painting this background in stylized, second-hand colours, reduces its action to that of one hollow fantasy played off against another. And when, after the couple has been arrested and the mundane truth about them comes out (Hulten was a married man who had never set foot in Chicago), the film simply comes to a stop, with only a disembodied voiceover to retail the subsequent events.

At the opening, the same stentorian voice has informed us: 'This is a true story. No facts have been altered.' But truth is, certainly in terms of a movie that adopts the procedures of dramatization, something of a chimera. *Bonnie and Clyde*, another story of a couple locked in destructive fantasy, is based on real events; but while the factual basis may provide historical perspective, what animates the whole is a quality of imaginative penetration. And imaginative penetration, as manifested by an organic style, is sadly what *Chicago Joe* lacks.

However much Orwell compels admiration in other respects, his evident disdain for the cinema leads cinephiles to qualify his judgements. Sad to say, however, the tawdriness of *Chicago Joe and the Showgirl*, with its resemblance to nothing so much as the kind of movie Jones and Hulten might have envisaged themselves being part of, tends to give him the last laugh.

TIM PULLEINE

CINEMA PARADISO

Cinema Paradiso is apparently in part an exercise in fictionalized autobiography; like his protagonist, Giuseppe Tornatore grew up in the Sicilian village of Giancaldo and began his working life as a projectionist at the local picture house. But it is autobiography displaced, as it were, in time. Tornatore is only in his 30s, and thus was born at about the time the main action of his film finishes – and also, of course, the time when the era of mass movie-going was coming to an end. In part what Cinema Paradiso resembles is a Valentine thrown to that vanished era; but only in part.

The film's form is that of sentimental-romanesque. In emblematic fashion, matters commence with news of a death and an impending funeral that occasions an imaginative journey into the past. De Vitta (Jacques Perrin) is 50-ish, a figure of some renown in the film industry in Rome; the death is that of Alfredo, his predecessor long ago as projectionist at the Paradiso, and the mentor of his youth.

Between this opening and the funeral itself, for which Da Vitta ('Toto' in boyhood) revisits his place of origin for the first time in countless years, comes the main body of the movie. This comprises his recollections of childhood and early manhood in the poverty-stricken village where the picture house provides not only the crucial influence in Toto's formation but the hub of community life.

Events begin during the war, when the child's father has, it transpires, been killed at the Russian front. The childless Alfredo – a rôle in which Philippe Noiret, expertly dubbed, gives a performance of nuance and density worthy of the pre-war heyday of French character acting – becomes a surrogate parent to him.

The relationship between them is inscribed both within the rituals of the projection booth (Alfredo can tell without looking when the image is out of focus) and within those of what is on the screen: Alfredo offers the boy a succession of apothegms on life and society which he then delightedly ascribes to John Wayne, Henry Fonda, et al.

Fittingly for the sense of symbiosis between the mechanism of showing movies and the experience of absorbing them, our first sight of Alfredo is of his face 'framed' in the window of the projection box. Just as the lion's head ornament through which the projector beam emerges is transmogrified in the child's imagining into a roaring beast unfurling its tongue, as if magically embodying a means of disseminating that 'universal language' which early film historians were so anxious to propound.

Among the Paradiso's patrons, the procedures of popular art and everyday life are depicted as intertwined: comedies and melodramas unfold on the screen; practical jokes are played and assignations kept in the auditorium.

As the other spectators shield their eyes from the depradations of Mr Hyde, two lovers gaze rapturously at each other, oblivious to the horrors in front of them; and in a flourish of black comedy, the blaze of tommy-guns in a gangster movie coincides with one elderly regular's demise, and subsequently a wreath occupies his habitual seat.

The blacker components of the picture are, however, not necessarily comic, and its central episode is one of tragedy: Alfredo is blinded in a fire when the celluloid ignites during his projection of a 'sold out' film on to a wall in the square outside – a bitterly ironic moment since his gesture had served to encapsulate the brunt of his earlier comment to Toto that what redeems the rigour of his life is the sense of being the instrument of bringing people happiness. (And there is grim subtlety in his having just beforehand jocularly likened the crowd outside the Paradiso to the mob in *Fury*, imparting to anyone familiar with Fritz Lang's film recall of its dreadful imagery of the burning of the jail.)

Even here, though, the horror is redeemed by heroic convention, since it is Toto who is able to save Alfredo's life by dragging him unconscious out of the blazing building. The Paradiso rises phoenix-like out of the ashes, under the aegis of a local inhabitant who has won a big lottery prize (and has reacted to the good news by falling, like a character from a René Clair comedy, into a dead faint). Alfredo's professional mantle falls on Toto, and as it does so, the action moves on several years to the boy's adolescence and his first love affair.

The resonances of this relationship are rhymed with the associations of Toto's continuing passion for the cinema, within a spectrum of moods – comic (the set piece at the church service with Toto and Elena in a lover's *tête-à-tête* in the confessional), melodramatic (his fruitless New Year's Eve vigil in the street outside the girl's home), lyrical (the couples running hand-in-hand through a giant cornfield).

In the latter part of the flashback, military service intervenes, the girl's family moves away, his letters go unanswered. Back in Giancaldo, he feels unable to settle; when he confides his deracination to Alfredo, the latter urges him to avoid the lure of the past ('Life isn't like the movies – life is harder') and to pursue a career to the north.

The spectator may experience slight dissatisfaction over Elena's disappearance from the narrative (less abrupt, it would appear, in the substantially longer version of the film which was initially released in Italy, then rapidly withdrawn), and the foreign viewer may also feel a degree of puzzlement over the Sicilian concern with nostalgia, or anti-nostalgia, which seemingly motivates Alfredo's extraction of his protégé's promise never to come back.

The concluding panel of the movie is, however, managed to superb effect, as Da Vitta once more sets foot in Giancaldo and in his mother's home. How succinct a visual symbol is the 'umbilical' thread of wool that unravels from the mother's knitting as she goes to greet him. And how fitting it is that the funeral, with its procession headed by an altar boy who recalls our first sight of Toto as a child, should come after the flashback, rather than prompt it, since the film's implication is that we can never truly grasp our own formation.

There is, in a sense, a double funeral, Alfredo's and that of the Paradiso itself, which a day or two later is bulldozed into a car park: it is as if Alfredo's decline has been occasioned by the cinema's closure and his death by its impending destruction. And though the film makes it properly evident that material and economic conditions in the village have immeasurably improved, Da Vitta tells his mother that when he looks about him, all he can see are ghosts.

But this is not quite the end: when he leaves, he takes with him a bequest from Alfredo's widow, a rusting can of film. Back in Rome he sees the contents projected: a seemingly endless succession of embraces, snipped from bygone movies (as we have seen earlier comically illustrated) at the censorious insistence of the village priest. The very fragmentation of this assemblage seems to make it into an embodiment of memory: the illusion of the movies and the illusoriness of our own pasts are conjoined in magical suspension.

As Tornatore throws his Valentine to the vanished age of mass movie-going, he briefly creates the sensation that in our hearts we really can go home again; and he demonstrates that the pleasure principle can be something a good deal more actual than part of a film theorist's litany.

TIM PULLEINE

CRIMES AND MISDEMEANORS

After *September* and *Another Woman* we prayed to see Woody Allen in one of his own films again, as people on a health farm pray for ice cream with chocolate sauce.

During recent years the Woody Allen Austerity Institute (speciality, humour deprivation) has subjected us to lecture courses on the following subjects: the angst of Ingmar Bergman; the autumnal colours of Chekhov as interpreted by Sven Nykvist; Mia Farrow – waif or saint; and how much spiritual masochism can a filmmaker insert in his oeuvre but still keep a Hollywood studio paying for it? (Or, when does Orion tighten its belt?)

Crimes and Misdemeanors risks being overrated simply because Allen is in it and he is funny. Here again is the human bug with the spindly limbs, lens-dilated eyes and mosquito-whine voice, homing in on self-importance like an insect on sugar. Allen plays a humble documentary movie-director who 'makes these little films on toxic waste and starving children'. He is in love with Public TV producer Mia Farrow. And he is the voice of complaining Everyman. It's the voice we fell in love with in *Annie Hall* and *Manhattan*.

Assigned to shoot a profile of smug media-man Alan Alda (TV producer and sitcom writer), fiction filmmaker Allen goes into action. 'He's an American phenomenon,' gushes Alda fan Farrow. 'So is acid rain,' says Woody. And before long the dissident lens-wielder is following the smooth pontificator all over Washington, capturing his face and apothegms ('Comedy is tragedy plus time') and then lacing them together in a first-draft documentary that intercuts Alda with Mussolini.

Allen's love-hate affair with authority figures is back, gloriously re-aired in *Crimes and Misdemeanors*. From God to TV pundits, from shrinks to politicians, few Woody Allen films unspool without some serious questioning of the beings we carelessly define as our 'betters'. (And even fewer unspool without a glancing blow at history's great tradition of totalitarian leaders. In this film Allen's wife stopped sleeping with him, he recalls, on April 20 – 'I remember the date exactly because it was Hitler's birthday.')

In *Crimes and Misdemeanors*, for the first time in Allen's work, the inquest on moral authority-figures is not a footnote, it's the whole text. The film is about variations on the theme of Big Brotherism. And the perspective is opened up to include the religious. Who watches us when we sin or err? Are the eyes of God upon us when we murder, lie or simply, in Alda's case, bullshit? Or in a godless age where moral truths are delivered to us from TV transmitters rather than stone tablets, has the eye of the camera lens replaced the eyes of God?

Two stories interconnect in the film. In one, Allen seeks to sort philosophical truth from philosophical claptrap as he pursues two gurus in rival documentary projects. (One is the assigned Alda; the other is a Jewish philosopher and concentration camp survivor he's saving for a labour-of-love TV profile.) In the second story, ophthalmologist Martin Landau seeks to murder querulous mistress Anjelica Huston, who has threatened to reveal their affair to the world and Landau's wife Claire Bloom. The murder happens; Huston is killed by Landau's gangster brother Jerry Orbach and the culprits go free. Ergo, the 'eyes of God' must be closed; or God must not exist.

Portentousness hovers over the movie like a cloud-mass. In her *New Yorker* review, Pauline Kael complained that Allen is becoming more of a DIY prophet-philosopher with each film: 'The years that he's been railing against the universe without definitive answers must have worn him down, so now he's supplying them.'

But Allen supplies few if any answers, religious or philosophical; and that's the film's strength. It argues, more with a shrug of the shoulders than with a flourish of rhetoric, that sin and deceit are common tender in an age when no agency exists for detecting counterfeit moral actions. No God; no shared religious convictions; almost no great moral thinkers. (The only one the Allen character looks up to, his Jewish death-camp survivor, commits suicide before the film's end.) Whether a man's sin is great or small – whether it's homicide (Landau) or humbug (Alda) – chances are he'll get away with it.

The movie's only major weakness is the character provided to knit the stories together, using a cumbersome skein of symbolism to do so. Sam Waterston plays a rabbi who is losing his sight. Allen's brother-in-law and Landau's friend and moral confidant, Waterston's character is also a walking (or rather sitting) metaphor. Representing God's clouding vision, the rabbi's failing powers of penetration in a spiritually murky world are contrasted with the keen but 'assisted' sight of ophthalmologist Landau, a man who makes artificial aids to vision, and media-man Alda who uses the fake eyes of TV.

Waterston's rôle is so schematic it belongs with the worst contrivances of *Interiors* and *September*. In a movie as effervescent as *Crimes and Misdemeanors*, he's a real party-pooper: a funeral guest who's strayed into a wedding or christening. Each time he appears on screen it's like a tap on the shoulder from a celestial white stick: 'Remember we're into spiritual admonishment here, my son. Close your eyes to the film's fun and one-liners. Turn them inwards on your own soul.'

Elsewhere the marvel of *Crimes and Misdemeanors* is that, like its characters, it's always one pace ahead of its own follies or pieties. It moves so fast that, unlike Allen's other stabs at morality drama, it has the semblance of life and surprise. Landau's brisk descent into the maelstrom of sin is thoroughly effective: swift, coldhearted and unfussy, an authentically twentieth-century murder. And in the lighter parallel story, Allen's comic snappings at Alda's heels, amplified by sexual jealousy as Alda and Farrow drift into a romance, join an anti-charlatanism message to the terrier wit of Allen at his best. ('He wants to produce something of mine,' says Farrow to Allen. 'Yes, your first child,' bleats Allen).

Woody Allen has played with multiple-story schemes before in his films.

Overtly in *Everything You Always Wanted to Know About Sex*; covertly in movies with overlapping plots and anecdotes like *Hannah and Her Sisters* and *Radio Days*. The filmmaker's apprenticeship as a stand-up comic, gag-writer and slim-volume humorist clearly sharpened his art as a creator of cameos rather than large canvases. And the uncertainties of films like *Interiors* and *September* lie in the mismatch between Allen's quick-sketch storytelling skills and the lumbering, pseudo-seamless dramas he tried to create in tribute to his heavy-mob culture heroes. In this film the only obvious Bergman resonance is in the title itself, an echo of *Cries and Whispers*.

In *Crimes and Misdemeanors*, the juggling of two stories in one film doesn't just sharpen the comedy and characterization. It allows Allen to play sophisticated games with time. Abandoning the airless neatness of *September*, in which the characters were trapped inside the Aristotelian unities as if within a designer hour-glass, the new film also moves beyond the 'stations of the cross' emotional-martyrdom scenario that constituted *Another Woman*.

Crimes and Misdemeanors is like two shaggy-dog stories chasing each other's tale. Each sharpens the other's speed and reflexes. And the intercutting of the two plots creates a mosaic of time in which the audience sees the rhyming of moral themes picked out more clearly thanks to the diffident, less attention-hogging impact of the narrative itself.

Indeed notions of time are so deftly discombobulated by the inter-threading of two stories – however much we can be sure of one story's time sequence, we can't so easily keep tabs on the relative time sequences of *two* tales – that even Allen's haunted psychodrama flashbacks work. When Martin Landau stands in the doorway of his childhood home, 'talking' to his long-gone parents, it is no more surprising than any other happening in a film with its own supple, free-range time scheme.

As a further, final bonus, *Crimes and Misdemeanors* displays more skill than any Allen movie since *Hannah and Her Sisters* at juggling the all-star cast that has lately become an Allen staple. Alda and Landau, Allen and Farrow find rôles that fit like gloves. Huston, Bloom and Orbach bring an edgy lustre to tinier parts. And even that wretched rabbi is made almost bearable by Waterston's delicate, ironized underplaying.

HARLAN KENNEDY

👎 DAD

Gary David Goldberg's background in sitcoms proves all too easy to deduce from this substantially altered and diluted treatment of William Wharton's novel. The resultant film is a cosmetic job in more than just the sense that Lemmon and Dukakis have manifestly been done over by the make-up department so as to resemble septuagenarians. The attempted mixture of laughter and tears which emanates from the return home to cope with his parents' illness of a businessman son (Danson, purveying plastic charm) – how he is able to brush off his commercial obligations goes blandly disregarded – varies in tenor from the merely awkward to the wholly excruciating, as Danson not only finds a new rapport with mom and dad, but establishes a new relationship with his own teenage offspring to boot. TP
Director *Gary David Goldberg* **producers** *Joseph Stern, Goldberg* **execs** *Steven Spielberg, Frank Marshall, Kathleen Kennedy* **script** *Goldberg, from novel by William Wharton* **camera** *Jan Kiesser* **editor** *Eric Sears* **design** *Jack DeGovia* **music** *James Horner* **cast** *Jack Lemmon, Ted Danson, Olympia Dukakis, Kathy Baker, Kevin Spacey, Ethan Hawke, Zakes Mokae, J. T. Walsh, Peter Michael Goetz, John Apicella, Richard McGonagle, Bill Morey, Art Frankel, Ray Girardin*
Running time: 118 mins
US release: Universal, Oct 27, 1989
UK release: UIP, Feb 23, 1990

DANCIN' THRU THE DARK

As might be expected from the playwright who brought us *Educating Rita and Shirley Valentine*, this centres around a woman's dilemma – should I marry my Scouse slob or run off to London with an old boyfriend, who's now a rising pop star? – but *Dancing' Thru the Dark* is an ensemble piece built with broader strokes than Willy Russell's other films. The result is funny and endearing but it lacks a dramatic core. As a group of hens and stags head towards the same kitsch nightclub on the eve of wedding day, the bride-to-be is drawn back to the musician she hasn't seen since he left Liverpool for London. He clearly carries a loaded pack and, after the groom has sicked up over his best friend's trousers in the first reel, there's really no contest. Some aggressive posturing by the groom's friends as they try to frighten off the rival, and some tragic looks from the would-be bride, can't make the ending seem any less predictable. JP
Director *Mike Ockrent* **producers** *Andrée Molyneux, Annie Rusell* **execs** *Richard Broke, Chris Brown, Charles Negus-Fancey* **script/music** *Willy Russell* **camera** *Philip Bonham-Carter* **editor** *John Stothart* **design** *Paul Joel* **cast** *Con O'Neill, Ben Murphy, Peter Beckett, Julian Littman, Claire Hackett, Julia Deakin, Angela Clark, Andrew Naylor, Peter Watts, Simon O'Brien, Conrad Nelson*
Running time: 95 mins
UK release: Palace, Mar 2, 1990

DANNY THE CHAMPION OF THE WORLD

The script of *Danny* is quite closely adapted from Roald Dahl's children's story, but backdating the period to 1955 has the effect of emphasizing the resemblance to a junior version of Ealing comedy. Allied to the depiction of an idealized village community, where iconoclasm and a spot of poaching are all very well so long as everyone knows their place in the scheme of things, is a proto-green theme of preserving rural living and putting paid to the property-speculating machinations of the *nouveau riche* villain. Pleasant enough in its way, but a bit twee and half-hearted: surely, for instance, the nasty schoolmaster (well depicted by Ronald Pickup) deserves some worse comeuppance than merely having the seat of his pants ripped open? TP
Director *Gavin Millar* **producer** *Eric Abraham* **execs** *Alan Horrox, Paulo de Oliveira, Carol Rubin, Jay Rayvid, Dale Bell, Simon Relph, Monica Sims* **script** *John Goldsmith, from novel by Roald Dahl* **camera** *Oliver Stapleton* **editors** *Peter Tanner, Angus Newton* **design** *Don Homfray* **music** *Stanley Myers* **cast** *Jeremy Irons, Robbie Coltrane, Samuel Irons, Cyril Cusack, Michael Hordern, Lionel Jeffries, Ronald Pickup, Jean Marsh, Jimmy Nail, William Armstrong*
Running time: 99 mins
UK release: Portobello, Jul 28, 1990

DAYS OF THUNDER

They should have called this 'Top Car'. Producers Simpson and Bruckheimer, director Tony Scott and star Tom Cruise here reprise their responsibilities in *Top Gun*. But unfortunately cars are less interesting than military jets and, unless one is wired into the filmmakers' apparent obsession with stock-car racing, the film seems an endless sequence of barely distinguishable cars going around interchangeable ovals, intercut with closeups of Cruise with grease on his face. Robert Duvall deserves some credit though. He plays the veteran mechanical genius as if he were in a real movie, and he's been given the best lines by screenwriter Robert Towne. Nicole Kidman, who had a striking Sigourney Weaver-type quality in *Dead Calm*, has little to do but sleep with the hero, give moralistic speeches about what a jerk he is, and finally realize that, although he may be an immature jerk, he's still a great immature jerk, and he's played by Tom Cruise, so he ought to be

given some slack. The film is curiously tensionless, especially by comparison with *Top Gun*. JH
Director *Tony Scott* **producers** *Don Simpson, Jerry Bruckheimer* **exec** *Jerry Molen* **script** *Robert Towne* **camera** *Ward Russell* **editors** *Billy Weber, Chris Lebenzon,* **design** *Benjamin Fernandez, Thomas E. Sanders* **music** *Hans Zimmer* **cast** *Tom Cruise, Robert Duvall, Randy Quaid, Nicole Kidman, Michael Rooker, Cary Elwes Fred Dalton Thampson, John C. Reilly, J. C. Quinn, Don Simpson*
Running time: 107 mins
US release: Paramount, Jun 27, 1990

◄▌ DEAD CALM

This feisty seagoing thriller is culled from the source novel for Orson Welles' never-completed *The Deep*. Holidaying in the Pacific, Sam Neill and wife have their lives taken over by a mystery survivor from a drifting schooner. Has he killed his comrades? Might he kill again? And when Sam goes off to investigate the schooner, should he leave his wife alone with the human enigma? Welles might have done more to play up the Pandora's Box of plot twists that follow; but the story keeps us guessing and gasping, and Dean Semler's photography is knockout. HK
Director *Phillip Noyce* **producers** *Terry Hayes, Doug Mitchell, George Miller* **script** *Hayes, from novel by Charles Williams* **camera** *Dean Semler* **editor** *Richard Francis-Bruce* **design** *Graham (Grace) Walker* **music** *Graeme Reville* **cast** *Sam Neill, Nicole Kidman, Billy Zane*
Running time: 96 mins
US release: Warner, Apr 7, 1989
UK release: Warner, Nov 3, 1990

DEAD POETS SOCIETY
D I S A P P O I N T M E N T

Director *Peter Weir* **producers** *Steven Haft, Paul Junger Witt, Tony Thomas* **script** *Tom Schulman* **camera** *John Seale* **design** *Wendy Stites* **music** *Maurice Jarre* **cast** *Robin Williams, Robert Sean Leonard, Ethan Hawke, Josh Charles, Gale Hansen, Dylan Kussman, Allelon Ruggiero, James Waterson, Norman Lloyd, Kurtwood Smith, Carla Belver, Leon Pownall*
Running time: 128 mins
US release: BV, Jun 2, 1989
UK release: Warner, Sep 22, 1989

▼ DEALERS

A British attempt at *Wall Street*, this is about a group of fundamentally nasty people making money hand over fist and dining out in style as they shuffle figures around without contributing anything to anyone. There's a token minute of wondering whether wheeler-dealing is morally sound, but that gets dropped like a hot potato to make room for some pretty posing from yuppie scum Paul McGann and Rebecca De Mornay, who play initially-at-odds, ultimately-in-bed dollar dealers out to haul a dodgy counting house out of its decline. Made with the soulless flair of an advert for a bank you don't want to trust, it pushes all the mechanical suspense buttons as people with striped shirts and braces prop three telephones on their shoulders and shout at each other, but it's more interesting in showing off the CDs and Italian cars that are the trappings of their useless lifestyle. McGann, for instance, escapes the commuter crush by coming in to work every morning via seaplane, and demonstrates his lovability by filling De Mornay's flat with balloons in an attempt to get off with her. One or two of the characters blow out their brains or have fatal heart attacks, but there are still too many of them left alive at the end. KN
Director *Colin Bucksey* **producer** *William P. Cartlidge* **execs** *Andrew Brown, John Hambley* **script** *Andrew MacLear* **camera** *Peter Sinclair* **editor** *Jon Costelloe* **design** *Peter J. Hampton* **music** *Richard Hartley* **cast** *Paul McGann, Rebecca De Mornay, Derrick O'Connor, John Castle, Paul Guilfoyle, Rosalind Bennett, Adrian Dunbar, Nicholas Hewetson, Sara Sugarman, Di Kraine Tulaine*
Running time: 91 mins
US release: Skouras, Nov 3, 1989
UK release: Rank, Aug 25, 1989

DEEPSTAR SIX

This underwater re-telling of *Alien* is competently done but still rates pretty low on the thrills meter. The monster from the deep looks like a certain sort of automatic car wash, and its murderous visitations are too heavily signposted to shock. The idea of the Thing Growing Inside is transmuted rather pathetically into a lady crew member's gestating baby. A couple of nuclear explosions may not destroy the beastie, but it's just too obvious that the nascent nuclear family will be the ones who make it back to the top. JP
Director *Sean S. Cunningham* **producers** *Cunningham, Patrick Markey* **execs** *Mario Kassar, Andrew Vajna* **script** *Lewis Abernathy, Geoff Miller* **camera** *Mac Ahlberg* **editor** *David Handman* **design** *John Reinhart* **music** *Harry Manfredini* **cast** *Taurean Blacque, Nancy Everhard, Greg Evigan, Miguel Ferrer, Nia Peeples, Matt McCoy, Cindy Pickett, Marius Weyers*
Running time: 99 mins
US release: Tri-Star, Jan 13, 1989
UK release: Guild, Dec 1, 1989

THE DELINQUENTS

Kylie Minogue does for cinema what she's already done for popular music in this gag-a-minute 1950s 'row-manse'. She gets to say 'We're just like Row-me-oh and Jool-yet', discreetly flash a breast (or was it a pimple?) and go to bed with this year's runner-up in the 'I think I look like Mel Gibson did at school . . .' competition, Charles Schlatter (if ever anyone deserved to die on the end of a Capulet's sword, 'tis he). She also gets to karate chop a chocolate cake and treat us to the best mad scene this side of a John Waters movie. What she doesn't do is convince us that she can act for more than a few seconds without looking bored. Although enough of her fans lied about their age to make The Delinquents a hit in the UK, its best chance for posterity lies with enthusiasts of bad movies. TW
Director Chris Thomson **producers** Alex Cutler, Michael Wilcox **execs** Greg Coote, John Tarnoff, Graham Burke **script** Mac Gudgeon, Clayton Froham, from novel by Criena Rohan **camera** Andrew Lesnie **editor** John Scott **design** Laurence Eastwood **music** Miles Goodman **cast** Kylie Minogue, Charlie Schlatter, Angela Punch-McGregor, Bruno Lawrence, Todd Boyce
Running time: 101 mins
UK release: Warner, Dec 26, 1989

DIAMOND SKULLS

Documentarist Nick Broomfield's first fiction feature is an attempt to do a late 1980s drama of aristocratic decadence in the spirit of such 1960s items as The Servant or The Breaking of Bumbo. After a car accident in which a lowly cook is killed, cueing a 'meals on wheels' joke, aristocratic guardsman Gabriel Byrne, the guilty party, is sheltered by his passengers, a bunch of toadying Establishment hangers-on, although the owner of the car, who happens to be Byrne's sister's boyfriend, starts to get worried that he is being set up to take the fall, and that Byrne was not casually splatting a nobody but trying to murder his ex-model wife (Donohoe). Byrne is boringly saturnine in an underwritten rôle, while Donohoe models and removes various high-fashion garments as is her wont, and most of the supporting cast are simply outdated caricatures of the rich and obnoxious. There are a few convincing moments, but the trite storyline and thin characterizations prevent the film from ever getting started. KN
Director Nick Broomfield **producer** Tim Bevan **script** Tim Rose Price **camera** Michael Coulter **editor** Rodney Holland **design** Jocelyn James **music** Hans Zimmer **cast** Gabriel Byrne, Amanda Donohoe, Michael Hordern, Judy Parfitt, Douglas Hodge, Sadie Frost, Struan Rodger, Ian Carmichael
Running time: 87 mins
UK release: Virgin, Jun 8, 1990

DICK TRACY

D I S A P P O I N T M E N T
Director/producer Warren Beatty **execs** Barrie M. Osborne, Art Linson, Floyd Mutrux **script** Jim Cash, Jack Epps Jr., from characters created by Chester Gould **camera** Vittorio Storaro **editor** Richard Marks **design** Richard Sylbert **music** Danny Elfman **cast** Warren Beatty, Charlie Korsmo, Glenne Headly, Madonna, Al Pacino, Dustin Hoffman, William Forsythe, Charles Durning, Mandy Patinkin, Paul Sorvino, R. G. Armstrong, Dick Van Dyke
Running time: 103 mins
US release: BV, Jun 15, 1990

THE DREAM TEAM

Actor Michael Keaton continues a career in which bonanza movies beginning with B – Beetlejuice, Batman – alternate with duds beginning with almost anything. This one starts with a plot premise you wouldn't wish on your least favourite filmmaker. Four mental patients are separated from their doctor during a trip to a baseball match, and have wacky adventures all over town. If this 'Let's laugh at the loonies' plot were not tasteless enough, how about the passel of over-the-top performances? Stephen Furst says little but fears much, Christopher Lloyd fusses over details, Peter Boyle strips and preaches at the slightest provocation and Keaton tends to act out hostility. Not so much a dream team, more a nightmare package from Tinseltown. HK
Director Howard Zieff **producer** Christopher W. Knight **exec** Joseph M. Caracciolo **script** Jon Connolly, David Loucka **camera** Adam Holender **editor** C. Timothy O'Meara **design** Todd Hallowellq **music** David McHugh **cast** Michael Keaton, Christopher Lloyd, Peter Boyle, Stephen Furst, Dennis Boutsikaris, Lorraine Bracco, Milo O'Shea, Philip Bosco, James Remar, Jack Gilpin, Macintyre Dixon, Michael Lembeck
Running time: 113 mins
US release: Universal, Apr 7, 1989
UK release: UIP, Dec 15, 1989

DREAMS

After the pyrotechnics of Kagemusha and Ran, Akira Kurosawa presents a dream diary. View it by plain light and its eight fantasy episodes on themes of youth, war, art and nature seem like an old man's barely legible doodlings. Hold it to the flame of your own imagination and its beauty glows bold against the page. The more message-bearing dreams are resistible – notably the eco-conscious witterings of the villagers in 'The Watermills' – but others have a classic Kurosawa ferocity. The corpse-like walking soldiers in a nightmare of war; the mountaineers battling with snow-gods; Mount Fuji in flames (courtesy of

George Lucas's ILM effects crew); even the voyage through Van Gogh's crow-haunted paintings – fiery and astonishing, so long as you can take Martin Scorsese as Van Gogh. **HK Director/script** Akira Kurosawa **producers** Hisao Kurosawa, Mike Y. Inoue **camera** Takao Saito Masaharu Ueda **editor** Tome Minami **design** Yoshiro Muraki, Akira Sakuragi **music** Shinichiro Ikebe **cast** Akira Terao, Mitsunori Isaki, Martin Scorsese, Chishu Ryu, Mieko Harada, Mitsuko Baisho, Chosuke Ikariya, Hisahi Igawa, Toshihiko Nakano
Running time: 119 mins
UK release: Warner, May 25, 1990

DRIVING MISS DAISY
HIT • HIT • HIT • HIT • HIT

Director Bruce Beresford **producers** Richard D. Zanuck, Lili Fini Zanuck **exec** David Brown **script** Alfred Uhry, from his play **camera** Peter James **editor** Mark Warner **design** Bruno Rubeo **music** Hans Zimmer **cast** Morgan Freeman, Jessica Tandy, Dan Aykroyd, Patti Lupone, Esther Rolle
Running time: 99 mins
US release: Warner, Dec 13, 1989
UK release: Warner, Feb 23, 1990

DRUGSTORE COWBOY
FILM • FILM • FILM • FILM

Director Gus Van Sant **producers** Nick Wechsler, Karen Murphy **exec** Cary Brokaw **script** Van Sant, Daniel Yost, from novel by James Fogle **camera** Robert Yeoman **editors** Curtiss Clayton, Mary Bauer **design** David Brisbin **music** Elliot Goldenthal **cast** Matt Dillon, Kelly Lynch, James Le Gros, Heather Graham, James Remar, Beah Richards, Grace Zabriskie, Max Perlich, William S. Burroughs
Running time: 101 mins
US release: Avenue, Oct 6, 1989
UK release: Virgin, Dec 8, 1989

A DRY WHITE SEASON
Earnest liberal drama about South Africa. Donald Sutherland glooms away as the schoolteacher seeking justice when his black gardener's child dies in the Soweto riots. Director Euzhan Palcy (Black Shack Alley) tries to pump some life in writer Colin Welland's pious re-tread of Cry Freedom. But only Marlon Brando springs any surprises. Returning to big-screen burglary, he steals all his scenes as a paunchy, crotchety, snow-haired lawyer, peering over half-moon specs at the world's folly. (Or at the Brando cue cards?) **HK Director** Euzhan Palcy **producer** Paula Weinstein **exec** Tim Hampton **script** Colin Welland, Palcy, from novel by André Brink **camera** Kelvin Pike, Pierre William Glenn **editors** Sam O'Steen,

Glenn Cunningham **design** John Fenner **music** Dave Grusin **cast** Donald Sutherland, Janet Suzman, Winston Ntshona, Zakes Mokae, Jürgen Prochnow, Susan Sarandon, Marlon Brando, Thoko Ntshinga, Leonard Maguire, Gérard Thoolen, Susannah Harker, Andrew Whaley, Rowen Elmes
Running time: 97 mins
US release: MGM, Sep 20, 1989
UK release: UIP, Jan 19, 1990

DUST IN THE WIND (Lianlian Feng Chen)
This retells the old story of the young man who leaves his humble rural family to find happiness in the big city (Taipei) and just drifts from job to job without showing any gumption. The young hero (Jingwen) returns from a year in the army to find that his girlfriend (Shufen) has married a mailman with more status than him. His scenes with the equally weedy girl are intended to convey timidity and awkwardness, but what you actually get is so minimal that it takes a long time to figure out that they are even supposed to be having a relationship. Everyday life trudges on in a series of static shots, trains trundle by, people moan, and boredom sets in as the film fails to find a focus or even make a genuine attempt to engage an audience. **KN Director** Hou Hsiao-Hsien **producers** Zhang Huakun, Li Xianzhang **execs** Xu Xinzhi, Lin Dengfei **script** Wu Nianzhen, Zhu Tianwen **camera** Li Pingbin **editor** Liao Qingsong **design** Liu Zhihua, Lin Ju **music** Chen Mingzhang **cast** Wang Jingwen, Xin Shufen, Li Tianlu, Chen Shufang, Lin Yang, Mei Fang, Lai Denan, Lin Yuping, Zhang Fuqin, Yang Liyin
Running time: 110 mins
UK release: ICA, Mar 30, 1990

D

DEAD POETS SOCIETY

D*ead Poets Society* took the Best Original Screenplay Oscar at this year's Academy Awards. It was also widely praised by critics for its 'mature approach' to 'intellectual issues', and managed, in the summer of *Batman* and *Indiana Jones and the Last Crusade*, to be the token Serious Film in the box-office top ten.

With Robin Williams in a secondary rôle behind a whole pile of neurotic young men who are inspired by his unconventional example to rebel against conformity, this is not actually a comedy, although at the press screening I attended I was not the only one to be paralyzed with laughter during the big suicide scene. In this impossibly arch sequence, a beautiful young man who's upset because his father doesn't want him to be an actor wanders around the house at night in a crown of thorns and finally tickles his tonsils with a .45. It's a passionless dirge of a death, obnoxiously calculated to twang your heartstrings and bring forth floods of tears.

The plot is simple stuff. In 1959, John Keating (Williams) arrives to teach English at hidebound, stuffy old Welton College, the most exclusive prep school in the country, and soon goes against the grain of the institution by having his students stand on their desks, tear chapters out of their text books, recite their own poetry and hide out in a cave smoking and discussing Thoreau. Keating believes in free expression and stuff like that, but the tyrannical headmaster and some even more tyrannical parents are into turning out rubber-stamped doctors and lawyers. So there's depression, gloom, scapegoating and suicide in prospect for everyone. In the end, after the artistic kid has snuffed himself, Keating gets the can from the straight-faced headmaster, and all his loyal pupils demonstrate their heroic regard for him, and their commitment to his ideals, by defiantly standing on their desks.

By this point, only the millions of people who loved the film could take it seriously any more. The cinema is full of great images of rebellion: remember Malcolm McDowell gunning down teachers in *If...?* Bogart and Rains walking off into the fog at the Moroccan airport in *Casablanca*? Marlon Brando coming into town on his motorbike in *The Wild One*, answering 'what are you rebelling against?' with 'what have you got?' Surely, there can be nothing more ridiculous than this spectacle, as a bunch of overprivileged brats with incredibly rich parents stand on tables. Let's face it, if John Keating wanted to do some good in 1959, what was he doing taking a job at Welton in the first place, rather than at a tough school in Watts or the Bronx. And isn't it about time the cinema stopped wasting its time on the agonized emotional and intellectual problems of people too rich to have any other kind?

Dead Poets Society is insidiously disguised as a good film: it has in Peter Weir a director who previously worked wonders with the enclosed society of a stuffy school in *Picnic at Hanging Rock*; the hot presence of Williams, an immensely talented performer who undoubtedly could manage to cross over from comedy to more weighty roles; pretty good performances from its young cast, presumably relieved that their first big break wasn't in a beer 'n' broads nerd movie; a neat orchestral score from Maurice Jarre that tinkles subtly in the background; and superb cinematography, capturing the rich autumnal hues of the grounds of Old Welton and the snowy wastes that arrive as Fall turns to Winter and the plot turns to misery. Furthermore, it wins very high points on the Barry Norman–Mary Whitehouse school of Cinematic Excellence by having not one whit of sex or nudity (one of the lads, Josh Charles, develops a crush on local girl Alexandra Powers, but nothing happens), explicit violence (the suicide is artful and offscreen) and only some very minor darning to stand in for bad language. But don't be fooled, this is a dog of the first water.

For a start, it really does believe that a group of rich teenagers standing on desks are making a significant statement against the dehumanizing process, and it claims to be a serious film while resorting to annoyingly hackneyed and manipulative plot-devices to beef up its slender storyline, uninvolving script and overwhelming pomposity. For instance, it's not enough that Neil Perry (Robert Sean Leonard), the martyr, is being crushed into a life of misery, but he also has to express his rebellion by taking the part of Puck in *A Midsummer Night's Dream*. Furthermore, he has to be saddled with a father who is marginally less villainous than Boris Karloff as Fu Manchu – he's played by Kurtwood Smith who was last seen as the chortling swine who performed untold acts of depravity throughout *RoboCop* – and set up throughout for a significant death just as surely as a teenage girl who has giggly sex is doomed to meet a meat-cleaver in a *Friday the 13th* sequel.

The film settles into a rut very early, and its whole idea of high culture, rebellion and dehumanization is essentially obvious, banal, patronizing and trite. It has very little feel for the claustrophobic school setting, and was indeed blown away by Keith Gordon's underrated *The Chocolate War*, which failed to get a theatrical release in Britain while this was clogging up the triplexes, and demonstrated the old rule that absurd things (a drive to sell chocolates) are far easier to turn into the subject of tragedy than actual tragedies like teenage suicide. *Dead Poets Society* is the worst kind of bad film, in that it gets treated seriously and respectfully while it force-feeds rubbish into your head. I'm giving it an 'F', and so will history.

KIM NEWMAN

DICK TRACY

Dick Tracy is a bold attempt by Warren Beatty to render the two-dimensional surface and pulp melodrama of Chester Gould's syndicated comic strip in live action without sacrificing its old-fashioned moral dynamics or essential naïveté. It succeeds in that aim, yielding neither to the crowd-pleasing demands of designer violence nor to the cynical heroism that was rife in the summer's other blockbusters (Total Recall, Robocop II, Die Hard 2). Prosthetic make-up artists John Caglione Jr. and Doug Drexler created a pullulating pop-art underworld of ghoul-mugged villains for the doughty, straight-arrow police detective Tracy (Beatty) to conquer. The film is magnificently mounted on Richard Sylbert's vast, glittering eternal city of night, and effulgently shot (in funny-paper primary colours) by Vittorio Storaro. Madonna – supplied with superb Sondheim songs – supplies a fine onscreen singing act, as Breathless Mahoney, and Al Pacino gives his funniest ever character performance as the garrulous, hunchbacked arch-villain Big Boy Caprice. Why then is Dick Tracy only intermittently interesting and frequently tedious?

Essentially a kid's movie programmed for adult appeal, Dick Tracy was marketed, like Batman a year earlier, as the 'buzz' movie of the summer, with the buzz focusing on an enigmatic crime fighter with his own line of customized crime-fighting paraphernalia – in this case a walkie-talkie watch. There were other similarities: Tracy has a Batman-like penchant for clambering about on roofs and peering into windows; he is shy in the presence of women (although he lacks the psychosexual neuroses that made Batman intriguing); he must fight to the death with his enemy in a shadowy, hazard-filled tower. (Also, as Jack Nicholson stole Batman from Michael Keaton, so Pacino stole Dick Tracy from Beatty.) Visually beautiful, both films lacked substance, but whereas Batman hovered in and out of darkness and was limned with cruel, camp wit, Dick Tracy was as flat textually as it was imagistically. You could say it was all up there on the screen, but that's all that was up there on the screen.

It has been nine years since Warren Beatty last directed a film, the Oscar-winning Reds – and the gap shows in the film's creakiness. A director with no directorial career to speak of, Beatty is a perfectionist who fusses over those films he does make to such an extent that they seem to sap his creative stamina. For all its impressive dressage and jokey stylization, Dick Tracy is a film without attitude, coherent rhythm or real narrative economy. One could almost forgive the hokey, negligible plot, if the film was directed less ponderously. Storaro's camera tracks prettily (with an opening crane-shot hommage to Welles's Touch of Evil), the villains are fascinatingly grotesque, but the crucial action sequences are drearily attenuated – Tracy climbing along a window ledge and jumping from a lamp post to a police car as a hood is blown to pieces beneath him; Tracy calculating how to bust his way into Big Boy's casino with the old fulcrum gag beloved of the Coyote

**Hey, tin man, you'll never clean up this patch
on your own.**

cartoon character; Tracy blazing away *ad nauseam* with a machine gun.

To give Beatty his due, the film this might have been is encapsulated in several thrilling visual flourishes. Best of all is a rapid-fire, surreal montage sequence describing Tracy's Ness-like thwarting of Big Boy (in one shot, he punches a handful of hoods to the ground with a single blow) while Breathless pines for him on the soundtrack; it ends, mordantly, with a large cockroach creeping through the detritus of the lair where the police surveillance man has successfully installed himself above Big Boy's headquarters.

Interwoven with Tracy's restless crime-busting are the scenes in which he courts the droll, pretty, girl-next-door horticulturalist Tess Trueheart (Glenne Headly) – they love each other but his refusal to take a desk job threatens their romance – and is furiously vamped by Breathless, the gangster's moll who has fallen in love with him; and the scenes in which Tracy and Tess adopt a tough-talking street urchin, Kid (Charlie Korsmo). The romantic triangle is as coy as it could possibly be: as Breathless, Madonna displays her alabaster Jessica Rabbit curves in sheer black negligées and taunts Tracy with a succession of innuendoes that Mae West wouldn't have touched with a ten-foot pole, like 'You don't know whether to kiss me or hit me. I get a lot of that.' Tracy responds to these come-ons with all the sexual excitement of a man being told he has a hernia. Although her performance doesn't yet suggest she could carry an entire movie, Madonna does convey – before the plot carries her into gothic never-never-land – the vague sense of a glamorous woman embittered by unrequited love.

Headly, though, is considerably more affecting, quietly bursting into tears when she catches Tracy kissing Breathless and the Kid unthinkingly applauds her: 'Now that's what I call a dame.' It's one of the movie's rare moments of genuine emotion (and it's followed by a quick, strange, and endearingly funny sequence in which the defeated Tess drives home to her pie-cooking mom somewhere in the country). That there aren't more such moments, because there is no chemistry in his relationship with either Tess or Breathless, has to be blamed on Beatty's listless performance in the leading rôle.

Not blessed, like Batman or Superman, with a secret identity, Tracy has to be characterized as a flesh-and-blood comic-strip hero but, as played by Beatty, the yellow-coated detective is almost incorporeal, a dreamer in a world of freaks. Beatty also suggests Tracy is impotent, as if that might somehow assuage the Hollywood Lothario's offscreen reputation. It's not enough to conclude that Beatty's performance was generous in its passivity, intended to highlight the fine work of Headly, Korsmo (tough and unsentimental as the Kid), Pacino, and an indulgent cameo by Dustin Hoffman (doing his *Rain Man* riff as Mumbles). Although there's a touchingly chivalrous, incorruptible quality about Beatty's Tracy, there is, diastrously, no passion in him, even in his feelings for Tess. Unlike such mild-mannered supermen as Bruce Wayne and Clark Kent, characters fraught with ambiguity, the strip Tracy was too emphatic and rugged a hero for Beatty to undercut with his characteristically genteel self-absorption. He could have made Tracy a suave Mike Hammer (troubled by his machismo) or a jejune Philip Marlowe; instead he made him a curiously limp dick.

GRAHAM FULLER

DRIVING MISS DAISY

*D*riving *Miss Daisy* is a nice enough little movie, smoothly charting the passing of seasons and years, and slipping down the throat like a perfect oyster. But a US gross of over $100 million must have seemed an extremely unlikely prospect at the outset, given a marketplace where only big-budget movies about bone-crunchers and superheroes now seem to stand a chance of making money.

Perhaps the film's secret lies in the distance it puts between itself and the rest of contemporary cinema. Audiences weary of fast-paced, incident-crammed, often violent, movies may have welcomed the respite provided by a film in which almost nothing happens: where the cops who approach a nigger with menace in their eyes drive away after merely letting drop a few racist aspersions; where nobody gets beaten up; where old age doesn't seem all that tough and where anything vicious that does happen — a Jewish Temple is fire-bombed — remains firmly off-screen.

But even if the surface of *Driving Miss Daisy* is so tranquil that you could almost mistake it for an English film, something else must explain its success beyond simple evasiveness and the uncinematic ways it betrays theatrical roots. Why, after all, should a contemporary audience be interested in the story of a cantankerous old woman who slowly discards her racist beliefs as she gets to know and sort of love her black chauffeur?

Following a back-garden accident in which she has written off her car, Miss Daisy gives two reasons for resisting her son Boolie (Dan Aykroyd) when he demands that she employ a driver: she doesn't want to be seen flaunting wealth, and she wants to hold on to her privacy. The driver, Hoke (Morgan Freeman), works hard to please her (tending the garden, expressing admiration for her home) but he succeeds only in causing irritation. And it turns out she's keeping careful watch, in the belief that: 'They all take things, you know.' The disappearance of a tin of salmon almost leads to his dismissal, but Hoke promptly vindicates himself by bringing a replacement.

Thus when Miss Daisy later asserts that: 'I've never been prejudiced in my life and you know it,' she's telling a lie. And having failed to persuade her son (Dan Aykroyd) to attend a dinner in honour of Martin Luther King, she's still incapable of making the gesture he suggests — taking Hoke with her instead. 'I think it's wonderful the way things is changing,' she says as she leaves him outside. 'Ain't changed all that much,' he ripostes under his breath.

Driving Miss Daisy presents a significant issue — racial prejudice — palatably wrapped up in the warming sight of a woman well on in years becoming increasingly enlightened — not a usual trajectory. But the film is also the story of any mismatched couple slowly defrosting the barriers that divide them, and it's this level that supplies the film's emotional warmth. They don't bicker and squabble quite like cops who've been assigned to the same beat, but Miss Daisy makes up for her servant's relative quiescence with continuous banter and reproaches. Hoke's first rebellion comes when he stops the car late at night so that he can 'make water'. 'I'm a man,' he asserts. 'I'm now 70 years old and I know when my bladder is full.'

'An old nigger and an old Jew woman taking off down the road together, that is one sorry sight,' comments an Alabama policeman. Miss Daisy's non-WASP origins, and allusions to her early poverty mute the barrier between black servant and white employer. In one scene, Hoke seeks to establish a sense of shared experience in their membership of persecuted groups. He's driving away from the traffic jam that blocks the road to the fire-bombed Temple, and recalls a horrific event from his childhood, when he saw a friend's father strung up from a tree. Miss Daisy refuses then to understand the significance of this story, but later reveals by attending that Martin Luther King dinner that she picked up the message.

Because Miss Daisy is so reluctant to give up beliefs she's sustained through a lifetime, the film allows the audience to celebrate her journey to relatively non-racist enlightenment and the capacity that we all have to change, while also looking back with some nostalgia at a world where different ethnic groups stayed firmly within their communities, and the races were kept as separate as the classes and the religious denominations. Miss Daisy despises her son's wife for the efforts she makes to ingratiate herself with Episcopalian society, just as she ensures that Hoke keeps his distance.

This divide between employer and employed is illustrated throughout by the ritual of separate dining. There seems nothing unnatural at first in Hoke taking his dinner with the maid, but when the maid has passed away, and the house's two remaining inhabitants do shared duty at the stove, it seems absurd that they should eat their meals in separate rooms. It's thus significant that the film's final shot shows him feeding her at the nursing home to which she has been consigned. From her initial insistence that 'I don't need you, I don't want you', Miss Daisy comes to acknowledge through a haze of senility that 'Hoke, you're my best friend.' Few declarations come more touching than that.

JAMES PARK

DRUGSTORE COWBOY

The studios set the pace in 1989 for the Disney-fication of Bush-era America, striving to build a cinematic suburbia wilfully ignorant of AIDS and crack. But between *Field of Dreams'* rampant populism (and patronizing nods to the threadbare survival of the hippie credo) and *Parenthood's* egregious celebration of the family unit (which absorbs even Keanu Reeve's dissentient punk) came Gus Van Sant's *Drugstore Cowboy*, an agreeably grungy and bitterly funny slice of nostalgia for the low-life junkie culture of the early 1970s, which supplied not only a much-needed shot in the arm for US independent cinema, but also a daring counter-cultural antidote to the Moral Majoritarian medicine prescribed by late-1980s Hollywood.

A painter and former adman with a film degree from Rhode Island School of Design, Van Sant previously demonstrated his unsentimental affinity for strung-out rebels with *Mala Noche*. Shot on 16mm for $25,000 in 1987, its story of a convenience-store manager's forlorn gay passion for an illegal immigrant from Mexico contrived to be both ironic and non-judgemental. *Drugstore Cowboy* was adapted by Van Sant and Daniel Yost from an unpublished novel by convicted felon James Fogle (who had based it on the career of a criminal friend), and it sacrificed neither the jaunty Skid Row lyricism nor the raw romanticism of the earlier film. And Van Sant's ability to poeticize the greedy, the squalid and the mundane was unhindered by a budget of $3.8 million and a star, Matt Dillon, with something to prove after a run of failures; indeed, the film's grim humour and grimy terrain seemed to shave years of acquired mannerisms and Brat Pack brittleness off the actor and to inspire in him a swashbuckling performance, with equal parts of lightness and authority.

Dillon plays Bob Hughes, the brains and undisputed leader of a crew of career junkies comprised of his cool and languid wife Dianne (Kelly Lynch), his dumb lieutenant Rick (James Le Gros) and Rick's baby-faced girlfriend Nadine (Heather Graham). Recounting their adventures in flashback as he bleeds from a gunshot wound in the back of an ambulance, Bob emerges as an instinctive, self-sufficient junkie-philosopher who has dedicated his life to getting high. It's his innate cunning, his professional pride in the gang's pharmacy raids and hospital heists, and the ingenious ploys he uses to outsmart the police which give the movie its juice – that and the desired fix. As he sets up one hapless surveillance man to be shot by a neighbour, Bob jubilantly drifts off into a heroin haze – a state depicted throughout the film by Van Sant as one of sublime well-being, in which the paraphernalia of Bob's craft (guns, spoons, pills) and the other disembodied flotsam and jetsam in his subconsciousness (trees, deers, hats) float in filigree miniature before his eyes.

Half road-movie, half outlaw-comedy, *Drugstore Cowboy* shares the Beat anomie of a Jim Jarmusch film (or a Robert Frank photograph): no matter how bloodied or beaten up he gets, Bob is almost nonchalant when he's on the job. Like Jarmusch, Van Sant recognizes that the splendid isolation of the existential desperado frequently borders on the banal, the farcical and the tragic. Accusations that *Drugstore Cowboy* glamorizes junkiedom seem ill-founded when you catch the homely Rick and a goofy apprentice pusher – David (Max Perlich), who resembles MAD magazine's gingery cover boy – talking about a kids' TV show midway through a deal. And there's a touching skewed domesticity in the scene where Bob and Dianne visit his chintzy mother at home and she refuses to admit them until she's hidden her money. In another sequence, Bob and Dianne, staying in a motel which is also hosting a sheriffs' convention, have to hide Nadine's blueing corpse – after she ODs in a fit of pique – in the attic of their room, and we watch in dismay as the body slides through the opening to the floor.

A dankness seeps into the movie when Bob buries Nadine in a forest, and the belief that he has failed to observe his codes and superstitions prompts him into rehab: he goes on a methadone programme and takes a job in a machine shop. Having previously framed each loving detail of the junkie's art, Van Sant now democratically closes in on the commonplace – the water Bob is boiling for tea, the words printed on a lightbulb – and the result is no less surreal than the Magritte-like imagery depicted in his hallucinations. Harsh reality may seem strange to the reformed junkie. And while it doesn't exactly condone drugs, there is a logic in Bob's explanation to his counsellor that people are drawn to dope 'to relieve the pressures of that everyday life – like having to tie their shoes.'

'I don't want to end up like Bonnie and Clyde,' a line from Desmond Dekker's reggae classic 'The Israelites', which Van Sant uses as his theme song, ruefully underpins the lovelessness in *Drugstore Cowboy* (like Bonnie and Clyde, Bob and Dianne no longer fuck), but also Bob's decision to clean up and Dianne's chronic continuing drug dependency. Kelly Lynch makes Dianne a tough, sexy and sardonic woman for four-fifths of the film, but you realize, as she struts down a corridor away from Bob and towards a probable early death, just how pathetic she really is.

It is in the same elegiac last passage that the movie's patron saint, William S. Burroughs (who was shown shooting up in Antony Balch's *Towers Open Fire*), appears as a skeletal defrocked junkie priest who Bob knew as a choirboy. As the camera prowls around his ravaged figure, he waxes polemical: 'Narcotics have been systematically scapegoated and demonized. I predict in the near future the right wing will use drug hysteria to set up an international police apparatus.' If at first this seems like the paranoid pontificating of an unrepentant addict excusing his own long-time deviance, it acknowledges, with the benefit of hindsight, the germ of the illiberalism and censoriousness which ran riot in America during 1989-90. In this context, hospital-bound Bob's realization at the end of the movie that 'the chickenshit cops were escorting me to the biggest pharmacy in town' is less of a pro-drug statement than a defiant declaration of independence.

GRAHAM FULLER

EARTH GIRLS ARE EASY

Hollywood manicurist Valerie (Davis) is having problems with her fickle and unresponsive fiancé when a spaceship crash-lands in her swimming pool and disgorges three colourful, hairy, fun-loving aliens. After a trip to the beauty shop, where the creatures are shaved into reasonable approximations of humanity, everyone goes out on the town. Mac (Goldblum), the least hyperactive of the aliens, falls for Valerie, and cars get crashed all over the shop. This zippy cross between *My Stepmother is an Alien* and *Beach Blanket Bingo*, which comes complete with bright colours, kitsch SF trappings, poolside parties and leftover jokes from *Carry On Doctor*, proves that Julien Temple can still get a job, although his arm-waving staging of Brown's material demonstrates that he can't really handle musical numbers. It's a colourful, distinctive movie and fast enough to get round its dud jokes, badly-mixed songs and general predictability. Geena Davis and Jeff Goldblum are a fetching couple again, and add some notes of sanity to the whole thing, which is otherwise eternally in danger of collapsing under the weight of its own jokiness. **KN**
Director *Julien Temple* **producer** *Tony Garnett* **script** *Julie Brown, Charlie Coffey, Terrence E. McNally* **camera** *Oliver Stapleton* **editor** *Richard Halsey* **design** *Dennis Gassner* **music** *Nile Rodgers* **cast** *Geena Davis, Jeff Goldblum, Julie Brown, Jim Carrey, Damon Wayans, Charles Rocket, Michael McKean, Charles Rocket*
Running time: 100 mins
US release: Vestron, May 12, 1989
UK release: Fox, Dec 22, 1989

EAT A BOWL OF TEA

Taking as its starting-point racist immigration laws that, until the 1940s, wouldn't allow the wives of Chinese men to enter the US, lest they unbalance the population's racial mix, Wayne Wang's latest film examines the strains placed on one of the first marriages after their abolition (to avoid miscegenation). The husband's loss of face and self-esteem when he is unable to give his Chinese-born wife a child leads to her infidelity and a re-examination of their respective cultures. While never hitting the high spots, the film rarely bores and avoids judgemental sentiments about the *mores* of either country. Quietly rewarding. **TW**
Director *Wayne Wang* **producer** *Tom Sternberg* **execs** *Lindsay Law, John K. Chan* **script** *Judith Rascoe, from novel by Louis Chu* **camera** *Amir Mokri* **editor** *Richard Candib* **design** *Bob Ziembicki* **music** *Mark Adler* **cast** *Victor Wong, Russell Wong, Cora Miao, Eric Tsang Chi Wai, Lau Siu Ming, Wu Ming Yu, Hui Fun, Law Fan, Lee Sau Kee, Yuen Yat Fai*

Running time: 103 mins
US release: Columbia, Jul 21, 1989
UK release: Artificial Eye, Dec 8, 1989

EIGHT MEN OUT

John Sayles challenges audience expectation that a sports picture will be about winning with this account of the 1919 Black Sox Scandal. It's a sorry tale of ballplayers who throw the World Series to take revenge on their meanie manager. But having been ripped off by the gamblers who made them do it, they are subsequently driven out of the game; even Buck Weaver (Cusack) who took no money and never dropped his batting average. Sayles can't quite turn the trick. If the film had worked, one would at least partially welcome the duff playing as an occasion when the players get their own back on the Establishment but, as it is, it's only when they do decide to play one game properly that the heart beats a little faster. Attempts to paint in individual motivations for the characters clutter the piece and make this a brave effort, characterized by colourful performances, that never quite cracks it. **JP**
Director *John Sayles* **producers** *Sarah Pillsbury, Midge Sanford* **execs** *Barbara Boyle, Jerry Offsay* **script** *Sayles, from book by Eliot Asinof* **camera** *Robert Richardson* **editor** *John Tintori* **design** *Nora Chavooshian* **music** *Mason Daring* **cast** *John Cusack, Clifton James, Michael Lerner, Christopher Lloyd, John Mahoney, Charlie Sheen, David Strathairn, D. B. Sweeney, Don Harvey, Michael Rooker, Perry Lang, James Read, Jace Alexander, Gordan Clapp, Richard Edson, Bill Irwin, Michael Mantell, Kevin Tighe, Studs Terkel, John Anderson, John Sayles, Wendy Makkena, Maggie Renzi*
Running time: 119 mins
US release: Orion, Sep 2, 1988
UK release: Rank, Jul 21, 1989

🐦 EL DORADO

Carlos Saura sets out to prove that the Germans aren't the only ones who can make a good Spanish-nutter-in-the-jungle movie. A lavish, revisionist version of *Aguirre, Wrath of God*, the film offers more for the eye than Herzog's film but ultimately becomes bogged down in repetitious assassinations and a lead performance that manifests the symptoms of Aguirre's paranoia without really showing us its roots. That said, there *are* some good moments as well as some of the most impressively-framed CinemaScope images of recent years. **TW**
Director/script *Carlos Saura* **producer** *Victor Albarrán* **execs** *Andrés Vicente Gómez* **camera** *Teo Escamilla* **editor** *Pedro del Rey* **design** *Terry Pritchard* **cast** *Omero Antonutti, Eusebio Poncela, Lambert Wilson, Gabriela Roel, José Sancho, Feodor*

Atkine, Patxi Bisquert, Francisco Algora, Francisco Merino
Running time: 123 mins
UK release: Palace, Aug 4, 1989

⚔ ENCOUNTER AT RAVEN'S GATE

What's going on down at Raven's Gate? Cassette players disgorge the wrong music. Dead birds fall out of the sky. Water evaporates mysteriously. Huge circular burns appear in an isolated pasture. And there are lights in the sky. Locating its bizarre storyline in a dried-up, mean-spirited rural Australia, *Encounter at Raven's Gate* starts a trifle awkwardly with an unnecessary flashback structure, but it's otherwise an outstanding, atmospheric nail-biter. On an isolated farm, a petty offender (Vidler) is sweating out his probation on his tyrannical brother's payroll. His problems are compounded by the local football thugs, who think he's stolen their trophy, and the local psycho, opera-loving cop who is obsessed with the barmaid he's been screwing. The film's fantastical elements are used to bring out the tensions of the human characters, which works because the characters are made credible before being forced into exaggerated behaviour by strange phenomena, and because director De Heer has a strong feeling for the loneliness, frustration and boredom of dead-end life on a dried-up farmstead. The film doesn't deliver any tentacled monstrosities, but it does have a few impressively unsettling moments in the invaded and transformed Raven's Gate farmhouse. **KN**
Director *Rolf de Heer* **producers** *de Heer, Marc Rosenberg* **exec** *Antony I. Ginnane* **script** *Marc Rosenberg, de Heer* **camera** *Richard Michalak* **editor** *Suresh Ayyar* **design** *Judi Russell* **music** *Graham Tardif, Roman Kronen* **cast** *Steven Vidler, Celin Griffin, Ritchie Singer, Vince Gil, Saturday Rosenberg, Terry Camilleri, Max Cullen*
Running time: 89 mins
US release: Hemdale, Jan 26, 1990
UK release: Castle Premier, Mar 9, 1990

ENEMIES, A LOVE STORY
FILM • FILM • FILM • FILM

Director/producer *Paul Mazursky* **execs** *James G. Robinson, Joe Roth* **script** *Roger L. Simon, Mazursky, from novel by Isaac Bashevis Singer* **camera** *Fred Murphy* **editor** *Stuart Pappé* **design** *Pato Guzman* **music** *Maurice Jarre* **cast** *Anjelica Huston, Ron Silver, Lena Olin, Margaret Sophie Stein, Judith Malina, Alan King, Rita Karin, Phil Leeds, Elya Baskin, Paul Mazursky*
Running time: 120 mins
US release: Fox, Dec 13, 1989
UK release: Fox, Apr 6, 1990

ENEMY OF THE PEOPLE
See Ganashatru

🏴 ERIK THE VIKING

Erik (Robbins) is a sensitive Viking who decides that he isn't terribly keen on rape and pillage, and leads a bunch of hairy dumb thugs on a not very funny voyage of discovery to find out something philosophical beyond the land of Hy-Brasil. Along the way, the gang encounters a large but unimpressive sea serpent and Terry Jones as the ruler of a doomed continent, but finally slip over the edge of the world to meet up with the childish and squabbling Gods of Asgard to learn why Fenrir the Wolf is eating up the Sun and men must kill each other. Jones did it all a lot better in a five-minute skit on *Monty Python's Flying Circus* some 20 years ago, and doesn't really have much to add these days, apart from a vomit joke or two. **KN**
Director/script *Terry Jones* **producer** *John Goldstone* **exec** *Terry Glinwood* **camera** *Ian Wilson* **editor** *George Akers* **design** *John Beard* **sfx** *Richard Conway, Peter Hutchinson* **music** *Neil Innes* **cast** *Tim Robbins, Mickey Rooney, Eartha Kitt, Terry Jones, Imogen Stubbs, John Cleese, Tsutomu Sekine, Antony Sher, Gary Cady, Charles McKeown, Tim McInnerny, John Gordon Sinclair, Richard Ridings, Samantha Bond, Freddie Jones, Danny Schiller, Jim Broadbent, Jim Carter, Matyelok Gibbs, Tilly Vosburgh*
Running time: 107 mins
US release: Orion, Oct 27, 1989
UK release: UIP, Sep 29, 1989

ERNEST GOES TO JAIL

Rubber-faced 'comedian' Jim Varney sets out with his evil twin for plenty o' special-effects-generated hilarity. He plays his trademark dumb act as a sanitary engineer, and also gets to play an oily convict who looks just like Ernest P. Worrell would if he had been born on planet Earth. The third in a lucrative, wilfully dumb series, *Ernest Goes to Jail* is, as it should be, as funny as a sitcom. There's a terrible rumour circulating round Hollywood that numbers four to ten in the series are already in development. **CB**
Director *John Cherry* **producer** *Stacy Williams* **exec** *Martin Erlichman* **script** *Charlie Cohen* **camera** *Peter Stein* **editors** *Sharyn L. Ross, Farrel Levy* **design** *Chris August* **music** *Bruce Arntson, Kirby Shelstad* **cast** *Jim Varney, Gailard Sartain, Bill Byrge, Barbara Bush, Barry Scott, Randall (Tex) Cobb, Dan Leegant, Charles Napier, Jim Conrad, Jackie Welch*
Running time: 81 mins
US release: BV, Apr 6, 1990

ERNEST SAVES CHRISTMAS

The second adventure of Ernest, an inimitable
klutz whose initial sleeper hit, Ernest Goes to
Camp, introduced Americans to the hapless
world of this cosmetically ravaged, but no less
frenetic, dumb nephew to Pee Wee Herman.
This time round he gets to meet Santa, satirize
the cynical ineptitude of Hollywood and rescue
Yuletide from cynical spoilers. MN
Director John Cherry producers Stacy Williams,
Doug Claybourne execs Martin Erlichman, Joseph
L. Akerman Jr. script B. Kline, Ed Turner camera
Peter Stein editor Sharyn L. Ross design Ian
Thomas music Mark Snow cast Jim Varney,
Douglas Seale, Oliver Clark, Nöelle Parker, Robert
Lesser, Gailard Sartain, Billie Bird, Bill Byrge,
Buddy Douglas, Patty Maloney
Running time: 89 mins
US release: BV, Nov 11, 1988
UK release: Warner, Nov 17, 1989

☛ EVERYBODY WINS

Had Bob Miller written Everybody Wins, it never
would have been made, but it was Arthur Miller's
first script since The Misfits, so Karel Reisz
directed it, and the results were such that Orion
opened it without a press screening. Nick Nolte is
a world-weary private eye hired by Debra Winger
(working terribly hard in an impossible rôle) to
investigate corruption in a small New England
town. Evil, of course, is everywhere, nobody wins,
and the story is an amateurish mess – at one
point, a character is about to deliver information
that would end the movie, so Miller has him run
over by a truck. JH
Director Karel Reisz producer Jeremy Thomas
execs Terry Glinwood, Linda Yellen script Arthur
Miller camera Ian Baker editor John Bloom
design Peter Larkin music Mark Isham cast Debra
Winger, Nick Nolte, Will Patton, Judith Ivey,
Kathleen Wilhoite, Jack Warden, Frank Converse,
Frank Military, Steve Skybell, Mary Louise Wilson
Running time: 97 mins
US release: Orion, Jan 19, 1990

ENEMIES, A LOVE STORY

N ovelist Isaac Bashevis Singer was born in Poland in 1904, emigrated to New York in 1935, and established himself as a newspaper columnist. Stories like *Yentl*, which recreated the vanished world of Eastern Jewry and was written in Yiddish, won him the Nobel Prize. *Enemies*, which first appeared as a serial in 1966, aroused some resentment, for uneasily mixing marital tragi-comedy, Holocaust memories and pessimism about the prospect for Jewish spiritual traditions in secular America. Paul Mazursky read the book on its publication in 1972 and set his heart on filming it.

New York circa 1948. Herman Broder (Ron Silver) lives by ghost-writing speeches for a fashionable rabbi. He shuttles between his wife Yadwiga (Margaret Sophie Stein) in Brooklyn, his mistress Masha (Lena Olin) in the Bronx, and Tamara (Anjelica Huston), his other wife, in Manhattan. Each has a powerful moral claim on him. Back in Poland, Yadwiga, a gentile peasant, hid him from the Nazis. Masha is the love of his life. Tamara, his wife by Jewish law, returned from the death camps where their children died. Gradually his arrangements for separating his three lives break down; his women start to negotiate around him, making the decisions for him, until all he can do is disappear. He leaves a baby daughter, which two of the women care for, giving it the name of the suicided third.

Mazursky's first big hit, *Bob and Carol and Ted and Alice*, was a high-grossing comedy about wife-swapping. It also beat the European art movie at its own game, treating sexual alienation with sharply finessed feeling, but with American zest and zip. Later experiments on similar lines included *Willie and Phil*, which played on Truffaut's *Jules et Jim*, and *Down and Out in Beverly Hills*, which transposed Renoir's *Boudu Saved From Drowning*. For a while market demographics put Hollywood in thrall to teenage tastes, so that comedies sexual or social had to be sweet and fizzy, or yuck-yock gross-out. But recently the market has reasserted the *thirtysomething* audience, encouraging Mazursky to return to his mellower, maturer, European tastes.

The mixture of themes in *Enemies* would scare off many producers, but Mazursky plays it straight. He concentrates on his character's everyday, practical encounters and interactions, with all their ambivalence and fumbling. He sometimes forces a comic tone, but it's a warm and gentle one. The human complications keep many moral and dramatic angles in play. One, no doubt, is post-Holocaust trauma; yet Herman's domestic chaos doesn't far exceed the scrapes everyday mediocrity gets into. His religious scepticism evokes a type of 'post-spiritual man'; as he can't believe in God, he can't commit, or resign, himself to anything, or stop messing with everything, and he ends as nothing.

Perhaps there's a psychological angle: for five years his whole life was hiding, and now the compulsion to hide stops him having a whole life; he gets his comeuppance while hiding in the gent's toilet at an important reception, goading a woman to shout at him through the door, and reveal his secrets to the whole world. Sometimes the plot bears out Singer's title theme, that 'ten thousand enemies can't harm a man as he can harm himself'. The refugee theme evokes other films about culture-shock in the Great American Melting Pot (*Moscow on the Hudson* was Mazursky too), touches on race prejudice *between* Jews (Russian, Polish . . .) and intimates the fragmentation of that ancient survival mechanism, the Jewish family.

About motherhood it's a heavy film. When Herman asks Tamara what became of their children in the camps, she replies 'Dead!', but in a quick, deep voice, and stiff-shouldered as a guardsman. Masha, though unquenchably lustful, is also inseparable from her mother; they quarrel and nag unstoppably; Masha suffers a hysterical pregnancy, or maybe it's a real pregnancy ended by abortion. Finally there's something disquieting about the two mothers crooning obliviously over their baby daughter, as if men were neither here nor there.

Herman fails in the Jewish male responsibility to become a father, and Singer discusses his 'fatalistic hedonism'. The phrase might just hint that Herman's tragic error was to combine fatalism (a Euro-Jewish weakness) with superficiality (an American one); he got the worst of both worlds. Not that Singer reduces his characters' destinies to one single attitude, or factor; for the story's concatenation of circumstance hints that the logic of a life would resemble chaos theory.

Herman's character poses fascinating problems of spectator identification. We have to feel with him, yet he's an enigma to others, and to himself. He's without ambition, almost without identity, often running on automatic. As compulsively as he deceives, he strives to maintain the responsibilities in which life has enmeshed him. He lies back in his bath, being lovingly soaped and pampered by Yadwiga, but he's smoking a cigar and reading the paper. He makes tigerish love with Masha, and the elevated roaring by the window makes the tenement shake, like a 'quote' from all those 1940s movies with trains roaring by to metaphor orgasm; but there's no relief from the heavy environment. He asks to sleep with Tamara like a five-year-old longing for a powerful mother.

The three women evoke traditional Jewish archetypes. Yadwiga adores and serves, and gradually takes up the faith he has lost, so that Jewish ethnicity continues through a gentile convert. Masha, passionate but sterile, is a Lilith who suffers. Tamara is the wife as strong mother, mother-as-fixer. But none of these women is 'true to type'; they're fully human, untidy, unpredictable.

The film's crazy situation is only everyday life writ large. As George Orwell put it, many ordinary people live 'lives of quiet desperation', in 'cells of fear'. Occasionally *Enemies* feels as dark as that, but in with the sadness the film mixes scandal, hope, comedy, drama and all the pleasures of artistic form; the tragic undertow only dominates in short scenes at the end. That may be a limitation, but it's not a cop-out, and indeed Singer doesn't pile on the tragic feeling either. He describes his characters in swift, terse, factual sentences, maintaining speed, detachment, uncertainty.

For the most part, Mazursky keeps us at appropriate distances from the characters, balancing criticism and sympathy. Sometimes Herman's faintly comic pathos evokes Woody Allen; sometimes his face is tight, mean, bleak and dead. It's a face which in 1940s movies would have typed its wearer as unsympathetic and expendable. It was Paddy Chayefsky's 1955 film *Marty* which first put a 'villain' face on an ordinary person; Ernest Borgnine, usually a dumb, cowardly, swarthy bully, played the Jewish butcher in Brooklyn whose life had made him 'a professor of pain.' That's the tradition Silver's quietly varied performance develops here.

Borgnine played larger-than-life; Silver starts gimlet deadpan, with short, cautious outbursts. His stealthy style gears in with the others. As Masha, Lena Olin (last seen in *The Unbearable Lightness of Being*), must dissimulate the death-wish working away within her. Judith Malina, from The Living Theater, is her loving, scolding, impossible mother. Anjelica Huston's narrow-eyed, high-nosed hatchet face would once have limited her to baleful women, barfly whores, hard-bitten Madams or wicked witches (and that's still on!). But none of these characters is conceived as a set type, whose keynote must be repeated in every detail. They're all open, vulnerable, unpredictable.

Singer, a very traditional novelist, more often *narrates* his story than he *dramatizes* it. That is to say, he frequently states facts and deep feelings quite baldly, as words quite naturally do, and not through scenes, actions and dialogue. The filmmakers must *first* invent all these, so as to obliquely *suggest* the point. This film is remarkably faithful to the novel, and a highly instructive example of the self-effacing art of adaptation. It looks as if they just 'filmed the novel'. But if you look closely, they had to invent *another* one.

Today's films recreate the past with a brilliance taken almost for granted. I for one feel strange vibrations when it's done well, especially when a certain fullness of description links up with other films set in the same time and place. Throughout *Enemies*, I half-expected to come across characters from *Five Corners*, or *Brighton Beach Memoirs*, even *Radio Days*. But these other films all work, in some way or other, the *Back to the Future* syndrome; they treat their past as innocence of what American will become. Whereas *Enemies* treats it as its own time; its characters aren't innocent of our knowledge, but imploding with their own. They're not in Nostalgia Time, they're in Injury Time.

Sometimes the acting gets a bit frantic, and faces zip through emotions hyperactively. As for that bright fairground wheel, Symbol of Life's Irony was stuck all over it. And Herman's mental-flashes only reminded me of *'Allo 'Allo*. It's not a perfect film, it's better than that: it's a moving and thought-provoking one.

RAYMOND DURGNAT

THE FABULOUS BAKER BOYS

A sharp, engaging little drama that finds brothers Jeff and Beau Bridges playing a pair of down-market lounge pianists who attempt to liven up their act by bringing in chanteuse Michelle Pfeiffer, and find that her disruptive presence gives their careers a boost while edging them nearer a break-up. It's understated in the manner of those 1970s films the Bridges Boys used to appear in before they became big stars, with the slender and familiar storyline spun out as the three central characters dance around each other – literally, in one New Year's Eve sequence – while their lifes go nowhere in particular. Jeff is the irresponsible bachelor who lives in a messy apartment and refuses to get involved, while Beau is the married, settled, balding brother, spraying paint on his hair and fussing like an aunt as he keeps the act together, and the impeccably turned-out Pfeiffer is an absolute revelation when singing 'Making Whoopee', convincingly striding through the picture as if aware that she's on her way to a somewhere that the Baker Boys haven't got a chance of getting to. KN
Director/script Steve Kloves producers Paula Weinstein, Mark Rosenberg exec Sydney Pollack camera Michael Ballhaus editor William Steinkamp design Jeffrey Townsend music Dave Grusin cast Jeff Bridges, Michelle Pfeiffer, Beau Bridges, Wendy Girard, Ellie Raab, Jennifer Tilly
Running time: 113 mins
US release: Fox, Oct 13, 1989
UK release: Rank, Oct 28, 1989

FAMILY BUSINESS

What a family; what a business. Sean Connery, Dustin Hoffman and Matthew Broderick are three generations of an Italian-Scottish-Jewish-American (sic) dynasty. One day they think, 'How about a robbery?' Sean, the ex-con, and Matthew, the college drop-out are keen, but meat-trader Dustin is worried. (Probably about his Italian accent.) Never mind: the heist happens and Junior is caught. What will dad and grandad do now? The suspense is bearable: which is more than can be said for the script, packed with top-heavy ironies about crime, punishment and family allegiance, or for Sidney Lumet's turgid direction. HK
Director Sidney Lumet producer Lawrence Gordon execs Jennifer Ogden, Burtt Harris script Vincent Patrick, from his novel camera Andrzej Bartkowiak editor Andrew Mondshein design Philip Rosenberg music Cy Coleman cast Sean Connery, Dustin Hoffman, Matthew Broderick, Rosana De Soto, Janet Carroll, Victoria Jackson
Running time: 113 mins
US release: Tri-Star, Dec 15, 1989
UK release: Palace, Feb 9, 1990

FAREWELL TO THE KING

Based on a novel but apparently deriving from real events, Farewell to the King would seem to offer John Milius an ideal subject – an exercise in heroic irony, in which the anomalies of history first create and then destroy a 'natural' leader, in the shape of an American deserter who becomes 'king' of a jungle-dwelling tribe in Borneo during World War 2. Yet while the locales are suitably daunting, the overall effect is inhibited, not only by awkwardness of exposition but by the frequent resort to stereotype. The pace and command of The Wind and the Lion are not to be found here, and though the movie ends on a cheerful note, with its protagonist apparently once more a free spirit, there is a feeling about the whole that the tragic elements of the tale have caused Milius to fall prey to self-conscious solemnity. TP
Director John Milius producers Albert S. Ruddy, André Morgan script Milius, from novel by Pierre Schoendoerffer camera Dean Semler editors Timothy O'Meara, Anne V. Coates design Gil Parrondo music Basil Poledouris cast Nick Nolte, Nigel Havers, James Fox, Marilyn Tokuda, Frank MacRae, Aki Aleong, William Wise, Gerry Lopez
Running time: 117 mins
US release: Orion, Mar 3, 1989
UK release: Vestron, Jul 7, 1989

FAR NORTH

Playwright-actor Sam Shepard's début as a writer-director is this slim little anecdote about a Minnesota family who love each other even while they can't stand each other. Charles Durning causes most of the trouble as the tyrannical old father who orders favourite daughter Jessica Lange to shoot the horse which put him in hospital, but the other characters – including Tess Harper as Lange's sister, and Patricia Arquette as her pregnant daughter – also get to snipe endlessly at each other. Lange demonstrates her sincerity by allowing her nose to shine redly, but otherwise looks improbably glamorous throughout. Durning blames it all on 'barbarian women', and has the occasional vision of galloping horses, but it all resolves itself in a traditional family gathering. The film is carefully acted, but it is a bit too meagre and whimsical for its own good, and the endless dialogue sequences have very little of the cinema about them. KN
Director/script Sam Shepard producers Carolyn Pfeiffer, Malcolm Harding exec Shep Gordon camera Robbie Greenberg, George Kohut editor Bill Yahraus design Peter Jamison music The Red Clay Ramblers cast Jessica Lange, Charles Durning, Tess Harper, Donald Moffat, Ann Wedgeworth, Patricia Arquette, Nina Draxten
Running time: 90 mins
US release: Alive, Nov 9, 1988
UK release: Rank, Feb 2, 1990

⁷ FAR OUT MAN

Far Out Man asks its audience to laugh at gross-out jokes, genitalia jokes and brat-packer Thomas C. Howell. Well, maybe it's not a total failure. But this solo attempt by the pothead comedian is chaotic, plotless and enormously stupid. Chong, never the funnier half of the Cheech and Chong comedy team, is here reduced to exploiting the dubious talents of his daughter, Rae Dawn, and his presumed friend, Howell, in a story that has him set up as a rich but witless slob. **CB**
Director/script Tommy Chong **producer** Lisa M. Hansen **exec** Paul Hertzberg **camera** Greg Gardiner, Eric Woster **editors** Stephen Myer, Gilberto Costa Nunes **design** David B. Miller **music** Jay Chattaway **cast** Tommy Chong, Shelby Chong, Paris Chong, C. Thomas Howell, Martin Mull, Rae Dawn Chong, Bobby Taylor, Reynald Taylor, Peggy F. Sands, Al Mancini, Judd Nelson, Paul Bartel, Cheech Marin
Running time: 91 mins
US release: New Line, May 11, 1990

FAT MAN AND LITTLE BOY (Shadowmakers in UK)

```
D I S A P P O I N T M E N T
```

Director Roland Joffé **producer** Tony Garnett **exec** John Calley **script** Bruce Robinson, Joffé **camera** Vilmos Zsigmond **editor** Françoise Bonnet **design** Gregg Fonseca **music** Ennio Morricone **cast** Paul Newman, Dwight Schultz, Bonnie Bedelia, John Cusack, Laura Dern, Ron Frazier, John C. McGinley, Natasha Richardson, Ron Vawter
Running time: 126 mins
US release: Paramount, Oct 20, 1989
UK release: UIP, Mar 9, 1990

⁴⁵ FELLOW TRAVELLER

Ron Silver plays an American writer in London during the early 1950s, who struggles with the meter in his digs and tries to write a script for a children's TV series, The Adventures of Robin Hood. Meanwhile in Beverly Hills, movie star Hart Bochner, his best friend, is drifting miserably about his mansion preparing to blow his brains out. Then, in flashback we return to the war years, when bejewelled Hollywood communists attended fund-raising drives for the Red Army, and all the neurotic film people were analyzed by head-shrinker Daniel Travanti, the only psychologist in town capable of squaring Marx and Freud. Of course, the HUAC comes along and ruins everybody's dreams. Fellow Traveller is an intriguing mix of character study, docu-drama and multi-media fantasy. And it's a British movie that manages to recreate the 1950s without looking as drab as We Think the World of You or Venus Peter or any of those other yawn-

inducers, and is daring enough to play a few tricks with film clips and flashbacks **KN**
Director Philip Saville **producer** Michael Wearing **execs** Colin MacCabe, Jill Pack **script** Michael Eaton **camera** John Kenway **editor** Greg Miller **design** Gavin Davies **music** Colin Towns **cast** Ron Silver, Imogen Stubbs, Hart Bochner, Daniel J. Travanti, Katherine Borowitz, Julian Fellowes, Richard Wilson, Doreen Mantle, David O'Hara, Allan Mitchell, Roger Hammond
Running time: 97 mins
UK release: BFI, Jan 5, 1990

FIELD OF DREAMS

```
F I L M  •  F I L M  •  F I L M  •  F I L M
```

Director Phil Alden Robinson **producers** Lawrence Gordon, Charles Gordon **exec** Brian Frankish **script** Robinson, from novel Shoeless Joe by W. P. Kinsella **camera** John Lindley **editor** Ian Crafford **design** Dennis Gassner **music** James Horner **cast** Kevin Costner, Amy Madigan, Gaby Hoffman, Ray Liotta, Timothy Busfield, James Earl Jones, Burt Lancaster, Frank Whaley, Dwyer Brown
Running time: 106 mins
US release: Universal, Apr 21, 1989
UK release: Guild, Nov 24, 1989

THE FIRST POWER

Lou Diamond Phillips plays a young police detective who's tracking a serial killer with Satanic connections. The killer is repeatedly executed but keeps coming back in different bodies. It's like The Hidden, though without that film's ferocity and, despite some great stunt work, there's little to recommend it. Phillips, as usual, is better than the material. **JH**
Director/script Robert Resnikoff **producer** David Madden **execs** Ted Field, Robert W. Cort, Melinda Jason **camera** Theo van de Sande **editor** Michael Bloecher **design** Joseph T. Garritz **music** Stewart Copeland **cast** Lou Diamond Phillips, Tracy Griffith, Jeff Kober, Mykel T. Williamson, Elizabeth Arlen, Dennis Lipscomb, Carmen Argenziano, Julianna McCarthy, Nada Despotovich, Sue Giosa
Running time: 98 mins
US release: Orion, Apr 6, 1989

FLASHBACK

'It takes more than just going down to your local video store and renting Easy Rider to be a rebel' intones Dennis Hopper himself in the part of a hippie activist left over from the 1960s who swops identities with the fed (Sutherland) who's escorting him on a jail transfer. The comedy is never quite astute or lowbrow enough and the clash between the radicalism of 1960s youth and the ultra-conformity of the yuppie generation is not really explored, but the film passes the time

amiably enough and at least it has its heart in the right place. **TW**
Director Franco Amurri **producer** Marvin Worth **exec** Richard Stenta **script** David Loughery **camera** Stefan Czapsky **editor** C. Timothy O'Meara **design** Vincent Crescimam **music** Barry Goldberg **cast** Dennis Hopper, Kiefer Sutherland, Carol Kane, Paul Dooley, Cliff De Young, Richard Masur, Michael McKean, Kathleen York, Tom O'Brien
Running time: 108 mins
US release: Paramount, Feb 2, 1990

THE FLY II

This is the sequel to David Cronenberg's remake of The Fly, (and therefore itself a remake of 1959's Return of the Fly) which has a reasonable script (if a silly storyline), mainly well-turned dialogue, generally good performances, some gloopy horror sequences, a fair approximation of the Cronenberg visual style and a seriousness of intent that almost makes the stupid ending work. Eric Stoltz plays the new-born son of the Jeff Goldblum character, who attains adulthood in five years, never sleeps, has a genius-capacity intelligence and is doomed by a plot contrivance and some caricatured corporate baddies to turn into an insectoid monstrosity. All the highlights of the first film are recapitulated, but on top of them we get a set of gross villains who provide cannon fodder for the make-up boys. By itself, The Fly II is head and shoulders above most monster movies, but as a sequel . . . well, who really needs it? **KN**
Director Chris Walas **producer** Steven-Charles Jaffe **exec** Stuart Cornfeld **script** Mick Garris, Jim Wheat, Ken Wheat, Frank Darabont, based on characters created by George Langelaan **camera** Robin Vidgeon **editor** Sean Barton **design** Michael S. Bolton **music** Christopher Young **cast** Eric Stoltz, Daphne Zuniga, Lee Richardson, John Getz, Frank Turner, Ann Marie Lee, Gary Chalk, Saffron Henderson, Harley Cross, Matthew Moore
Running time: 105 mins
US release: Fox, Feb 10, 1989
UK release: Fox, Sep 8, 1989

FOOLS OF FORTUNE

Memories are famously long in Ireland, with resentments that were formed in the sixteenth century still motivating stone-throwing in Derry today. But while it makes sense to spread a tale of Ireland's Troubles over an extended period, the story needs a screenwriter who can fit together the various episodes into some sort of whole. Fools of Fortune tells the promising story of a boy who sees his father and sisters killed by a vicious British soldier, grows up, watches his embittered mother take to the bottle and falls in love with

lovely Marianne (Mastrantonio) but is plotting all the while his revenge on the man who murdered his family. Framing its chronological episodes between shots of Willie (Glen) recovering on a desolate island from his one brutal act, the film prepares us for some sort of epiphanic healing moment, but all it delivers is a Willie's sudden switch from unshaven desperado to besuited smoothie, as he readies for a tentative reunion with his former beloved and their crazed love-child. Christie gives a glowing performance as Willie's dipso mother, and Pat O'Connor shoots the early scenes of terrorist violence and brutality with the same intensity he brought to parts of Cal, but there's a complete absence of narrative drive or moral framework. **JP**
Director Pat O'Connor **producer** Sarah Radclyffe **execs** Tim Bevan, Graham Bradstreet **script** Michael Hirst, from novel by William Trevor **camera** Jerzy Zielinski **editor** Michael Bradsell **design** Jamie Leonard **music** Hans Zimmer **cast** Mary Elizabeth Mastrantonio, Iain Glen, Julie Christie, Michael Kitchen, Sean T. McClory, Frankie McCafferty, Niamh Cusack, Neil Dudgeon, Catherine McFadden
Running time: 104 mins
UK release: Palace, Jun 22, 1990

ⴲ THE FOURTH WAR

After showing some improvement with 52 Pick Up and Dead Bang, John Frankenheimer has gone straight back to the gutter with this bodged and boring tale of two Cold Warriors who so need an enemy to defend their own existence that they start their own private war on the Czech-German border. Any hope of a return to the style of The Manchurian Candidate or Seven Days in May is shattered by amateur direction (silly angles and missed cues) and some remarkably bad performances: Roy Scheider comes across more like a good corporate lawyer than a good soldier and Harry Dean Stanton gives an embarrassing impersonation of Robert Mitchum. Jürgen Prochnow does emerge with some credit, but his key rôle is so underwritten as to be a virtual cameo. Even the action sequences are completely uninvolving – not so surprising from a director whose true gift was putting action in an emotional, political and narrative context that made the audience genuinely interested in the outcome. With such poorly-defined characters and such an undeveloped script, the only suspense is if you'll make it through the full 90 minutes. **TW**
Director John Frankenheimer **producer** Wolf Schmidt **execs** William Stuart, Sam Perlmutter **script** Stephen Peters, Kenneth Ross from novel by Peters **camera** Gerry Fisher **editor** Robert F. Shugrue **design** Alan Manzer **music** Bill Conti **cast** Roy Scheider, Jürgen Prochnow, Tim Reid,

Lara Harris, Harry Dean Stanton, Dale Dye, Bill MacDonald
Running time: 91 mins
US release: New Age, Mar 23, 1990
UK release: Guild, Jun 22, 1990

▼ FRESH HORSES

Fresh Horses is part of the detritus left over after the collapse of Weintraub Entertainment. The film tries to be a backwoods *Of Human Bondage*, with Andrew McCarthy, the Brat Pack's Leslie Howard, as a sensitive college student falling for Molly Ringwald's backwoods siren. It almost works, but someone (director David Anspaugh, perhaps?) keeps rubbing the rough edges off the material. JH
Director *David Anspaugh* **producer** *Dick Berg* **exec** *Allan Marcil* **script** *Larry Ketron, from his play* **camera** *Fred Murphy* **editor** *David Rosenbloom* **design** *Paul Sylbert* **music** *David Foster, Patrick Williams* **cast** *Molly Ringwald, Andrew McCarthy, Patti D'Arbanville, Ben Stiller, Leon Russom, Molly Hagan, Viggo Mortensen, Doug Hutchinson, Chiara Peacock, Marita Geraghty, Rachel Jones, Welker White*
Running time: 105 mins
US release: Weintraub, Nov 18, 1988
UK release: Col/Tri-Star, Jun 19, 1990

FRIDAY THE 13th VIII: ▼ JASON TAKES MANHATTAN

If they're going to call it *Jason Takes Manhattan*, then let's see Jason harassed by street gangs, Jason trying to take a cab to the village, Jason on the subway. *Friday the 13th VIII* was filmed on location. In British Columbia, where Jason gets on a cruise boat that's going to New York (How? By the Panama Canal?) and kills teenagers. They did a night of pickups in Times Square with Jason and the two teenage leads. What a ripoff! JH
Director/script *Rob Hedden* **producer** *Randolph Cheveldave* **camera** *Bryan England* **editor** *Steve Mirkovich* **design** *David Fischer* **music** *Fred Mollin* **cast** *Jensen Daggett, Scott Reeves, Peter Mark Richman, Barbara Bingham, V. C. Dupree, Kane Hodder, Sharlene Martin, Martin Cummins, Timothy Burr Mirkovich, Amber Pawlick*
Running time: 100 mins
US release: Paramount, Jul 28, 1989

FROM HOLLYWOOD TO DEADWOOD

This intricate story, with its doubling back of plot and sympathy, would have been better served by the written word. Two self-consciously alienated detectives, an ex-actor and an ex-writer, are hired to pursue a runaway actress whose disappearance has shut down a ten million dollar film. Cast with a couple of familiar faces (Paulin, Mulkey), and directed with some skill, the script too plainly hears the footsteps of Raymond Chandler and Ross MacDonald on its trail. JH
Director/script *Rex Pickett* **producer** *Jo Peterson* **exec** *Bill Byrne* **camera** *Peter Deming* **editors** *Stuart Adrianson, Robert Erickson* **design** *Tori Hourafchan* **music** *Alex Gibson, Gregory Kuehn* **cast** *Scott Paulin, Chris Mulkey, Jim Haynie, Barbara Schock, Jurgen Doeres, Mike Genovese, Norbert Weisser, Tom Dahlgren, Campbell Scott*
Running time: 102 mins
US release: Island, Apr 6, 1990

FULL MOON IN BLUE WATER

It comes as little surprise to find that Bill Bozzone's script derives from an unproduced play, and location shooting on the Texas Gulf Coast tends to throw into relief, rather than to obscure, the theatricality of this tragi-comedy of rum doings at a rundown bar. The material is a bit like *The Petrified Forest* crossed with one of the eccentric late works of Tennessee Williams, with suicide, arson and gunplay intruding noisily into the already less than quiet desperation of the *dramatis personae*. Chief of these is the proprietor (Hackman), sunk in maudlin inability to accept his wife's death, while Teri Garr is the lady of a certain age who aims to step into the deceased spouse's shoes. The director fails to find a unifying tone, and as a result some of the humour is of the unintended variety. TP
Director *Peter Masterson* **producers** *Lawrence Turman, David Foster, John Turman* **execs** *Moshe Diamant, Eduard Sarlui* **script** *Bill Bozzone* **camera** *Fred Murphy* **editor** *Jill Savitt* **music** *Phil Marshall* **cast** *Gene Hackman, Teri Garr, Burgess Meredith, Elias Koteas, Kevin Cooney, David Doty, Gil Glasgow*
Running time: 94 mins
US release: Trans World Nov 23, 1988
UK release: Entertainment, Jul 7, 1989

FAT MAN AND LITTLE BOY

There's almost never a good reason for changing a film title. There are odd exceptions – *Shoot to Kill* became *Deadly Pursuit* in the UK to avoid audience confusion in the wake of the John Stalker affair – but substituting *Fat Man and Little Boy* for *Shadowmakers*, reportedly because Joe Public in the US thought it sounded like a comedy, isn't one of them. If Paramount hoped to prevent the film becoming as big a flop in the UK as it was in the US, they failed.

The film deals with America's race to build the first atomic bomb and the Mephistophelean relationship that develops between the military and the scientists, particularly between the conservative General Groves (Paul Newman) and the liberal Robert Oppenheimer (Dwight Schultz). By no means a new subject, having already been covered on TV in *Oppenheimer* and *Day One*, Roland Joffé's pitch was to bring a huge budget to the moral debate. But the result is a procession of tired stereotypes – garrulous general, idealistic scientist juggling wife and mistress who embodies a larger morality, comic-relief doctor, nice young physicist and the nice young nurse he loves – for which Joffé, having rewritten Bruce Robinson's original script amid much acrimony, must take most of the blame. Like *The Mission*, and unlike that previous Joffé-Robinson 'collaboration' *The Killing Fields*, *Fat Man and Little Boy* shows Joffé's ability to take an epic and emotional subject, then leave audiences occasionally impressed but totally unmoved.

The first half of the film is a mess. It's filled with earnest but obviously simplified science-speak, delivered with the sort of academic urgency that manages to keep audiences at a distance from the protagonists without really explaining what is going on until, hey presto, some bright spark has the idea of squashing an orange. Having got all the theory and the pep talk out of the way, the film shows the device being assembled through easily-digestible and rapidly-resolved chunks of conflict between Groves and Oppie. The more intriguing of these (such as the bugging and constant surveillance of the scientists) are left hanging in a manner that suggests the first half of the film took the brunt of *Fat Man*'s heavy pre-release cutting (the original ending is also missing). Unfortunately there's nothing in the first 50 minutes or so of the film to hint that anything important was lost in this process.

What makes it so hard to sit through *Fat Man and Little Boy* is the film's failure to involve us in any of the characters. The surprisingly impressive Schultz catches the nervy precision of Oppenheimer, but makes it hard to sympathize with his fall from grace, while Newman's Groves is such an unconvincing string of clichés haphazardly arranged into sentences (such as 'It's all about ass – you kick it or you lick it' or 'My primadonnas better come through or you are lookin' at a piece of dead meat') that the relationship never becomes the stuff of drama.

The supporting cast are equally off-the-peg. Laura Dern is one-note banal, John Cusak is equally dull as her lover, and the usually wonderfully Bonnie Bedelia is an inaccurate reworking of Oppie's wife – a gifted scientist herself in reality – as a near-alcoholic Hausfrau whose only talent is having babies and turning a blind eye to her husband's infidelities. If any of these characters was a cliché we could care about maybe the damage wouldn't be so bad, but they are all performed with such a total lack of zest as to render the question of involvement academic. And since we already know the ending, there's never much by way of suspense.

We do learn, however, that the bomb was conceived as much as a weapon against the Soviets as the Nazis, and that the military exploited the Judaism of the (often communist) scientists to ensure their cooperation: it is only after Germany's defeat that they start to seriously question the morality of the device. And Groves' race to perfect the bomb before the Japanese can surrender does help the film pick up energy in the second half. But it's never enough to make the hard slog of getting to the big bang seem worth the effort.

Despite all the money spent on building a huge re-creation of the Los Alamos site, Joffé gives us no sense of time or place. And the film ultimately seems to lack a point of view, as it reduces its subject to the level of a purely American tragedy: Hiroshima and Nagasaki are never specifically mentioned, and the film's sole victim of radiation poisoning is an American scientist.

It was the latter contrivance that took the brunt of American critics' wrath, provoking a truth vs. reality debate in which neither side played by the rules. Experts were wheeled out to point up every minor inaccuracy, forcing Joffé to admit that he took liberties with the chronology of events to create an 'impression of reality', while producer Tony Garnett insisted it was a work of fiction (which isn't going to be any comfort to the Japanese). Eventually the film's failure was blamed on the critics' resentment at the British-in-Hollywood treatment of an American subject – a hoary old excuse for the failure of films that aren't any good, previously wheeled out for *Revolution* and *A Chorus Line*.

The film does offer some small rewards – the image of a dormant Fat Man blotting out the rising sun as it falls into place; Oppenheimer's shadow turning into that of Little Boy; the demented grin on his face as the wind from the first nuclear explosion distorts his features; his triumphant return to Los Alamos where Groves' look of approval suddenly reminds him of his own mortality and responsibility. But it's something of a comment on the banality of Joffé's dialogue that the only such moments are pure visuals.

Offsetting the effect of these scenes are moments of sledgehammer symbolism: Groves watching a ballet version of *The Sorcerer's Apprentice*, Laura Dern releasing doves, a final freeze-frame of Mother Earth. Despite the odd stunning image, Vilmos Zsigmond's photography brings not so much a caramel-coated past to mind as a melted Mars bar on the lens; Ennio Morricone's score is devoid of humanity until the beautiful final theme. Every aspect of the production is an infuriating mixture of the sublime and the amateur, with no single vision strong enough to keep the film on an even keel.

TREVOR WILLSMER

FIELD OF DREAMS

Although two of the best fantasy films of all time – The Wizard of Oz and It's a Wonderful Life – were made in Hollywood, the American cinema has always been decidedly uneasy with the blurring of reality and desire that is central to the genre. It's as though, having pragmatically accepted that there are no second chances in American life, that in America (unless you're Dorothy) you can't go hor . again, the drive to wish fulfilment has been savagely suppressed in the one art whose very form is most suited to treat it.

On one level, Field of Dreams is part of a recent slew of films about America's national sport, and one supposes that the baseball connection had a large part in raising the finance. But the tack it adopts is very much its own. At one point in the film, the James Earl Jones character says, 'The one constant through all the years has been baseball. It reminds us of all that once was good, and could be again,' making it very clear that this is a film dealing with the game as a metaphor. That's suggested at the opening when a heavenly voice declares, 'If you build it he will come,' so setting in motion the personal quest of Kevin Costner's Ray Kinsella.

The voice's 'he' initially seems to refer to Shoeless Jackson, a fabled and disgraced member of the Chicago White Sox team of 1929, which threw the World Series. It's a ghostly Jackson (played by Ray Liotta with a sense of detachment appropriate to an inhabitant of the after-life) who comes when Costner builds the required baseball diamond on his Iowa farm. But, like Jones and Burt Lancaster's small-town doctor, both of whom Costner is then asked to find, Shoeless Jackson's rôle is only as a guide. For it is the unresolved relationship between father and son that is the central theme of Field of Dreams.

In the wake of The Big Chill, which first articulated the need of the newly middle-aged to find a balance between youthful idealism and present-day realities, the American cinema has become besotted with the family. A preoccupation with the body beautiful and a desire to live forever have been overlaid by an interest in the quality of life as well as the problems and delights of parenthood. What marks out Field of Dreams from the rest of the pack is that its thirtysomething hero is required to sort out the past before he can confront the future. Thus the film's climactic moment shows Costner playing catch with his father, for the first time able to see his parent for what he is. And the film's wish-fulfilment ending is an endless convoy of cars converging on the field to witness this verity of family life transformed into the innocence of baseball.

As a child Costner has been introduced to baseball by his father, only to reject the sport because he cannot penetrate the dreams of a once-young man bowed down by a difficult present. In a key sequence, Costner recounts to Jones how he spat on his father's dreams, telling him that he can no longer respect anyone who has a criminal (Shoeless Jackson) as a hero. 'Why did you say that?' asks the incredulous Jones. 'Because I was seventeen,' replies Costner, admitting for the first time his insensitivity.

The businessmen who want to take away Costner's ailing farm lack the crude but vigorous characterization given to John Barrymore in *It's a Wonderful Life*. And Amy Madigan is irritatingly complacent and compliant as Costner's wife. In particular, the attempt to give the film an edge by having her champion the writings of Jones – he plays a J. D. Salinger-like writer who, though he's lost faith in himself, articulated the dreams of the 1960s – against her book-burning neighbours, is distressingly weak. But then, Phil Alden Robinson's concept of politics is as simplistic as Capra's. Moreover, these infelicities come with the territory. In John Ford's *The Sun Shines Bright*, the impossible dream of an idealized and harmonious community feeds a set of sequences and luminescent images that testify to the power of that dream but the broken-backed narrative makes no attempt to integrate the diverse stories. The flaws in *Field of Dreams* are similar. Occasionally the film almost seems to fall over itself. Thus, there's an embarrassing sequence in which Costner's daughter nearly chokes on a hot dog and is only saved when Burt Lancaster's Doctor Graham forgoes his dream of playing against the ghostly baseball team – in his brief career he never played against a major-league pitcher – by re-crossing the line that separates reality from fantasy. That said, his action confirms Lancaster's previous statement that, though the loss of his baseball career is a personal tragedy, it would have been a real tragedy if he'd only been a doctor for five minutes. It's the flaws in Robinson's film that demonstrate the impossibility of self-redemption.

Jones' impassioned, burnt-out author, and Lancaster's calm, accepting town doctor give the dream of redemption its social element, but it is when the film focuses on Costner's personal vision that it works best. Criss-crossing America as part of his attempt to force Jones to admit his love for baseball, and in a midnight conversation with the dead Lancaster, from whom he learns the simple importance of good works, Costner slowly realizes his need to come to terms with his father. In this he is aided by Robinson's understated direction and the low-key special effects. These give an intense other-worldly feel to the baseball diamond and the fluttering corn into which the ghostly players disappear, neatly and subtly demarcating the line between fantasy and reality.

Field of Dreams is, of course, a sentimental fable – you really can't go back home again – but the dream remains compelling. Like an elliptical Paul Simon song, it conveys both a nostalgia for a time of innocence and a knowing that it cannot be.

PHIL HARDY

GANASHATRU
(An Enemy of the People)

The film which marks Ray's return to directing after an enforced absence through illness is appropriately concerned with health – of the body and by metaphoric extension of the body politic. The drama in this updated transposition of Ibsen may be stylized (the premise of the original is not altogether tenable in an era of mass communication) but nonetheless it tackles head-on the ills of Indian society – demagoguery, superstition, vested interests – and evinces in its working-out a dynamic belief in democracy. The film was made wholly in the studio (required by Ray's convalescence) and occasionally the elimination of exteriors seems contrived; but on the whole the consciously theatrical manner of decoration and performance merges with and amplifies the hortatory tone of the screenplay. Hardly likely to be counted among Ray's most noteworthy achievements, the film still bears the hallmarks of its director's humanism. **TP**
Director/music Satyajit Ray **exec** Ravi Malik **script** Ray, based on play by Henryk Ibsen **camera** Barun Raha **editor** Dulal Dutta **design** Ashok Bose **cast** Soumitra Chatterjee, Ruma Guhathakurta, Dhritiman Chatterjee, Mamata Shankar, Dipankar Dey, Subhendu Chatterjee, Vischwa Guhathakurta
Running time: 100 mins
UK release: Electric, Dec 29, 1989

GETTING IT RIGHT

Randal Kleiser admired 1960s British sex comedies so much he went to London and made one himself. The result, set today only in terms of the calendar, isn't quite up to The Knack but surpasses Smashing Time. Jesse Birdsall is a 30-year-old virgin until he meets rich twit Helena Bonham Carter, rich tigress Lynn Redgrave and poor hairdresser's assistant Jane Horrocks. The hairdresser she assists is Birdsall who, despite having a gay best friend, isn't gay himself – just very, very shy. Peter Cook is funny as the owner of the salon, and likewise Sir John Gielgud as Bonham Carter's nouveau riche father. **BM**
Director Randal Kleiser **producer** Jonathan D. Krane, Kleiser **exec** Rusty Lemorande **script** Elizabeth Jane Howard, from her novel **camera** Clive Tickner **editor** Chris Kelly **design** Caroline Amies **music** Colin Towns **cast** Jesse Birdsall, Helena Bonham Carter, Peter Cook, Lynn Redgrave, Jane Horrocks, Richard Huw, John Gielgud, Pat Heywood, Judy Parfitt, Bryan Pringle
Running time: 102 mins
US release: MCEG, May 5, 1989
UK release: Medusa, Oct 20, 1989

GHOSTBUSTERS II

As the animated TV spin-off has shown, the format of Ghostbusters is ideally suited to further adventures, but Ghostbusters II opts to remake the first film, only not as well. All the major characters are brought back, and the plot gets off to a slow start as it fills us in on what's been happening to them in the intervening five years. Then we go through an only-slightly-varied rerun of the original movie's story, winding-up with a giant creature stalking the streets of New York and the ghostbusters trying to save the world. Although the cast more or less do the things that worked for them last time round, the whole film seems a beat or two off the mark. The special effects are surprisingly ropy, and only a few odd dialogue exchanges raise much in the way of laughter. Probably the most irritating aspect of the film, aside from the blender-worthy baby, is the non-stop 'get on down' score which intrudes into almost every scene as if the filmmakers were desperate to squeeze a soundtrack album out of the picture. **KN**
Director/producer Ivan Reitman **execs** Bernie Brillstein, Joe Medjuck, Michael C. Gross **script** Harold Ramis, Dan Aykroyd **camera** Michael Chapman **editors** Sheldon Kahn, Donn Cambern **design** Bo Welch **sfx** Dennis Muren, Pamela Easley, ILM **music** Randy Edelman **cast** Bill Murray, Dan Aykroyd, Sigourney Weaver, Harold Ramis, Rick Moranis, Ernie Hudson, Annie Potts, Peter MacNichol, Harris Yulin, David Margulies, Kurt Fuller, Janet Margolin, Wilhelm von Homburg
Running time: 108 mins
US release: Columbia, Jun 16, 1989
UK release: Columbia Tri-Star, Dec 1, 1989

⚑ GLEAMING THE CUBE

A fair idea for a TV movie gets turned into an embarrassing feature as a 'skateboard rebel' sets out to avenge the death of his adopted Vietnamese brother, with the aid of a hip-talking rebel cop who shouts at his superiors and impresses all the skateboarders with his amazing knowledge of skateboarding moves. Michael Tolkin's script never makes up its mind what it wants to be when it grows up, and Graeme Clifford's perfunctory direction lets the cast get away with murder: Steven Bauer sneers a lot to prove he's cool and Christian Slater seems under the delusion he's got the most pervasive smile since Tom Cruise (he even grins when he finds out his brother is dead!). As much fun as falling off a skateboard, and a lot less exciting. **TW**
Director Graeme Clifford **producers** Lawrence Turman, David Foster **script** Michael Tolkin **camera** Reed Smoot **editor** John Wright **design** John Muto **music** Jay Ferguson **cast** Christian Slater, Steven Bauer, Min Luong, Art Chudabala, Le Tuan, Richard Herd, Le Tuan, Ed Lauter,

Micole Mercurio, Peter Kwong
Running time: 105 mins
US release: Fox, Feb 17, 1989
UK release: Rank, Oct 20, 1989

GLORY
FILM • FILM • FILM • FILM

Director Edward Zwick **producer** Freddie Fields
script Kevin Jarre, from Lay This Laurel by Lincoln
Kirsten and One Gallant Rush by Peter Burchard,
and the letters of Robert Gould Shaw **camera**
Freddie Francis **editor** Steven Rosenblum **design**
Norman Garwood **music** James Horner **cast**
Matthew Broderick, Denzel Washington, Cary
Elwes, Morgan Freeman, Jihmi Kennedy, André
Braugher, John Finn, Donovan Leitch, John David
Cullum, Alan North, Raymond St. Jacques, Jane
Alexander, Bob Gunton
Running time: 122 mins
US release: Tri-Star, Dec 14, 1989
UK release: Columbia Tri-Star, Mar 2, 1990

THE GODS MUST BE CRAZY II
More of the same, with Nǃxau, the world's only
Bushman movie star, trying to find his children,
who have accidentally hitched a ride on a
poacher's truck. There are the usual jokes
involving stupid white people, and some third-
rate footage of the veldt. Low, broad comedy
predominates, though director Jamie Uys lacks
comic timing and rhythm. **JH**
Director/script Jamie Uys **producer** Boet
Troeskie **camera** Buster Reynolds **editors** Renée
Engelbrecht, Ivan Hall **music** Charles Fox **cast**
Nǃxau, Lena Farugia, Hans Strydom, Eiros, Nadies,
Erick Bowen, Treasure Tshabalala, Pierre Van
Pletzen, Lourens Swanepoel
Running time: 99 mins
US release: Columbia, Apr 13, 1990
UK release: Fox, May 18, 1990

GREAT BALLS OF FIRE!
Jim McBride's old-fashioned biopic of Jerry Lee
Lewis makes an infectious rock 'n' roll comedy
but, somewhere along the line, Great Balls of Fire
got gelded. As a lovable hick with a surfeit of
Southern arrogance, Quaid rides on his
undeniable charm and energy, but there's only
the barest hint of psychological complexity. Still,
Winona Ryder, as his incredulous thirteen-year-
old bride, and Alec Baldwin, as a perspiring
Jimmy Swaggart, excel as do the late Trey Wilson
as Sam Phillips and Michael St Gerard as a
depressive Elvis. The songs, by the man himself,
don't miss a beat. **GF**
Director Jim McBride **producer** Adam Fields
execs Michael Grais, Mark Victor **script** Jack
Baran, McBride, from book by Myra Lewis, Murray

Silver **camera** Affonso Beato **editors** Lisa Day,
Pembroke Herring, Bert Lovitt **design** David
Nichols **cast** Dennis Quaid, Winona Ryder, John
Doe, Joe Bob Briggs, Stephen Tobolowsky, Trey
Wilson, Alec Baldwin, Steve Allen, Lisa Blount,
Joshua Sheffield, Mojo Nixon, Jimmie Vaughan,
David Ferguson, Robert Lesser, Lisa Jane Persky,
Paula Person, Valerie Wellington
Running time: 107 mins
US release: Orion, Jun 30, 1989
UK release: Rank, Nov 10, 1989

GREMLINS 2: THE NEW BATCH
Not content to repeat himself, director Joe Dante
(and screenwriter Charlie Haas) turn Gremlins 2
into a post-modern assault on contemporary
cinema, locking most of the story into a large
steel and glass skyscraper owned by Donald
Clamp (Glover), a tycoon who combines the least
appealing aspects of Ted Turner and Donald
Trump – his cable network offers 'Casablanca in
living colour, with a new, happier ending.' There
are allusions to, and assaults upon: chic
Manhattan restaurants ('It's Canadian – they
clean the fish right at your table!') and their
careerist clientele; Hollywood action movies
(especially Die Hard); self-referential TV
programmes and talk shows; old science fiction
movies; Batman and much else. Great fun! **JH**
Director Joe Dante **producer** Michael Finnell
execs Steven Spielberg, Frank Marshall, Kathleen
Kennedy **script** Charlie Haas, from characters
created by Chris Columbus **camera** John Hora
editor Kent Beyda **design** James Spencer **music**
Jerry Goldsmith **cast** Zach Galligan, Phoebe Cates,
John Glover, Robert Prosky, Robert Picardo,
Christopher Lee, Haviland Morris, Dick Miller,
Jackie Joseph, Gedde Watanabe, Keye Luke,
Kathleen Freeman, Howie Mandel, Tony Randall,
Jeff Bergman
Running time: 105 mins
US release: Warner, Jun 15, 1989
UK release: Warner, Jul 27, 1990

GROSS ANATOMY
This is product, ground fine and deprived of
personality. Matthew Modine is a rebellious
working-class kid who goes to medical school,
seemingly to show off his street smarts and shame
his bourgeois classmates. It's The Paper Chase
with doctors, and we are expected to sympathize
because of how hard the work is. Why? Medical
school is notoriously tough, and nobody drafted
them – they're volunteers who will one day make
a lot of money. The bright spot is Christine
Lahti, in the John Houseman rôle, who never
realizes she's not playing in a great picture. **JH**
Director Thom Eberhardt **producers** Howard

Rosenman, Debra Hill **execs** Sandy Gallin, Carol
Baum **script** Ron Nyswaner, Mark Spragg **camera**
Steve Yaconelli **editors** Bud Smith, Scott Smith
design William F. Matthews **music** David
Newman **cast** Matthew Modine, Daphne Zuniga,
Christine Lahti, Todd Field, John Scott Clough,
Alice Carter, Robert Desiderio, Zakes Mokae,
J. C. Quinn, Rutanya Alda
Running time: 107 mins
US release: BV, Oct 20, 1989

THE GUARDIAN

Possible disadvantages of being rich and famous
in America. One, your English nanny (Jenny
Seagrove) could be an evil tree-nymph
determined to steal your baby. Two, the young
architect who built your house could be horribly
murdered by Miss S. Three, your own life could
be threatened by a crescendo of terror. Only
comfort: your story could be filmed by William
Exorcist Friedkin. This stylishly deranged thriller
is short on plausibility but long on virtuoso lens-
work and special effects. Marvel at Ms Seagrove's
on-screen metamorphosis, the most startling
thing since Daphne performed the same trick for
Apollo. **HK**
Director William Friedkin **producer** Joe Wizan
exec David Salven **script** Steven Volk, Dan
Greenburg, Friedkin **camera** John A. Alonzo **editor**
Seth Flaum **design** Gregg Fonseca **music** Jack
Hues **cast** Jenny Seagrove, Dwier Brown, Carey
Lowell, Brad Hall, Miguel Ferrer, Natalia Nogulich
Running time: 98 mins
US release: Universal, Apr 27, 1990

G

GLORY

Glory is not the film you'd expect from Edward Zwick. But whether he undertook the project out of sheer perversity given the current unfashionability of historical dramas, or as a riposte to critics who blasted his TV series, *thirtysomething*, for its whites-only view of suburban Philadelphia, it's a film that makes a significant contribution to the debate about the black experience in America by recounting an event, the formation of the first black regiment, that arguably changed the direction of the American Civil War. Along the way it also offers a commentary on contemporary US black-white relations.

While recent films like *Mississippi Burning* or *Do the Right Thing* showed the incendiary reactions of respectively the incensed white liberal and the disenfranchized urban black to racism, Zwick's film argues for a conciliatory attitude to racial conflict, as it follows the evolution of black solidarity under white leadership that leads to the 'glory' of the 54th Massachusetts infantry's suicidal assault on Fort Wagner, a Confederate earthwork defending the entrance to Charleston Harbour.

The title could also refer to the affectionate nickname for the American flag, 'Old Glory', since the film is as much about the unity imposed by a national cause on a dissolute gathering of dispossessed runaway slaves as it is about about the individual heroism that bestowed glory upon the regiment. Yet it is such old-fashioned values as heroism, dignity, integrity and valour that inspire Zwick's delineation of his leading characters.

The opening battle deliberately shakes loose the grandiose connotations hanging round the civil war theme. The camera doggedly follows Robert Gould Shaw (Matthew Broderick) as he charges behind his squadron leader towards the rebel lines at Antietam. Cannons belch out shot and the squadron leader's head disintegrates in front of a stunned Broderick, graphically elevating the film above the costume-drama ethics of a genre largely sated with Southern Belles, mint juleps and damn Yankees.

Broderick comes to after the battle is over. As a surgeon tends to a slight neck wound, he tells Broderick, who is staring hollow-eyed at a man being amputated on while conscious, that Lincoln has issued his Emancipation Proclamation. Zwick thus implies that Broderick's half-hearted attempt on the battlefield was due to a lack of faith in his cause.

At a party in the Boston home of Broderick's abolitionist parents, he is asked to head up the north's first black regiment. The black leader Frederick Douglass says the regiment will 'offer pride and dignity to those who have known only degradation'. This remark echoes through the film, and applies as much to Broderick, and his horrific experience of war, as to the three former slaves, André Braugher, Morgan Freeman and Denzel Washington, whose transformation into fighting men Zwick's camera records with probing intensity.

Zwick's TV movie *Special Bulletin* – a nuclear incident in Charleston seen through a series of TV news bulletins – and the film *About Last Night* . . ., based on David Mamet's play about sexual relationships – demonstrated his skills with narrative. But it is *thirtysomething*, the TV series he co-created, which has the strongest visual links with *Glory*. This contemporary soap about upper-middle-class families, examined through the minutiae of their angst-ridden relationships, thrives on the incestuously close relationship the camera maintains with each member of the ensemble.

Zwick employs the same plethora of medium close-up shots in *Glory* to telling effect. The soldiers' faces are constantly cut into the film's progress, and might render it stilted were it not for the insights they capture, as they monitor the characters' changing attitudes to themselves and each other. Freeman, weathered and wise, finds his way to stoical indifference, while Braugher, humiliated by his own assumptions regarding his standing in the troop – a consequence of his childhood friendship with Broderick – finds a new independence. But it is Denzel Washington, with his malignant hatred of anything white, who burns feverishly at the centre of the film.

Washington, more than any of the other characters, sounds a contemporary note of outrage and hatred against white oppression. In one of the film's strongest scenes, Broderick orders Washington whipped for desertion. His shirt is pulled off his back to reveal a mass of scar tissue from previous flagellations. Zwick cuts back and forth from the angry defiance etched in Washington's face to the slight quivering of Broderick's features as he orders the punishment to continue.

One tear rolls down Washington's face as he stares at Broderick, while the lash comes down on his back off-screen. The slow, probing pace of Zwick's cutting accentuates the quiet anger that claws out of the scene, making you almost feel Broderick jump every time the whip cracks.

Broderick's is the most demanding performance. Zwick's camera dwells on him constantly, but his determined features, masked under the burden of authority, rarely betray emotion. It is with his eyes, in the climactic scene before he leads the march on the fort, that Broderick displays the conflicting sensations of fear and bravery that are struggling for control of him.

Broderick's perception of his troops, articulated through voiceovers from his letters home, lets the film explore the sense of distance he feels in the face of their camaraderie, music and humour. But constantly the barriers of race and authority are broken down, as Broderick requests Freeman's help in meeting the needs of the soldiers, and also attempts to bring Washington into the fold by offering him an opportunity to carry the flag into battle.

It is not until a later scene that these embryonic seeds of unity finally start to flower. The film finds a sense of honour and dignity in the regiment, nowhere more eloquently realized than when, around the camp fire, the soldiers have an informal church gathering, some singing and clapping as others take it in turns to testify to their new-found purpose as they prepare for the fight the next day. 'We're men ain't we,' says Washington to Freeman. The suggestion is that they have finally shaken off the shackles of slavery by giving up their individuality for the sake of a common cause, rather than at the behest of an overseer's whip.

But it is the assault on Fort Wagner that cements the unity between officers and men, as well as between the soldiers themselves. Broderick, trying to rally his men in the face of an onslaught of Confederate rifles, falls back dead. The troops, watching his tumbling body, freeze in a moment of awful silence, which is swallowed up by the volleys of Confederate gunfire. Then Washington takes up the flag and the troops rally with him, breaking through the Confederate defences. Zwick's camera races alongside the men, lending a majestic gracefulness to the charge, as they reach the heart of the Southern defense and a cannon is turned on them, while James Horner's choral score adds an elegiac quality to an exquisite moment of doomed glory.

Zwick cuts from the smoke after the cannon fires to a slow-motion sequence, where the soldiers' bodies are tipped into a sandy grave. First Broderick, then Washington roll in, one on top of the other, Washington's arm coming to rest across Broderick, almost in a protective embrace.

Earlier in the narrative, Freeman tells some black children, 'We're runaway slaves but we come back fighting men.' That desire to provide rôle models infuses the narrative. The inspiration that the storming of Fort Wagner generated during the war – black troops making up over ten per cent of the North's armed forces by the end of the conflict – Zwick seems to be suggesting is still relevant now.

If Zwick 'writes within history', as he has described the manipulation of the true events on which Glory is based, it is to interpret the story as a rite of passage, not to manhood, but to a unified multi-racial society. What was in terms of the war a minor skirmish – and largely a marginalized footnote in the history of the war – becomes in Glory a symbol of the potential emergence of a national identity predicated on a belief in equality for which both black and white men fought and died. Of course Mississippi Burning and Do the Right Thing showed that what might have been, has yet to come about.

STEPHEN DARK

HALLOWEEN 4: THE RETURN OF MICHAEL MYERS

Whereas *Halloween 3: Season of the Witch* was a brave experiment that didn't come off, this is as unimaginative, uninspiring, predictable and dumb as the disappointing *Halloween 2* or any of the other psycho sequels currently clogging the marketplace. It's ten years since unstoppable psycho Michael Myers last put on his mask and terrorized his home town. When he goes after the orphaned daughter of the old Jamie Lee Curtis character, Dr Loomis (Pleasence) heads for Haddonfield, Illinois, to stop the slaughter. It's incredible that a film could be so closely patterned on Carpenter's still-thrilling original movie and yet be so suspenseless, stupid, unscary and plodding as this. Miraculously, something interesting happens in the last two minutes, but by that time it's far, far too late. **KN**
Director *Dwight H. Little* **producer** *Paul Freeman* **exec** *Moustapha Akkad* **script** *Alan B. McElroy* **camera** *Peter Lyons Collister* **editor** *Curtiss Clayton* **design** *Roger S. Crandall* **music** *Alan Howarth* **cast** *Donald Pleasence, Ellie Cornell, Danielle Harris, George R. Wilbur, Michael Pataki, Beau Starr, Kathleen Kinmont, Sasha Jenson, Gene Ross, Carmen Filpi*
Running time: 88 mins
US release: Galaxy, Oct 21, 1988
UK release: Fox, Nov 3, 1989

HAMLET GOES BUSINESS (Hamlet Liikemaailmassa)

The prolific Aki Kaurismäki turns, after a fashion, to the Bard, with a modern-dress version of his famous tragedy which converts it into a farcical pastiche of boardroom melodrama (the court of Denmark has been substituted for a furniture business), treated rather in the manner of some old Allied Artists B-thriller, complete with looming shadows, menacing footsteps and percussive score. Almost inevitably, the result is hit and miss, and suitably manic embellishments rub shoulders with stretches of near-ineptitude. The mixture of inconsequentiality and mock-fatalism is piquant, but insufficiently so to stave off the feeling that the whole thing might have worked better as a half-hour sketch. **TP**
Director/producer/script *Aki Kaurismäki* **camera** *Timo Salminen* **editor** *Raija Talvio* **design** *Pertti Hilkamo* **cast** *Pirkka-Pekka Petelius, Esko Salminen, Kati Outinen, Elina Salo, Esko Nikkari, Kari Väänänen, Hannu Valtonen, Mari Rantasila, Turo Pajala, Aake Kalliala, Pentti Auer*
Running time: 86 mins
UK release: Electric, Feb 23, 1990

THE HANDMAID'S TALE

Outside the walls of Gilead, the corrupt and repressive theocracy that America has become by the 21st century, a young family escaping in the snow is apprehended and the husband shot. Inducted as a surrogate mother and as the mistress of the commander (Duvall), the young widow (Richardson) leads the inevitable insurrection by slitting his throat. The political rhetoric of Margaret Atwood's novel has not been betrayed by Harold Pinter's adaptation and the acting is universally excellent, but director Volker Schlöndorff looks uncomfortable with the material throughout. The colour-coded costuming and half-baked futurism of this feminist *1984* look incredibly dated, and it's a pity that no-one thought to supply an ending. **GF**
Director *Volker Schlöndorff* **producer** *Danny Wilson* **exec** *Wolfgang Glattes* **script** *Harold Pinter*, from *Margaret Atwood's* novel **camera** *Igor Luther* **editor** *David Ray* **design** *Tom Walsh* **music** *Ryuichi Sakamoto* **cast** *Natasha Richardson, Robert Duvall, Faye Dunaway, Aidan Quinn, Elizabeth McGovern, Victoria Tennant, Blanche Baker, Traci Lind, David Dukes, Zoey Wilson, Kathryn Doby, Lucile McIntyre*
Running time: 109 mins
US release: Cinecom, Mar 7, 1990

HARD TO KILL

Yes indeed. If a seven-year coma cannot kill ex-cop Steven Seagal, what can? His wife is murdered one night before his eyes while watching the Johnny Carson show. (He told her TV was bad for her health.) Bullet-riddled himself, Mr Seagal retires into a Rip Van Winkle state and wakes up 2,000 shopping days later to find beautiful nurse Kelly Le Brock by his bed. 'You're famous all over the hospital' she trills. But no time for conversation, the baddies are back. Then it's guns, fists and car chases, deafeningly permutated till end title – all laced with a bit of Zen buddhism. Foolish nonsense, fit for a rainy day when the VCR is your only friend. **HK**
Director *Bruce Malmuth* **producers** *Gary Adelson, Joel Simon, Bill Todman Jr.* **execs** *Lee Rich, Michael Rachmil* **script** *Steven McKay* **camera** *Matthew F. Leonetti* **editor** *John F. Link* **design** *Robb Wilson King* **music** *David Michael Frank* **cast** *Steven Seagal, Kelly Le Brock, Bill Sadler, Frederick Coffin, Bonnie Burroughs, Zachary Rosencrantz, Branscombe Richmond*
Running time: 95 mins
US release: Warner, Feb 9, 1990
UK release: Warner, Jun 2, 1990

▼ HARLEM NIGHTS

This is the kind of movie that makes racism seem respectable. All the black characters are pimps, prostitutes, liars, cheats or murderers. And they're the good guys; none more so than Eddie Murphy, who proves it by shooting the foot off the madam of his brothel and murdering the girl he sleeps with. All women are 'bitches' or 'property' to be abused, insulted, tortured or killed by him. Misogyny doesn't even begin to describe the pure hatred this film expresses towards women. Why one of the few black stars with the muscle to bankroll any film he wants should make a movie that portrays blacks in such a low light is almost as much of a mystery as why the black press, which so vociferously protested a white director's version of *The Color Purple*, praised Murphy's portrayal of a 'strong black leading man'. **TW**
Director/exec/script Eddie Murphy **producers** Robert D. Wachs, Mark Lipsky **camera** Woody Omens **editor** George Bowers **design** Lawrence G. Paull **music** Herbie Hancock **cast** Eddie Murphy, Richard Pryor, Redd Foxx, Danny Aiello, Michael Lerner, Della Reese, Jasmine Guy, Arsenio Hall
Running time: 118 mins
US release: Paramount, Nov 17, 1989
UK release: UIP, May 25, 1990

HAWKS

This sporadically entertaining black comedy is just two decades too late. Whilst the early scenes in a terminal ward occasionally hit the right note of desperate black humour, as Timothy Dalton draws Anthony Edwards into his world of bitter practical jokes, the film's heavily signposted moments of grotesquerie and a misconceived escape to visit Amsterdam's biggest brothel lead the film into sentimentality and an unconvincing, morally redeeming romance that is as incurable as its main characters. With drastic surgery and another doctor on the case, the script could have been something but, as it is, my prescription is to wait for it to come on the telly and turn off at the halfway point. It doesn't get any better, and neither do they. **TW**
Director Robert Ellis Miller **producers** Stephen Lanning, Keith Cavele **exec** Morrie Eisenman, Richard Becker **script** Roy Clarke, based on idea by Barry Gibb, David English **camera** Doug Milsome **editor** Malcolm Cooke **design** Peter Howitt **music** Barry Gibb, John Cameron **cast** Timothy Dalton, Anthony Edwards, Janet McTeer, Camille Coduri, Jill Bennett, Robert Lang, Pat Starr, Bruce Boa, Sheila Hancock, Geoffrey Palmer, Caroline Langrishe, Benjamin Whitrow, Robyn Moore, Connie Booth
Running time: 109 mins
US release: Skouras, Nov 10, 1989
UK release: Rank, Aug 5, 1988

HEART CONDITION

This has enough high concept to last just the length of its trailer. Denzel Washington plays a rich (and eventually dead) lawyer whose heart is transplanted into Bob Hoskins, a working-class cop with racist leanings and a massive cholesterol count. Getting by on the strengths of its actors, it's like *48 Hours* mixed with the middle part of *Always* and a hint of *All of Me*. If that's an awkward description, it fits. **CB**
Director/script James D. Parriott **producer** Steve Tisch **exec** Robert Shaye **camera** Arthur Albert **editor** David Finter **design** John Muto **music** Patrick Leonard **cast** Bob Hoskins, Denzel Washington, Chloe Webb, Roger E. Mosley, Janet DuBois, Alan Rachins, Ray Baker, Jeffrey Meek
Running time: 95 mins
US release: New Line, Feb 2, 1990
UK release: Enterprise, Oct 26, 1990

◀▮ HEATHERS

This is a bravely comic, totally astonishing variation on the 'youth problem' movie – a deeply unsettling fable that bristles with repeatable lines, appalling but hilarious lapses in taste, a clutch of spot-on performances and a unique combination of cruelty and subversive wit. Winona Ryder is fortunate to be one of the high school's élite clique along with three glamorous and variously obnoxious girls called Heather. But she is burdened with a conscience and doesn't want to go along with the ruthless persecution, emotional torture and shallow vacuity that the Miss Popularity crown entails. Cue arrival of Christian Slater as Ryder's psycho boyfriend, who proposes they murder Bitch Queen Heather Number One and pass it off as suicide. The suicide then turns the school upside-down, with the dead monster canonized. Slater then thinks of a plan to get even with a couple of football thugs, and gradually things get even more gruesome. First-time director Michael Lehman, working from a super-smart script by Daniel Waters, choreographs the stylized violence and sick humour with equal ease. The film's strength is that it refuses to slot into any of the genres one expects it to try for, and its success is that it manages to be cynical, merciless and riotous while still making valid moral points. **KN**
Director Michael Lehmann **producer** Denise Di Novi **exec** Christopher Webster **script** Daniel Waters **camera** Francis Kenney **editor** Norman Hollyn **design** Jon Hutman **music** David Newman **cast** Winona Ryder, Christian Slater, Shannen Doherty, Lisanne Falk, Kim Walker, Penelope Milford, Glenn Shadix, Lance Fenton, Patrick Labyorteaux, Jeremy Applegate, Jon Matthews
Running time: 103 mins
US release: New World, Mar 31, 1989
UK release: Premier, Nov 17, 1989

HEAVY PETTING

For those who need to know, Sandra Bernhard once let a little boy give her 'a shot in the butt' – they were playing doctor – in return for a Fudgsicle. In this survey of the Eisenhower-era mating rituals of heterosexual white America, Obie Benz mixes interviews with people who grew up to be famous New Yorkers – David Byrne, Laurie Anderson, Ann Magnuson – with clips from old movies and 'health education' films. But his humour comes wrapped in a fog of nostalgia. Weren't the 1950s a time of sexual repression and entrenched misogyny? Was it this much fun? CB
Director/producer *Obie Benz* **camera** *Sandi Sissell* **editor** *Josh Waletzky*
Running time: 80 mins
US release: Skouras, Sep 22, 1989

🖓 HENRY V

Kenneth Branagh, as director and star, is obviously guilty of hubris in trying to match Olivier's achievement in the same rôles for the 1945 film version of Shakespeare's play. Still, it's an honourable attempt to do something with intractable material that's consistently striking visually on a limited budget The potato-faced Branagh's performance as the snotty tearaway turned militarist monarch is adequate. He is more effective as a director, doing his best to handle a selection of Britain's finest classical hams and turning in a Peckinpah-ish mud and blood update of the Battle of Agincourt for the post-Falklands era. The highlight is a long, show-offy, budget-spending tracking shot featuring hordes of extras, piles of corpses, and a gorgeous bit of Latin chanting, an effect only slightly marred by the impaled and giggling extra in the foreground who can hardly have been Branagh's favourite person after the rushes were screened. KN
Director *Kenneth Branagh* **producer** *Bruce Sharman* **exec** *Stephen Evans* **script** *Branagh, from play by William Shakespeare* **camera** *Kenneth MacMillan* **editor** *Mike Bradsell* **design** *Tim Harvey* **music** *Patrick Doyle* **cast** *Kenneth Branagh, Derek Jacobi, Simon Shepherd, James Larkin, Brian Blessed, James Simmons, Paul Gregory, Charles Kay, Alec McCowen, Fabian Cartwright, Stephen Simms, Jay Villiers, Edward Jewesbury, Ian Holm, Daniel Webb, Jimmy Yuill, John Sessions, Shaun Prendergast, Pat Doyle, Michael Williams, Richard Briers, Geoffrey Hutchings, Robert Stephens, Robbie Coltrane, Christian Bale, Judi Dench, Paul Scofield, Michael Maloney, Harold Innocent, Richard Clifford, Emma Thompson, Geraldine McEwan, David Lloyd Meredith, David Parfitt*
Running time: 137 mins
US release: Goldwyn, Nov 8, 1989
UK release: Curzon, Oct 6, 1989

🖓 HENRY ... PORTRAIT OF A SERIAL KILLER

This is a chilling masterpiece of low-budget intellectual splatter. Shot in Chicago for about $100,000, *Henry* is inspired by the confessions of Henry Lee Lucas, who left a couple of hundred bodies in roadside graves in Texas. Showing a horrified restraint for the first hour (we see the aftermath of the killings, rather than the killings themselves), the film explodes into a finale of baroque, stomach-turning violence that shames the last decade's dead-babysitter/camp counsellor movies and their aestheticized violence – this shows the skull beneath the skin. JH
Director *John McNaughton* **producers** *McNaughton, Lisa Dedmond, Steven A. Jones* **script** *Richard Fire, McNaughton* **camera** *Charlie Lieberman* **editor** *Elena Maganini* **design** *Rick Paul* **music** *McNaughton, Ken Hale, Jones* **cast** *Michael Rooker, Tom Towles, Tracy Arnold*
Running time: 83 mins
US release: Greycat, Mar 23, 1990

HIDER IN THE HOUSE

If it were presented with a bit more gothic flair, the central premise of this draggy thriller might almost be scary, if not believable. Gary Busey plays Tom Sykes who murdered his nasty parents when he was a child and has just been released from the nut house. He finds an empty luxury home, and moves into the attic, constructing himself a concealed hidey-hole and bugging the whole house. The Dryer family moves in and the rest follows. Heavily influenced by *Fatal Attraction*, this is another attempt to make a semi-serious slasher movie. Busey is a barrel-chested presence, and makes the film less unbearable than it might have been, but everyone else is a total vacuum. The storyline never remotely threatens to make any sense, and the film shamelessly re-uses the same old clichés you've seen in a hundred other slasher movies. KN
Director *Matthew Patrick* **producers** *Edward Teets, Michael Taylor* **execs** *Steven Reuther, Diane Nabotoff* **script** *Lem Dobbs* **camera** *Jeff Jur* **editor** *Debra T. Smith* **design** *Victoria T. Paul* **music** *Christopher Young* **cast** *Gary Busey, Mimi Rogers, Michael McKean, Kurt Christopher Kinder, Candy Hutson, Elizabeth Ruscio, Chuck Lafont, Bruce Glover, Leonard Termo*
Running time: 108 mins
UK release: Vestron, Dec 1, 1989

🖓 HOMEBOY

Johnny Walker (Rourke), a boxer so punch-drunk, inarticulate and sleazy that he makes Rocky Balboa look like Cary Grant, arrives in a run-down resort to build a new career by getting

beaten to a pulp. He falls in with Wesley (Walken), a small-time crook and nightclub entertainer and finds himself being pulled towards a life of crime. However, he also meets Ruby (Feuer), a gentle soul who owns a run-down carnival and she tries to bring out his notional finer side by having him help restore her broken carousel. No sooner than you can say cliché, a doctor (Blades) is diagnosing a skull fracture which means Johnny could die if he gets hit in the head one more time, and he is given a choice between a comeback fight with a top contender or putting on a false Hassidic beard and helping Wesley heist a jeweler. Mickey Rourke, who was once a boxer, developed his own storyline for *Homeboy*, and shamelessly uses the film as an excuse to show off his Method mumbling. Unfortunately, this kind of dogged sluggishess also characterizes the laughably simplistic exposition. **KN**
Director Michael Seresin **producers** Alan Marshall, Elliott Kastner **script** Eddie Cook, from story by Mickey Rourke **camera** Gale Tattersall **editor** Ray Lovejoy **design** Brian Morris **music** Eric Clapton, Michael Kamen **cast** Mickey Rourke, Christopher Walken, Debra Feuer, Thomas Quinn, Kevin Conway, Anthony Alda, Jon Polito
Running time: 112 mins
UK release: Fox, Jul 14, 1989

HONEY, I SHRUNK THE KIDS

When an inventor (Moranis) zaps his teenage daughter, the boy next door and two younger brothers with his latest invention, they are suddenly Lilliputians who – accidentally put out with the garbage – have to make an incredible journey through the backyard. There's nothing reductive about this exuberant Disney family comedy – with its friendly ant, three-storey Lego bricks, and monstrous lawnmower – which delights not only in turning the garden into a prehistoric jungle but also in its wry observation of generational conflicts. Rick Moranis and Matt Frewer, the neurotically sporty neighbour, are terrific as dads preoccupied with their own adolescent fantasies. **GF**
Director Joe Johnston **producer** Penney Finkelman Cox **exec** Thomas G. Smith **script** Ed Naha, Tom Schulman **camera** Hiro Narita **editor** Michael A. Stevenson **design** Gregg Fonseca **sfx** Marianne Ray, Robin D'Arcy, Image Engineering **music** James Horner **cast** Rick Moranis, Matt Frewer, Marcia Strassman, Kristine Sutherland, Thomas Brown, Jared Rushton, Amy O'Neill, Robert Oliveri, Carl Steven, Mark L. Taylor, Kimmy Robertson, Lou Cutell, Laura Waterbury
Running time: 86 mins
US release: BV, Jun 23, 1989
UK release: Warner, Feb 9, 1990

THE HOUSE OF BERNARDA ALBA (La Casa de Bernarda Alba)

Director Mario Camus unscrolls the sacred text of Federico García Lorca. Less reverence and more liberty-taking might have saved this stagey account of Lorca's play, in which five love-starved sisters are locked into a mourning vigil by their semi-crazed mother. Artful claustrophobia is one thing in a drama about sexual and spiritual cabin fever. But a camera nailed to the floor and inertly ogling 'great' performances is another. The cream of Spanish theatre is here; but instead of pouring it lovingly over a living drama Camus lets it sour and congeal in histrionics. **HK**
Director Mario Camus **execs** Jaime Borrell, José Miguel Juárez, Antonio Oliver **script** Camus, Antonio Larreta, from play by Federico García Lorca **camera** Fernando Arribas **editor** José M. Biurrun **design** Rafael Palmero **cast** Irene Gutierrez Caba, Ana Belén, Florinda Chico, Enriqueta Carballeira, Vicky Peña, Aurora Pastor, Mercedes Lezcano
Running time: 103 mins
UK release: Gala, Mar 2, 1990

HOUSE PARTY

Somewhere in America, in a black neighbourhood, Christopher Martin has the house to himself while his parents are out of town, and so he decides to throw a party– which is disrupted by a trio of hoods and a couple of white cops who cruise around the neighbourhood looking for blacks to victimize. *House Party* is a low-budget comedy about black youth culture that provides a contrast to *Beat Street*, *Breakdance* or *Rappin'* – films that get laughed at in the movie – by presenting the music the kids like as nothing special aside from an excuse to have fun. While it manages to be funny and likeable, it also dares to be socially responsible by omitting all but the merest token mention of drugs. It's not a moralizing movie, but it does break some new ground by depicting black kids as neither juvenile delinquents nor martyrs. The ordinary background is a realistic version of the way most blacks genuinely do live in America. Incredibly, despite the three hoods pouring petrol, the film doesn't even get round to trashing the host's house. It's rough around the edges, but well worth seeking out. **KN**
Director/script Reginald Hudlin **producer** Warrington Hudlin **exec** Gerald Olson **camera** Peter Deming **editor** Earl Watson **design** Bryan Jones **music** Marcus Miller **cast** Christopher Reid, Robin Harris, Christopher Martin, Martin Lawrence, Tisha Campbell, A. J. Johnson
Running time: 100 mins
US release: New Line, Mar 9, 1990
UK release: Enterprise, Aug 31, 1990

HOW TO GET AHEAD IN ADVERTISING

When Richard E. Grant isn't ranting his way through this movie, he's running around the garden half-naked. A hysterical diatribe, *How to Get Ahead in Advertising* sounds off about a 'conspiracy' but doesn't offer any sort of coherent polemic, and largely wastes its central idea – a boil grows on ad man Grant's shoulder as he starts to nurse doubts about his profession. Since Grant's two personalities, as boil and well-meaning human, both behave in such an extreme fashion, there's no contest between them, and neither character is sufficiently revealed to give the excrescence much value as metaphor. Robinson, who can write scenes and direct actors, can't structure a script.or orchestrate a movie. **JP**
Director/script *Bruce Robinson* **producer** *David Wimbury* **execs** *George Harrison, Denis O'Brien* **camera** *Peter Hannan* **editor** *Alan Strachan* **design** *Michael Pickwoad* **music** *David Dundas, Rick Wentworth* **cast** *Richard E. Grant, Rachel Ward, Richard Wilson, Jacqueline Tong, John Shrapnel, Susan Wooldridge, Mick Ford*
Running time: 95 mins
US release: Warner, May 5, 1989
UK release: Virgin, Jul 28, 1989

THE HUNT FOR RED OCTOBER

Because of recent shifts in east-west relations, *The Hunt for Red October* is forced to establish that its hi-tech, seemingly near-future events are actually taking place in 1984, well before the Gorbachev era, and that the fiendish Red October, a nuclear submarine that dissident skipper Sean Connery plans to turn over to the West, is the kind of war toy prized by the Chernenko régime. However, even without the tripwire of current events, this is a remarkably turgid and old-fashioned affair. While Richard Jordan and Joss Ackland trade cynical political equivocations topside, the higher-billed performers dangle out of helicopters in high winds over freezing waters, cling to the bulkheads as torpedoes are avoided, fire ricochet bullets around the nuclear weapons and strain to look nervous. Even John McTiernan (*Predator, Die Hard*) can hardly do much with this overlong, humourless suspense picture given that it consists almost entirely of drab-uniformed men in confined spaces arguing with each other as the complex but unbelievable plot is laboriously worked through. **KN**
Director *John McTiernan* **producer** *Mace Neufeld* **execs** *Larry DeWaay, Jerry Sherlock* **script** *Larry Ferguson, Donald Stewart, from novel by Tom Clancy* **camera** *Jan de Bont* **editors** *Dennis Virkler, John Wright* **design** *Terence Marsh* **sfx** *Scott Squires, ILM* **music** *Basil Poledouris* **cast** *Sean Connery, Alec Baldwin, Scott Glenn, Sam Neill,*

James Earl Jones, Joss Ackland, Richard Jordan, Peter Firth, Tim Curry, Courtney B. Vance, Stella Skarsgard, Jeffrey Jones, Timothy Carhart, Larry Ferguson
Running time: 137 mins
US release: Paramount, May 2, 1990
UK release: UIP, Apr 20, 1990

I LOVE YOU TO DEATH

This fact-based comedy creates an interesting disjunction between farcical situations and delicate performances. Tracy Ullman is a housewife who discovers that her husband, pizzeria owner Kevin Kline, is cheating on her, and decides to kill him. The hilarity of her unsuccessful attempts – and her inept minions (notably Keanu Reeves, who here takes his blitzed teen speciality into new realms) – are the comic spine of the picture. If one is attuned to the film's mood of murderous good cheer, it is among the year's best entertainments. JH
Director *Lawrence Kasdan* **producers** *Jeffrey Lurie, Ron Moler* **execs** *Charles Okun, Michael Grillo* **script** *John Kostmayer* **camera** *Owen Roizman* **editor** *Anne V. Coates* **design** *Lilly Kilvert* **music** *James Horner* **cast** *Kevin Kline, Tracey Ullman, Joan Plowright, River Phoenix, William Hurt, Keanu Reeves, James Gammon, Victoria Jackson, Miriam Margolyes, Jack Kehler, Phoebe Cates, Kathleen York, Heather Graham, Lawrence Kasdan*
Running time: 96 mins
US release: Tri-Star, Apr 6, 1990

I'M GONNA GIT YOU SUCKA

Ultracool Jack Spade and his hip sidekicks (Brown, Hayes, Casey) take on the Mr Big of city crime in this sporadic, but often very funny shafting of the blacksploitation movie of the early 1970s. Aiming at the same audience as *Hollywood Shuffle*, the film lacks Robert Townsend's sure touch and runs out of steam too soon, but it has more than enough great moments to make up for its failings. TW
Director/script *Keenen Ivory Wayans* **producers** *Peter McCarthy, Carl Craig* **execs** *Raymond Katz, Eric L. Gold* **camera** *Tom Richmond* **editor** *Michael R. Miller* **design** *Melba Farquhar, Catherine Hardwicke* **music** *David Michael Frank* **cast** *Keenen Ivory Wayans, Bernie Casey, Antonio Fargas, Steve James, Isaac Hayes, Jim Brown, Ja'net DuBois, Dawn Lewis, John Vernon*
Running time: 87 mins
US release: UA, Dec 14, 1988
UK release: UIP, Nov 10, 1989

IMMEDIATE FAMILY

Glenn Close and James Woods are a well-off, happily married couple who yearn for but can't conceive a baby; Mary Stuart Masterson is the blue-collar teenager who contracts to give them her child as soon as it is born and then changes her mind when she holds it in her arms. The Baby M. surrogate mother case was barely out of the headlines when this tepid bleeding-heart screen version emerged, its drama a pale shadow of that endured by the real-life protagonists.

Blessed by Masterson's unsentimental performance as the worldy-wise young mother, director Jonathan Kaplan addresses the social problems of a young proletarian woman with the same tact and adroitness he showed in *The Accused*, but the conclusion of *Immediate Family* is a cop-out. GF
Director *Jonathan Kaplan* **producers** *Sarah Pillsbury, Midge Sanford* **exec** *Lawrence Kasdan* **script** *Barbara Benedek* **camera** *John W. Lindley* **editor** *Jane Kurson* **design** *Mark Freeborn* **music** *Brad Fiedel* **cast** *Glenn Close, James Woods, Mary Stuart Masterson, Kevin Dillon, Linda Darlow, Jane Greer, Jessica James, Mimi Kennedy, Charles Levin, Harrison Mohr, Matthew Moore, Kristin Sanderson, Merrilyn Gann*
Running time: 95 mins
US release: Columbia, Oct 27, 1989

IMPULSE

For this year's second woman-directed, woman-centred cop thriller – Kathryn Bigelow's *Blue Steel* is the other – the focus is on psychology rather than action, with Theresa Russell as an undercover vice cop who gets trapped in a world of nocturnal sleaze. Locke's past association with Clint Eastwood may have done the film more harm than good – the only thing this has in common with his thrillers is an obsessively dark lighting scheme. She does her best with the material but, given a plot that has the consistency of Swiss cheese, the script just ain't happening. CB
Director *Sondra Locke* **producers** *Albert S. Ruddy, André Morgan* **exec** *Dan Kolsrud* **script** *John De Marco, Leigh Chapman* **camera** *Dean Semler* **editor** *John W. Wheeler* **design** *William A. Elliott* **music** *Michel Colombier* **cast** *Theresa Russell, Jeff Fahey, George Dzundza, Alan Rosenberg, Nicholas Mele, Eli Danker, Charles McCaughan, Lynne Thigpen, Shawn Elliott*
Running time: 108 mins
US release: Warner, Apr 6, 1990

IN COUNTRY

Another instalment in the American cinema's obsessive chronicling of the legacy of Vietnam, Norman Jewison's film centres on a teenage girl whose father died in the conflict, and her relationship with a withdrawn uncle who also fought in the war. The Kentucky small-town background is all too convincingly drab, and the style is suitably plain and direct. But the screenplay, lacking density of characterization as well as clarity of structure, cannot carry the requisite thematic weight, so that the final effect is of well-meaning vagueness. Emily Lloyd, a little oddly cast, manages to be quite persuasive, and Bruce Willis, as the shambling uncle, deserves

some sort of award for so ruthlessly eschewing glamour. **TP**
Director Norman Jewison **producers** Jewison, Richard Roth **exec** Charles Mulvehill **script** Frank Pierson, Cynthia Cidre, from novel by Bobbie Ann Mason **camera** Russell Boyd **editors** Antony Gibbs, Lou Lombardo **design** Jackson DeGovia **music** James Horner **cast** Bruce Willis, Emily Lloyd, Joan Allen, Kevin Anderson, Richard Hamilton, Judith Ivey, Peggy Rea, John Terry, Dan Jenkins, Stephen Tobolowsky
Running time: 115 mins
US release: Warner, Sep 15, 1989
UK release: Warner, Jan 12, 1990

AN INNOCENT MAN

Tom Selleck hides his dimples under a bushel in this Serious Drama, where he's framed by drug-dealing cops and set upon by menacing black men in jail. He kills one, becomes a man as a result, and orchestrates a drawn-out revenge. A perfunctory mixture of 'big house' yarn and revenge melodrama, the picture is often implausible in detail and, quite apart from its failure of imaginative nerve in dramatizing the protagonist's metamorphosis, is crucially undermined by the casting of Selleck, an actor whose screen persona is one of cocky self-confidence. The graphic violence and four-letter language only serve to emphasize by default the resemblance elsewhere to the more mechanical species of TV movie. **TP**
Director Peter Yates **producers** Ted Field, Robert W. Cort **exec** Scott Kroopf **script** Larry Brothers **camera** William A. Fraker **editors** Stephen A. Rotter, William S. Scharf **design** Stuart Wurtzel **music** Howard Shore **cast** Tom Selleck, F. Murray Abraham, Laila Robins, David Rasche, Richard Young, Badja Djola, Todd Graff
Running time: 113 mins
US release: BV, Oct 6, 1989
UK release: Warner, Jun 22, 1990

◀▤ INTERNAL AFFAIRS

Hollywood film noir meets Shakespeare's Othello. What can Andy Garcia of the LA internal affairs division (cops investigating cops) do about corrupt fellow policeman and murder suspect Richard Gere? Is Gere, the force's Casanova, getting off with Garcia's own wife? With tumbling shadows and moody electronic music, British director Mike Figgis (Stormy Monday) creates a nervy melodrama of jealousy. In this gutter Othello, a pair of knickers serves for the tell-tale handkerchief and Gere's villain prances balletically around Garcia's bull-at-bay hero. Splendid. **HK**

Director Mike Figgis **producer** Franc Mancuso Jr. **execs** Pierre David, René Malo **script** Henry Bean **camera** John A. Alonzo **editor** Robert Estrin **design** Waldemar Kalinowski **music** Figgis, Anthony Marinelli, Brian Banks **cast** Richard Gere, Andy Garcia, Nancy Travis, Laurie Metcalf, Richard Bradford, William Baldwin, Michael Beach, Katherine Borowitz, Faye Grant, John Kapelos, Xander Berkeley, Annabella Sciorra
Running time: 115 mins
US release: Paramount, Jan 12, 1990
UK release: UIP, May 4, 1990

THE IRON TRIANGLE

This is the first Vietnam War movie to try to see the conflict from both sides, which unfortunately means that the Viet Cong are allowed to be as two-dimensional as the Americans. Liam Whatley, a teenage idealist in black pyjamas, confides to a diary his feelings as he fights against the Americans. His counterpart is a humane Beau Bridges, who becomes his captive at one point, and with whom he reaches an unbelievable truce. The film's charity is not extended to the South Vietnamese, who are represented as atrocity-committing troops who disgust their clean American allies. The film ends ridiculously when Bridges calls down an entire air strike to get one man out of the jungle, and misses. **KN**
Director Eric Weston **producers** Angela P. Schapiro, Tony Scotti **execs** Ben Scotti, Fred Scotti **script** Eric Weston, John Bushelman, Lawrence Hilbrand, based on the diary of an unknown Viet cong soldier **camera** Irv Goodnoff **editor** Roy Watts **design** Errol Kelly **music** Michael Lloyd, John D'Andrea, Nick Strimple **cast** Beau Bridges, Haing S. Ngor, Liem Whatley, Johnny Hallyday, Jim Ishida, Ping Wu, Jack Ong
Running time: 91 mins
UK release: Medusa, Sep 29, 1989

JACKNIFE

Will you watch another drama about Vietnam vets who can't cope, even one as well acted as this? Robert De Niro plays a trout fisher, not a deer hunter this time, who takes himself to the brink of death in order to bring back a buddy, Ed Harris, whose combat memories are killing him. Kathy Baker is the sub-Streepian woman they left behind. The characters are such stock figures by now and the stagebound situation so trite that only performers as magnetic as De Niro and Harris could give it any life at all. David Jones, good as he is with actors, should pick his American scripts more carefully. **BM**
Director *David Jones* **producers** *Robert Schaffel, Carol Baum* **script** *Stephen Metcalfe, from his play* Strange Snow **camera** *Brian West* **editor** *John Bloom* **design** *Edward Pisoni* **music** *Bruce Broughton* **cast** *Robert De Niro, Ed Harris, Kathy Baker, Charles Dutton, Loudon Wainwright III, Tom Isbell, Sloane Shelton, Ivan Brogger*
Running time: 102 mins
US release: Cineplex, Mar 10, 1989
UK release: Vestron, Sep 8, 1989

JESUS OF MONTREAL
(Jésus de Montréal)

Denys Arcand's film is a clever vision of a contemporary Christ – seen through the eyes of an actor hired to revitalize a Mystery play, and whose integration of modern historical research and theological debate into the Gospel leads to a very different Messiah from the one the church expected or will accept. The film offers so much to both theologian and cinema-goer in its clever satire on the commercialization of religion, art and human feeling that it would be a sin to miss it. Arcand makes some serious points without ever seeming heavy-handed, while Lothaire Bluteau, as the actor transformed by his work, gives a performance of quiet magnetic power that illuminates both the man and the message. It's a film that delivers far more than it promises. **TW**
Director/script *Denys Arcand* **producers** *Roger Frappier, Pierre Gendron* **camera** *Guy Dufaux* **editor** *Isabelle Dedieu* **design** *François Séguin* **music** *Yves Laferrière, François Dompierre, Jean-Marie Benoît* **cast** *Lothaire Bluteau, Catherine Wilkening, Johanne-Marie Tremblay, Rémy Girard, Robert Lepage, Gilles Pelletier, Yves Jacques, Denys Arcand*
Running time: 119 mins
US release: Orion Classics, May 25, 1990
UK release: Artificial Eye, Jan 19, 1990

JOE VERSUS THE VOLCANO

You are Tom Hanks and you have six months to live according to Dr Robert Stack, who diagnoses a terminal 'brain cloud'. Would you (a) get a second opinion? (b) stay in your humdrum job in a surgical goods factor apparently designed by Fritz Lang or (c) take off to the South Seas to throw yourself into a volcano. This would be a nice gesture from a dying man to appease the local lava gods, argues philanthropist Lloyd Bridges, who will foot all the bills. Steven Spielberg footed the bill for this rambling, sub-*Candide* fantasy from writer-director John Patrick Shanley (*Moonstruck*). A series of non-sequitur scenes searching for a point, the film is relieved only by a couple of visual coups (a giant moon at sea, a raft made of travelling trunks) and by Meg Ryan bubbling merrily in three different rôles. **HK**
Director/script *John Patrick Shanley* **producer** *Teri Schwartz* **execs** *Steven Spielberg, Kathleen Kennedy, Frank Marshall* **camera** *Stephen Goldblatt* **editor** *Richard Halsey* **design** *Bo Welch* **music** *Georges Delerue* **cast** *Tom Hanks, Meg Ryan, Lloyd Bridges, Robert Stack, Abe Vigoda, Dan Hedaya, Ossie Davis, Barry McGovern, Amanda Plummer, Carol Kane*
Running time: 102 mins
US release: Warner, Mar 9, 1989
UK release: Warner, Jul 6, 1990

JOHNNY HANDSOME

Walter Hill's still razor-sharp action movie skills are again wasted on a screenplay that keeps tripping over its own implausibility. Mickey Rourke is Johnny Handsome, a congenitally malformed New Orleans criminal with a genius for planning meticulous heists. While knocking over a numismatics store, Johnny is double-crossed by a couple of scumbag crooks (Barkin, Henriksen). Johnny gets sent up the river and is stabbed in prison, whereupon an unbelievably philanthropic doctor (Whitaker) offers to remake his face, turning him, after a series of painful operations, into Mickey Rourke without the latex. Then, in quick succession, Johnny is unbelievably let out of prison, almost believably falls in love with clerk Elizabeth McGovern and unbelievably sets in motion an elaborately stupid plan, involving another robbery, for revenge. Rourke is remarkable as the reformed freak, that even if the character doesn't make sense, the performance papers over the cracks; Hill stages the heists and shoot-outs and confrontations with his usual flair; and Barkin and Henriksen make a wonderful pair of human vermin villains. But, while the movie looks nice and the actors do what they can, it still cannot leap-frog its continually ridiculous storyline. **KN**
Director *Walter Hill* **producer** *Charles Roven* **execs** *Mario Kassar, Andrew Vajna* **script** *Ken Friedman, from book* The Three Worlds of Johnny Handsome *by John Godey* **camera** *Matthew F. Leonetti* **editor** *Freeman Davies* **design** *Gene*

Rudolf **music** *Ry Cooder* **cast** *Mickey Rourke, Ellen Barkin, Elizabeth McGovern, Morgan Freeman, Forest Whitaker, Lance Henriksen, Scott Wilson, David Schramm, Yvonne Bryceland, Peter Jason*
Running time: 94 mins
US release: Tri-Star, Sep 29, 1989
UK release: Guild, May 11, 1990

JUDGEMENT IN BERLIN
A dramatized account of how the 1978 hijacking of a Polish airliner by East German escapers led to its being subjected, under West German and US auspices, to a sort of show trial for air piracy. The issues involved are genuinely interesting, and not rendered retrospectively any less so by the coincidence of the film's opening in Britain at the time the Berlin Wall was finally demolished. But the dramatization is ploddingly banal, with judicial processes made a mere excuse for histrionics, and the American judge who refuses to bow to external pressures turned into a ridiculous star turn for Martin Sheen. **TP**
Director *Leo Penn* **producers** *Joshua Sinclair, Ingrid Windisch* **execs** *Martin Sheen, William R. Greenblatt, Jeffrey Auerbach* **script** *Joshua Sinclair, Penn, from book by Herbert J. Stern* **camera** *Gabor Pogany* **editor** *Teddy Darvas* **design** *Jan Schlubach, Peter Alteneder* **music** *Peter Goldfoot* **cast** *Martin Sheen, Sam Wanamaker, Max Gail, Juergen Heinrich, Heinz Hoenig, Carl Lumbly, Max Volkert Martens, Christine Rose, Marie-Louise Sinclair, Joshua Sinclair, Jutta Speidel, Harris Yulin, Sean Penn, Burt Nelson*
Running time: 96 mins
UK release: Hobo, Mar 23, 1990

K-9

First off in the canine-cop buddy movie stakes, this isn't as good as the Tom Hanks outing but offers a considerably less repellent (albeit psychologically disturbed) four-legged friend and fairly good value for money so long as you don't expect great art or a life-changing experience. The laughs are fairly evenly divided between the members of its double act, albeit frequently aimed at the lowest common denominator. Rod Daniels' direction shows a considerable improvement on the flashy and misconceived pyrotechnics of *Like Father, Like Son*, although he never quite manages to hide the perfunctory nature of the plot. Only Mel Harris, as a particularly soppy love interest who seems to take the whole thing seriously, fails to strike the right note. Not one of the year's best but, as production-line product goes, an entertaining diversion. **TW**
Director *Rod Daniel* **producers** *Lawrence Gordon, Charles Gordon* **exec** *Donna Smith* **script** *Steven Siegel, Scott Myers* **camera** *Dean Semler* **editor** *Lois Freeman-Fox* **design** *George Costello* **music** *Miles Goodman* **cast** *James Belushi, Mel Harris, Kevin Tighe, Ed O'Neill, Jerry Lee, James Handy, Cotter Smith*
Running time: 102 mins
US release: Universal, Apr 28, 1989
UK release: UIP, Oct 6, 1989

THE KARATE KID PART III

Venerable martial arts whizz-kid (Macchio) gesticulates his way through another rites-of-passage teen pic, this time betraying the stoic catechisms of his kung fu mentor (Morita) in favour of the brutal tactics employed by a rival – who's made a pile from dumping chemical wastes in Third World countries and is determined to revenge the team vanquished in Part II. Since most of the Oriental profundities were explored in the first two movies, it's only Macchio's stupidity that keeps the plot stumbling through until the hero's final, inevitable victory. **MN**
Director *John G. Avildsen* **producer** *Jerry Weintraub* **exec** *Sheldon Schrager* **script** *Robert Mark Kamen* **camera** *Stephen Yaconelli* **editors** *John Carter, Avildsen* **design** *William F. Matthews* **music** *Bill Conti* **cast** *Ralph Macchio, Noriyuki "Pat" Morita, Robyn Lively, Thomas Ian Griffith, Martin L. Kove, Sean Kanan, Jonathan Avildsen*
Running time: 112 mins
US release: Columbia, Jun 30, 1989
UK release: Col/Tri-Star, Jul 28, 1989

KICKBOXER

When his brash kickboxing champ brother (Alexio) is crippled by a psychotic Thai martial-arts champ (Po), Jean-Claude Van Damme, a sensitive soul who has cautioned his brother against over-confidence, swears that he will avenge his chair-bound relative. He signs up with a little old man in white pyjamas (Chan) and is taught lots of ancient wisdom by having coconuts dropped on his stomach. Finally, he gets back in the ring with the baddie and restores his family honour in blood-dripping colour, making especially destructive use of resin-smeared bandage gloves dipped in broken glass to get more gore into the picture. A laughably stupid film, but certainly an accomplished little piece of action exploitation, and far preferable in its lack of smugness to the *Karate Kid* series upon which it is modelled. **KN**
Directors *Mark DiSalle, David Worth* **producer** *DiSalle* **script** *Glenn Bruce* **camera** *Jon Kranhouse* **editor** *Wayne Wahrman* **design** *Shay Austin* **music** *Paul Hertzog* **cast** *Jean Claude Van Damme, Dennis Alexio, Dennis Chan, Tong Po, Haskell Anderson, Rochelle Ashana, Steve Lee, Richard Foo, Ricky Liu*
Running time: 102 mins
US release: Cannon-Pathé, Sep 8, 1989
UK release: Entertainment, Aug 18, 1989

THE KILL-OFF

Things is bad, real bad, in Jim Thompson country. Bedridden gossip Luane (Gross) scorches the phone lines with her vocal venom. A young couple hang themselves for no good reason. Luane's not-too-bright hubby takes up with the local bar's not-too-young stripper. And two drug-soaked teenagers plan to rob and elope. All in a day's work for novelist Thompson (*The Getaway*), whose tale is filmed with maggoty relish by Maggie Greenwald. She pans her camera along the toxic telephone wires; sears into close-up on seedy Luane; and ranges her barflies in the shadows like fugitives from an Ed Hopper painting. Mean, moody and mesmerizing. **HK**
Director *Maggie Greenwald* **producer** *Lydia Dean Pilcher* **execs** *Alexander W. Kogan Jr., Barry Tucker* **script** *Greenwald, from novel by Jim Thompson* **camera** *Declan Quinn* **editor** *James Y. Kwei* **design** *Pamela Woodbridge* **music** *Evan Lurie* **cast** *Loretta Gross, Andrew Lee Barrett, Jackson Sims, Steve Monroe, Cathy Haase, William Russell, Jorjan Fox*
Running time: 97 mins
UK release: Palace, Feb 9, 1990

KILLING DAD

An odd, if not wholly misbegotten, venture into comic grotesquerie of a sub-Joe Orton sort, *Killing Dad* tells of a repressed suburban mother's boy journeying to out-of-season Southend with the intention of despatching his drunkard of a father, who had vanished years before but is now

threatening to return to the domestic hearth. A strong cast – Elliott and Grant as father and son, Walters as the former's blowsy new companion – isn't given much to work with, and, possibly because the source is a novel rather than a play, the development of the situation lacks the proper (or in this case improper) farcical rigour. **TP**
Director Michael Austin **producer** Iain Smith **exec** Gus MacDonald **script** Austin, from novel Berg by Ann Quinn **camera** Gabriel Beristain **editors** Edward Marnier, Derek Trigg **design** Adrienne Atkinson **music** Chaz Jankel, David Storrs, Juan Martin **cast** Denholm Elliott, Julie Walters, Richard E. Grant, Anna Massey, Laura Del Sol, Ann Way, Tom Radcliffe, Jonathan Phillips, Kevin Williams
Running time: 93 mins
UK release: Palace, Sep 1, 1989

KING OF THE WIND

An exercise in juvenile picaresque which may have worked in the source novel but comes out as excessively episodic in this dramatization. Relating the adventures of an Arab stallion and his mute groom in eighteenth-century Arabia, France and England, leading to a somehow anti-climactic finale at Newmarket races, the picture is peopled by familiar British mummers, who peer out from brocades and rustic togs and speak in idioms which range from bland anachronism ('doing the accounts', 'more than, my job's worth') to utterances like 'Bring me a pot of ale, Master Williams'. The production's rather under-funded look cannot be said to lend much help.**TP**
Director Peter Duffell **producers** Michael Guest, Paul Sarony, Peter S. Davis, William Panzer **execs** Patrick Dromgoole, Johnny Goodman, Guy Collins **script** Phil Frey, from novel by Marguerite Henry **camera** Brian Morgan **editor** Lyndon Matthews **design** Ken Sharp **sfx** Mirage Effects **music** John Scott **cast** Frank Finlay, Jenny Agutter, Nigel Hawthorne, Navin Chowdhry, Ralph Bates, Neil Dickson, Barry Foster, Jill Gascoine, Joan Hickson, Anthony Quayle, Ian Richardson, Norman Rodway, Peter Vaughan, Richard Harris, Glenda Jackson, Melvyn Hayes
Running time: 102 mins
UK release: Enterprise, May 25, 1990

THE KISS

In the age of AIDS, something fatally slimy could easily inhabit anyone's body – even your beautiful aunt's. In this horror fantasy, Joanna Pacula carries a snake-like monster within her that craves transmission to a family member. But it can only pass into another's body via a big wet kiss. Niece Meredith Salenger is the target of this sloppy assault, but first the infected Pacula must dispose of her sister and her niece's boyfriend.

The monster is wisely kept behind closed lips most of the movie; for when it emerges at the end, it provokes laughter, not terror. **BM**
Director Pen Densham **producers** Densham, John Watson **exec** Richard B. Lewis **script** Stephen Volk, Tom Ropelewski **camera** François Protat **editor** Stan Cole **design** Roy Forge Smith **music** J. Peter Robinson **cast** Nicholas Kilbertus, Joanna Pacula, Meredith Salenger, Mimi Kuzyk
Running time: 101 mins
US release: Tri-Star, Oct 14, 1988
UK release: Col/Tri-Star, Jul 21, 1989

👍 THE KRAYS

Given its gossip column casting – Gary and Martin Kemp from the band Spandau Ballet as Ron and Reggie Kray – and return to the currently fashionable British movie turf of the seamy side of the 1950s and 1960s, one hardly expects The Krays to turn into something as twisted, bizarre and interesting as this – with a genuinely hypnotic twinned performance from the leads, and some very un-British splatter effects. The film plays off the expected screen image of the criminals by invoking all the family associations of the Godfather movies and then depicting a different, matriarchal underworld. The Krays hold their business meetings in mum's cosy terraced house in Bethnal Green and, for all her tea-making and manners-minding, she is as responsible for the brief, horrifying explosions of violence as her sons. While the film perhaps inevitably sails into a plot doldrums with Reggie's drunken nervous breakdown and can only haul itself out with a double murder, it's otherwise a confident and gripping glide through the crimes of the recent past. **KN**
Director Peter Medak **producers** Dominic Anciano, Ray Burdis **execs** Jim Beach, Michele Kimche **script** Philip Ridley **camera** Alex Thomson **editor** Martin Walsh **design** Michael Pickwoad **music** Michael Kamen **cast** Billie Whitelaw, Tom Bell, Gary Kemp, Martin Kemp, Susan Fleetwood, Charlotte Cornwell, Kate Hardie, Avis Bunnage, Gary Love, Steven Berkoff, Jimmy Jewel, Barbara Ferris, Victor Spinetti, John McEnery, Philip Bloomfield, Norman Rossington, Patti Love, Michael Balfour, Roger Monk, Jimmy Flint, Andrew Kitchen, Michael Carr
Running time: 119 mins
UK release: Rank, Apr 27, 1990

K

🔻 LADDER OF SWORDS

There's weird things afoot up on t'moor. Travelling circus man Martin Shaw has this dancing bear that's a bit poorly, plus he's married to drunken harpy Eleanor David. This Juliet Stevenson girl, though, from the local town, she's a bit of all right, isn't she? Ah well, if wishes were fishes. Crash, bang. What was that? Good God, the drunken old cow's dead. Must've fallen over and hit her head on the script. Better bury her quick and pretend it's the bear that copped it. Juliet? Let's elope. Oo-er, here's copper Bob Peck. Will he dig up and discover? He's digging. What's that body under there. It's – it's – why, it's the corpse of the British film industry. Is that thing still around? Quick, dig it back in and pretend it's a dead bear. HK

Director *Norman Hull* **producer** *Jennifer Howarth* **script** *Neil Clark* **camera** *Thaddeus O'Sullivan* **editor** *Scott Thomas* **design** *Caroline Hanania* **music** *Stanley Myers* **cast** *Martin Shaw, Eleanor David, Juliet Stevenson, Bob Peck, Simon Molloy, Pearce Quigley, Anthony Benson*
Running time: 98 mins
UK release: Hobo, Jan 12, 1990

LAMBADA

From the makers of *Breakin'* (and *Breakin' 2: Electric Boogaloo*) comes the first movie to cash-in on the lamest dance craze since Dick Clark looked his age. This one has a few buttock-baring numbers, but it's really 'To Sir With Lust', featuring a hunky teacher who inspires Beverly Hills brats and East LA street kids to make something of their lives. Enormously stupid, it still holds appeal for those fascinated with youth exploitation films. CB

Director *Joel Silberg* **producer** *Peter Shepherd* **exec** *Dick Griffey* **script** *Silberg, Sheldon Renan* **camera** *Roberto D'Ettore Piazzoli* **editor** *Marcus Manton* **design** *Bill Cornford* **music** *Greg De Belles* **cast** *J. Eddie Peck, Melora Hardin, Shabba-Doo, Ricky Paull Goldin, Basil Hoffman, Dennis Burkley, Keene Curtis*
Running time: 98 mins
US release: Warner, Mar 16, 1990
UK release: Pathé, Apr 13, 1990

THE LAND BEFORE TIME

Before God created the wrist-watch, dinosaurs roamed the earth. And lo! They had no sense of time nor respect for normal human attention spans. And it happened that one dinosaur family, as drawn by animator Don Bluth, was cute and gambolling and pinkish-grey and went in search of the Great Valley (large and fertile), accompanied by much lolloping music. Onward, onward they trekked, through earthquake, bereavement (momma dinosaur snuffs it) and the antics of a funny pterodactyl. Finally they reach their goal: a vast, lush, empty space, untrod by other beings. (In this case it might be the movie auditorium.) A turgid brush-and-paint epic from the Spielberg studios, unleavened by wit or visual panache and sentenced to as certain an extinction as its subjects. HK

Director/design *Don Bluth* **producers** *Bluth, Gary Goldman, John Pomeroy* **execs** *Steven Spielberg, George Lucas* **script** *Stu Krieger* **camera** *Jim Mann, Tony Geiss* **editors** *Dan Molina, John K. Carr* **animators** *John Pomeroy, Linda Miller, Ralph Zondag, Dan Kuenster, Lorna Pomeroy, Dick Zondag* **music** *James Horner* **voices** *Pat Hingle, Gabriel Damon, Helen Shaver, Candice Houston, Judith Barsi, Will Ryan, Burke Barnes*
Running time: 69 mins
US release: Universal, Nov 18, 1988
UK release: UIP, Aug 4, 1989

◀️ LAST EXIT TO BROOKLYN (Letzte Ausfahrt Brooklyn)

Given his previous, rather pointlessly depressing, work on *Christiane F*, Ulrich Edel has surprisingly managed to catch exactly the horrified and yet tender tone of Hubert Selby's book, presenting the 1950s as a Hell as tangible as any of Dickens' London slums. Isolated incidents could almost have come from an early John Waters film, but the almost comic sleaze jostles with the genuinely horrific. Rather than attempt to duplicate the semi-beat experimental style of the prose, screenwriter Desmond Nakano has dug out the dialogue from the stream-of-consciousness rants of the book, and Edel has been lucky in his choice of performers. While Burt Young merely continues to incarnate the ultimate in blue-collar comic scumminess, Stephen Lang makes something of the obnoxious, self-destructive Harry Black, while Jennifer Jason Leigh adds to her run of 'victim' rôles as the pathetic Tralala, managing convincingly the transition from street-corner vamp to used-up drudge. KN

Director *Ulrich Edel* **producer** *Bernd Eichinger* **script** *Desmond Nakano, from novel by Hubert Selby Jr.* **camera** *Stefan Czapsky* **editor** *Peter Przygodda* **design** *David Chapman* **music** *Mark Knopfler* **cast** *Stephen Lang, Jennifer Jason Leigh, Burt Young, Peter Dobson, Jerry Orbach, Alexis Arquette, Steve Baldwin, Cameron Johann*
Running time: 98 mins
US release: Cinecom Apr 27, 1990
UK release: Guild, Jan 5, 1990

THE LAST OF THE FINEST

In a great year for cop films (*Blue Steel, Internal Affairs, Sea of Love*) – it's a pity that this enjoyable effort is so muddled and ordinary. The notion of renegade cops uncovering government

plans to trade drugs for arms is not particularly new and, despite the pace and tension John Mackenzie brings to the direction, the film's over-reliance on generic clichés – the cops all have limited vocabularies and the female characters are simply appendages to accentuate their masculinity – and have-it-all-ways morality render it only an average time-waster. **TW**
Director John Mackenzie **producer** John A. Davis **exec** Jere Cunningham **script** Cunningham, Thomas Lee Wright, George Armitage **camera** Juan Ruiz-Anchia **editor** Graham Walker **design** Laurence G. Paull **music** Jack Nitzsche **cast** Brian Dennehy, Joe Pantoliano, Jeff Fahey, Bill Paxton, Deborra-Lee Furness, Guy Boyd, Henry Darrow, Lisa Jane Persky, Michael C. Gwynne, Henry Stolow, John Finnegan, J. Kenneth Campbell, Patricia Clipper, Michelle Little, Xander Berkeley, Pam Gidley
Running time: 106 mins
US release: Orion, Mar 9, 1990

LEATHERFACE: TEXAS CHAINSAW MASSACRE III

New Line's attempt to turn The Texas Chainsaw Massacre into another successful series franchise falls down because the result has a listless sequel feel, almost as if it were a collection of reels pulled at random out of the middle of a movie. Another heroine (Hodge) wanders into the territory of the cannibal clan from the first film, and falls foul of a group of degenerates led by cowboy-ish Viggo Mortensen. Leatherface (Mihailoff), still suffering from the leg-wound inflicted in the last scene of the first film, limps with a leg-brace, which slows him down and prevents him being the mountainous menace he used to be, and the few attempts at characterizing him certainly don't make him into a cult figure to equal Freddy Krueger. Splatter-punk novelist David Schow's screenplay has a few memorably brutal lines, but director Jeff Burr, responsible also for Stepfather 2, neither matches the overdrive pacing of Hooper's original nor brings any individual personality to the project. **KN**
Director Jeff Burr **producer** Robert Engelman **script** David J. Schow **camera** James L. Carter **editor** Brent A. Schoenfeld **design** Mick Strawn **music** Jim Manzie **cast** Kate Hodge, Viggo Mortensen, William Butler, Ken Foree, Joe Unger, Tom Everett, Toni Hudson, Miriam Byrd-Nethery, R. A. Mihailoff
Running time: 81 mins
US release: New Line, Jan 12, 1990

THE LEGEND OF THE HOLY DRINKER (La leggenda del santo bevitore)

Whereas Olmi's previous films have seemed innately Italian, this one – set in a misty Paris of uncertain period and spoken largely in English with occasional music by Stravinsky – is in a sense a stateless work. Yet this very statelessness contributes to the overall effect of events occurring in a dream. The film is adapted closely (perhaps too closely for dramatic comfort) from Joseph Roth's novella about the last two weeks in the life of an alcoholic drifter, subsequent to his meeting with an enigmatic benefactor. The tone, though, is subtly changed: Roth's ironic denial of the apparent biblical intimations is suppressed, so that the protagonist's ultimate oblivion – he expires in a church – seems to become the gaining of a state of grace. Though slow, and occasionally stilted in verbal idiom, the film is graced by evocative use of settings and locations, as well as by the impressive performance of Rutger Hauer. **TP**
Director/editor Ermanno Olmi **producers** Roberto Cicutto, Vincenzo De Leo **exec** Marcello Siena **script** Tullio Kezich, Olmi, from novel by Joseph Roth **camera** Dante Spinotti **design** Gianni Quaranta **cast** Rutger Hauer, Anthony Quayle, Sandrine Dumas, Dominique Pinon, Sophie Segalen, Jean Maurice Chanet, Cecile Paoli
Running time: 128 mins
UK release: Artificial Eye, Sep 1, 1989

LENINGRAD COWBOYS GO AMERICA

A live-action cartoon in which a horrendously untalented Russian pop group tries to makes its name in the States. Predictably they don't have much success, although at the movie's end they are poised to become big names in Mexico. The humour reflects a sort of juvenile surrealism, while the consciously artless style underlines the prevailing resemblance to a home movie, complete with a cameo appearance in the guise of a used car dealer by Jim Jarmusch, as well as persona propra incidental characters like the bartenders identified in the credits as 'Mr and Mrs Morris'. Alternately appealing and exasperating, Cowboys unmistakably bears its maker's signature as it contrives to imbue inconsequence with a kind of pugnacity. **TP**
Director/script Aki Kaurismäki **producers** Kaurismäki, Klas Olofsson, Katinka Farago **camera** Timo Salminen **editor** Raija Talvio **design** Heikki Ukkonen, Kari Laine **music** Mauri Sumén **cast** Matti Pellonpää, Nicky Tesco, Kari Väänänen, Jim Jarmusch, Sakke Järvenpää, Heikki Keskinen, Pimme Korhonen, Sakari Kuosmanen
Running time: 79 mins
UK release: Artificial Eye, Feb 16, 1990

LENNY LIVE AND UNLEASHED

In an attempt to stave off the sameyness of all comedian-in-concert movies, this opens with a cameo by Robbie Coltrane as an obnoxious and not-particularly-amusing taxi driver and then has Lenny Henry give himself advice in brilliantly executed impersonations of Steve Martin, Richard Pryor and Eddie Murphy. Then comes the main business of the evening, Henry doing his stand-up act at the Hackney Empire, and trotting out his TV-advertised characters – Brixton DJ Delbert Wilkins, political reggae activist Fred Dread, legendary blues singer Low-Down-Finger-Lickin'-Hound-Dog Smith, ruminative and ancient Jamaican immigrant Deakus and macho showbiz moron Theophilus P. Wildebeeste. Henry survives the embalmed-on-film process rather better than Pryor or Murphy have done, probably because the canny mix of regular routines, spoof songs and familiar characters is more appealing than an hour and a half of straight star stand-up. KN
Director *Andy Harries* **producers** *Harries, Martyn Auty* **execs** *Stephen Woolley, Nik Powell* **script** *Lenny Henry, Kim Fuller* **camera** *Peter Sinclair* **editor** *Gerry Hambling* **design** *Christopher Hobbs* **music** *Steve Nieve, Jo Dworniak, Duncan Bridgeman, Dennis Bovell, Kim Fuller* **cast** *Lenny Henry, Robbie Coltrane, Jeff Beck*
Running time: 97 mins
UK release: Palace, Jul 27, 1989

LET'S GET LOST

Jazzman Chet Baker died in 1988, after a lifetime of cool horn-playing, brawling, tomcatting around and immense drug consumption. Fashion snapper-turned-documentarist Bruce Weber had already used Baker on the soundtrack of his *Broken Noses* before deciding to do a whole film about him, and this is the result; a mixture of interview, archive, performance and home-movie footage that shows how you can turn from James Dean lookalike into the splitting image of Jack Palance with only 30 years of self-abuse. A beautifully-shot, black-and-white movie, this is an effective portrait of someone who would probably be unbearable if he weren't so talented, and the cracked voice of Baker becomes ultimately as hypnotic as his music while he either does peculiar things to jazz standards in performance or reminisces about his life and hard times. KN
Director/producer *Bruce Weber* **exec** *Nan Bush* **script** *Susan Stribling* **camera** *Jeff Preiss* **editor** *Angelo Corrao* **design** *Sam Shahid, Donald Sterzin, Rise Daniels*
Running time: 120 mins
UK release: Mainline, Feb 2, 1990

LETHAL WEAPON 2

If *Lethal Weapon* was a prime example of the machine-made action man movie of the 1980s, then this buddy cop comedy-actioner is an absolute model of sequel-craft. Without repeating too much of the plot of the original, it brings back the main characters with their tics intact, and dumps them in a plot that gets them out of their familiar mean streets and into a super-Bondian world of master villains, mass destruction and over-the-top stunts. With Joss Ackland and Derrick O'Connor as blonde-rinsed neo-Nazis proving how convenient it is for Hollywood to have a racial group unable to complain when they are stereotyped as grotesque villains, *Lethal Weapon 2* trots out a succession of Aryan thugs in designer suits who can be mown down without conscience by the heroes. Donner pulls out all the stops in the set-pieces, but remembers to give his personable stars enough quiet moments to exchange jokes or half-choked admissions of manly love. And womanly love is taken care of by Patsy Kensit, who takes off her clothes and gets killed, without getting in the way of the boys too much. KN
Director *Richard Donner* **producers** *Donner, Joel Silver* **script** *Jeffrey Boam* **camera** *Stephen Goldblatt* **editor** *Stuart Baird* **design** *J. Michael Riva* **music** *Michael Kamen, Eric Clapton, David Sanborn* **cast** *Mel Gibson, Danny Glover, Joe Pesci, Joss Ackland, Derrick O'Connor, Patsy Kensit, Darlene Love*
Running time: 113 mins
US release: Warner, Jul 7, 1989
UK release: Warner, Sep 15, 1989

LET IT RIDE

Remember the episode of *Bilko* when Ernie just couldn't lose, even on the wildest long shots? Well, now you can see it three times as long, ten times more expensive and not even half as funny. Richard Dreyfuss vows to give up his compulsive gambling only to be faced with the ultimate winning streak, which of course turns him into a big head who stands to lose the love of his life before he is redeemed by misfortune. With a better script, better direction and a straight face, this might have stood a chance but, as it is, only Robbie Coltrane shines, as a philosophical bookie. There are a few jokes and it's not particularly offensive. But it's not particularly good either. TW
Director *Joe Pytka* **producer** *David Giler* **script** *'Ernest Morton' (Nancy Dowd), from novel Good Vibes by Jay Cronley* **camera** *Curtis J. Wehr* **editors** *Dede Allen, Jim Miller* **design** *Wolf Kroeger* **music** *Giorgio Moroder* **cast** *Richard Dreyfuss, David Johansen, Teri Garr, Jennifer Tilly, Allen Garfield, Ed Walsh, Michelle Phillips, Mary Woronov, Robbie Coltrane*
Running time: 86 mins
US release: Paramount, Aug 18, 1989

LEVIATHAN

It's just too soon to remake *Alien* again. George Cosmatos's adventure is perfectly serviceable but boringly predictable nevertheless. Peter Weller is the hesitant commander of a group of undersea miners who come upon the wreckage of a Soviet ship and unwisely lift from it some genetically super-charged vodka. Daniel Stern is the first to succumb to the ichtheo-hominoid strain, which proceeds to absorb one after another of the crew members. Hector Elizondo plays the John Hurt scene, turning green when the thing bursts out of his chest. As in *Alien*, the ultimate villain is private enterprise, in the person of Meg Foster, who is righteously slugged by Weller when he gets topside. **BM**
Director *George Pan Cosmatos* **producers** *Luigi De Laurentiis, Aurelio De Laurentiis* **execs** *Lawrence Gordon, Charles Gordon* **script** *David Peoples, Jeb Stuart* **camera** *Alex Thomson* **editors** *Roberto Silvi, John F. Burnett* **design** *Ron Cobb* **music** *Jerry Goldsmith* **cast** *Peter Weller, Richard Crenna, Amanda Pays, Daniel Stern, Ernie Hudson, Michael Carmine, Lisa Eilbacher, Hector Elizondo, Meg Foster*
Running time: 98 mins
US release: MGM, Mar 17, 1989
UK release: Fox, May 11, 1990

LICENCE TO KILL

The somewhat more realistic, or anyway less unrealistic, approach of *The Living Daylights* is continued here, with Bond tracking down a sadistic Latin drugs baron. Although the latter, as played by Robert Davi, is a genuinely nasty piece of work rather than one of the stagey megalomaniacs of some earlier Bonds, it is he who tends to be provided with the quips which used to issue from OO7's lips – e.g., of a victim fed to sharks, 'He disagreed with something that ate him'. Elsewhere, glimmerings of feminism penetrate the traditionally masculine domain: when Bond passes off a woman accomplice as his 'executive secretary', she grumpily ripostes, 'You could have pretended that you were mine.' Fantastication still reassuringly clings, however, to the action set pieces; and not for the first time in the series, the proceedings seem to be stretched out much longer than necessary. **TP**
Director *John Glen* **producers** *Albert R. Broccoli, Michael G. Wilson* **script** *Wilson, Richard Maibaum* **camera** *Alec Mills* **editor** *John Grover* **design** *Peter Lamont* **music** *Michael Kamen* **cast** *Timothy Dalton, Carey Lowell, Robert Davi, Talisa Soto, Anthony Zerbe, Frank McRae, Everett McGill, Wayne Newton, Benicio Del Toro, Desmond Llewelyn, David Hedison*
Running time: 133 mins
US release: UA, Jul 14, 1989
UK release: UIP, Jun 14, 1989

♠ LIFE AND NOTHING BUT (La Vie et rien d'autre)

All the best anti-war movies take place after the battle has ended, and this ranks alongside *J'accuse, La Grande Illusion* and *Paths of Glory* as one of the very best of them all, as well as providing all the proof you'll ever need that Philippe Noiret is the greatest actor in continental cinema. For his hundredth film he turns in a moving, yet never lachrymose, performance as a French officer assigned the task of identifying what's left of the dead and dying from France's post-World War 1 battlefields, as well as choosing a corpse for ceremonial interment as the official 'unknown soldier'. His attempt to avoid emotional involvement with two women from different social strata, as they search for lost loves amid the lost lives, facilitates his gradual return to a world of feeling. Meanwhile, the women are drawn into a shared destiny that shatters the remnants of their pre-war world and serves as a simple, but effective, metaphor for the nation's healing. Photographed with stunning images of stark simplicity and filled with touchingly understated irony and an enormous sense of compassion, Life and *Nothing But* is simply magnificent. **TW**
Director *Bertrand Tavernier* **execs** *Frédéric Bourboulon, Albert Prévost* **producer** *René Cleitman* **script** *Jean Cosmos, Tavernier* **camera** *Bruno de Keyzer* **editor** *Armand Psenny* **design** *Guy-Claude François* **music** *Oswald d'Andrea* **cast** *Philippe Noiret, Sabine Azéma, Pascale Vignal, Maurice Barrier, François Perrot, Jean-Pol Dubois, Daniel Russo, Michael Duchaussoy*
Running time: 134 mins
UK release: Artificial Eye, Oct 27, 1989

LIFE IS A LONG QUIET RIVER (La Vie est une longue fleuve tranquille)

This would-be Buñuelian comic tale of two families comes from first-time French director Etienne Chatiliez. But the spirit of San Luis never blesses this surrealist shaggy-dog story in which two children from different families swap homes and income brackets. (Pretext: they were mixed up at birth.) Working-class Momo goes to live with the rich Le Quesnoys. And dainty Bernadette must slum it with the Groseilles, whose mum seems to be in training for a Roseanne Barr lookalike (and act-alike) contest. The cross-class ironies are trowelled on, the acting is in the wink-and-nod style and the movie runs out of plot after an hour. Chatiliez' previous experience in pop promos has prepared him ill for the disciplines of feature-making. **HK**
Director *Etienne Chatiliez* **producer** *Charles Gassot* **exec** *Florence Quentin* **script** *Quentin, Chatiliez* **camera** *Pascal Lebègue* **editor** *Chantal Delattre*

design *Geoffroy Larcher* music *Gérard Kawczynski*
cast *Benoît Magimel, Valerie Lalande, Tara Romer,
Jérôme Floc'h, Sylvie Cubertafon, Emmanuel
Cendrier, Guillaume Hacquebart, Jean-Brice Van
Keer, Praline Le Moult, Axel Vicart*
Running time: 91 mins
UK release: Electric, Oct 27, 1989

▼ LIMIT UP

In this ill-considered fusion of *Working Girl,
Dealers* and *Dr Faustus*, Nancy Allen is a lowly
stock-market runner who longs to be the first
woman to scale the heights of success and live
the life of a soya-bean trader. She is approached
by a dreadlocked agent of the Devil and given the
chance to get in the pit and shout numbers with
the men. This tiresomely laugh-free picture is
based on the notion that soya-bean trading is as
cinematic an occupation as flying a fighter-plane
or being a cowboy. It turns out to be a moralistic
and unbelievable trifle as well, when the villainess
is revealed as an angel manipulating the stock
market in order to solve the world hunger
problem. **KN**
Director *Richard Martini* **producer** *Jonathan D.
Krane* **script** *Martini, Luana Anders* **camera** *Peter
Lyons Collister* **editor** *Sonny Baskin* **design** *R.
Clifford Searcy* **music** *John Tesh* **cast** *Nancy Allen,
Dean Stockwell, Brad Hall, Danitra Vance, Ray
Charles, Rance Howard, Sandra Bogan, William J.
Woff, Ava Fabian, Robbie Martini*
Running time: 88 mins
UK release: Medusa, Jun 22, 1990

LISA

This inter-penetrates (and that's the only word)
two Hollywood genres, the psycho-killer suspense
film and the teen-girl sitcom. For most of the film
Gary Sherman keeps up the interest in the
schlocky story of a girl stalking an adult hunk
who happens to be a serial killer, generating
moments of true suspense, but the climax spills
over into self-parody. Cheryl Ladd, who had
turned in a credible performance as Lisa's mom
up to that point, suddenly reveals herself to be
Cheryl Ladd and, with the rest of the cast, cranks
up the silliness to an unbearable level. **CB**
Director *Gary Sherman* **producers** *Frank Yablans*
script *Sherman, Karen Clark* **camera** *Alex
Nepomniaschy* **editor** *Ross Albert* **design** *Patricia
VanRyker* **music** *Joe Renzetti* **cast** *Cheryl Ladd, D.
W. Moffett, Staci Keanan, Tanya Fenmore, Jeffrey
Tambor, Edan Gross, Julie Cobb*
Running time: 93 mins
US release: MGM/UA, Apr 20, 1990

THE LITTLE MERMAID

Everything you wanted to know about sub-
aquatic life forms but were afraid to ask. Yes,
animated nymphets do dash about the pearly
depths in brightly-coloured bikinis. Yes, they fall
in love with princes passing overhead. And yes,
King Neptune is a merry old sole with a singing
Caribbean crab for chief adviser. (His calypso
number, 'Under the Sea', steals the show and
won Best Song Oscar.) When all other forms of
power fail to save the Disney animated feature,
here comes wave energy to do so. Full of wit and
colour and mercifully schmaltz-free: the best
paint-and-brush show the studio has given us
since *The Jungle Book*. **HK**
Directors *John Musker, Ron Clements* **producers**
Howard Ashman, Musker **script** *Musker, Clements,
from fairy tale by Hans Christian Andersen* **editor**
John Carnochan **design** *Michael A. Peraza Jr.,
Donald A. Towns* **music** *Alan Menken* **voices** *Jodi
Benson, Pat Carroll, Samuel Wright, Kenneth
Mars, Buddy Hackett, Jason Marin, Christopher
Daniel Barnes, René Auberjonois, Ben Wright*
Running time: 82 mins
US release: BV, Nov 15, 1989

▼ LITTLE MONSTERS

Fred Savage finds a monster and a gateway to
another world under his bed in this botched
Beetlejuice rip-off. Unfortunately the monster is
played by the devastatingly unfunny Howie
Mandel and the other world is filled with
unimaginative lumps of prosthetics (sorry,
creatures) and seems to have been designed by a
Taiwanese toymaker heavily under the influence
of Dr Seuss. There is one good effects joke when
Mandel loses his temper, but it's not worth
sitting through the whole film for. **TW**
Director *Richard Alan Greenberg* **producers**
Jeffrey Mueller, Andrew Licht, John A. Davis **execs**
Mitchell Cannold, Dori B. Wasserman **script** *Terry
Rossio, Ted Elliott* **camera** *Dick Bush* **editor**
Patrick McMahon **design** *Paul Peters* **music** *David
Newman* **cast** *Fred Savage, Howie Mandel, Daniel
Stern, Margaret Whitton, Rick Ducommun, Frank
Whaley, Ben Savage, William Murray Weiss, Deven
Ratray, Amber Barretto*
Running time: 100 mins
US release: UA, Aug 25, 1989

THE LITTLE THIEF
(La Petite Voleuse)

Some 30 years after *Les Quatres cent coups* comes
this tale of a sultry teenage femme kleptomaniac,
scripted from an outline by Truffaut. What might
once have been fresh and challenging here seems
calculated and contrived. Not that Charlotte
Gainsbourg misses a beat in a careful
performance as the parentless child who attempts

to compensate for a lack of love with fantasy (at the cinema, inevitably), and seeks entry into the adult work through petty thieving and a calculated loss of virginity. It's just that the film's makers never give the impression of trying to explore her predicament or say anything about its source. **JP**
Director *Claude Miller* **exec** *Jean-Rose Richer* **script** *Miller, Luc Beraud, Annie Miller from story by François Truffaut, Claude De Givray* **camera** *Dominique Chapuis* **editor** *Albert Jurgenson* **design** *Jean-Pierre Kohut-Svelko* **music** *Alain Jomy* **cast** *Charlotte Gainsbourg, Didier Bezace, Simon De La Brosse, Raoul Billerey, Chantal Banlier, Nathalie Cardonne, Clotilde De Bayser*
Running time: 110 mins
US release: Miramax, Aug 25, 1989
UK release: Pathé, Jun 23, 1989

LOCK-UP

Sylvester Stallone, a low-risk prisoner with only six months left to serve, is planning for his future outside. However, one night he is transferred to a maximum security hell-hole run by Warden Donald Sutherland, a sadistic megalomaniac with a grudge against him. Given the premise of 'Sylvester Stallone in jail', *Lock Up* is precisely the film as expected, with the regulation elements from previous prison movies thrown into a plot structured around Stallone's usual hymn to the indomitability of the blue-collar spirit. Unlike most action movie stars, Stallone has yet to cast himself as a professional criminal hero, and too much of the running time is taken up with elaborations on his essential decency (looking after the vulnerable prisoners) and modest ambitions (he wants to open a garage when he gets out). **KN**
Director *John Flynn* **producers** *Lawrence Gordon, Charles Gordon* **exec** *Michael S. Glick* **script** *Richard Smith, Jeb Stuart, Henry Rosenbaum* **camera** *Donald E. Thorin* **editors** *Michael N. Knue, Donald Brochu* **design** *Bill Kenney* **music** *Bill Conti* **cast** *Sylvester Stallone, Donald Sutherland, John Amos, Sonny Landham, Tom Sizemore, Frank McRae, Darlanne Fluegel, William Allen Young, Larry Romano, Jordan Lund, John Lilla, Dean Duval*
Running time: 109 mins
US release: Tri-Star, Aug 4, 1989
UK release: Guild, Feb 2, 1990

LOOK WHO'S TALKING
TURKEY • TURKEY • TURKEY

Director/script *Amy Heckerling* **producer** *Jonathan D. Krane* **camera** *Thomas Del Ruth* **editor** *Debra Chiate* **design** *Reuben Freed, Graeme Murray* **music** *David Kitay* **cast** *John Travolta, Kirstie Alley, Olympia Dukakis, George Segal, Abe*

Vigoda, Bruce Willis (voice), Twink Caplan, Joy Boushel, Don S. Davis, Louis Heckerling, Brenda Crichlow, (Jason Schaller, Jaryd Waterhouse, Jacob Haines, Christopher Aydon)
Running time: 96 mins
US release: Tri-Star, Oct 13, 1989
UK release: Col/Tri-Star, Apr 6, 1990

🍷 LOOSE CANNONS

Loose Cannons is another mismatched cops movie, with Gene Hackman as the cagey veteran partnered with the nervous Dan Aykroyd. Aykroyd responds to stress by manifesting other personalities, most of whom are familiar from TV and movies. The plot, which involves an ageing Nazi and the Israeli secret service, has holes big enough to drive Arnold Schwarzenegger through, and Hackman, the most likeable of American actors, is the only relief from the tedium. **JH**
Director *Bob Clark* **producers** *Aaron Spelling, Alan Greisman* **exec** *René Dupont* **script** *Richard Matheson, Clark* **camera** *Reginald H. Morris* **editor** *Stan Cole* **design** *Harry Pottle* **music** *Paul Zaza* **cast** *Gene Hackman, Dan Aykroyd, Dom DeLuise, Ronny Cox, Nancy Travis, Robert Prosky, Paul Koslo, Dick O'Neill*
Running time: 93 mins
US release: Tri-Star, Feb 9, 1990

LORD OF THE FLIES

William Golding's storm-tossed schoolboys fetch up on the beach again. This time, though, the only English accent is behind the camera: that of director Harry Hook (*The Kitchen Toto*). With the cast transformed into US military school cadets, the switch from civilization to savagery loses all its bite. While English milksops were believably at sea in Golding's savage Eden, these youngsters look as if they could handle any amount of pig-sticking or stick-rubbing. Damply directed, the tale itself never catches fire: a shock-value fable robbed of its shocks. **HK**
Director *Harry Hook* **producer** *Ross Milloy* **execs** *Lewis Allen, Peter Newman* **script** *Sara Schiff, from novel by William Golding* **camera** *Martin Fuhrer* **editor** *Tom Priestley* **design** *Jamie Leonard* **music** *Philippe Sarde* **cast** *Balthazar Getty, Chris Furrh, Danuel Pipoly, Badgett Dale, Edward Taft, Andrew Taft, Bob Peck, Bill Schoppert, Michael Greene*
Running time: 90 mins
US release: Columbia, Mar 16, 1990
UK release: Palace, Jul 6, 1990

LOVE AT LARGE

Like most of Alan Rudolph's woozy romances, *Love at Large* is an inconsequential anecdote about a bunch of characters each utterly disconnected from everything except his or her

own private reality. Tom Berenger plays a dumb
hard-boiled dick hired by a half-mad vamp
(Archer) to follow her philandering ex-lover. He
spends most of the movie tailing the wrong guy
and trying to shrug off the persistent would-be
gumshoe (Perkins) who's tailing him. After
watching the wrong man's wife (Capshaw) fooling
with a farmhand (O'Connor), these hapless
investigators predictably start striking sparks off
one another. The result is something sweet and
funny – but it's the kind of movie that requires a
patience thoroughly lacking in the modern
American audience. **GF**
Director/script *Alan Rudolph* **producer** *David
Blocker* **camera** *Elliot Davis* **editor** *Lisa Churgin*
design *Steven Legler* **music** *Mark Isham* **cast** *Tom
Berenger, Elizabeth Perkins, Anne Archer, Ted
Levine, Annette O'Toole, Kate Capshaw, Ann
Magnuson, Barry Miller, Kevin J. O'Connor, Neil
Young*
Running time: 97 mins
US release: Orion, Mar 9, 1990
UK release: Rank, Nov 2, 1990

LOVERBOY

Joan Micklin Silver continues her move into the
mainstream with this polished and sporadically
very funny comedy in which a pizza delivery boy
(Dempsey) finds that his 'extra anchovies' rapidly
become the hottest item on the menu with the
local ladies. The words 'male prostitution' are
never mentioned (all they want is a little
attention), and there's something a bit dodgy
about the idea he's only servicing the locals so as
to save enough money to get back to college and
his girlfriend. But despite a contrived ending, the
farce is for the most part adroitly handled, and
Robert Ginty is outstanding in a generally good
cast as Dempsey's muddled father. **TW**
Director *Joan Micklin Silver* **producers** *Gary
Foster, Willie Hunt* **execs** *Leslie Dixon, Tom
Ropelewski* **script** *Robin Schiff, Ropelewski, Dixon*
camera *John Hora* **editor** *Rick Shaine* **design** *Dan
Leigh* **music** *Michel Colombier* **cast** *Patrick
Dempsey, Kate Jackson, Kirstie Alley, Carrie
Fisher, Robert Ginty, Nancy Valen, Charles Hunter
Walsh, Barbara Carrera, Bernie Coulson, Ray
Girardin, Robert Camilletti, Vic Tayback, Kim
Miyori, Robert Picardo, Peter Koch*
Running time: 99 mins
US release: Tri-Star, Apr 28, 1989
UK release: Col/Tri-Star, May 25, 1990

LOOK WHO'S TALKING

This is one of those rare films that induces instant and squirm-inducing hatred in the viewer. It is common knowledge in the industry that the film's enormous success took everyone by surprise, and that several highly-placed insiders were of the opinion that it was 'unreleasably bad' before it had opened. They were right, but millions of people in America and around the world still plonked down their ticket money and subjected themselves to this inexcusable tripe.

The film's sole conceivable justification could be that it finally gives a substantial screen role to Kirstie Alley, who has shown how good she can be on TV's *Cheers* but has been wasted in a succession of bits and bobs (*Shoot to Kill, Blind Date, Champions*) since her pointy-eared début in *Star Trek II: The Wrath of Khan*. But the shapely comedienne is submerged here into an ordeal which manages to combine more horrible ideas, awful people and glutinous smarm in one package than any picture in living memory. Alley plays one of those smart-suited 'independent' Hollywood heroines, in this case a high-powered accountant whose ability with figures must be far greater than her smarts when it comes to contraception. For she turns into a clod-hopping Lucille Ball clone at the first whiff of oestrogen, when she is impregnated by her married lover (George Segal), and gives birth in the back of John Travolta's taxi to a little pile of cutesy babyfat who worms its way into everyone's hearts. By the end of the film, she has even birthed another bundle of joy, this time with Big John, who has stepped in and become the ideal man in her life, as the actual rather than substitute Daddy.

The gimmick is that the film is narrated in voiceover by the baby – just like those horrid nappy adverts of a few years ago – and the baby has a hip, cool, wisecracking Bruce Willis sort of character, allowing Bruce Willis to pick up a lot of money and publicity for breezing into a studio one morning and reading out some crudola jokes. The whole genre is descended from *Bobbikins*, the 1960 Max Bygraves vehicle in which a fourteen-month toddler could speak out loud and give stock market tips, but *Look Who's Talking* manages to be even more repulsive, witless and laugh-free than that mercifully forgotten dud. This is yet another demonstration of the horrid idea – see *Three Men and a Baby, Baby Boom, For Keeps, She's Having a Baby,* and even the excellent *Raising Arizona* – that the ultimate fashion accessory for the *thirtysomething* generation is a cutely gurgling, cutely puking, cutely crapping infant. The cumulative effect of these movies, of which this is indubitably the worst, is to make you nostalgic for the good old days of the 1970s where babies in movies like *Rosemary's Baby* and *It's Alive* were insidious and brutal monsters who should be shot on sight. Perhaps the time is right for Clive Barker to get the rights to all those school playground jokes and make 'Dead Baby; the Movie' to end the whole genre.

Unable to stand the shock of being in a successful film after all these post-*Saturday Night Fever* years on Skid Row with losers like *Moment to Moment*, *Staying Alive*, and *Two of a Kind*, Travolta goes through an incredible display of perky little grins and eye-rolling mannerisms, as if determined to be the first leading man in a baby movie not to be upstaged by the brat. He gets to fly a plane and dance, demonstrating his own off-screen interests, but he is prevented from trying to convert the kid to Scientology, which is a shame because his co-star, Alley, is also a devout follower of L. Ron Hubbard's cranky put-on of a religion, making you suspect that this whole thing is some sinister mind control plot. But the film also features a minor comeback from George Segal, whose career has also been in the video-only doldrums of late, and he almost manages to get away with it as the vacillating swine who is 'going through a selfish phase at the moment', only to lose out at the last minute in some humiliating slapstick as Alley smashes up his office. As if Travolta and the rug rat weren't enough abuse for one movie, you also get some hilarious senility jokes from Abe Vigoda (yup, if there's one thing guaranteed to get millions of Americans rolling in the aisles it's a senility joke) and another fussy, motherly, pain-in-the-ass performance from Olympia Dukakis, who is fast becoming the most irritating woman in the cinema and here reveals that her comic timing is just about on a par with her cousin's flair for getting elected to the presidency.

But the thing I really hate most about the movie is its sneaky insistence – along with a whole slew of recent American pictures from *Parenthood* through *Fatal Attraction* to *Child's Play* – that men should go to work, women should stay at home, babies should puke up and that they should all arrange themselves in an unreal 1950s sitcom family unit for the betterment of God and country.

If the film proves anything, it's that a woman in Hollywood – Amy Heckerling – can make films just as dreadful as any male hack director. So, how does one explain its incredible, sequel-generating popular success? My guess is that it's all down to demographics: this is a movie that appeals to a large and usually neglected audience – women in their mid-to-late 20s – and women in their mid-to-late 20s were girls in their mid-teens when Travolta was at the height of his popularity, and so they are relishing the chance to leave their boyfriends – who never even liked Olivia Newton-John, let alone rubberlips Travolta – at home, with their optional puke accessory – and relive their disco youth while being reminded that all men except John are gits and that the best thing a woman can do is have a baby. We're talking horrible, horrible, horrible . . .

KIM NEWMAN

⚑ MACK THE KNIFE

Menahem Golan 'directed' this adaptation of Brecht's *The Threepenny Opera*. In the process he had Kurt Weill's music re-orchestrated (and Weill had a genius for orchestration), used the old Mark Blitzstein translation of Bertolt Brecht's lyrics (big mistake) and managed to throw away a dream cast – Raul Julia as Macheath, Julia Migenes as Jenny, Roger Daltrey as the Street Singer. *The Threepenny Opera* is almost director-proof, but then Golan's no director. **JH** **Director** *Menahem Golan* **producer** *Stanley Chase* **script** *Golan, from The Threepenny Opera by Bertolt Brecht and Kurt Weill* **camera** *Elemer Ragalyi* **editor** *Alain Jakubowicz* **design** *Tivadar Bertalan* **cast** *Raul Julia, Richard Harris, Julia Migenes, Roger Daltrey, Julie Walters, Rachel Robertson, Clive Revill, Bill Nighy, Erin Donovan, Julie T. Wallace* **Running time:** 120 mins **US release:** 21st Century, Feb 2, 1990

MADHOUSE

Night Court's John Larroquette and *Cheers'* Kirstie Alley star as self-centred yuppies whose home is invaded by 'house-guests from hell'. The film has a good theme, but nothing is made of the house-proud self-absorption of the characters and their response to such unlikely and unwanted guests. Very like TV – when Alley does a striptease, she's behind a curtain. **JH** **Director/script** *Tom Ropelewski* **producer** *Leslie Dixon* **camera** *Denis Lewiston* **editor** *Michael Jablow* **design** *Dan Leigh* **music** *David Newman* **cast** *John Larroquette, Kirstie Alley, Alison LaPlaca, John Diehl, Jessica Lundy, Bradley Gregg, Dennis Miller, Robert Ginty* **Running time:** 90 mins **US release:** Orion, Feb 16, 1990 **UK release:** Rank, Nov 16, 1990

MAJOR LEAGUE

Police Academy meets *Eight Men Out* in this amiable baseball comedy that boasts an above-average cast and a few good jokes (though not many new ones) among the old reliables, as coach Tom Berenger – displaying a nice comic touch – puts together the worst team imaginable in an effort to get relocated to Miami. The film does nothing to advance the art of motion pictures, but it does make you laugh – which is all it sets out to do. And how many other movies this year offer the sight of a voodoo worshipper sacrificing Kentucky Fried Chicken? **TW** **Director/script** *David S. Ward* **producers** *Chris Chesser, Irby Smith* **exec** *Mark Rosenberg* **camera** *Reynaldo Villalobos* **editor** *Dennis M. Hill* **design** *Jeffrey Howard* **music** *James Newton Howard* **cast** *Tom Berenger, Charlie Sheen, Corbin Bernsen,*

Margaret Whitton, James Gammon, Rene Russo, Wesley Snipes, Charles Cyphers, Chelcie Ross, Dennis Haysbert, Andy Romano, Bob Uecker **Running time:** 107 mins **US release:** Paramount, Apr 7, 1989 **UK release:** Fox, Sep 22, 1989

MAMA, THERE'S A MAN IN YOUR BED (Romuald et Juliette)

Coline Serreau, who gave us *Three Men and a Cradle*, translates the Western colonial encounter into a French romantic comedy – no mean feat. A white executive named Romuald has his financial and emotional life saved by a black cleaning woman named Juliette (geddit?). Best news: Serrault is canny enough to give us a black ending, where Juliette goes off on Romuald and all he represents, and a white ending, where they live happily ever after. Worst news: an American remake is planned, starring Whoopi Goldberg and Richard Dreyfus. **CB** **Director/script** *Coline Serreau* **producers** *Philippe Carcassonne, Jean-Louis Piel* **camera** *Jean-Noël Ferragut* **editor** *Catherine Renault* **design** *Jean-Marc Stehle* **cast** *Firmine Richard, Pierre Vernier, Maxime Leroux, Gilles Privat, Muriel Combeau, Catherine Salviat* **Running time:** 111 mins **US release:** Miramax, Apr 13, 1990 **UK release:** Gala, Aug 10, 1990

MAX MON AMOUR

If this looks more like Buñuel than Oshima, that may be due to the presence of the Spanish master's producer Serge Silberman and writer Jean-Claude Carrière. Buñuel, of course, isn't making movies any more, and Oshima has enough sureal impulses to move into his territory, among the discretely charming bourgeoisie, with this story of a diplomat's wife (Rampling) who rejects propriety to have an affair with a chimp. It's bright and funny, with Anthony Higgins as the husband who moves from amusement over his wife's paramour to homicidal rage. **JH** **Director** *Nagisa Oshima* **producer** *Serge Silberman* **script** *Oshima, Jean-Claude Carrière* **camera** *Raoul Coutard* **editor** *Hélène Plemiannikov* **design** *Pierre Guffroy* **music** *Michel Portal* **cast** *Charlotte Rampling, Anthony Higgins, Bernard-Pierre Donnadieu, Victoria Abril, Anne-Marie Besse, Nicole Calfan, Pierre Etaix, Bernard Haller, Sabine Haudepin, Christopher Hovik, Fabrice Luchini, Diana Quick* **Running time:** 97 mins **UK release:** Electric, May 18, 1990

👍 MELANCHOLIA

Film distributor Andi Engel turns filmmaker.
A middle-aged German living and working in
London, Engel has made a film about – a middle-
aged German living and working in London. But
fears of dressed-up autobiography soon vanish.
Jeroen Krabbé's art critic hero is a living, self-
sufficient creation: a drink-prone, doubt-racked
survivor of the 1960s, looking for a wake-up call
to his slumbering idealism. One day he gets it:
'Assassinate a Latin American torturer visiting
England.' The wheels of fate roll, the landscape
of fear unfurls, and Engel's camera beautifully
dovetails film noir German-style with lapidary
manners English-style. **HK**
Director Andi Engel **producer** Colin MacCabe
script Engel, Lewis Rodia **camera** Denis Crossan
editor Christopher Roth **design** Jock Scott **music**
Simon Fisher Turner **cast** Jeroen Krabbé, Susannah
York, Ulrich Wildgruber, Jane Gurnett, Kate
Hardie, Saul Reichlin, John Sparkes,
Running time: 87 mins
UK release: BFI, Oct 20, 1989

MEN DON'T LEAVE

Jessica Lange stars as a woman widowed and
forced to move to Baltimore in order to support
her two young sons. This is a very uneven
comedy drama from the director of Risky Business
and the author of Immediate Family. Lange
spends a great deal of time polishing her halo.
With her dippy grin and otherworldly timing she
allows Joan Cusack to steal the film, as an
eminently practical nurse with a taste for teenage
boys (notably Lange's older son). Further proof
that there is no such thing as a great movie
containing hot-air balloon scenes. **JH**
Director/exec Paul Brickman **producer** Jon Avnet
script Barbara Benedek, Brickman **camera** Bruce
Surtees **editor** Richard Chew **design** Barbara Ling
music Thomas Newman **cast** Jessica Lange, Chris
O'Donnell, Charlie Korsmo, Arliss Howard, Tom
Mason, Joan Cusack, Kathy Bates, Core Carrier,
Jim Haynie, Belita Moreno, Shannon Moffett, Lora
Zane, Theresa Wozniak
Running time: 113 mins
US release: Warner, Feb 2, 1990

👍 MIAMI BLUES

Wonderful adaptation of Charles Willeford's
novel about a 'blithe psychopath'. Alec Baldwin
waltzes into Miami with a smile, a shoeshine, a
suitcase full of dollars and a hand-squeeze that
kills. (Well, it kills the Hari-Krishna chap seeking
donations at the airport.) Soon mad, bad Baldwin
is tangling with slow, dodo policeman Fred Ward,
and bodies are littering the littoral. Will justice
triumph? Or evil mischief? It's a fine scene-
stealing contest between Ward, all frowns, double

takes and lost-denture grins, and Baldwin, rasping
out pastel-coloured charm as if he were Cary
Grant reborn into the age of Don Johnson. **HK**
Director George Armitage **producers** Jonathan
Demme, Gary Goetzman **execs** Edward Saxon, Fred
Ward **script** Armitage, from novel by Charles
Willeford **camera** Tak Fujimoto **editor** Craig
McKay **design** Maher Ahmad **music** Gary Chang
cast Alec Baldwin, Fred Ward, Jennifer Jason Leigh,
Nora Dunn, Charles Napier, Jose Perez, Paul
Gleason
Running time: 99 mins
US release: Orion, Apr 20, 1990
UK release: Rank, Dec 7, 1990

👎 MILLENNIUM

At the heart of this sci-fi film is a good idea for a
half-hour Twilight Zone episode. But once the
basic premise is revealed – time travellers from a
sterile future rescue passengers from doomed
airplanes in the twentieth century as a way of
replenishing their stock – it doesn't have
anywhere to go and seems stumped for an ending.
A pity, because the early scenes of crash
investigator Kris Kristofferson rooting through
the wreckage of one crash too many are quite
impressive, which is more than can be said for
the bargain-basement future or Cheryl Ladd,
accurately described by one character as being
'as subtle as a lead pipe'. Michael Anderson's
complete disinterest in sci-fi (despite Logan's Run)
is apparent throughout while John Varley's TV-
movie-of-the-week script seems aimed directly at
the homevideo market, stranding a good
supporting cast who deserve – and should have
known – better. **TW**
Director Michael Anderson **producer** Douglas
Leiterman **execs** Freddie Fields, John Foreman,
Louis M. Silverstein, P. Gael Mourant **script** John
Varley **camera** René Ohashi **editor** Ron Wisman
design Gene Rudolf **music** Eric N. Robertson **cast**
Kris Kristofferson, Cheryl Ladd, Daniel J. Travanti,
Robert Joy, Lloyd Bochner, Brent Carver, David
McIlwraith, Maury Chaykin, Al Waxman,
Lawrence Dane, Thomas Hauff
Running time: 108 mins
US release: Fox, Aug 25, 1989
UK release: Rank, Oct 20, 1989

MISS FIRECRACKER

Like her Crimes of the Heart, this new Beth
Henley comic gothic is peopled with characters
too strong for its slender plot. Holly Hunter is a
Mississippi plain-Jane striving one last time to win
her town's annual beauty-talent contest. One
cousin, past winner Mary Steenburgen, is back
home to crown the winner and speak on My Life
as a Beauty. Other cousin Tim Robbins is home
too, one step away from the booby hatch. Half-

wit Alfre Woodard hovers amusingly. Hunter does nothing halfway, from frizzing her hair to doing the splits, but the effort expended produces slightly too few laughs. **BM**
Director Thomas Schlamme **producer** Fred Berner **execs** Lewis Allen, Ross E. Milloy **script** Beth Henley, from her play The Miss Firecracker Contest **camera** Arthur Albert **editor** Peter C. Frank **design** Kristi Zea **music** David Mansfield **cast** Holly Hunter, Mary Steenburgen, Tim Robbins, Alfre Woodard, Scott Glenn, Veanne Cox, Ann Wedgeworth, Trey Wilson
Running time: 102 mins
US release: Corsair, Apr 28, 1989
UK release: Rank, Jun 15, 1990

MONKEY SHINES
FILM • FILM • FILM • FILM
Director George A. Romero **producer** Charles Evans **execs** Peter Grunwald, Gerald S. Paonessa **script** Romero, from novel by Michael Stewart **camera** James A. Contner **editor** Pasquale Buba **design** Cletus Anderson **music** David Shire **cast** Jason Beghe, John Pankow, Kate McNeil, Joyce Van Patten, Christine Forrest, Stephen Root, Stanley Tucci, Janine Turner, William Newman
Running time: 115 mins
US release: Orion, Jul 29, 1988
UK release: Rank, Feb 23, 1990

MONSIEUR HIRE
FILM • FILM • FILM • FILM
Director Patrice Leconte **producers** Philippe Carcassonne, René Cleitman **script** Leconte, Patrick Dewolf, from the novel Les fiançailles de M. Hire by Georges Simenon **camera** Denis Lenoir **editor** Joëlle Hache **design** Ivan Maussion **music** Michael Nyman **cast** Michel Blanc, Sandrine Bonnaire, Luc Thuillier, André Wilms
Running time: 79 mins
US release: Orion Classics, Apr 20, 1990
UK release: Palace, Apr 27, 1990

MOUNTAINS OF THE MOON
An account of the exploits of, and fraught relationship between, the Victorian explorers Burton and Speke seems an odd project for director Bob Rafelson, despite his known penchant for travel in remote realms. The result is a hybrid, a miniseries-like exotic adventure crossed with intimations of 'modern' psychology. The film proceeds by fits and starts towards the rather anti-climactic ending which history dictates but which might also be taken to reflect a lack of clarity in the conception. Vivid details here and there are not enough to sustain the over-generous length. **TP**

Director Bob Rafelson **producer** Daniel Melnick **execs** Mario Kassar, Andrew Vajna **script** William Harrison, Rafelson, based on Burton and Speke by Harrison, and original journals by Richard Burton, John Hanning Speke **camera** Roger Deakins **editor** Thom Noble **design** Norman Reynolds **cast** Patrick Bergin, Iain Glen, Richard E. Grant, Fiona Shaw, John Savident, James Villiers, Adrian Rawlins, Peter Vaughan, Delroy Lindo, Bernard Hill, Anna Massey, Leslie Phillips, Delroy Lindo, Paul Onsongo
Running time: 136 mins
US release: Tri-Star, Feb 23, 1990
UK release: Guild, Apr 20, 199

👍 MUSIC BOX
Although at first sight a composite of Eszterhas's scripts for Betrayed and Jagged Edge, this knocks spots off both as lawyer Jessica Lange defends her father from deportation to face trial for war crimes. Costa-Gavras captures the horror of the familiar suddenly perverted as Lange has to reconcile her knowledge of a loving family man who teaches his grandson push-ups with the testimony of strangers that he forced them to do the same over bayonets planted in the ground after acts of rape, torture and murder. The film does not stop at the question of his guilt, but also invokes America's post-war complicity: it's not her father, but her highly respected father-in-law, who tells her son the Holocaust was an exaggeration and uses his influence to turn the trial. By the end of the film, Lange's world has been turned inside out and, in the film's most chilling image, she cannot look into the Danube without the reflected sunset invoking memories of the days when it ran red with blood. With a trio of superb performances from Lange, Armin Mueller-Stahl and Frederic Forrest, Music Box is one of the most thoughtful and disturbing of this year's mainstream films. Its faults pale into insignificance beside its achievements. **TW**
Director Costa-Gavras **producer** Irwin Winkler **execs** Joe Eszterhas, Hal W. Polaire **script** Eszterhas **camera** Patrick Blossier **editor** Joele Van Effenterre **design** Jeanine Claudia Oppewall **music** Philippe Sarde **cast** Jessica Lange, Armin Mueller-Stahl, Frederic Forrest, Donald Moffat, Lukas Haas, Cheryl Lynn Bruce, Mari Torocsik, J. S. Block, Sol Frieder, Michael Rooker,
Running time: 126 mins
US release: Tri-Star, Dec 25, 1989
UK release: Guild, Jun 15, 1990

👎 MY FIRST FORTY YEARS
Based on a popular Italian volume of scandal-mongering memoirs, this 'erotic' movie has been dubbed into English with such strangulated ineptitude as to make it impossible to judge whether it may once have possessed any quality.

M

On the damaged evidence, however, this seems unlikely – given, for instance, the conspicuous lack of any evolving period background in a narrative that spreads itself over more than 20 years. Elliott Gould, heavily bearded as if in search of anonymity, pops up briefly as a caricature journalist (a grotesque figure even judged by prevailing movie notions of the Fourth Estate), and the late Capucine makes a sad farewell appearance in an irrelevant rôle as the objectionable heroine's mother-in-law. **TP**
Director Carlo Vanzina **producers** Mario Cecchi Gori, Vittorio Cecchi Gori **script** Enrico Vanzina, Carlo Vanzina, from book by Marina Ripa Di Meana **camera** Luigi Kuveiller **editor** Ruggero Mastroianni **design** Mario Chiari **music** Umberto Smaila **cast** Carol Alt, Elliott Gould, Jean Rochefort, Pierre Cosso, Massimo Venturiello, Isabel Russinova, Paola Quattrini, Riccardo Garrone, Capucine
Running time: 107 mins
UK release: Col/Tri-Star, Sep 8, 1989

MY LEFT FOOT
DISAPPOINTMENT

Director Jim Sheridan **producer** Noel Pearson **execs** Paul Heller, Steve Morrison **script** Shane Connaughton, Sheridan, from book by Christy Brown **camera** Jack Conroy **editor** J. Patrick Duffner **design** Austen Spriggs **music** Elmer Bernstein **cast** Daniel Day-Lewis, Ray McAnally, Brenda Fricker, Ruth McCabe, Fiona Shaw, Eanna MacLiam, Alison Whelan, Declan Croghan, Hugh O'Conor, Cyril Cusack
Running time: 103 mins
US release: Miramax, Nov 10, 1989
UK release: Palace, Aug 18, 1989

⁌ MYSTERY TRAIN

Jim Jarmusch spins together three offbeat stories set one night in Memphis, revolving around a series of lost souls who, for one reason or another, find themselves staying in a run-down hotel. The characters of the snappily-dressed night clerk (bluesman Hawkins) and his bellboy (Lee) crop up in all three episodes, as does – in various forms – the ghost of Elvis Presley. But essentially this is a three-bite selection of mini-movies. 'Far From Yokohama' concerns a pair of Japanese teenagers (Nagase, Kudoh), who visit the town to assess the roots of rock 'n' roll and find themselves wandering through a nearly abandoned wasteland that looks like Yokohama with 60 per cent of the buildings taken away. He shows off his rockabilly quiff, flip-top lighter and drainpipes, and stubbornly insists on the superiority of Carl Perkins, while she is dedicated

to 'the Kingu, Elvisu Pu-res-lieh' and hoards 200 T-shirts in the bright red suitcase they carry around on a pole. Nothing much happens to the tourists, but this episode makes a stronger impression than the more densely-plotted follow-ups. 'Ghosts' is about a stranded Italian Luisa (Braschi), stopping over in the city with her recently-deceased husband's coffin, who has a brush with the befuddled spectre of Elvis. And 'Lost in Space' is about a barber (Buscemi) and an ex-English loser (Strummer) who drift around town with black dude Will Robinson (Aviles) and wind up committing a stupid liquor store hold-up. The film is much more than its spaced-out stories suggest it should be, and offers an affecting vision of one city living with its disappointments. **KN**
Director/script Jim Jarmusch **producer** Jim Stark **execs** Kunijiro Hirata, Hideaki Suda **camera** Robby Müller **editor** Melody London **design** Dan Bishop **music** John Lurie **cast** Masatoshi Nagase, Youki Kudoh, Screamin' Jay Hawkins, Cinqué Lee, Nicoletta Braschi, Elizabeth Bracco, Joe Strummer, Rick Aviles, Steve Buscemi, Vondie Curtis-Hall
Running time: 110 mins
US release: Orion Classics, Nov 17, 1989
UK release: Palace, Dec 8, 1989

MYSTIC PIZZA

Female buddy films may be the next Hollywood genre. It's a shame, though, that Donald Petrie's effort to make a Diner for women simply flips the gender rôles, making the men into shallow sex objects. Still, there's plenty of comedy and honesty in this slight film about three young women who waitress at a pizza parlour in Connecticut. Julia Roberts is the beautiful one, strong enough to cope with the shortcomings of her yuppie beau. Lili Taylor is energetic and emotion-driven, unable to commit to her simple fisherman boyfriend. Annabeth Gish is the clever one, but naïve enough to lay down for a wishy-washy older man. The film's stronger character moments make up for the trite plot. **BM**
Director Donald Petrie **producers** Mark Levinson, Scott Rosenfelt **exec** Samuel Goldwyn Jr. **script** Amy Jones, Perry Howze, Randy Howze, Alfred Uhry **camera** Tim Suhrstedt **editor** Marion Rothman **design** David Chapman **music** David McHugh **cast** Julia Roberts, Annabeth Gish, Lili Taylor, Vincent D'Onofrio, William R. Moses, Adam Storke, Conchata Ferrell, Joanna Merlin
Running time: 104 mins
US release: Goldwyn, Oct 21, 1988
UK release: Virgin, Jan 5, 1990

MONKEY SHINES

The prospect of a monkey movie does not normally fire one with boundless enthusiasm. For every *King Kong* and *Planet of the Apes*, there are hundreds of *Greystokes* and *Gorillas in the Mist*, featuring the primate as noble savage and ecological statement. Occasionally, the monkey takes the Freddy Krueger rôle (psycho chimps on the loose in *Link*); sometimes it's the Steve McQueen part (*Project X*, a simian variation on *The Great Escape*); sometimes it's even a monkeyfied Marcello Mastroianni (*Max, Mon Amour*). Monkeys are gimmicks of anthopomorphization, ideal to be dressed up and given mugs of tea to drink.

The premise of *Monkey Shines*, based on an Oxford-set thriller by British writer Michael Stewart, is enough to make one's heart sink: quadriplegic ex-jock develops meaningful relationship with a capuchin monkey which has been specially trained to do his bidding. But Stewart covers a surprising amount of scientific and ethical ground, and – in the hands of one of America's most talented and uncompromising directors – the plot becomes a hook on which is hung more food for thought than can be gleaned from any number of 'serious issue' films by the likes of Costa-Gavras and Martin Ritt. Just because George A. Romero is best known for his zombie movies (*Night of the Living Dead, Dawn of the Dead, Day of the Dead*), he tends to get overlooked by mainstream critics who refuse to dig deeper than the flesh-ripping surface.

Fiction films are rarely so truthful about the specifics of disablement, and seldom have we been drawn so thoroughly into seeing things from the disabled person's point of view. At the beginning of the film, Allan is a promising law student and athlete with everything to live for. After his accident – he is struck by a truck while out jogging – he is left a quadriplegic, incapable of movement except in his neck and head (Jason Beghe does wonders with a rôle which is mostly restricted to facial expression). His girlfriend leaves him for the oily specialist who operated on him after the accident, and he finds himself returned to the humiliating state of helpless infancy, with his mother only too delighted to reassert her early rôle by moving back in, fussing around and giving him embarrassing sponge-baths. Allan's life is reduced to dependence on other people and an obstacle course of wheelchairs, straps and pulleys. When his nurse's budgerigar lands on his face and pecks at his eyes, he is unable to brush it off. He can turn the pages of a book only by sucking through a straw.

Allan reacts the way one imagines most of us would react; he rails bitterly against his fate. He is not a model patient, he does not suffer nobly and he is mortified by the loss of his sexual faculties – the limitations of a quadriplegic's sex life are broached here with a fine balance of candour and tact. But then Allan is a fully-fledged person as opposed to a one-dimensional cipher with a handicap to keep the plot ticking over; he is likeable, but no saint. We are not expected to sympathize with him purely because he suffers.

The mad doc rôle is taken by Geoffrey (John Pankow), a driven man who chops up human brains to inject into his capuchins, shooting himself full of drugs so he doesn't have to waste time on sleep. He is also Allan's best friend, and his motives in producing a monkey with abnormally high intelligence are mixed – he is an amiable chap, he really does want to help Allan (especially after he attempts suicide), but there is also something of the Dr Frankenstein about him. Ella is his brainchild; he is keen to see her strut her stuff.

And so she does, after a crash course in how to be a home-help from Melanie (Kate McNeil), an animal trainer. This bit of the film is based on fact; the Helping Hands Program at Boston University trains capuchin monkeys for just such purposes. But that's where fact stops and fiction starts; the credits, rather shamefacedly, point out that 'none of the incidents portrayed have ever been recorded in the ten-year history of the program.' Of course not; this is a *story*.

Allan and Ella develop a close affinity; rather *too* close. Allan sinks into trances and imagines he's running at lightning speed through the undergrowth outside; he imagines he can see things through Ella's eyes. He begins to fly into violent rages, and he imagines Ella is drawing them out of him; man and monkey, spitting and snarling, lay bare sets of teeth which appear uncomfortably similar. Allan is beginning to suspect that Ella is his instinct incarnate, an evil imp who can fulfil his animal urges without the binds of civilization. 'That's what the devil is, Geoff,' he says. 'It's instinct, animal instinct.' For when the laws of the jungle come into force, the fragile restraints of society are shattered and it's every man, or monkey, for himself.

Up to this point, Romero's build-up has been slow and measured, favouring character and situation over shock effects. But, from here on, anyone who rubs Allan up the wrong way is in danger of being visited by a small furry creature with a penchant for holding lighted matches against drapes or throwing electric appliances into the bath. The director who in his zombie movies has built up something of a partnership with Tom Savini, one of the best splatter make-up specialists in the business, is here almost decorous in his depiction of violent death; the screen fades ominously to black before we see anything, or a shower curtain obscures the grisly details. But the preparation has paid off; for the last section of the film is one of the most relentless half-hours of suspense in recent cinema. An electrical storm is raging around the house, the malevolent capuchin has chomped through the telephone wires and, while Allan's mother, Geoff and Melanie all come under threat, the hero has to find ways of using his head, in all senses of the word, to fight back against his rampaging helpmate.

There are signs of studio-inflicted strain in the film's coda, an ending which is rather too pat. But there is also a last-minute shock effect which isn't quite as gratuitous as it might seem; Allan dreams that Ella is inside him and forces her way out. It's the standard bad-dream epilogue, but also an apt reminder that Ella is indeed inside him. Allan has overcome his animal instincts for the time being, but they're still there. They're inside all of us, ready to burst out and raise hell.

ANNE BILLSON

MONSIEUR HIRE

Film-watchers know Simenon mostly from the smug screen Maigrets parodied by Peter Sellers' Inspector Clouseau, and naturally they prefer American-type *noir*. But some Euro-highbrows see Simenon as the twentieth century's Balzac. Where Balzac's 'romantic realism' described the monstrous energy of nineteenth-century man, Simenon's 'criminal realism' is geared to the sleazy pathos of the modern mass.

The hero, or butt, of *Les fiançailles de M. Hire* (1933) is one of Simenon's 'victims whom one cannot pity'. A middle-aged Parisian tailor, of Polish-Jewish extraction, his creepy-yet-prickly manner gets him shunned by all and suspected of murder. Each night he watches a maidservant, Alice, undress in her room across the way; she catches him at it, and has her reasons for leading him on. In classical fashion, this detective story works backwards to discover whodunnit. But it also surges forwards and outwards, as police investigations follow up neighbours' gossip. Julien Duvivier filmed the novel in 1946, as *Panique*. Supreme pessimist of French movies, Duvivier slipped in sly needle about so many Parisians having denounced one another to the Gestapo, and stressed not so much gossip by malicious individuals as a surge of herd-instinct. Whodunnit? Human nature dunnit.

Patrice Leconte makes his own changes, and like Duvivier's they're not betrayals of Simenon's vision, but supporting testimony. He updates the story, but minimally (he sought a 'timeless' feeling). Alice is now a shop-assistant who maybe models a bit. The flowing, gregarious crowds of the 1930s have been replaced by choppy little groups. An LP of Brahms accompanies Hire's voyeurism, expressing its sacred yearnings. This time the community's prejudice is concentrated into the police inspector (André Wilms), a lean, sad, angry man in a tired pullover and duffle coat. He personifies a tireless, bitter indignation against a filthy world.

Michel Blanc makes Hire a sad, defiant loner: his oily, fatalistic eyes brimming with anger, his insolence tautly controlled, his flesh as pale as candle-grease. So constrained a character risks being one-dimensional, but he's a bundle of contradictions. His first remarks to the cop, about hating and being hated, are so lucid you want to applaud; but so chilling you can't. Meeting a neighbour on the stairs he's tensely oblivious, like Death passing by to collect someone else; but at the local bowling-alley he's a star. There, his eerie skills at bowling, blindfold or backwards, give him golden moments of, not extroversion exactly, but pseudo-interaction, of a mercurial kind. When he lays his hands on a child's head you can't decide if it's from extreme loneliness, or tragic lack of *savoir-faire*, or imminent paedophilia, or the whole lot. A cop sneers, 'How long since you came inside a woman?', and Hire is silent. But it's not assent, only dumb insolence, and a prostitute whose regular he is takes more trouble over him than necessary. Only, the moment she shows a personal interest in him, he angrily demands a different girl. No doubt about it, he's a very bad egg. But which came first, the egg of perversity or the chicken of solitude? Is Alice his way out from this vicious circle? Of the doom of his fragile equilibrium?

This is a nearly religious film, about moral suicide and despair. It's almost appropriate that lightning from on high betrays the watcher to the watched. Alice is played by Sandrine Bonnaire, who played Mouchette, the defiant and perverse heroine, in Pialat's *Sous le soleil de Satan*, from Bernanos's grimly Catholic novel. Whatever the motives of this silent, tenacious girl in befriending a likely sex-killer, there's an 'elective affinity' between them. It's not 'love' exactly, more a gravitational attraction. Undressing in her room, she senses a dark watcher, pauses, hesitates and proceeds. Whatever else is on her mind, there's a fellow-feeling for his devious infatuation, for an emptiness like her own. Her young lover is a high-spirited, handsome extrovert; his conscience is as clear as a rottweiler's.

The film's final confrontation, a thing of twists, is indescribable without giving away the plot. The speech beginning 'You will think me stupid, but . . .' goes way beyond *Blue Velvet* in exploring 'the dark side of the moon' of human nature, its mixtures of obstinacy and masochism, self-destruction and chilly shame. For all its other qualities, the Lynch film's knowledge of evil stops at weirdo clues and odd scraps of behaviour until the whole corny association of gays, drugs, gangs and evil rolls in. But Simenon understands, from inside and 'in the round', the spider-dances of intimacy, the strange moves between a man made passive by years of suspicion and despair, and a young girl with a peasant's silent, cautious, active strength.

Leconte reconciles Simenon's loose (not to say slipshod) plot mechanics with the tight structure desirable in movies, by making the story a succession of riddles. It's an ever more common tactic, here taken so far that the spectator often feels like another detective, assembling a story from a jigsaw of clues. Is this a park, or a photograph of a park? What's that whitish patch – litter, a dress, a corpse? Why is this middle-aged man so obsessed with it? Why does the film dwell on Hire keeping mice? What are those white little objects he tosses into the Seine? The answers emerge slowly, the last two being, if I guessed right, of a sexual vileness hitherto unfilmed, though known to low-class folklore.

With the clues go some, not so much red herrings, as ironic echoes. That placid old lady is feeding pigeons, but feeding them what? There are carefully plotted continuity misleads, so that what looks like a scene of Hire resignedly watching Alice and a friend making love turns out to be inter-cutting between the lovers in one place and him in another. Maybe the inter-cutting expresses jealous thoughts; its ambiguity makes the relationship between the scenes even eerier.

This 'prism of riddles' suits the detective genre, which depends on suspicion, paranoia, irony. Hire is the butt of others' paranoia (though perhaps he deserves it – for other reasons, which they *don't* suspect!). He overcomes his own paranoia, by a heroic effort; result: an ironic miscarriage of justice. It's as if every friendship is equally a betrayal, as if we're all condemned to be detectives, criminals, victims, executioners, of one another. Yet, so starved for affection is even Hire, that when Alice lies back and unbuttons a cardigan, as if to show that she feels at home with him, its sexual impact, like Rita Hayworth removing one long black glove in *Gilda*, hits like striptease. That was all Alice need do, and maybe she knew it . . .

Whether Hire stands in his dark window, eyes sucking in the spectacle of Woman, or walks abroad with eyes rigidly forward, this is not a tale of mere voyeurism. Far from Hire's 'male look' being aggressive, phallic, judgemental, he's absorbing, saturating himself, with Alice; and far from fearing the gaze of others, his very despair compels him to disdain it. True, the film involves Polaroids and other telescopes, and one might think that detection itself is a kind of voyeurism. But the last proposition is significant; for it reverses the argument. Detection isn't about voyeurism, voyeurism is about detection; that is, knowledge. Hire's voyeurism is only one of his odd, sad habits, and to fixate on it is to overlook too much, in the way of thoughts, suspicions, hopes, surmises. Not to mention the body's other 'media': scent, touch, kinaesthesia. It's a major visual moment when Hire's heavily-gloved hand fastidiously lifts perfume to his precisely appraising nose.

Leconte's short (97 minutes) movie feels more like three hours, not because it drags, but because its reticence sets one thinking fast. It's part of a new idiom in French cinema. Leconte, like Beineix and Carax, tells the story less through a *dramatic* continuity, a flow of actions and declarations, than by a jigsaw of moments, making suggestions *pictorially*. It could come from modern comic-strips, of the sort which all three directors devised before turning to films. Leconte, however, made his name, like Blanc, in intimate-satirical theatre; its in-jokey spirit is said to permeate his eight earlier films, all too esoteric for export. So it's hard to say how far *Hire* represents his own vision and how far it's Simenon's illustrated. In some ways its style suggests a more aloof kind of pessimism, closer to Bresson and Pialat. But it also restores contact, somehow, with the spirit of 'poetic realism' which Simenon shared with Duvivier and so many classic French movies. And it steers clear of neo-romantic gloss (Beineix, Carax) and slapdash caricature of the bourgeoisie (Chabrol, Fassbinder). Perhaps it represents a sort of 'realism revisited', along with *Jean de Florette* and *Manon des sources*, Berri's remake of 1930s Pagnol movies. French movies lost the knack of 'realism' around 1960, and it's good to see the old richness creep back.

RAYMOND DURGNAT

MY LEFT FOOT

Experience has taught me caution. Many years ago, I wrote a less than enthusiastic review of a film based on the true story of a one-legged cancer sufferer's charity-hop across Canada, and was immediately swamped with letters from angry readers, some of whom expressed the hope that I would shortly be riddled with some form of the Big C for which there is no known cure.

Suffering is perceived as a holy condition, and those who suffer are accorded a form of sainthood. By extension, anything to which their name is attached is also perceived as holy, and so it follows that criticism of films based on the lives of real-life sufferers is apt to be construed as directed at the sufferers themselves. So let me get all the obvious stuff out of the way: there is *no question* that Christy Brown was a fellow of rare spirit, possessed of extraordinary reserves of courage and determination, and we should be so lucky to have even a tenth of his zest for life. A shame, then, that *My Left Foot* turns out to be such a zest-free experience.

The British love a Performance; none of this pointing-the-suit-and-mumbling nonsense. You get the feeling that inside every British actor there's a Robert Newton itching to leap out and do Long John Silver impersonations – funny walks and even funnier accents. And Daniel Day Lewis, whose embarrassing cod-Czech accent was inexplicably overlooked by admirers of 'The Unbearable Boringness of Being', is working hard at becoming Britain's answer to Meryl Streep.

It's one of life's more interesting little quirks that Day Lewis's closest rival for the 1990 Academy Award for Best Actor was Tom Cruise, nominated for his rôle as a paraplegic Vietnam veteran in *Born on the Fourth of July*. The battle of the wheelchairs! But alas, poor Tom – wheels apart, all he had to get his teeth into were an infra-dig haircut, an attitude problem and a couple of common or garden crying jags. Whereas for *My Left Foot*, Day Lewis gets to drool, suffer from cerebral palsy *and* do an Irish accent – all at the same time. No wonder he got the Best Actor Oscar – and no wonder they never gave it to Cary Grant, who throughout his career made the mistake of making screen acting look effortless.

My Left Foot is firmly rooted in the British small-screen tradition. Working-class life in pre-war Dublin is everything you ever imagined it would be – the Brown family ekes out an existence on porridge-scrapings and stolen coal; their day-to-day activities have that (appropriately) *brownish* tinge which in British television terms denotes nostalgia, honest poverty and/or home-baked bread.

Of course, there is nothing as viewer-friendly as a *story* for the film-goer to fix on, no point, no beacon on the horizon to signal where the action is headed. But neither are there any surprises. Instead, the narrative ambles on from one scene to the next without prospect of respite: edited highlights from its subject's life, a few chuckles, some tears – it's nothing but a social-realist soap opera that could barely pass muster as an American how-I-triumphed-over-my-disease TV Movie of the Week. Only a requisite sprinkling of fine old Irish character actors saves the day, with Brenda Fricker and the late Ray McAnally being solid and supportive as Christy's parents.

It's worth comparing My Left Foot with another wheelchair film, one which was dismissed by most critics as worthless exploitation; the hero of George A. Romero's Monkey Shines is left quadriplegic after a road accident, able to move only from the neck up. Within the format of a psychological thriller with horrific trappings (mad scientist, brain experiments, trained monkey running amok), Romero tackles head-on all the issues of emotional and physical dependency which My Left Foot ducks. And he does it with pace and pizzazz; he is making a film, not airing his sensitivity and compassion.

One might argue that we could always do with more films about people in wheelchairs, a deserving minority often overlooked in the stampede to flaunt plastic surgeon perfection. My Left Foot, however, is not so much a film with a handicapped subject as a film with a handicap as its subject; cerebral palsy comes in from the cold and does a soft-shoe shuffle to attract attention. But it also encourages viewers to keep their distance, to marvel at Christy's sainthood from afar, rather than identify with him.

In some ways, Christy's handicap is almost passed over. There is a tendency to concentrate on the end results of his achievements at the expense of what were, one assumes, arduous learning processes. We watch him chalk the word 'mother' on the floor with the eponymous left foot – the only part of his body over which he exercises control – but this is depicted as one of the holy miracles of the blessed St Sufferer; we have no more idea than his startled family how he taught himself to write and spell. Later, he suddenly produces the manuscript of his first book as if he were Paul Daniels conjuring a rabbit out of a hat; we are never allowed to share the tortuous process of composing and typing. All this has a diminishing effect on Christy's character and is an insult to us, the audience – he is presented as not so much a human being who has surmounted incredible odds as a chair-bound superhero. But this is no superman or saint; Christy was extra-ordinary precisely because he was an ordinary, everyday man afflicted with an ordinary, everyday handicap. And there is considerable cowardice in the happy-ever-after ending which freeze-frames the artist-writer and his wife-to-be with a celebratory bottle of champagne – conveniently ignoring the hardships of his later life and its premature end.

In one scene only do writer-director Jim Sheridan and his co-writer Shane Connaughton succeed in setting out the dilemmas and limitations of Brown's condition. Christy learns that the lady doctor on whom he has developed a crush has become engaged to the owner of the art gallery that has just exhibited his paintings and, halfway through a celebratory dinner, explodes into a drunken fury of helpless jealousy. This is the Cinema of Embarrassment at its most spectacular, and it does what the rest of the film cannot: it engages the emotions, hooks up the intellect and, for an all-too-brief moment, enables the audience to exercise its imagination and take a guess at what life must really have been like for a heart and soul trapped in the broken body of Christy Brown.

ANNE BILLSON

NATIONAL LAMPOON'S CHRISTMAS VACATION

Having turned much of North America and most of Europe into a wasteland, the horrendous Griswold family decides to spend Christmas at home- – only to find their even more horrific relatives turning up uninvited. Some of the film is so accurate that it's impossible to laugh, but there's enough lowest-common-denominator humour and belly-laughs to make the vacation worthwhile for all but the most humourless. **TW** **Director** Jeremiah S. Chechik **producer/script** John Hughes **exec** Matty Simmons **camera** Thomas Ackerman **editor** Jerry Greenberg **design** Stephen Marsh **music** Angelo Badalamenti **cast** Chevy Chase, Beverly D'Angelo, Randy Quaid, Diane Ladd, John Randolph, E. G. Marshall, Doris Roberts, Julia Louis-Dreyfus, Mae Questel, William Hickey, Brian Doyle-Murray, Juliette Lewis, Johnny Galecki, Nicholas Guest, Miriam Flynn **Running time:** 97 mins **US release:** Warner, Dec 1, 1989

NEW YORK STORIES

Martin Scorsese essays comedy and nearly succeeds, Francis Coppola tries whimsy and gets covered in goo and Woody Allen returns to fantasy with hilarious results. This rare triptych started with Allen and should have stayed with him. In Scorsese's opening episode, Nick Nolte is an artist amusingly besotted with his youthful assistant. Coppola and daughter Sofia wrote his truly awful contribution, in which a little girl lives alone in a fancy New York hotel and wastes a lot of money bringing her globetrotting parents together. Allen stars in his own episode, in which his mother, the Jewish mother to end all Jewish mothers, hounds him from the sky above Manhattan. **BM** **Producer** Robert Greenhut **execs** Jack Rollins, Charles H. Joffe LIFE LESSONS **Director** Martin Scorsese **producer** Barbara De Fina **script** Richard Price **camera** Nestor Almendros **editor** Thelma Schoonmaker **design** Kristi Zea **cast** Nick Nolte, Rosanna Arquette, Patrick O'Neal, Jesse Borrego, Steve Buscemi, Peter Gabriel LIFE WITHOUT ZOE **Director** Francis Coppola **producers** Fred Roos, Fred Rucks **script** Francis Coppola, Sofia Coppola **camera** Vittorio Storaro **editor** Barry Malkin **design** Dean Tavoularis **music** Carmine Coppola **cast** Heather McComb, Talia Shire, Giancarlo Giannini, Paul Herman, James Keane, Don Novello, Selim Tlili, Carmine Coppola, Carole Bouquet OEDIPUS WRECKS **Director/script** Woody Allen **producer** Robert Greenhut **execs** Jacky Rollins, Charles H. Joffe **camera** Sven Nykvist **editor** Susan E. Morse

design Santo Loquasto **cast** Woody Allen, Mia Farrow, Julie Kavner, Mae Questel, Marvin Chatinover, Jessie Keosian, George Schindler, Bridgit Ryan, Mayor Koch **Running time:** 123 mins **US release:** BV, Mar 1, 1989 **UK release:** Warner, Nov 10, 1989

NEXT OF KIN

When a Chicago hillbilly van driver (Paxton) is iced by the mob, his two brothers swear revenge. One is a by-the-book big city cop (Neeson) who vows to let due process take its course, the other an unshaved backwoods psycho (Swayze) who believes in an eye for an eye and a pump shotgun in the face for a dead brother. It's a glum action-man movie, very similar in tone to John Irvin's earlier Raw Deal, albeit with Swayze as a slow-to-burn hero rather than the casually genocidal Arnold Schwarzenegger. Given that the film's appeal is predicated on the need for violent revenge, it seems to take an eternity for the hero to come round to the cause, while Neeson, oddly cast as the secondary hero brother, handles far more of the action. The film might have been more enjoyable if it had junked its discussion on the ethics of revenge and concentrated instead on Neeson's crusade against the anachronistic mafia tycoons. **KN** **Director** John Irvin **producers** Les Alexander, Don Enright **exec** Larry De Waay **script** Michael Jenning **camera** Stephen Poster **editor** Peter Honess **design** Jack T. Collis **music** Jack Nitzsche **cast** Patrick Swayze, Liam Neeson, Adam Baldwin, Helen Hunt, Andreas Katsulas, Bill Paxton, Ben Stiller, Michael J. Pollard, Ted Levine, Del Close, Valentino Cimo, Paul Greco, Vincent Guastaferro, Paul Herman **Running time:** 108 mins **US release:** Warner, Oct 20, 1989 **UK release:** Warner, Apr 27, 1990

🌶 NIGHTBREED

Clive Barker's second film as a writer-director lacks the claustrophobic tightness of his début feature, Hellraiser. Its weak and illogical central storyline fails to yoke together the film's bizarre and visionary elements. Craig Sheffer, a psychiatric patient with a Californian haircut, is convinced by his sombre-suited psychoanalyst (Cronenberg) that he is a masked serial murderer. Obsessed with the myth of Midian, a legendary city rumoured to be home to the monsters of the world, Sheffer then encounters some monsters who infect him. He is shot dead by the police, but returns in a changed form. Featuring a startling array of briefly-seen monsters, the film doesn't find much for them to do except be unhelpful bystanders in the battle between the

blandly unmonstrous hero and the mad doctor. The characters never quite come together, and the film is too eager to leap over holes in the narrative in order to set up its visual effects. Much rewritten and tinkered-with during nearly a year of shooting, *Nightbreed* is ultimately a rather bewildering picture despite the impressive achievements in make-up, music, production design, costume and effects. **KN**
Director *Clive Barker* **producer** *Gabriella Martinelli* **execs** *James G. Robinson, Joe Roth* **script** *Barker, from his novel* Cabal **camera** *Robin Vidgeon* **editors** *Richard Marden, Mark Goldblatt* **design** *Steve Hardie* **music** *Danny Elfman* **cast** *Craig Sheffer, Anne Bobby, David Cronenberg, Charles Haid, Hugh Quarshie, Hugh Ross, Doug Bradley, Catherine Chevalier, Malcolm Smith, Bob Sessions, Oliver Parker, Debora Weston*
Running time: 99 mins
US release: Fox, Feb 16, 1990

A NIGHTMARE ON ELM STREET 5 - THE DREAM CHILD

While the *Elm Street* films get more and more impressive visually, their scripts make less and less sense. The heroine of the last film (Wilcox) is still around, newly pregnant by her quickly-disposed-of boyfriend, and the evil Freddy Krueger (Englund) is trying to return to real life by possessing the unborn child. There are the usual excellent effects/dream scenes, but the story advances through disorienting lapses and leaps as another uninteresting selection of teenagers are brought on and killed off. Stephen Hopkins does an astonishing job of making the film visually engaging, but his overdrive style is constantly undercut by the terrible, much-rewritten screenplay. The scariest idea in the film, underlined by yet another open ending, is the possibility that this nightmare will never end, the non-existent story spinning out forever, until the profits stop coming in. **KN**
Director *Stephen Hopkins* **producers** *Robert Shaye, Rupert Harvey* **execs** *Sara Risher, Jon Turtle* **script** *Leslie Bohem* **camera** *Peter Levy* **editors** *Chuck Weiss, Brent Schoenfeld* **design** *C. J. Strawn* **sfx** *Alan Munro, Ted Rae, Doug Beswick, Visual Concept Engineering, 'Cinema Research Corporation* **music** *Jay Ferguson* **cast** *Robert Englund, Lisa Wilcox, Kelly Jo Minter, Danny Hassel, Erika Anderson, Nick Mele, Whitby Hertford, Joe Seely, Valorie Armstrong, Burr DeBenning, Clarence Felder, Michael Ashton*
Running time: 89 mins
US release: New Line, Aug 11, 1989
UK release: Enterprise, May 11, 1990

▼ NUNS ON THE RUN

Eric Idle and Robbie Coltrane here join the elephants' graveyard of British TV comedians who have humiliated themselves on the big screen. An excruciatingly over-plotted farce, *Nuns on the Run* vaguely takes off from the premise of *Some Like It Hot*; two soft-hearted gangsters on the run from their vicious boss, the police and hatchet-wielding gangsters, dress up as nuns and take refuge in an inner-city convent. The film moves from the girls' showers in the convent to bedpans and black suspenders in a hospital as it hunts for cheap laughs, wasting a lot of time before the story gets going, and failing horribly in romantic sequences that are supposed to be played straight. Based on the common British misconception that fat people, men in drag and nuns are automatically hilarious. **KN**
Director/script *Jonathan Lynn* **producer** *Michael White* **execs** *George Harrison, Denis O'Brien* **camera** *Michael Garfath* **editor** *David Martin* **design** *Simon Holland* **music** *Yello, Hidden Faces* **cast** *Eric Idle, Robbie Coltrane, Camille Coduri, Janet Suzman, Doris Hare, Lila Kaye, Robert Patterson, Robert Morgan, Winston Dennis, Tom Hickey*
Running time: 90 mins
US release: Fox, Mar 16, 1990
UK release: Palace, May 4, 1990

N

OLD GRINGO

TURKEY • TURKEY • TURKEY

Director Luis Puenzo **producer** Lois Bonfiglio **exec** David Wisnievitz **script** Aida Bortnik, Puenzo, from novel by Carlos Fuentes **camera** Felix Monti **editor** Juan Carlos Macias, William Anderson, Glenn Farr **design** Stuart Wurtzel, Bruno Rubeo **music** Lee Holdridge **cast** Jane Fonda, Gregory Peck, Jimmy Smits, Patricio Contreras, Jenny Gago, Gabriela Roel, Sergio Calderon, Guillermo Rios, Jim Metzler, Samuel Valadez, Anne Pitoniak, Pedro Armendariz Jr., Stanley Grover, Josefina Echanove, Pedro Damian, Maya Zapata
Running time: 120 mins
US release: Columbia, Oct 6, 1989
UK release: Col/Tri-Star, Oct 20, 1989

OLIVER AND COMPANY

Based on an inherently lousy premise – a modern-day version of *Oliver Twist* with cats and dogs in the lead rôles – this isn't quite the ordeal one might have expected. What you get is bright but forgettable songs, characterful animation, some voice artists having a good time hamming it up and an absolute minimum of waifish cuteness. The plot is the usual mix of chases, comic bits, songs and sentiment, but enough happens to keep the adults awake while the kids are screaming and shouting. Disturbingly insubstantial by the standards of classic Disney, *Oliver and Company* is nevertheless 20 times better than the average Thunder-He-Man and the My Little Transformer Go-Bears cartoon. **KN**
Director George Scribner **script** Jim Cox, Timothy J. Disney, James Mangold **editor** Jim Melton, Mark Hester **animators** Mike Gabriel, Hendel Butoy, Glen Keane, Mark Henn, Ruben A. Aquino, Doug Krohn **design** Dan Hansen **music** J. A. C. Redford **voices** Joey Lawrence, Billy Joel, Cheech Marin, Richard Mulligan, Roscoe Lee Browne, Sheryl Lee Ralph, Dom DeLuise, Taurean Blacque, Carl Weintraub, Robert Loggia, Natalie Gregory, William Glover, Bette Midler
Running time: 74 mins
US release: BV, Nov 18, 1988
UK release: Warner, Dec 15, 1989

🏆 OPPORTUNITY KNOCKS

Saturday Night Live comic Dana Carvey plays centre-screen as a con man who grows to like his dupes. Robert Loggia sleepwalks through his rôle as the industrialist charmed by Carvey, and comic Todd Graff shows up at inopportune times to approximate Jerry Lewis. Even if the script had managed to be funny, Carvey is far too lightweight to fill up a movie screen. He mugs, he smirks and he floats away. **CB**
Director Donald Petrie **producers** Mark R. Gordon, Christopher Meledandri **exec** Brad Grey

script Michael Katlin, Nat Bernstein **camera** Steven Poster **editor** Marion Rothman **design** David Chapman **music** Miles Goodman **cast** Dana Carvey, Robert Loggia, Todd Graff, Julia Campbell, Milo O'Shea, James Tolkan, Doris Belack, Sally Gracie, Mike Bacarella, John M. Watson Snr., Beatrice Fredman
Running time: 105 mins
US release: Universal, Mar 30, 1990

OLD GRINGO

Stranded like a beached whale between the safe, secure grounds of the 'art' film, and the lapping, enticing waters of blockbusterdom, *Old Gringo* ends up as nothing but a very bad movie. The 'literary adaptation' is a notoriously difficult thing to pull off when you're aiming at a mainstream audience. Even in Britain where the translation of literary works into images is done with a certain élan, the siren calls of bigger stars and bigger budgets have blunted many a promising project. But in America, where actions speak louder than words, it's a form that is fraught with danger.

On paper, *Old Gringo* certainly has promise: Jane Fonda as the middle-aged virgin brought to life by the love of Jimmy Smits' Mexican revolutionary; a part for a crusty character actor as the old man who stands and watches, dispensing witticisms while the bullets and maracas thunder. Sadly only the crusty character part is brought off at all successfully. Gregory Peck plays Ambrose Bierce with the world-weary air that's needed to convey the feelings of a man who's come to Mexico seeking the oblivion of death, taking his last chance to ride a horse and do derring-do. But all around him the characters fall into a torpor relieved only by pointlessly elongated action sequences.

It's not that the film can be castigated for being, like *Reds* for example, just another tale of love set against a revolutionary backdrop, in which the ideas behind the events take second fiddle to the need for 'mature' on-screen couplings and romantic declarations. For neither the novel nor the film are about the Mexican Revolution as such. That said, the action sequences (and the celebratory shoot-ups that follow) are mostly exotic bustle and sub-Peckinpah theatrics to no purpose.

Far more damaging is the simplification of the novel in the interests of shifting the focus of the film onto the Fonda character. In the process she's made into a much cruder figure than she was on the page. And although she smoulders with passion when aroused from spinsterhood, she's left with little to do in the long central section of the film where Smits anguishes about the past. The script is at fault for trivializing the passion it unleashes.

There's also a lack of imagination applied to the stasis that Smits falls into. Having captured a hacienda with the active assistance of Peck and the passive aid of Fonda, the camera explores every cranny of the place and its new inhabitants, but it never establishes a relationship between Smits and his surroundings. It transpires that the reason he refuses to follow orders and lead his troops to Pancho Villa's assistance is because the hacienda is where he was born, and the master he has killed is his father, who raped his peasant mother. Instead of fighting for the future, Smits, Hamlet-like in his indecision, dwells on the past and the pointless legal documents that he mistakenly believes will return the hacienda and its land to the people. A marvellous gothic conceit, this is visualized in the paltriest of images: Smits poring over papers, reiterating to his followers that he is their commander, wandering through the household and taking his pleasure with Fonda.

The climax – for legalistic reasons Peck, who has been shot by Smits, is exhumed and 'executed' alongside his killer in the presence of Fonda – is similarly lacking in the gothic overtones it so clearly requires. Presented to us from the perspective of a shocked Fonda and introduced with too much revolutionary rhetoric from Smits, it seems like a gimmick ending rather than a moment of high (melo)drama. It's not that the novel is all talk and the film all action, just that the characters, so rich and rounded in the novel, are hollow. Where in the novel the Bierce character grows to despise the cruel stance he had adopted in his writings, in the film he is lionized – the opening sequence sees him denounce not his writings but the false backslapping of his publishers – as a writer.

Of course, literary novels have to be altered for the screen when they're being propelled by a $24 million budget. But the tragedy of *Old Gringo* is that, instead of an imaginative reshaping of Carlos Fuentes's material, Fonda (whose company produced the film) and Columbia have opted for a flat and unconvincing storyline. It's a film one hoped to like, but which one can never forgive for wasting the opportunity it represented.

PHIL HARDY

THE PACKAGE

A hit man is hired by neo-fascists in both the US and USSR armies to kill Gorbachev when he visits America on a peace mission. He's transported from East Berlin to America by an unwitting Hackman, who spends most of the movie uncovering the plot after his 'package' escapes at the airport. The script, which owes something to *Day of the Jackal*, and even more to the real-life assassination of JFK, doesn't quite crack it as a politically credible post-glasnost thriller. It's a so-so movie with some well-handled, albeit predictable, set pieces that only partially redeem the elementary characterization – both Joanna Cassidy and Tommy Lee Jones are wasted as usual and Gene Hackman is pretty much on auto-pilot throughout. **TW**
Director *Andrew Davis* **producers** *Beverly J. Camhe* **exec** *Arne L. Schmidt* **script** *John Bishop* **camera** *Frank Tidy* **editors** *Don Zimmerman, Billy Weber* **design** *Michael Levesque* **music** *James Newton Howard* **cast** *Gene Hackman, Joanna Cassidy, Tommy Lee Jones, Dennis Franz, Reni Santoni, Pam Grier, Chelcie Ross, Ron Dean, Kevin Crowley, Thalmus Rasulala, Marco St. John, John Heard, Nathan Davis, Joe Greco, Ike Pappas*
Running time: 108 mins
US release: Orion, Aug 25, 1989
UK release: Rank, Jun 8, 1990

PARENTHOOD

An all-star cast of distinguished actors appear here as five generations of an extended and messy family of middle-class Americans who have fouled up their relationships with their kids and/or their parents. Result is an easygoing, mainly amusing, fundamentally empty comedy-drama that seems designed to be the pilot for a TV series. Steve Martin gets most of the laughs as a manic father who is torn between the pressures of a demanding job and an even more demanding family, and he almost redeems the film's sogginess with sheer energy. It's riotously funny in spurts, but it also has that congealed gooey centre familiar from too many Hollywood films and you end up wishing that Americans weren't quite so keen on expressing their love for each other. **KN**
Director *Ron Howard* **producer** *Brian Grazer* **exec** *Joseph M. Caracciolo* **script** *Lowell Ganz, Babaloo Mandel* **camera** *Donald McAlpine* **editors** *Michael Hill, Daniel Hanley* **design** *Todd Hallowell* **music** *Randy Newman* **cast** *Steve Martin, Mary Steenburgen, Dianne Wiest, Jason Robards, Rick Moranis, Tom Hulce, Martha Plimpton, Keanu Reeves, Harley Kozak, Dennis Dugan, Leaf Phoenix, Eileen Ryan, Helen Shaw, Jasen Fisher*
Running time: 124 mins
US release: Universal, Aug 2, 1989
UK release: UIP, Jan 12, 1990

PATHFINDER (Veiviseren/Ofelas)

The first film ever made in the Lapp language is a genuine wide-screen surprise. The hollow-eyed Tchudes come on as brutally and remorselessly as any horror-film monster, pursuing the boy (Mikkel Gaup) whose family they have already killed, but writer-director Nils Gaup lays in sufficient fresh material from Northern legend to enliven any generic borrowings. And, despite some careless camera work, the snowy landscape is deployed to impressive effect, particularly in a climactic sequence when the boy leads the Tchudes to their demise on a snow-swept rockface and the powerhouse killing machines become desperate men struggling on the end of a rope. The script doesn't care enough about the community saved through the boy's actions to render the ending, when he's acknowledged to be their new 'pathfinder', as epiphanic as may have been intended, but this was one of the most refreshing movie experiences of the year. **JP**
Director/script *Nils Gaup* **producer** *John M. Jacobsen* **camera** *Erling Thurmann-Andersen* **editor** *Niels Pagh Andersen* **design** *Harald Egede-Nissen* **music** *Nils Aslak Valkeapää, Marius Müller, Kjetil Bjerkestrand* **cast** *Mikkel Gaup, Ingvald Guttorm, Ellen Anne Buljo, Inger Utsi, Svein Scharffenberg, Helgi Skulasin, Knut Walle*
Running time: 86 mins
UK release: Guild, Sep 23, 1988
US release: IFEX, May 11, 1990

PATTI ROCKS

A sequel to David Morris's *Loose Ends*, which was made in 1976 but not distributed in the UK, *Patti Rocks* begins like a road movie but turns into psycho-drama as it unfolds over a single day and night. Two blue-collar friends in their mid-30s travel to visit the girlfriend of one of them, who has disclosed that she is pregnant. The film's earlier sequences ironically and scatologically annotate aspects of male insecurity; the concluding passage offers a subdued assertion of female resilience. While the construction may be a little shaky, the effect is frequently acerbic, with the emotional impact no doubt ascribable in part to the screenplay having been devised by the director in collaboration with the three principal players. The budget, it's worth noting, was a mere $300,000. **TP**
Director *David Burton Morris* **producers** *Gwen Field, Gregory M. Cummins* **exec** *Sam Grogg* **script** *Morris, Chris Mulkey, John Jenkins, Karen Landry* **camera/editor** *Cummins* **design** *Charlotte Whitaker* **music** *Doug Maynard* **cast** *Chris Mulkey, John Jenkins, Karen Landry, David L. Turk, Stephen Yoakam*
Running time: 87 mins
UK release: Premier, Sep 15, 1989

PENN AND TELLER GET KILLED

Post-modern magic act Penn and Teller start a plot whereby someone will try to murder Penn (the tall, noisy one with the bad hair), and the convolutions pile up from there. There are funny moments, but the P&T are not as funny as they think they are. The ending, however, is gruesomely hilarious – a fulfilment of the title's promise and a supremely logical joke on contemporary Hollywood comedy. JH
Director/producer Arthur Penn script Penn Jillette and Teller camera Jan Weincke editor Jeffrey Wolf design John Arnone music Paul Chihara cast Penn Jillette, Teller, Caitlin Clarke, David Patrick Kelly, Leonardo Cimino, Christopher Durang, Alan North
Running time: 89 mins
US release: Warner, Sep 22, 1989

👍 PET SEMATARY

Based on Stephen King's bestseller, Pet Sematary concerns an animal graveyard built, like the Overlook Hotel in The Shining, on an Indian burial ground that has turned sour. Dad (Midkiff) is impressed when the family cat, despatched (by one of the gleaming juggernauts that dominate the rural routes) and duly interred, is resurrected – albeit as a mangy demon – and makes the mistake of planting his squashed two-year-old in the same place. Despite schlocky flashbacks and abysmal performances (except for creepy neighbour Fred Gwynne and the tot), Mary Lambert's chiller fully comprehends the evil in children and comes up smelling of death and Blue Velvet, white picket fences and all. GF
Director Mary Lambert producer Richard P. Rubinstein exec Tim Zinnemann script Stephen King, from his novel camera Peter Stein editors Michael Hill, Daniel Hanley design Michael Z. Hanan sfx Fantasy II Film Effects music Elliot Goldenthal cast Dale Midkiff, Fred Gwynne, Denise Crosby, Brad Greenquist, Michael Lombard, Blaze Berdahl, Miko Hughes, Susan Blommaert
Running time: 102 mins
US release: Paramount, Apr 21, 1989
UK release: UIP, Nov 17, 1989

📯 THE PHANTOM OF THE OPERA

Relocated to London, with the masque and chandelier sequences omitted, this version of Phantom of the Opera has one praying for the Andrew Lloyd Webber version. Robert Englund simply runs through his Freddy routine in different make-up, and there's a silly prologue which has the heroine (Schoelen) passing out and waking up a century earlier. TW
Director Dwight H. Little producer Harry Alan Towers exec Menahem Golan script Duke

Sandefur, from screenplay by Gerry O'Hara camera Elemer Ragalyi, Peter Collister editor Charles Bornstein design Tivadar Bertalan music Misha Segal cast Robert Englund, Jill Schoelen, Alex Hyde-White, Bill Nighy, Terence Harvey, Stephanie Lawrence, Nathan Lewis, Peter Clapham, Molly Shannon, Emma Rawson, Mark Ryan, Yehuda Efroni
Running time: 93 mins
US release: 21st Century, Nov 2, 1989
UK release: Castle Premier, Jun 15, 1990

PHYSICAL EVIDENCE

A blackmailing mobster is found dead, and everyone concerned would like to pin the killing on beaten-up, frequently drunk, invariably suspended low-life cop Burt Reynolds. Theresa Russell, an ambitious public defender, takes up the case and tries to prove Reynolds' innocence. Unfortunately, he's the only person in town with more enemies than the deceased, and he's had a mental blackout about the evening of the murder. Physical Evidence follows Suspect in its focus on a committed lady lawyer whose personal life gets mixed up with the case she's working on, and while this one doesn't have as much slush as the Cher vehicle, it does have several too many unlikely plot twists. Reynolds doesn't so much deconstruct his he-man persona as flounder about in its wake, and Russell – despite an impressive wardrobe – has to bear the burden of far too many courtroom clichés. Director Crichton pulls off a neat opening, with a would-be suicide discovering a corpse stashed under the bridge from which he wants to hang himself, but thereafter fails to get much out of the film noir plotline. KN
Director Michael Crichton producer Martin Ransohoff exec Don Carmody script Bill Phillips camera John A. Alonzo editor Glenn Farr design Dan Yarhi music Henry Mancini cast Burt Reynolds, Theresa Russell, Ned Beatty, Kay Lenz, Ted McGinley, Tom O'Brien, Kenneth Welsh, Ray Baker
Running time: 99 mins
US release: Columbia, Jan 27, 1989
UK release: Rank, Aug 18, 1989

👍 PIRAVI (The Birth)

Masterly Indian film, pieced together mosaic-like from abstract colours, shapes and sounds: a rain-battered mansion in rural India; a river curling dark and silent between it and the village, and a white-stubbled old Brahmin who daily crosses it in the hope of meeting his son at the bus-stop. But the son never comes. Rumours of arrest in the city (it's the time of Indira Gandhi's emergency) whisper around the father's head. And the days tick on, haunted by fear and the ghostly patterings

of a wife and sister. First-time director Shaji orchestrates sense impressions like a symphony: the infinite percussive sounds of rain, the loamy colours of soaked earth, even the rowing motions of a boatman's arm circling like a clock-hand as day by day, hour by hour, time eats up hope. **HK**
Director Shaji N. Karun **producer** Sethu **script** S. Jayachandran Nair, Ragunath Paleri, Shaji **camera** Sunny Joseph **editor** Venugopal **design** Devan **music** G. Aravindan, Mohan Sitara **cast** Premji, C.V. Sreeraman, Krishna Moorty, Chandran Nair, Mullaneyi, Kottara Gopalakrishnan
Running time: 110 mins
UK release: Contemporary, Jan 26, 1990

PLAFF!

Plaff is an onomatopoeic approximation of a raw egg hitting a wall, and the raw eggs hitting Concha's house are the least of her problems in this wacky Cuban satire (that is not a misprint). Director Juan Carlos Tablo plainly views Godard as the supreme comedy director of the post-World War 2 era, and Plaff! is filled with terrible edits, missed cues, and visible camera crews, as well as comic commentary on sexual prejudice, bureaucracy and romance under Castro. It's overlong but still hilarious. **JH**
Director Juan Carlos Tabio **script** Daniel Chavarria Reynoso **cast** Daisy Granados, Thais Valdés, Raul Pomares, Luis Alberto García, Alicia Bustamante, Jorge Cao
Running time: 90 mins
UK release: Metro, Mar 9, 1990

🎞 THE PLOT AGAINST HARRY

Watching this two decades-old mob comedy, brought out of the limbo to which it was consigned by financing problems, one can imagine how the Russians felt on finding an intact woolly mammoth frozen in the tundra. In the low-key, New York realist mode of the time, it charts a few weeks in the life of an ex-bookie who finds his world crumbling after a nine-month prison stretch. Amid the Woodstock anniversary hype, it's fascinating to see a 1969 American cultural product that has nothing to do with hippies, peace, love or Jefferson Airplane, offering instead an eerie prefiguring of Cookie and Married to the Mob. **JH**
Director/script Michael Roemer **producers** Robert Young, Roemer **camera** Young **editors** Terry Lewis, Georges Klotz **design** Howard Mandel **music** Frank Lewin **cast** Martin Priest, Ben Lang, Henry Nemo
Running time: 80 mins
US release: New Yorker, Jan 12, 1990

POLICE ACADEMY 6: CITY UNDER SIEGE

This entry puts the series back on track, after a very rough patch, with plenty of mindless slapstick based on the box-office standards of revenge, debunking of authority figures and incompetents winning out over their social superiors. This time the excuse for a plot is a master criminal ruining local business through having obtained inside information from the police, but it never gets in the way of the jokes, which are executed throughout with a good-natured sense of innocent fun. **TW**
Director Peter Bonerz **producer** Paul Maslansky **script** Stephen J. Curwick **camera** Charles Rosher Jr. **editor** Hubert De La Bouillerie **design** Tho E. Azzari **music** Robert Folk **cast** Bubba Smith, David Graf, Michael Winslow, Leslie Easterbrook, Marion Ramsey, Lance Kinsey, Matt McCoy, Bruce Mahler, G. W. Bailey, George Gaynes
Running time: 83 mins
US release: Warner, Mar 10, 1989
UK release: Warner, Jul 21, 1989

🎞 POWWOW HIGHWAY

Coming after a string of ill-fated, offbeat projects from Britain's HandMade Productions, Powwow Highway turns out to be a surprisingly mature and funny road movie about a pair of Native Americans on a quest to discover their cultural heritage that becomes an almost mythical (but never pretentious) journey of self discovery. Beautifully acted, especially by Gary Farmer as the road warrior, and photographed with a good eye for the characters' relations to the landscape, it is an enjoyable surprise. **TW**
Director Jonathan Wacks **producer** Jan Wieringa **execs** George Harrison, Denis O'Brie **script** Janet Heany, Jean Stawarz, from novel by David Seals **camera** Toyomichi Kurita **editor** James Austin Stewart **design** Cynthia Sowder **music** Barry Goldberg **cast** A. Martinez, Gary Farmer, Amanda Wyss, Joanelle Nadine Romero, Sam Vlanos, Wayne Waterman, Margo Kane, Geoff Rivas, Roscoe Born
Running time: 91 mins
US release: Warner, Mar 24, 1989
UK release: HandMade, May 11, 1990

PRANCER

A little girl (Harrell) discovers a wounded reindeer and hides it from her father in the belief that it's one of Santa's and that, without her help, Christmas won't happen. The film is aided by a self-deprecating sense of humour and some superb photography – the girl's discovery of Prancer under the full moon is wonderfully atmospheric – and it has enough charm to win over most audiences. That said, cynics with a low whimsy tolerance will hate it. **TW**

Director John Hancock producer Raffaella De Laurentiis script Greg Taylor camera Misha Suslov editor Dennis O'Connor design Chester Kaczenski music Maurice Jarre cast Sam Elliott, Rebecca Harrell, Cloris Leachman, Rutanya Alda, John Joseph Duda, Abe Vigoda, Michael Constantine
Running time: 103 mins
US release: Orion, Nov 17, 1989

PRETTY WOMAN

For Richard Gere's second comeback film of the year, he compliments his evil cop in Internal Affairs with the emotionally uneasy Prince Charming in this comedy Pygmalion. A corporate raider by trade, he hires an innocent hooker (Roberts) as escort and falls in love with her in a story that throws in elements of Cinderella, the Frog Prince and Rapunzel. It's formula filmmaking at its slickest, celebrating the American dream (limousines and gold credit cards) with little self-criticism but some surprisingly subtle class comedy. There's something hollow and almost unlikeable about Roberts' immensely professional performance, but Gere's comic touch keeps the film on track. **KN**
Director Garry Marshall producers Arnon Milchan, Steven Reuther exec Laura Ziskin script J. F. Lawton camera Charles Minsky editor Priscilla Nedd design Albert Brenner music James Newton Howard cast Richard Gere, Julia Roberts, Ralph Bellamy, Jason Alexander, Laura San Giacomo, Alex Hyde-White, Amy Yasbeck, Elinor Donahue, Hector Elizondo
Running time: 119 mins
US release: BV, Mar 23, 1990
UK release: Warner, May 11, 1990

A PRIVATE LIFE

Truth-based tale of love across the colour bar in post-war South Africa. When white policeman Jack (Flynn) marries 'coloured' woman Stella (Cilliers), a 30-year nightmare begins. Stella's unjust racial classification – adopted by a coloured family, she never knew her untraced mother – becomes a curse shared with her husband and handed down to three children (one of whom kills himself). Writer Andrew Davies and director Francis Gerard adopt a fine-tuned, delicately humanist style, allowing anger to well up in us unasked rather than be bullied out of us with rhetoric. **HK**
Director Francis Gerard producers Gerard, Roland Robinson exec Innes Lloyd script Andrew Davies camera Nat Crosby editor Robin Sales design Mark Wilby music Trevor Jones cast Bill Flynn, Jana Cilliers, Kevin Smith, Ian Roberts, Anthony Fridjhon, Joanna Weinberg
Running time: 93 mins
UK release: Hobo, Nov 24, 1989

THE PUNISHER

Dolph Lundgren single-handedly wipes out most of the mafia and a few ninjas in the sort of film on which it would have been worth securing the body-bag concession. Despite a certain comic-strip energy, The Punisher lacks the stylization of the strip that inspired it, and Lundgren's performance leaves a hole in the film's centre. A movie to watch when the pubs are shut and there's nothing on TV. **TW**
Director Mark Goldblatt **producer** Robert Kamen **exec** Robert Guralnick **script** Kamen, Boaz Yakin **camera** Ian Baker **editor** Tim Wellburn, Stephanie Flack **design** Norma Moriceau **sfx** Cinema Research Corporation, Steve Courtley **music** Dennis Dreith **cast** Dolph Lundgren, Louis Gossett Jr., Jeroen Krabbé, Kim Miyori, Bryan Marshall, Nancy Everhard, Barry Otto, Brian Rooney, Zoshka Mizak, Kenji Yamaki, Hirofumi Kanayama, Todd Boyce
Running time: 89 mins
UK release: Castle Premier, Jun 2, 1990

Q&A

An angry study of New York law enforcement, Q&A focuses on the cops as exemplars of the city's problems. Nick Nolte stars – and is almost extraordinary – as a racist police lieutenant involved in a homicide which he claims was self-defence. Idealistic DA Timothy Hutton has trouble believing him, and eventually starts to uncover the details of a conspiracy that's far too filthy for him to handle. The plot is extremely complex and gradually spins out of control: whole rôles could have been excised and it could all have been told much more simply. Armand Assante, as a Puerto Rican drug dealer, and Broadway actor Lee Richardson, as a veteran District Attorney, are the best things here. What's most obviously lacking is any real emotional insight to Hutton's predicament – apart from an incredible sub-plot which has him trying to win back his ex from dope dealer Assante. **JH**

Director *Sidney Lumet* **producers** *Arnon Milchan, Burtt Harris* **exec** *Patrick Wachsberger* **script** *Lumet, from Edwin Torres' novel* **camera** *Andrzej Bartkowiak* **editor** *Richard Cirincione* **design** *Philip Rosenberg* **music** *Rubén Blades* **cast** *Nick Nolte, Timothy Hutton, Armand Assante, Patrick O'Neal, Lee Richardson, Luis Guzman, Charles Dutton, Jenny Lumet, Paul Calderon*
Running time: 132 mins
US Release: Tri-Star, Apr 27, 1990

QUEEN OF HEARTS

A thoroughly disarming, highly unusual little film set mainly in a semi-imaginary London-Italian community where the 1950s and the 1980s seem to co-exist, *Queen of Hearts* feels more like an Italian movie than a British one. Narrated by a romantic young lad (Spagnoli) whose father (Long) runs a café that boasts a gleaming expresso machine, it's partly an episodic family comedy, but there's also a melodramatic and sometimes magical plot about a vendetta spanning the decades which takes the film into the realm of the bizarre. Poker games in Italian clubs, visits from elderly and not-entirely-welcome relatives, and a complicated set of relationships among the family and patrons of the restaurant are gradually worked through, and the film's gradual accumulation of nice little moments adds up into an entrancing spell. **KN**

Director *Jon Amiel* **producer** *John Hardy* **exec** *Graham Benson* **script** *Tony Grisoni* **camera** *Mike Southon* **editor** *Peter Boyle* **design** *Jim Clay* **music** *Michael Convertino* **cast** *Vittorio Duse, Joseph Long, Anita Zagaria, Eileen Way, Vittorio Amandola, Roberto Scateni, Stefano Spagnoli, Alec Bregonzi, Ronan Vibert, Matilda Thorpe*
Running time: 112 mins
US release: Cinecom, Sep 20, 1989
UK release: Enterprise, Sep 29, 1989

🏆 RABID GRANNIES

As Belgian splatter movies dubbed into English
go, *Rabid Grannies* is pretty awful. A group of
grasping relatives who caricature various 'vices' –
a cowardly priest, a fat condom manufacturer, a
French arms dealer, a lesbian fashion editor –
arrive at the country estate of two dear old ladies
(Aymerie, Broekman) to worm their way into the
will. A Satanist who has been disinherited sends a
present which emits a smoke that turns the
women into cackling monsters who proceed to
slaughter everyone in sight. Although only a
pick-up for Troma Films, the film displays the
company's usual style, mixing slapstick splatter
with genuinely offensive material, plus bad pacing
and hideous overacting. Incidentally, the
monsters are aunts, not grannies. **KN**
Director/script *Emmanuel Kervyn* **producers**
James Desert, Jonathan Rambert **exec** *Desert*
camera *Hugh Labye* **editor** *Philippe Ravoet* **design**
Luke Bertrand **music** *Peter Castelain, J. B.
Castelain* **cast** *Catherine Aymerie, Caroline
Broekman, Danielle Daven, Raymond Lescot, Elliot
Lison, Michael Lombet, Anne Marie Fox, Paule
Herreman, Bobette Jouret, Françoise Lamoureux,
Jack Mayar*
Running time: 83 mins
US release: Troma, Sep 29, 1989

🏆 THE RACHEL PAPERS

Another American star is imported into a solidly
British subject in an attempt to get London
swinging again while pretending to be an
American-style teen movie. Updating Martin
Amis's novel to such a degree that the title
becomes redundant, this follows thick-lipped
Brit-brat Dexter Fletcher as he scientifically
attempts to manage his affair with an American
girl (Skye) by entering all manner of information
into his computer, and still going through a
typically contrived on-off romantic plot that ends
not in tears but in tedium. There is some fairly
exploitative bathroom sex, while Fletcher's
chatting to camera evokes both *Alfie* and *Annie
Hall* to no particularly useful end and the trendy
London backgrounds are unconvincing. Mildly
disastrous. **KN**
Director *Damian Harris* **producer** *Andrew S.
Karsch* **execs** *Eric Fellner, James T. Roe III* **script**
Harris, based on novel by Martin Amis **camera**
Alex Thomson **editor** *David Martin* **design** *Andrew
McAlpine* **music** *Chaz Jankel, David Storrs* **cast**
*Dexter Fletcher, Ione Skye, Jonathan Pryce, James
Spader, Bill Paterson, Shirley Anne Field, Michael
Gambon, Lesley Sharp, Jared Harris, Aubrey Morris*
Running time: 95 mins
UK release: Virgin, Oct 27, 1989

THE RAINBOW

Ken Russell returns to Nottinghamshire with this
'prequel' to his 1970 film *Women in Love*. He fills
the screen with Lawrentian images of thundering
horses, nymphs in ponds, swains breasting
hillsides, and of course the title optical illusion.
His otherwise faithful adaptation of the last third
of D. H. Lawrence's classic omits, however, a
strong enough actress at the centre. Sammi Davis
is nude enough but lacks the range to do more
than stick her snub nose in the air and look cross
when thwarted. Glenda Jackson as her mother
and Amanda Donohoe as her co-nymph do more
with less. We never get any sense from Davis of
Ursula's struggle against the limitation of her
roots or her uncompromising need to be free, and
so, however honourable, we are left with just
another costume drama with nude scenes. **BM**
Director/producer *Ken Russell* **execs** *William J.
Quigley, Dan Ireland* **script** *Russell, Vivian Russell,
from novel by D. H. Lawrence* **camera** *Billy
Williams* **editor** *Peter Davies* **design** *Luciana
Arrighi* **music** *Carl Davis* **cast** *Sammi Davis, Paul
McGann, Amanda Donohoe, Christopher Gable,
David Hemmings, Glenda Jackson, Dudley Sutton,
Jim Carter, Judith Paris, Ken Colley, Glenda
McKay, Molly Russell, Rupert Russell*
Running time: 112 mins
US release: Vestron, May 5, 1989
UK release: Vestron, Nov 3, 1989

👍 REEFER AND THE MODEL

A winningly weatherbeaten Irish love-and-crime
yarn in which ex-IRA man Ian McIlhenny teams
up with two pals and ageing girlfriend Carol
Scanlan to go bank-robbing. They and the movie,
rife with doomy wit and wisdom, tack to and fro
across the land, weaving a picture of Ireland
where dreams and despair, cynicism and idealism,
are scarcely distinguishable through the socio-
political turmoils. With plucky acting and a
surprise-primed plot, this is a 'watch for more'
début by director Joe Comerford. **HK**
Director/script *Joe Comerford* **producer** *Lelia
Doolan* **camera** *Breffni Byrne* **editor** *Sé Merry*
design *John Lucas* **music** *Johnny Duhan* **cast** *Ian
McElhinney, Eve Watkinson, Carol Scanlan, Birdy
Sweeney, Sean Lawlor, Ray McBride, Fionn
Comerford, John Lillis, Henry Comerford, Sabina
Higgins, Henry Waters*
Running time: 93 mins
UK release: Metro, Nov 17, 1989

RENEGADES

Director Jack Sholder's *The Hidden* was a triumph
of crashed cars, machine-gun shoot-outs,
energetic running-around and trashed public
property, and *Renegades* is more of the same.
Philadelphia cop Kiefer Sutherland is working

undercover on his own time to get the crook in his department and has been duped into taking part in a big jewel heist by a pretty-boy psycho gangster (Knepper) who shoots him in the stomach for good measure. During a chase, Knepper also detours through a museum of American History and steals a sacred spear that has been in the Lakota Sioux tribe forever and which Phillips, a passing Indian, swears to get back at all costs, up to and including the deaths of his entire family. Phillips gets his witch doctor father to nurse Sutherland back to health and soon they're on the streets looking for Knepper, when they're not crashing cars, leaping between trains, shooting it out in restaurants or beauty parlours, torturing people, insulting each other and doing the regulation action movie things. There is a great deal of action in *Renegades*, but it still manages to be a faintly boring film. Clichés and plot contrivances abound, and all the frenetic running-about doesn't disguise the fundamental stupidity of the heroes or the silliness of the plot. **KN**
Director *Jack Sholder* **producer** *David Madden* **exec** *James G. Robinson, Joe Roth, Ted Field, Robert Cort* **script** *David Rich* **camera** *Phil Meheux* **editor** *Caroline Biggerstaff* **design** *Carol Spier* **music** *Michael Kamen* **cast** *Kiefer Sutherland, Lou Diamond Phillips, Jami Gertz, Rob Knepper, Bill Smitrovich, Floyd Westerman*
Running time: 106 mins
US release: Universal, Jun 2, 1989
UK release: Virgin, Mar 9, 1990

RESURRECTED

A North Country location setting, Tom Bell and Rita Tushingham in the cast . . . *Resurrected* is in some senses a throwback to the regional realism of the early 1960s, complete with the *de rigueur* Woodfall component of a seaside outing and a visit to a clangorous amusement arcade. The time, though, is 1982 and the aftermath of the Falklands War; a young soldier, supposed heroically dead, turns up weeks later and is then unofficially alleged to have deserted. In a way, the film draws, too, on the *fantastique* tradition in British cinema, with the boy returning as a kind of ghost, so as to render him a witness to a heightened vision of British values, or lack of the same – on the one hand, the traditional village community seen behind the credits; on the other, the admass sub-culture manifested by the tabloid press coverage. The various elements do not quite mesh together and the ending seems oddly abrupt; but despite these shortcomings and some evidence of budgetary restriction, *Resurrected* is a British movie of more than usual interest. **TP**
Director *Paul Greengrass* **producer** *Tara Prem, Adrian Hughes* **script** *Martin Allen* **camera** *Ivan*

Strasburg **editor** *Dan Rae* **design** *Chris Burke* **music** *John Keane* **cast** *David Thewlis, Tom Bell, Rita Tushingham, Michael Pollitt, Rudi Davies, William Hoyland, Ewan Stewart, Christopher Fulford, David Lonsdale, Peter Gunn*
Running time: 92 mins
UK release: Hobo, Sep 29, 1989

▼ THE RETURN OF THE MUSKETEERS

Coming seventeen years after Richard Lester's *The Three Musketeers*, this sequel has more than enough plot to go round, but absolutely *nothing* works. The main problem is that George C. MacDonald Fraser's screenplay casts the four – five including C. Thomas Howell as Athos's drippy adopted son – musketeers as total buffoons. They consistently fail in their daring missions, and even manage to be bested frequently in hand-to hand combat by Kim Cattrall, whose awkwardness with a sword is equalled only by her lack of facility with dialogue. All the fat old musketeers look pretty ridiculous in fights, with the exception of Richard Chamberlain who wisely relegates himself to a supporting rôle. The earlier movies were rollicking adventures, with just the right touch of semi-spoof to leaven the mix, but this is a plodding slapstick comedy that consistently fails to take fire. **KN**
Director *Richard Lester* **producer** *Pierre Spengler* **execs** *Mario Sotela, Wayne Drizin* **script** *George MacDonald Fraser from novel by Alexandre Dumas* **camera** *Bernard Lutic* **editor** *John Victor Smith* **design** *Gil Parrondo* **music** *Jean-Claude Petit* **cast** *Michael York, Oliver Reed, Frank Finlay, C. Thomas Howell, Kim Cattrall, Geraldine Chaplin, Roy Kinnear, Christopher Lee, Philippe Noiret, Richard Chamberlain, Eusebio Lazaro, Alan Howard, David Birkin, Bill Paterson, Jean-Pierre Cassel, Servane Ducorps, William J. Fletcher, Laure Sabardin, Marcelline Collard*
Running time: 101 mins
UK release: Entertainment, Aug 4, 1989 ·

▼ THE RETURN OF THE SWAMP THING

The first *Swamp Thing* was pretty dire. However, next to this follow-up, it was a masterpiece. Jim Wynorski specializes in directing sequels to films you didn't want followed-up (*Deathstalker II*, *Big Bad Mama II*), and his style is an annoying blend of kidvid juvenilia and tits 'n' ass 'n' blood. Here, the hero is an eight-foot tall stunt man (Durock) in a rubbery vegetable suit, and he falls for a vacuous bubblehead (Locklear), who is being threatened with hideous mutation by her evil stepfather (Jourdan). Mainly it's a succession of appalling comedy turns, interrupted by clumsy

action scenes. The highlight comes when Jourdan recites the lyrics of one of his old songs from Gigi to an understandably startled parrot. **KN**
Director *Jim Wynorski* producers *Benjamin Melniker, Michael E. Uslan* execs *Tom Kuhn, Charles Mitchell* script *Derek Spencer, Grant Morris* camera *Zoran Hochstatter* editor *Leslie Rosenthal* design *Robb Wilson King* sfx *Jim Stewart, Bob Shelley's Special Effects International* music *Chuck Cirino* cast *Louis Jourdan, Heather Locklear, Sarah Douglas, Dick Durock, Joey Sagal, Ace Mask, Chris Doyle, Daniel Taylor, Ronreaco Lee, Monique Gabrielle, Tony Cecere, Timothy Birch, Alex Van, Ralph Pace, Rex Pierson*
Running time: 87 mins
UK release: Medusa, Dec 22, 1989

REVENGE
TURKEY • TURKEY • TURKEY
Director *Tony Scott* producers *Hunt Lowry, Stanley Rubin* exec *Kevin Costner* script *Jim Harrison, Jerry Fiskin, from novella by Harrison* camera *Jeffrey Kimball* editor *Chris Lebenzon* design *Michael Seymour, Benjamin Fernandez* music *Jack Nitzsche* cast *Kevin Costner, Anthony Quinn, Madeleine Stowe, Tomas Milian, Joaquin Martinez, James Gammon, Jesse Corti, Sally Kirkland, Miguel Ferrer*
Running time: 124 mins
US release: Columbia, Feb 16, 1990
UK release: Columbia, Jun 22, 1990

THE REVOLVING DOORS (Les Portes tournantes)
A French-Canadian exercise in nostalgic regret, *The Revolving Doors* ladles on period 'charm' at the expense of conviction and narrative structure, and rapidly becomes altogether exasperating. The apology for a story centres on a dying woman whose memoirs of her early life in provincial Quebec during the 1920s and 1930s (flashbacks provide the main body of the action) are recorded in a diary which she sends to the son from whom melodramatic contrivance long ago caused her to be separated. In the event, it's her young grandson who makes the trip to New York to find her but, when he finally arrives, the picture comes to an abrupt, if merciful, end. **TP**
Director *Francis Mankiewicz* producers *René Malo, Francyne Morin* exec *Pierre Latour* script *Jacques Savoie* camera *Thomas Vamos* editor *André Corriveau* design *Anne Pritchard* music *François Dompierre* cast *Monique Spaziani, Gabriel Arcand, Miou-Miou, François Méthé*
Running time: 102 mins
UK release: Gala, Feb 16, 1990

ROAD HOUSE
FILM • FILM • FILM • FILM
Director *Rowdy Herrington* producer *Joel Silver* execs *Steve Perry, Tim Moore* script *David Lee Henry, Hilary Henkin* camera *Dean Cundey* editors *Frank Urioste, John Link* music *Michael Kamen* cast *Patrick Swayze, Kelly Lynch, Sam Elliott, Ben Gazzara, Marshall Teague, Julie Michaels, Red West, Sunshine Parker, Jeff Healey, Kevin Tighe*
Running time: 114 mins
US release: UA, May 19, 1989
UK release: UIP, Nov 10, 1989

ROBOCOP 2
This sequel to the political satire/action thriller hit of 1987 has a promising new team behind the camera: writer Frank Miller, creator of the graphic novel, *Batman: The Dark Knight Returns*, and Irvin Kershner, who specializes in superior sequels (*Never Say Never Again, The Empire Strikes Back*). But the producers hovering over the project seem to have been so concerned to keep some good material back for part three that the resulting film is rather thin. Despite state-of-the-art bang-bang, Peter Weller doing stalwart duty as the guy in the sardine can, and a funny interlude when RoboCop gets his prime directives screwed up, it's a film that never quite delivers on its promise. It's a shame because there are just enough good scenes to indicate that *RoboCop 2* could have been a hilarious, weird sequel. **JH**
Director *Irvin Kershner* producer *Jon Davison* exec *Patrick Crowley* script *Frank Miller, Walon Green, from characters created by Edward Neumeier, Michael Miner* camera *Mark Irwin* editor *William Anderson* design *Peter Jamison* sfx *Dale Martin, William Greg Curtis, Peter Kuran/VCE* music *Leonard Rosenman* cast *Peter Weller, Nancy Allen, Daniel O'Herlihy, Belinda Bauer, Tom Noonan, Gabriel Damon, Felton Perry, Robert Do'Qui, Galyn Görg, Stephen Lee, Willard Pugh, Roger Aaron Brown, Patricia Charbonneau, Jeff McCarthy*
Running time: 118 mins
US release: Orion, Jun 22, 1990

ROGER & ME
Michael Moore is a native of Flint, Michigan, a town which was once at the heart of the mighty Ford motor industry, but which has been going downhill since General Motors shut down all the auto factories in order to relocate in Mexico. He flips through the history of his community in a folksy, funny style, reflecting a disenchanted vision of 1950s go-ahead America rather than the expected radical sassiness, and then spends the rest of the film trying to persuade Roger Smith, the chairman of GM, to come to Flint and

confront the havoc that he has personally — the film alleges — wreaked. Moore recounts the town's failed and ridiculous attempts to establish itself as a tourist haven, and interviews various Flint celebrities. We get glimpses of Smith, and there is a horrific sequence intercutting his benevolent reading from A Christmas Carol at a GM party with shots of Flint Sheriff Fred Ross evicting people from their homes. It's been called the first 'feel-good atrocity film', and it could be accused of being too funny, too entertaining, too audience-friendly for its own political good. **KN**
Director/producer/script Michael Moore **camera** Christopher Beaver, John Prusak, Kevin Rafferty, Bruce Schermer **editors** Wendy Stanzler, Jennifer Beman
Running time: 90 mins
US release: Warner, Dec 20, 1989
UK release: Warner, Apr 20, 1990

ROMERO

An account of the last three years in the life of Oscar Romero, from his appointment in 1977 as Roman Catholic archbishop in San Salvador until his assassination by a government gunman – a consequence of his growing readiness to speak out against official corruption and political violence. The central portrait, of a reclusive priest rising almost in spite of himself to the demands of spiritual leadership, is quite persuasively presented. But the predominantly external treatment, underscored by sometimes stilted speech patterns, means that characterization is not pursued in depth, and the dramatization elsewhere tends to lean on stereotypes, so that the succession of horrifying events is at risk of becoming numbing in the wrong sense. **TP**
Director John Duigan **producer** Ellwood E. Kieser **execs** Lawrence Mortoff, John Sacret Young, Tricia Riordan **script** Young **camera** Geoff Burton **editor** Frans Vandenburg **design** Roger Ford **music** Gabriel Yared **cast** Raul Julia, Richard Jordan, Ana Alicia, Eddie Vélez, Alejandro Bracho, Tony Plana, Harold Gould, Lucy Reina, Al Ruscio, Tony Perez, Robert Viharo, Harold Cannon-Lopez, Claudio Brook, Martin Lasalle
Running time: 105 mins
US release: Four Seasons, Aug 25, 1989
UK release: Warner, Feb 23, 1990

ROOFTOPS

In Manhattan's run-down Alphabet City, there is a thriving community of healthy runaways who get their kicks from combat dancing or spray-painting graffiti. Our hero is T (Gedrick), who lives in a water tank and cultivates a rooftop garden, and he is in trouble because the local crack-dealing scumbag in a shiny suit (Velez)

wants him out of the way so he can set up a drugs concession. When Vélez kills T's best pal, our man graduates from aggressive dancercise to of the dance-based Brazilian martial art of Capoeira and goes after the bad guys. Director Robert Wise is 76 years old and presumably got this bopsical assignment on the strength of having done West Side Story in 1960. However, the weedy, posy dance/fight sequences on view here just serve to remind you that choreographer Jerome Robbins was responsible for all the best scenes of Story. If it were not for the participation of Wise this would be just another annoying, primary-coloured, cliché-ridden action-youth-music movie you could just ignore. As it is, it's hard not to imagine the grand old man tottering around the set asking the young cast to turn the music down. **KN**
Director Robert Wise **producer** Howard W. Koch Jr. **execs** Taylor Hackford, Stuart Benjamin **script** Terence Brennan, from story by Allan Goldstein, Tony Mark **camera** Theo Van de Sande **editor** William Reynolds **design** Jeannine C. Oppewall **music** David A. Stewart, Michael Kamen **cast** Jason Gedrick, Troy Beyer, Eddie Vélez, Alexis Cruz, Tisha Campbell, Allen Payne
Running time: 95 mins
US release: New Century/Vista, Mar 17, 1989
UK release: Fox, Feb 9, 1990

ROSALIE GOES SHOPPING

Following the endearing Sugarbaby and the slightly less endearing Bagdad Cafe, this third collaboration between Adlon and Sägebrecht finds the law of diminishing returns setting in. The hefty Frau Sägebrecht presides over an Arkansas family of eccentrics, including dim-witted macho hubby Carl Davis and a brood of bizarre children, and keeps them living beyond her means thanks to credit cards, cheque fraud, computer hacking and plain overspending. She confesses all her sins to priest Judge Reinhold, in the mistaken belief that Catholic absolution excuses all her legal misdemeanours and makes her loveable in the eyes of the audience. The fragile charm of the earlier pictures has become definitely strained, and one becomes increasingly impatient with the smugly larcenous Sägebrecht, almost to the point of identifying with those who want to curb her financial irregularities. **KN**
Director Percy Adlon **producers/script** Percy Adlon, Eleonore Adlon **camera** Bernd Heinl **editor** Jean-Claude Piroué **design** Stephen Lineweaver **music** Bob Telson **cast** Marianne Sägebrecht, Brad Davis, Judge Reinhold, Erika Blumberger, Willy Harlander, John Hawkes, Patricia Zehentmayr, Courtney Kraus, Alex Winter, Lisa Fitzhugh
Running time: 94 mins
US release: Four Seasons, Feb 24, 1990
UK release: Mainline, Jan 12, 1990

ROSELYNE AND THE LIONS (Roselyne et les lions)

Like all of Beineix's films, *Roselyne* is to some degree an exercise in the perverse, and its tale of a teenage boy fixated on the vocation of lion training, and in particular on a glamorous female exponent of the craft, appears at first to be a fantasy of escape from adult domination (a model which perhaps owes more to Scandinavian than to French cinema). But in a way the perversity resides in the manner in which expectations are turned inside out: despite a few sado-masochistic sidelights, the course of love and fulfilment run smooth. The unfaked lion taming sequences do create a frisson (albeit one that will hardly be appreciated by spectators who dislike the notion of performing animals) but as the film proceeds on its over-extended way, the feeling grows that these rituals contain no meaning beyond themselves, and that the fantastication does not succeed in interacting with real experience. **TP**
Director/producer *Jean-Jacques Beineix* **script** *Beineix, Jacques Forgeas* **camera** *Jean-François Robin* **editors** *Marie Castro-Bréchignac, Annick Baly, Danielle Fillios, Oswald Bargero* **design** *Carlos Conti* **music** *Reinhardt Wagner* **cast** *Isabelle Pasco, Gérard Sandoz, Philippe Clevenot, Gunter Meisner, Wolf Harnisch, Gabriel Monnet, Jacques Le Carpentier, Dimitri Furdui, Melih Duzenli, Carlos Pavlidis, Joroslav Vizner*
Running time: 137 mins
UK release: Palace, Dec 15, 1989

◄╪ ROUGE (Yanzhi Kou)

A ghost story from Hong Kong, *Rouge* has less to do with the home-grown supernatural genre of *A Chinese Ghost Story* than the lush, romantic Hollywood fantasy tradition of *The Ghost and Mrs Muir*. The fragile Anita Mui is perfectly cast as a 1930s courtesan who enters into a suicide pact with her well-born lover and then finds herself alone in limbo. She returns to the world 50 years later to try and find her lost and possibly faithless love, falling in with a mildly cynical reporter who becomes fascinated with her naïve and touching flashbacks. It's a wonderfully old-fashioned tragic love story, and Mui is marvellous as the ghostly gamine, especially in the finale where she finally discovers the embittered and wasted old man who should have joined her in death years before. Honestly sentimental in a way Western films are mainly afraid to be these days, delicately wistful in its telling use of minor details, *Rouge* is highly seductive. **KN**
Director *Stanley Kwan* **producer** *Jackie Chan* **script** *Li Bihua, Qiu-Dai Anping, from novel by Bihua* **camera** *Bill Wong* **editor** *Peter Cheung* **design** *Piao Ruomu, Horace Ma* **music** *Michael Lai* **cast** *Anita Mui, Leslie Cheung, Alex Man, Emily Chu, Irene Wan, Patrick Tse, Wang Yu, Tan*

Qianhong, Zhu Ruitang, Bruce Lau, Hui Yinghong
Running time: 96 mins
UK release: ICA Projects, Oct 20, 1989

👎 RUDE AWAKENING

Two 1960s hippies have to take it on the lam and spend 20 years in Central American seclusion; when circumstances bring them back to New York, culture shock awaits them. The scenario seems to offer some satirical possibilities, but none of them are realized in this dismally inept farce. There is no plot to speak of, which renders the impoverishment of the incidental humour all the more glaring. Not only that, but the playing is uniformly charmless, with look-ins by Buck Henry and Louise Lasser sadly attesting to their past presence in infinitely superior comedies on not unrelated themes. **TP**
Directors *Aaron Russo, David Greenwalt* **producer** *Russo* **script** *Neil Levy, Richard La Gravenese* **camera** *Tim Sigel* **editor** *Paul Fried* **design** *Mel Bourne* **music** *Jonathan Elias* **cast** *Cheech Marin, Eric Roberts, Julie Hagerty, Robert Carradine, Buck Henry, Louise Lasser, Cindy Williams, Andrea Martin, Cliff DeYoung, Aaron Russo*
Running time: 100 mins
US release: Orion, Aug 16, 1989
UK release: Rank, Mar 23, 1990

RUNNING ON EMPTY

As in *Daniel*, Sidney Lumet tells a story of what happens to the children when a couple of radicals go too far into political action. Judd Hirsch and Christine Lahti bombed a building in their anti-war years, but somebody got hurt and they spent the ensuing two decades on the run. Now their son River Phoenix is ready to leave the nest to study music and he's also in love with his music teacher's daughter, Martha Plimpton. Do they hold on to him forever or let him go and risk their safety? The teen romance is treated as seriously as the film's 'problem', resulting in a typically gripping Lumetian melodrama. **BM**
Director *Sidney Lumet* **producers** *Amy Robinson, Griffin Dunne* **execs** *Naomi Foner, Burtt Harris* **script** *Foner* **camera** *Gerry Fisher* **editor** *Andrew Mondshein* **design** *Philip Rosenberg* **music** *Tony Mottola* **cast** *Christine Lahti, River Phoenix, Judd Hirsch, Martha Plimpton, Jonas Abry, Ed Crowley, L.M. Kit Carson, Steven Hill, Augusta Dabney, David Margulies*
Running time: 116 mins
US release: Warner, Sep 9, 1988
UK release: Warner, Jul 28, 1989

REVENGE

Among Britain's more dubious exports of the past decade are those filmmakers who used to make TV commercials, and in some cases still do: Tony Scott, Adrian Lyne, Hugh Hudson and the erratic Ridley Scott all have a tendency to live beyond their aesthetic means. They are masterful creators of beautiful images that sag under the weight of their self-importance.

Tony Scott is the whoring technician par excellence. The chic trash of *The Hunger*, the noisy chases and gunplay of *Beverly Hills Cop II* and the all-American jingoism of *Top Gun* create an image of a man who has no ideas and no soul. (The worst thing about Ridley's *Black Rain* was that it was the closest he had come to his brother's unique soul-dead technical panache.)

Which brings us to *Revenge*, Tony's longest, most ambitious and worst movie. However one felt about the earlier films, at least they had action and movement: Catherine Deneuve–Susan Sarandon sex scenes, superb aerial combat sequences or car chases made each picture noisily enjoyable.

Revenge, however, is a film destroyed by ambition. It wants to be an existential story about the price to be paid for love in a corrupt world. It wants perhaps to be a John Huston movie.

Kevin Costner, for whom this is something of a vanity production, plays a fighter pilot who is retiring young (no good reason is given) to kick around the American South-West. One assumes that Scott had leftover fighter footage from *Top Gun*, so they used it here and made Costner a pilot.

Costner heads for Mexico to visit an old friend, a fantastically wealthy and powerful criminal (Anthony Quinn) with a beautiful young wife (Madeleine Stowe). She is wan and barely has a personality. He is so mean he'll toss his dog in the swimming pool if it offends him.

Can you guess what happens? Stowe doesn't love Quinn, and Costner has the same reckless streak as Tom Cruise in *Top Gun* – ah, those impetuous pilots – so Costner and Stowe, not the brightest couple ever to appear on the silver screen, have an affair, then run away to the cabin he is building in the mountains. The cabin everyone *knows* he is building in the mountains.

Up to this point *Revenge* is simply dull. Arthritically paced, staid, with postcard-pretty cinematography and all romantic explosions rapidly defused by a couple who develop no chemistry. (Since Stowe managed to strike sparks with Richard Dreyfuss, of all people, in *Stakeout*, we can't blame this one on her.) Now *Revenge* becomes genuinely offensive.

Quinn and his thugs show up. They beat the living hell out of Costner, set fire to his cabin. Then Quinn takes a razor, slashes Stowe's cheek, and has her sold to a brothel where she will practise unsafe sex and be shot up with drugs.

There's a logic problem here. If Quinn would sell his wife to a brothel for adultery, then he wouldn't let Costner off with a beating. He would probably perform a little surgery. But then this is a Hollywood movie, and in Hollywood movies one does not castrate executive producers. (Though it's worth considering.)

Costner crawls away from the burning wreck. He finds an old Mexican who helps him recuperate. He gives him his money and goes off in search of revenge. Aha! At last! Let the bad times roll!

(Brief, pleasant aside: three actors show up and give the film what life it has. James Gammon, the amiable Shorty in *The Milagro Beanfield War*, appears as an ornery, tubercular cattle-buyer. Sally Kirkland has a few scenes as a rock singer in a sleazy tavern, and she's great fun in these rowdy, borderline slut rôles. Miguel Ferrer, son of José, has a supporting rôle as a thug with a grudge against Anthony Quinn.

Costner then kills Quinn's henchmen, who show up, singly and seemingly unaware that anyone might wish them harm. Then he and Ferrer track down Quinn. They have him at gunpoint and don't kill him. (It turns out he bought Stowe back from the whorehouse and sent her to a convent.)

It's called *Revenge*. Aren't there laws about honesty in advertising? This is like *Metalstorm: The Destruction of Jared-Syn*, where there was no storm, metal or otherwise, and Jared-Syn was not destroyed. If you're going to call the wretched thing *Revenge* the hero had better take his revenge. Audiences don't expect to sit through more than two hours in order to watch Costner leave Quinn standing so he can go off to have Stowe die in his arms. They didn't spend good money for closeups of Costner staring soulfully off into the distance.

Revenge needs a complex, slightly dishonest, tainted hero (it needs an existential brooder like Bogart or James Woods). This is a hero willing to betray his best friend with said friend's wife. But what we're given is Kevin Costner, now in control of his career, making star decisions rather than dramatic decisions.

He is supposed to betray this friend because of his passion for a woman. I could buy Maria Conchita Alonso in this rôle. Or Rachel Ticotin. Or Elizabeth Peña. It needs someone with fire and passion – someone over whom a man would willingly participate in his own destruction. What it doesn't need is Madeleine Stowe, who looks and acts like a slumming *Vogue* model.

But what the film needs most of all is a director who understands out-of-control passion. Tony Scott is not that director.

If a character dies – as Stowe does – it should not be an event that simply allows the other lead to learn a lesson; it should be a shattering experience. In any case, the disproportionate punishment meted out to her reeks of the sort of neolithic sexism that saw numerous 'bad women' in Westerns take bullets so the men they loved could go off with the schoolmarm.

When Stowe is dragged off to become a junkie whore, she is clutching Costner's dogtags in her hand. When she is servicing fat, sweaty Mexicans and being shot up with heroin, she is clutching his dogtags in her hand. When she dies in Costner's arms, her hand falls open, and she's still holding the damn dogtags. Didn't the nuns ever wash her hands?

JOHN HARKNESS

THE WAR OF THE ROSES

CRIMES AND MISDEMEANORS

SWEETIE

ENEMIES, A LOVE STORY

CINEMA PARADISO

JEAN-CLAUDE VAN DAMME IN
KICKBOXER

MONKEY SHINES

ANDY GARCIA IN AMERICAN ROULETTE

FIELD OF DREAMS

JULIA ROBERTS IN STEEL MAGNOLIAS

JULIA ROBERTS IN PRETTY WOMAN

MORGAN FREEMAN IN DRIVING
MISS DAISY

LAURA SAN GIACOMO IN SEX, LIES
AND VIDEOTAPE

ROAD HOUSE

With enough echoes in its characters' names – Dalton, Garrett, Younger, Doc, Cody, Tilghman, Bass, Ketchum, etc. – and dialogue – 'I hear you're the new marshal in town' – to qualify as a latterday Western (its Missouri setting was created in LA's Santa Clarita Valley, the location of an estimated 10,000 early Hollywood Westerns), *Road House* is very nearly the perfect exploitation movie. In its blending of the lurid, the silly and the ambitious, it is pleasantly reminiscent of the populist Roger Corman-produced New World rural action movies (*Fighting Back*, *The Black Oak Conspiracy*, *Moving Violation*) of the 1970s.

Its natural home, and the place where its homely virtues would truly shine, would be a drive-in dusk-till-dawn bill in rural USA, with Coca-Cola cartons littering the lot between the speakers, a teenage audience high on weed and moonshine gazing up at the screen, and the cicadas trilling along to the soundtrack rock 'n' roll. Given the choice, 99 out of 100 real people would rather sit down with their loved ones and watch *Road House* than *The Sacrifice*, *The Story of Apu* or *Space Sluts in the Slammer*, and they would be right.

On the Joe Bob Briggs Four Bs scale, the film lacks only Beasts, but it features plentiful Blood, Breasts and Boots. In fact, it's a film with Everything: a charismatic star performance from hang-dog hunk Patrick Swayze as the enigmatic Dalton, a 'cooler' (high-powered bouncer) who is hired to take over security at the Double Deuce, a roadside saloon which is suffering from the rowdiness of its clientele; a marvellously slimy and obnoxious villain in Ben Gazzara's Wesley, a road-hog gangster who runs the town of Jasper with his band of filthy verminos and does destructive things like drive a monster tractor through a car show-room to make a point; totally gratuitous nudity courtesy of a group of strange women who wander into bars to dance on tables and Swayze who decides to wander around with no clothes on at several important plot points; and more-or-less non-stop kung-fu action as Swayze and his merry band of bouncers take on the endless succession of grudge-holding Gazzara minions who try it on in the saloon.

Swayze's hero is a philosophy graduate martial artist who sets about adding respectability to the Double Deuce – described as 'the kind of place where they sweep up the eyeballs after closing' – with the zeal that Errol Flynn once brought to keeping the outlaws out of Dodge City, and he expands his heroism by encouraging the small businessmen of Jasper to stand up to the cattle baron analogue Wesley just as Alan Ladd's *Shane* or Clint Eastwood's *Pale Rider* similarly rallied the oppressed against rotten business interests. Swayze, who gets the chance to display his pin-up body in energetic, nude bedroom scenes and when being stitched up in hospital, has enough self-awareness to be a superior action hero. In the bare-knuckled he-man stakes, he's a born American beefcake in contrast to such foreign-accented musclemen as Arnold Schwarzenegger,

Jean-Claude Van Damme, Bruce Lee and Sho Kosugi. He also stays far enough away from the Sylvester Stallone school of grunting to import a touch of real acting into the sweat-and-strain genre while retaining a sense of comedy, pitching himself somewhere between Clint Eastwood and Burt Reynolds, and leaving such pretenders as Chuck Norris, Michael Dudikoff, Steven Seagal and Robert Ginty standing with their big guns on the direct-to-video racks.

Swayze slyly sends himself up through extravagant gestures like refusing an anaesthetic as Doc, the heroine (Kelly Lynch), takes a stapler to his side or laying aside an impeccably intellectual tome in his loft apartment to gaze at the raucous partying that takes place at Wesley's mansion on the other side of the lake. After looking dopey in his last few films (*Dirty Dancing, Tiger Warsaw*), Swayze is here in his element as an intellectual action man who has to overcome his trauma-induced inability to rip out a baddie's throat, happily emerging in the finale as a complete man who can read poetry with one hand while he kills a redneck villain with the other. A comparison of this with the later, soggier Swayze action vehicle, *Next of Kin*, shows just how far ahead of the pack *Road House* is in its perfect understanding of the requirements of the genre, and of the need to play everything with just the right combination of self-mockery to prevent the familiarity of the plot from getting on an audience's nerves.

Although there's some attempt to show the workings of Dalton's highly-paid profession – he drives a 560 Mercedes Benz but buys a clunker to leave in the parking lot of the Double Deuce to serve as the butt for the anger of those he has evicted from the place – we learn very little about the art of 'cooling', and the film is always more interested in exploiting its Western parallels as a way of adding mythic resonance to the storyline than in any serious examination of how the bar business works. To the casual viewer, the old Double Deuce, with its non-stop brawling and a band performing Blues Brothers-style behind chickenwire, might even seem more appealing than the bland nightspot, with uniformed bouncers and day-glo décor, which the manager (Kevin Tighe) turns it into when the bad element has been kicked out. Indeed, the music, which comes courtesy of Dalton's blind keyboards-playing sidekick and guest star waitress Kathleen Wilhoite, gets notably less enjoyable when order has been restored. But Gazzara doesn't let peace and quiet come easy and keeps making trouble right up to the final scene, after which he isn't in any shape to return in a sequel unless Wesley has an evil twin brother stashed away somewhere.

It's perhaps symptomatic of the film's excess that Dalton should need four surrogate fathers to give him helpful words of cracker-barrel wisdom, but this at least brings in some extra suspense as we are never sure which of them will be sacrificed by the plot to spur the hero's inevitable final revenge spree. Sam Elliott, an actor who gained immensely in credibility when his stubble started to go grey, adds to his run of amiable, whiskery action men (see also *Shakedown* aka *Blue Jean Cop*, which would make a perfect double-bill partner with *Road House* at that drive-in just down the interstate from the Double Deuce) as the actual victim. Gazzara has also been allowed to have fun as the thoroughly rotten Wesley ('Brad Wesley is an evil, evil, evil man,' says Gazzara, 'that's why I like him'), who is introduced as he weaves inconsiderately all over the road in time to the song –

'Sh-Boom' – he is singing at the wheel of his gas-guzzler, and who meets his justly deserved fate amid the stuffed animals of his trophy room ('the only thing missing,' he tells Dalton of his collection, 'is your ass'). And the rest of the supporting cast grunt, sweat, wisecrack and take their punches gamely, the women more than pulling their weight for some equal-opportunity exploitation.

Otherwise, this is the sort of film where the stuntmen are more vital to the success of the venture than the speaking performers, and director Rowdy Herrington certainly lives up to the promise of his name in the kick-boxing stakes. Herrington, following up his interesting modern Jack the Ripper movie *Jack's Back*, has some trouble with the two awkward scenes between Dalton and Doc towards the end when the woman is serving too well her traditional generic purpose of trying in vain to dissuade the hero from taking the violent stand necessary to bring the film to a climax and just slowing down the inevitable, but he otherwise stages an exemplary series of kung-fu battles, bar-room brawls, G-string dance contests, explosions, car crashes, rock 'n' roll numbers, shoot-outs, knife fights and macho dialogue exchanges. By no means unsophisticated, widely misunderstood (of course) by the snotty critics, and cinematic to its last frame, *Road House* is where movies should be headed in the 1990s.

KIM NEWMAN

R

SANTA SANGRE

Alejandro Jodorowsky, purveyor of fine-bone shockers to the gentry (*El Topo*, *The Holy Mountain*), sets out to scandalize again. This time he has crafted the tale of an armless Mexican priestess with a possessive interest in her son. When not performing a look-no-arms vaudeville act with the lad, she spurs him on to murder women. Must be something Freudian here. Either that or Jodorowsky has been at the old kitsch-and-horror classics again. The film plays like a cross between *The Hands of Orlac*, Buñuel's *El* and *The Greatest Show on Earth*. Ersatz surrealism for those who can't afford or wouldn't recognize the real thing. **HK**
Director *Alejandro Jodorowsky* **producer** *Claudio Argento* **execs** *René Cardona Jr., Angelo Lacono* **script** *Jodorowsky, Roberto Leoni, Argento* **camera** *Daniele Nannuzzi* **editor** *Maura Bonanni* **design** *Alejandro Luna* **music** *Simon Boswell* **cast** *Axel Jodorowsky, Blanca Guerra, Guy Stockwell, Thelma Tixou, Sabrina Dennison, Adan Jodorowsky, Faviola Elenka Tapia, Teo Jodorowsky, Ma. de Jesus Aranzabal, Jesus Jurez*
Running time: 123 mins
US release: Expanded Entertainment, Apr 20, 1990
UK release: Mainline, Apr 13, 1990

SCENES FROM THE CLASS STRUGGLE IN BEVERLY HILLS

This is Paul Bartel's funniest-yet concoction of camp, knockabout, farce, irony, dry wit, dirty jokes and every other way to get a laugh in a dark room. Into a disgustingly rich household in Beverly Hills, Bartel tosses such types as a relieved widow (Bisset), a bisexual houseboy (Sharkey), a houseboy who resists bisexuality (Beltran), a fat diet doctor (Bartel), the ghost of Bisset's hubby (Mazursky), a lusty neighbour (Woronov), her faithless ex-husband (Shawn) and others. Bartel keeps his *Scenes* moving quickly from style to style, ensuring that everybody will find something offensive, or funny or both. **BM**
Director *Paul Bartel* **producer** *James C. Katz* **execs** *Amir J. Malin, Ira Deutchman* **script** *Bruce Wagner* **camera** *Steven Fierberg* **editor** *Alan Toomayan* **design** *Alex Tavoularis* **music** *Stanley Myers* **cast** *Jacqueline Bisset, Ray Sharkey, Robert Beltran, Mary Woronov, Ed Begley Jr., Wallace Shawn, Arnetia Walker, Rebecca Schaeffer, Barret Oliver, Edith Diaz, Paul Bartel, Paul Mazursky, Jerry Tondo, Susan Saiger*
Running time: 103 mins
US release: Cinecom, Jun 9, 1989
UK release: Rank, Jan 19, 1990

SEA OF LOVE

FILM • FILM • FILM • FILM

Director *Harold Becker* **producers** *Martin Bregman, Louis A. Stroller* **script** *Richard Price* **camera** *Ronnie Taylor* **editor** *David Bretherton* **design** *John Jay Moore* **music** *Trevor Jones* **cast** *Al Pacino, Ellen Barkin, John Goodman, Michael Rooker, William Hickey, Richard Jenkins, Paul Calderon, Gene Canfield, Larry Joshua, John Spencer, Christine Estabrook, Barbara Baxley, Patricia Barry, Jacqueline Brookes, Michael O'Neill*
Running time: 113 mins
US release: Universal, Sep 15, 1989
UK release: UIP, Feb 6, 1990

SEE NO EVIL, HEAR NO EVIL

Richard Pryor and Gene Wilder re-team hilariously as a blind man and a deaf man, respectively, who collectively 'witness' a murder. The blind man heard the shot, the deaf man saw the legs of the murderess (Severance). Without demeaning the seeing-deprived and hearing-impaired, Arthur Hiller's film is a slapstick compendium of blind and deaf jokes (yes, Pryor drives a car; yes, Wilder gets steamed when people shout at him). Non-handicap jokes abound, too. Severance is about to execute our two heroes, but first she grants Wilder's wish – a kiss. Pryor pipes up, 'I suppose a fuck is out of the question?' **BM**
Director *Arthur Hiller* **producer** *Marvin Worth* **execs** *Burtt Harris, Earl Barret, Arne Sultan* **script** *Barret, Sultan, Eliot Wald, Andrew Kurtzman, Gene Wilder* **camera** *Victor J. Kemper* **editor** *Robert C. Jones* **design** *Robert Gundlach* **music** *Stewart Copeland* **cast** *Richard Pryor, Gene Wilder, Joan Severance, Kevin Spacey, Kirsten Childs, Alan North*
Running time: 103 mins
US release: Tri-Star, May 12, 1989
UK release: Col/Tri-Star, Sep 1, 1989

SEE YOU IN THE MORNING

See You in the Morning betrays its origins as a semi-autobiographical tale, laced with burnished pop-psychology, about the anxieties of a man torn between two marriages and two families. Jeff Bridges, playing a Manhattan psychiatrist, stresses the sensitive side of his harassed sensitive guy persona as a character who eventually gets to achieve the moral high ground after learning the value of quality time with spouse and impossibly articulate kids. After a good first hour (the script is aimed at adults!) the treacle starts to set. Impossible to watch. **CB**
Director/script *Alan J. Pakula* **producers** *Pakula,*

Susan Solt **camera** Donald McAlpine **editor** Evan
Lottman **design** George Jenkins **music** Michael
Small **cast** Jeff Bridges, Alice Krige, Farrah Fawcett,
Drew Barrymore, Lukas Haas, David Dukes,
Frances Sternhagen, George Hearn, Theodore Bikel,
Linda Lavin, Heather Lilly
UK release: Warner, May 4, 1990

SEX, LIES AND VIDEOTAPE
F I L M • F I L M • F I L M • F I L M

Director/script/editor Steven Soderbergh
producers Robert Newmyer, John Hardy **execs**
Nancy Tenenbaum, Nick Wechsler, Morgan Mason
camera Walt Lloyd **design** Joanne Schmidt **music**
Cliff Martinez **cast** James Spader, Andie
MacDowell, Peter Gallagher, Laura San Giacomo,
Ron Vawter, Steven Brill
Running time: 101 mins
US release: Miramax, Aug 4, 1989
UK release: Virgin, Sep 8, 1989

SHADOW MAKERS
See Fat Man and Little Boy

SHAG
With its succession of retro-chic music, cars and
fashion, Shag is the latest in a line of teen
nostalgia films that stretches from American
Graffiti to Dirty Dancing. It resurrects the
character types and plot incidentals of Glendon
Swarthout's Where the Boys Are, mixed in with
familiar bits and pieces from other teen movies,
with the result that the film seems like a greatest-
hits compilation album of the genre. We are
presented with a wild party that trashes an
elegant mansion, a crucial dance contest in which
the underdogs suddenly display amazing footwork,
the black maid who is always wandering into
rooms where teenagers are clinching ('you is the
horniest bunch of white folks I's ever seen!'), a
mean and macho rebel who prods the soon-to-be-
settled-down queen out of her complacency, the
self-involved teen star who provides a
disappointment to his gold-digging fans, playful
defiance of parental authority, trips to the
fairground and the local lovers' lane, and the
awkward but touching relationship between two
teens who realize they aren't quite the geeks they
think themselves to be. In a young and lively
cast, only Annabeth Gish really comes across
well. **KN**
Director Zelda Barron **producers** Stephen
Woolley, Julia Chasman **execs** John Daly, Derek
Gibson, Nik Powell **script** Robin Swicord, Lanier
Laney, Terry Sweeney **camera** Peter MacDonald
editor Laurence Méry Clark **design** Buddy Cone
cast Phoebe Cates, Scott Coffey, Bridget Fonda,
Annabeth Gish, Page Hannah, Robert Rusler,

Tyrone Power Jr., Jeff Yagher
Running time: 98 mins
US release: Hemdale, Jul 21, 1989
UK release: Palace, Aug 12, 1988

SHE-DEVIL
T U R K E Y • T U R K E Y • T U R K E Y

Director Susan Seidelman **producers** Jonathan
Brett, Seidelman **script** Barry Strugatz, Mark R.
Burns, **from novel** The Life and Loves of a She-
Devil by Fay Weldon **camera** Oliver Stapleton
editor Craig McKay **design** Santo Loquasto **music**
Howard Shore **cast** Meryl Streep, Roseanne Barr,
Ed Begley Jr., Sylvia Miles, Linda Hunt, Elisebeth
Peters, Bryan Larkin, A. Martinez, Maria Pitillo,
Mary Louise Wilson
Running time: 99 mins
US release: Orion, Dec 8, 1989
UK release: Rank, May 11, 1989

SHE'S BEEN AWAY
Dear old 'Lilian' – that's Dame Peggy Ashcroft
looking pixillated – is coming out of the mental
home. The place has been closed thanks to Mrs
Thatcher, and now the nice old bat can come
and stay with rich nephew James Fox and his
pregnant wife Geraldine James. Soon Miss J and
Dame P are quarelling all over the Laura Ashley
furniture; until suddenly, recognizing a kinship
beneath the banter, they decide to run away
together. Why? I have no idea. Ask writer
Stephen Poliakoff. Possibly they have just seen
Rain Man. Anyway, they whoop it up across
England while Mr Fox frets to the police and
director Peter Hall tries to urge some sense into
an increasingly silly story. Nice acting; some
timely tilts at Tory health cuts; otherwise a blend
of coyness and contrivance. **HK**
Director Peter Hall **producer** Kenith Trodd **script**
Stephen Poliakoff **camera** Philip Bonham-Carter
editor Ardan Fisher **design** Gary Wilkinson **music**
Richard Hardley **cast** Peggy Ashcroft, Geraldine
James, James Fox, Jackson Kyle, Rebecca Pidgeon,
Rosalie Crutchley, Rachel Kempson, Hugh Lloyd
Running time: 106 mins
UK release: BBC Enterprises, Sep 22, 1989

SHIRLEY VALENTINE
There's something reassuringly old-fashioned
about this second Willy Russell–Lewis Gilbert
collaboration (Educating Rita was the first) which
gives it a charm usually lacking in British films.
Convincingly opened out from Russell's original
one-hander, it's still very much Pauline Collins'
show; she plays a Liverpool housewife worn down
by routine who rediscovers what she used to like
about herself while on a holiday to Mykonos. The
rest of the cast are also impressive, even though

Tom Conti lays on the Zorba accent a bit thick and, with its snappy, accurate one-liners and refreshingly likeable characters, the film never lets its wish fulfilment get the better of its humanity. **TW**
Director/producer *Lewis Gilbert* **exec** *John Dark* **script** *Willy Russell, from his play* **camera** *Alan Hume* **editor** *Lesley Walker* **design** *John Stoll* **music** *George Hadjinassios, Russell* **cast** *Pauline Collins, Tom Conti, Julia McKenzie, Alison Steadman, Joanna Lumley, Sylvia Syms, Bernard Hill, George Costigan, Anna Keaveney, Tracie Bennett, Ken Sharrock, Karen Craig, Gareth Jefferson*
Running time: 108 mins
US release: Paramount, Aug 20, 1989
UK release: UIP, Oct 13, 1989

▼ A SHOCK TO THE SYSTEM

Not a lot of people know this, but missing out on promotion can make men murderous. Take Michael Caine. He's been passed over for a top job in his New York firm by smoothie colleague Peter Riegert. So what does he do? Naturally he goes home and murders the wife (Kurtz). Electrocutes her in the cellar. There. Now, what next? Well, detective Will Patton gets suspicious and so does girlfriend Elizabeth McGovern, anxious Mr Caine develops a nasty case of the voice-over soliloquies; and the film grinds on like an Edgar Lustgarten quickie translated to New England. Can Mr C escape the law? Can director Jan Egleson make us care? Is there another film showing in the cinema? **HK**
Director *Jan Egleson* **producer** *Patrick McCormick* **exec** *Leslie Morgan* **script** *Andrew Klavan, from novel by Simon Brett* **camera** *Paul Goldsmith* **editor** *Peter C. Frank, William A. Anderson* **design** *Howard Cummings* **music** *Gary Chang* **cast** *Michael Caine, Elizabeth McGovern, Peter Riegert, Swoosie Kurtz, Will Patton, Jenny Wright, John McMartin, Barbara Baxley, Haviland Morris, Philip Moon*
Running time: 87 mins
US release: Corsair, Mar 23, 1990

SHOCKER

Having lost control of the *Nightmare on Elm Street* series, Wes Craven attempts with *Shocker* to kick-start a new splatter series. While it's by no means down in the trough with the worst of Craven (*Deadly Friend*), it doesn't really hang together either, and the baneful spectre of the razor-fingered Freddy loiters around in the background, tactfully reminding you that, despite a few new ideas, this film is very obviously patterned on the initial *Elm Street* movie. There's a serial killer slaughtering families in a small American town, and the hero (Berg) has bad

dreams in which he sees the maniac at work. When he dreams of the murder of his adopted mother and siblings, Jonathan helps his cop pop (Murphy) identify TV repairman Horace Pinker (Pileggi) as the killer. The police manage to track down Pinker and he gets condemned to the electric chair. In the execution chamber, Pinker dramatically reveals the source of his psychic link with Jonathan and vows to return from beyond the grave. After the fry-up, Pinker inhabits the same section of the afterlife as Freddy, and keeps popping up to make trouble. Craven's script is all over the place – and the last act is almost impossible to follow – but he can still stage individual suspense sequences with flair. **KN**
Director/script *Wes Craven* **producers** *Marianne Maddalena, Barin Kumar* **execs** *Shep Gordon, Craven* **camera** *Jacques Haitkin* **editor** *Andy Blumenthal* **design** *Cynthia Kay Charette* **music** *William Goldstein* **cast** *Michael Murphy, Peter Berg, Cami Cooper, Mitch Pileggi, John Tesh, Heather Langenkamp, Jessica Craven, Richard Brooks, Sam Scarber, Timothy Leary*
Running time: 110 mins
US release: Universal, Oct 27, 1989
UK release: Guild, Apr 20, 1990

A SHORT FILM ABOUT KILLING (Krótki Film o Zabijaniu)

Featurized like *A Short Film About Love* from an episode in Krzysztof Kieślowski's *Ten Commandments* TV series, *A Short Film About Killing* is played off against the implacable streets and public buildings of Warsaw, and shot through filters to achieve a drained and 'sicklied over' look. The film is at once rigorously pared down and oppressively detailed as it recounts two acts of murder – the killing of a taxi driver for small change by a young drifter, and the youth's subsequent execution for the crime. The intermediary is the humane lawyer who defends the boy at his trial, but he is not utilized as a propagandist instrument. It is, in fact, the very impossibility of feeling any sympathy for the reptilian murderer which renders him vulnerable, and makes his hanging particularly horrific. Arguably gratuitous, it's a work of existential intensity, whose images the mind's eye proves disconcertingly unwilling to shed. **TP**
Director *Krzysztof Kieślowski* **producer** *Ryszard Chutkowski* **script** *Krzysztof Piesiewicz, Kieślowski* **camera** *Slawomir Idziak* **design** *Ewa Smal* **editor** *Ewa Smal* **design** *Halina Dobrowolska* **music** *Zbigniew Preisner* **cast** *Miroslaw Baka, Krzysztof Globisz, Jan Tesarz, Zbigniew Zapasiewicz, Barbara Dziekan-Vajda, Aleksander Bednarz, Jerzy Zass, Zdzislaw Tobiasz, Artur Barciś*
Running time: 84 mins
UK release: Gala, Nov 17, 1989

👎 A SHORT FILM ABOUT LOVE (Krótki Film o Milosci)

Another featurized episode from Krzysztof Kieślowski's *Ten Commandments* TV series, this gem-like masterpiece is the tale of a young peeping Tom who falls for the beautiful, uncurtained neighbour. It's at once romantic and seditious, touching and satirical. Bureaucratic intervention is spoofed in the boy's attempt to reach his quarry. (He interferes in her post, her gas supply, her milk deliveries.) And when hunter and hunted finally meet, they start to exchange rôles. Perhaps in pre-freedom Poland, a surveillance culture teaches you to love your watchers. Perhaps too – as voyeur movies have shown us from *Rear Window* to *Stakeout* – the romance of spying communicates its passion even to the spied-on. Riveting. **HK**
Director *Krzysztof Kieślowski* **producer** *Ryszard Chutkowski* **script** *Krzysztof Piesiewicz, Kieślowski* **camera** *Witold Adamek* **editor** *Ewa Smal* **design** *Halina Dobrowolska* **music** *Zbigniew Preisner* **cast** *Grażyna Szapolowska, Olaf Lubaszenko, Stefania Iwińska, Piotr Machalica, Artur Barciś*
Running time: 87 mins
UK release: Gala, Mar 30, 1990

SIDEWALK STORIES

At a time when Spike Lee and the Hudlin Brothers are outdoing each other in the hyperkinetic department, Charles Lane weighs in with a black and white, *silent* film about homeless New Yorkers. Clearly indebted to Chaplin's *The Kid*, *Sidewalk Stories* features Lane as a sensitive street artist who winds up as custodian of an enormously cute little girl. The script (and the canny use of the kid) often match Chaplin's blend of comedy and pathos, but Lane himself isn't quite the actor that the rôle demands. **CB**
Director/producers/script *Charles Lane* **execs** *Howard M. Brickner, Vicki Lebenbaum* **camera** *Bill Dill* **editors** *Anne Stein, Lane* **design** *Ina Mayhew* **music** *Marc Marder* **cast** *Charles Lane, Nicole Alysia, Sandye Wilson, Darnell Williams, Trula Hoosier*
Running time: 97 mins
US release: Island, Nov 3, 1989

👎 SISTERS (Some Girls in US)

A smart, intelligent and often very funny movie about one of those weekends that just doesn't work out the way it was planned. College student Patrick Dempsey goes with girlfriend Connolly to her family home and finds her running hot and cold on him, while he becomes caught up with her two captivating sisters. If that isn't confusing enough, her father writes in the nude (clothes constrict his imagination), her mother is fiercely religious and their amazing house is Alice's Wonderland relocated to an art gallery. Plot is not the strong point here; ambience and illusion are all as Dempsey's Everyman tries vainly to make sense of a group of people who so deeply live their notions of art – even the sisters think they are Botticelli's Three Graces – that they can never quite grasp the real world. A genuine original. **TW**
Director *Michael Hoffman* **producer** *Rick Stevenson* **script** *Rupert Walters* **camera** *Ueli Steiger* **editor** *David Spiers* **cast** *Patrick Dempsey, Jennifer Connelly, Sheila Kelly, André Gregory, Lance Edwards, Lila Kedrova, Florinda Bolkan, Ashley Greenfield, Jean-Louis Millette*
Running time: 94 mins
US release: MGM, Sep 9, 1988
UK release: UIP, Jan 19, 1990

👎 SKI PATROL

This is *Police Academy* on skis, without jokes. The scenery is nice but life has so much more to offer than films like this. **TW**
Director *Richard Correll* **producers** *Philip B. Goldfine, Donald L. West* **exec** *Paul Maslansky* **script** *Steven Long Mitchell, Craig W. Van Sickle* **camera** *John Stephens* **editor** *Scott Wallace* **design** *Fred Weiler* **music** *Bruce Miller* **cast** *Roger Rose, Corby Timbrok, T.K. Carter, Leslie Jordan, George Lopez, Martin Mull, Ray Walston, Paul Fieg, Tess, Sean Gregory Sullivan*
Running time: 91 mins
US release: Triumph, Jan 12, 1990
UK release: Entertainment, Jun 15, 1990

SKIN DEEP

This Blake Edwards sex comedy may be his best work of recent years – and contains the funniest safe-sex scene to date – but still ends up being rather superficial. John Ritter plays yet another self-obsessed Californian writer sleeping his way through most of the supporting cast before seeing the light in time for yet another Dreadful Warning finale (wife leaves him, best friend dies). We never really care, despite John Ritter's boy-next-door charm, but it's a painless couple of hours, and the luminous condom joke (the main selling point in the ad campaign) is almost worth the price of admission. **TW**
Director/script *Blake Edwards* **producer** *Tony Adams* **execs** *James G. Robinson, Joe Roth* **camera** *Isidore Mankofsky* **editor** *Robert Pergament* **design** *Rodger Maus* **cast** *John Ritter, Vincent Gardenia, Alyson Reed, Joel Brooks, Julianne Phillips, Chelsea Field, Peter Donat, Don Gordon, Nina Foch, Denise Crosby, Michael Kidd*
Running time: 101 mins
US release: Fox, Mar 3, 1989
UK release: Fox, Jul 7, 1989

SLAVES OF NEW YORK

James Ivory, never one to raise many smiles, reproduces the milieu from Tama Janowitz's book of interlocked stories about struggling artists in lower Manhattan but omits the humour. Bernadette Peters, about twice the age of Janowitz's heroine and far too pretty, can't afford Manhattan unless she keeps rooming with cretinous artist Colman Howard. She makes hats out of junk she finds in bins but has yet to make a commercial connection. Others in the gallery world push and thrive but Peters just cooks and irons for Howard. In a tacked-on resolution, she finally gets her millinery accepted and moves into a place of her own. **BM**
Director *James Ivory* **producers** *Ismail Merchant, Gary Hendler* **script** *Tama Janowitz, from her stories* **camera** *Tony Pierce-Roberts* **editor** *Katherine Wenning* **design** *David Gropman* **music** *Richard Robbins* **cast** *Bernadette Peters, Adam Coleman Howard, Nick Corri, Madeleine Potter, Charles McCaughan, Chris Sarandon, Mary Beth Hurt, Mercedes Ruehl, John Harkins, Anna Katarina, Bruce Peter Young, Michael Schoeffling, Steve Buscemi, Christine Dunford*
Running time: 121 mins
US release: Tri-Star, Mar 17, 1989
UK release: Col/Tri-Star, Aug 18, 1989

SOCIETY

Brian Yuzna's film offers reassuring proof that the rich really are different — a species of incestuous blue-bloods in fact who rearrange their bodies and literally (in the case of a psychiatrist) talk out of their arses whilst preying on the under-privileged. A finale of amazing special effects and literal-minded social satire is preceded by a rather under-nourished build-up as Billy Warlock is driven by suspicion of his family to increasing paranoia, fueled by the prompt disappearance of anyone who tells him they have information to impart. Like a lot of genre items, this is a film that exists almost entirely for its finale. But when the finale is this good, who cares? **TW**
Director *Brian Yuzna* **producer** *Keith Walley* **execs** *Paul White, Keizo Kabata, Terry Ogisu* **script** *Woody Keith, Rick Fry* **camera** *Rick Fichter* **editor** *Peter Teschner* **design** *Matthew C. Jacobs* **music** *Mark Ryder, Phil Davies* **cast** *Bill Warlock, Devin DeVasquez, Evan Richards, Ben Meyerson, Charles Lucia, Connie Danese, Patrice Jennings, Heidi Kozak, Ben Slack, David Wiley, Tim Bartell, Brian Bremer, Maria Claire, Conan Yuzna*
Running time: 99 mins
UK release: Medusa, Apr 6, 1990

☞ SPACED INVADERS

This alien-creature parody positively creaks with each scene change. Little green standup comics in latex monster suits (well, they're supposed to be an alien invading force) show up in a small town and almost destroy the place with their 'amusing' stupidity. The joke is that they arrive on Halloween night just as Orson Welles' *War of the Worlds* is being re-broadcast. Most adults will find the film unwatchable though it holds some appeal for the adolescent-minded. **CB**
Director *Patrick Read Johnson* **producer** *Luigi Cingolani* **exec** *George Zecevic* **script** *Johnson, Scott Lawrence Alexander* **camera** *James L. Carter* **editors** *Seth Gaven, Daniel Gross* **design** *Tony Tremblay* **music** *David Russo* **cast** *Douglas Barr, Royal Dano, Ariana Richards, J. J. Anderson, Gregg Berger, Wayne Alexander, Kevin Thompson*
Running time: 100 mins
US release: BV, April 27, 1990

SPEAKING PARTS

The cinema's answer to the Rubik cube. Atom (*Family Viewing*) Egoyan's movie presents four characters in a hotel and defies you to work out their relationships. Gigolo, chambermaid, film director and screenwriter: two men, two women and many a weird encounter in bedroom and boardroom and on video screen. Is life in a hi-tech Marienbad worth the price of room service? Egoyan's film is sleekly shot and acted. But despite flashes of surreal wit and video-age satire, suspicion grows that when the cube is solved all it will reveal is the message 'Breakdown of communication in a golden age of communications'. **HK**
Director/script *Atom Egoyan* **exec** *Don Ranvaud* **camera** *Paul Sarossy* **editor** *Bruce McDonald* **design** *Linda Del Rosario* **music** *Mychael Danna* **cast** *Michael McManus, Arsinée Khanjian, Gabrielle Rose, Tony Nardi, David Hemblen, Patricia Collins, Gerard Parkes*
Running time: 92 mins
US release: Zeitgeist, Feb 16, 1990
UK release: Recorded Releasing (Oasis), Sep 15, 1989

SPLENDOR

Recounting the life and times of a small Italian cinema from its opening (in 1937 with *Scipio L'Africano*) to its decline and fall in the 1980s, *Splendor* culminates in literally Capraesque fashion with a re-enactment of the Christmas climax from *It's a Wonderful Life* as the old regulars flood back to prevent the picture palace's closure. The project is a sympathetic one, but the effect it creates is oddly muddled: the fortunes of the cinema owner (Mastroianni) and sundry other characters seem hardly to bisect with those of the Splendor itself, and the selection of extracts tends, with name-dropping implausibility, towards movies by such as Bergman and Truffaut. One or two irresistible

moments, however, such as that in which the movie-mad projectionist improvises a bedtime story for his girlfriend's offspring by recounting the plot of *Ace in the Hole*. **TP**
Director/script *Ettore Scola* **producers** *Mario Cecchi Gori, Vittorio Cecchi Gori* **camera** *Luciano Tovoli* **editor** *Francesco Malvestito* **design** *Luciano Ricceri* **music** *Armando Trovaioli* **cast** *Marcello Mastroianni, Massimo Troisi, Marina Vlady, Paolo Panelli, Pamela Villoresi, Giacomo Piperno, Massimo Bartocini, Mauro Bosco, Ferruccio Castronuovo*
Running time: 99 mins
UK release: Warner, Aug 4, 1989

STANLEY & IRIS

Jane Fonda betrays Pat Barker's source novel (a hymn to the solidarity of working women in the north of England) by relocating it and Reaganizing it into a tale of two no-hopers pulling themselves up to where they belong by their own endeavours. The film bears so little resemblance to its supposed source that you wonder why they bothered to buy the novel in the first place. Iris works in a factory; Stanley is the illiterate handyman who asks her to teach him to read. And hey, guess what, not only does he regain his self-respect but he falls in love with her and, just to show how far he has come, invents an assembly-line robot that will put all Fonda's pals at the factory on the dole queue. Fonda excludes from the script anything that threatens to make her look bad without thinking about the knock-on effect on narrative, character or theme and she ensures De Niro doesn't get enough of a rôle to threaten her limelight. **TW**
Director *Martin Ritt* **producers** *Arlene Sellers, Alex Winitsky* **exec** *Patrick Palmer* **script** *Harriet Frank Jr, Irving Ravetch, from novel* Union Street *by Pat Barker* **camera** *Donald McAlpine* **editor** *Sidney Levin* **design** *Joel Schiller* **music** *John Williams* **cast** *Jane Fonda, Robert De Niro, Swoosie Kurtz, Martha Plimpton, Harley Cross, Jamey Sheridan, Feodor Chaliapin*
Running time: 105 mins
US release: MGM, Feb 9, 1990
UK release: UIP, Jun 22, 1990

STAR TREK V: THE FINAL FRONTIER

Jaw-dropping in its ghastliness, the fifth big-screen *Star Trek* opens unpromisingly with a Vulcan mystic (Luckinbill) using some Californian est therapy to dissuade an alien with a bad gum condition from killing him, and then hilariously cuts to a young, fit he-man scrambling up the side of a mountain in Yosemite National Park. No sooner has the stunt man reached the top

than he turns to the camera and is replaced by the wheezing, podgy William Shatner, who is back not only as Captain Kirk but as the megaphone man. Leonard Nimoy didn't do such a good job on the last two 'Treks', but Shatner's work here makes old pointy-ears look like Martin Scorsese. The plot has to do with Luckinbill hijacking the USS Enterprise and taking it on a remarkably unperilous trip through the great barrier, and on to meet God. With a rubbishy script, a cast who are well past their sell-by stardate and some remarkably ugly visuals, this is the least appetizing sci-fi spectacular since *The Black Hole*. **KN**
Director *William Shatner* **producer** *Harve Bennett* **exec** *Ralph Winter* **script** *David Loughery, from story by Shatner, Bennett and Loughery based on TV series created by Gene Roddenberry* **camera** *Andrew Laszlo* **editor** *Peter Berger* **design** *Herman Zimmerman* **sfx** *Bran Ferren* **music** *Jerry Goldsmith* **cast** *William Shatner, Leonard Nimoy, DeForest Kelley, James Doohan, Walter Koenig, Nichell Nichols, George Takei, David Warner*
Running time: 106 mins
US release: Paramount, Jun 9, 1989
UK release: UIP, Oct 20, 1989

STAYING TOGETHER

This makes all those warm-hearted family-boosters Hollywood keeps churning out look like the kandy-coloured TV-schlock they are. Set in a small Carolina town, *Staying Together* follows three sons and their imperfect parents as they make the mistakes and brave decisions involved in living with families. No major surprises here, only superb performances, assured direction and warmth that doesn't depend on punchlines and insta-crises. It's no surprise that Lee Grant's greatest skill is with actors. Even the smallest rôles are fully drawn. **CB**
Director *Lee Grant* **producer** *Joseph Feury* **execs** *John Daly, Derek Gibson* **script** *Monte Merrick* **camera** *Dick Bush* **editor** *Katherine Wenning* **design** *W. Steven Graham* **cast** *Sean Astin, Stockard Channing, Melinda Dillon, Jim Haynie, Levon Helm, Dinah Manoff, Dermot Mulroney, Tim Quill, Keith Szarabajka, Daphne Zuniga*
Running time: 91 mins
US release: Hemdale, Nov 19, 1989

STEEL MAGNOLIAS

This is what happens when a group of high-profile actresses get together in a three-hankie weepie about a young mother (Roberts) who has a fatal disease. Feckless menfolk loiter in the background as the drama staggers from festival to festival – with Daryl Hannah giving a different terrible performance in each episode – and the sad, sad story develops in the background.

Tiresomely dotty, *Steel Magnolias* is set in the Deep South and never lets you forget it, with plentiful strained accents and picturesque eccentricities. Essentially a cat fight as to who gets the Oscar, Field emerges as the frontrunner with the biggest emotional breakdown scene. Unquestionably the most irksome pretence at character acting comes from MacLaine as the horrible neighbourhood hag who turns out to be quite decent really and is dragged around everywhere by a huge hound. **KN**
Director *Herbert Ross* **producer** *Ray Stark* **exec** *Victoria White* **script** *Robert Harling, from his play* **camera** *John A. Alonzo* **editor** *Paul Hirsch* **design** *Gene Callahan, Edward Pisoni* **music** *Georges Delerue* **cast** *Sally Field, Dolly Parton, Shirley MacLaine, Daryl Hannah, Olympia Dukakis, Julia Roberts, Tom Skerritt, Sam Shepard, Dylan McDermott, Kevin J. O'Connor, Bill McCutcheon*
Running time: 117 mins
US release: Tri-Star, Nov 15, 1989
UK release: Columbia-Tri-Star, Feb 9, 1990

STELLA

This remake of *Stella Dallas* is a vehicle for Bette Midler, but the material was old at the time of the King Vidor/Barbara Stanwyck version, and has not been re-thought to make sense in a modern context. Midler, who probably cannot spell 'subtle', plays the sacrificing mom as an emotional terrorist, and doesn't notice that her co-stars steal scenes simply by being attentive. Unbelievably bad. **JH**
Director *John Erman* **producers** *Samuel Goldwyn Jr.* **exec** *David V. Picker* **script** *Robert Getchell* **camera** *Billy Williams* **editor** *Jerrold L. Ludwig* **design** *Jeffrey Ginn* **music** *John Morris* **cast** *Bette Midler, John Goodman, Trini Alvarado, Stephen Collins, Marsha Mason, Eileen Brennan, Linda Hart*
Running time: 114 mins
US release: BV, Feb 2, 1990
UK release: Rank, Sep 7, 1990

STEPFATHER II

Joseph Ruben's *The Stepfather* had Donald Westlake's brilliant script, working the conceit that a man without identity might move from town to town, inserting himself in broken families in a pathological quest for the utopia of the American. The sequel doesn't have Ruben or Westlake. It is standard horror sequel-making, and one wonders why they bothered. **JH**
Director *Jeff Burr* **producers** *William Burr, Darin Scott* **exec** *Carol Lampman* **script** *John Auerbach* **camera** *Jacek Laskus* **editor** *Pasquale A. Buba* **design** *Bernadette Disanto* **music** *Jim Manzie* **cast** *Terry O'Quinn, Meg Foster, Caroline Williams, Jonathan Brandis, Henry Brown, Mitchell Laurance*

Running time: 86 mins
US release: Millimeter, Nov 3, 1989

A STRANGE PLACE TO MEET (Drôle d'endroit pour une rencontre)

Strange is the word for this exercise in watered-down *amour fou* and minimalist drama. The entire action passes at a motorway lay-by and cafeteria, where Catherine Deneuve, an abandoned middle-class wife, meets up with Gérard Depardieu, an enigmatic doctor whose car has (symbolically?) broken down. The setting is quite strikingly caught in Charlie Van Damme's camerawork, but once the non-relationship at the centre has been set up, the film proves to have next to nothing to make of it, other than to let Deneuve have a fling with some loutishly priapic lorry drivers. The two stars drive away together at the end, but only in a predictable spirit of anti-climax. **TP**
Director *François Dupeyron* **producer** *Patrick Bordier* **script** *Dupeyron, Dominique Faysse* **camera** *Charlie Van Damme* **editor** *Françoise Collin* **design** *Carlos Conti* **cast** *Catherine Deneuve, Gérard Depardieu, André Wilms, Nathalie Cardone, Jean-Pierre Sentier, Alain Rimoux, Vincent Martin, Philippe Faure*
Running time: 98 mins
UK release: Artificial Eye, Sep 8, 1989

STRAPLESS

DISAPPOINTMENT

Director/script *David Hare* **producer** *Rick McCallum* **camera** *Andrew Dunn* **editor** *Edward Marnier* **design** *Roger Hall* **music** *Nick Bicât* **cast** *Blair Brown, Bruno Ganz, Bridget Fonda, Alan Howard, Michael Gough, Hugh Laurie, Suzanne Burden, Rohan McCullough, Billie Roche, Camille Coduri, Gary O'Brien, Spencer Leigh*
Running time: 100 mins
US release: Miramax, May 20, 1990
UK release: Virgin, Mar 23, 1990

THE SUMMER OF AVIYA (Hakayitz shel Aviya)

In an Israeli village during the early 1950s, the ten-year-old Aviya, poor and completely shorn by her mother for having lice, escapes into a fantasy life to avoid maternal dominance. Her mother bears a mark deeper than her poverty – a serial number tattooed on her forearm. In this village swelled by Holocaust survivors, the pressure to conform seems even greater, driving both Aviya and her mother into craziness. The pathos here often seems manipulative but, with performances this good, one can almost forgive the easy sentiment. **CB**

Director Eli Cohen **producers** Eitan Evan, Gila Almagor **script** Cohen, Almagor, Chaim Buzaglo, from novel and play by Almagor **camera** David Gurfinkel **editor** Tova Ne'eman **design** Yoram Shayer **music** Shem-Tov Levi **cast** Gila Almagor, Kaipo Cohen, Eli Cohen, Marina Rossetti, Avital Dicker, Dina Avrech, Y'Akov Ayali, Rami Baruch, Yossi Kanz, Ruth Weinsbik
Running time: 95 mins
UK release: Mutual, Mar 9, 1990

THAT SUMMER OF WHITE ROSES

A British-Yugoslav coproduction, White Roses adheres to some of the most threadbare conventions of East European cinema in purveying a tragi-comic tale set in a backwater community in Yugoslavia near the end of the war. Violence and bloodshed hover on the margins of the situation, and then erupt centre-stage in an incoherently ironic climax. The director brings a notable lack of cinematic rhythm to the tale, quite apart from a seeming unfamiliarity with the rhythms of English speech. Pleasant performances by Tom Conti, playing a sort of 'holy fool' beach lifeguard, and by his attractive mongrel dog, afford only meagre compensation. **TP**
Director Rjako Grlic **producers** Simon MacCorkindale, Zdrauko Mihalic **execs** Susan George, Suljeman Kapic **script** Borislav Pekic, Kajko Grlic, MacCorkindale, from novel Defense and the Last Days by Pekic **camera** Tomislav Pinter **editor** Damir German **design** Dinka Jericevic **music** Bane Zivkovic, Junior Campbell, Mike O'Donnell **cast** Tom Conti, Susan George, Rod Steiger, Nitzan Sharron, Alun Armstrong, John Gill, John Sharp, Geoffrey Whitehead, Miljenko Brlecic, Vanja Drach, Slobodan Sembera
Running time: 103 mins
UK release: Premier, Feb 9, 1990

SUR

Latin American political 'musical' from the once-estimable, now apparently write-off Fernando Solanas (Hour of the Furnaces). Released from five years in prison under the Argentinian junta, Floreal (Sola) returns home one night. But what a night: padded out with flashbacks, kitsched up with shoestring scenic effects (billowing pamphlets, studio mist) and scored for woozy tunes from a barber-shop combo who stand and deliver in the middle of the street. The film plays as if Ken Russell had turned up one day, sketched out a few wacky ideas, then realized money was short and pushed off to the nearest pub. No chance for the struggling love story to come through, let alone any cogent political theme or thesis. **HK**

Director/script/design Fernando E. Solanas **producers** Envar El Kadri, Solanas, Patricia Novat, Pierre Novat **execs** Sabina Sigler, Djamila Olivesi **camera** Felix Monti **editor** Juan Carlos Macias, Pablo Mari **music** Astor Piazzolla, Anibal Troilo **cast** Miguel Angel Sola, Susu Pecoraro, Philippe Léotard, Lito Cruz, Ulises Dumont, Robert Goyeneche, Gabriela Toscano, Mario Lozano, Nathan Pinzon, Antonio Ameijeiras, Ines Molina, Fito Paez, Nini Gambiert, Chany Mallo
Running time: 119 mins (127 originally)
UK release: Gala, Feb 2, 1990

SWEETIE

FILM • FILM • FILM • FILM

Director Jane Campion **producer** John Maynard **script** Gerard Lee, Campion **camera** Sally Bongers **editor** Veronika Haussler **design** Peter Long, Peter Harris **music** Martin Armiger **cast** Genevieve Lemon, Karen Colston, Tom Lycos, Jon Darling, Dorothy Barry, Michael Lake, André Pataczek, Jean Hadgraft, Paul Livingston, Louise Fox, Ann Merchant, Robyn Frank, Bronwyn Morgan
Running time: 100 mins
US release: Avenue, Jan 19, 1990
UK release: Electric, May 4, 1990

SEA OF LOVE

I t has been very strange to follow Hollywood's response to the AIDS plague. During the condom summer of a year or two ago, Janet Maslin of the *New York Times* accused *The Squeeze* of having a 'pre-AIDS consciousness' because the hero went to bed with a villainous woman whom he'd just met in a bar while giving no evidence that any form of protection had been used. This was a pretty strange charge to lay on *The Squeeze*, which was really just a bad movie. But apart from occasional coy condom scenes in movies from *Dragnet* to *Cross My Heart*, and outside defiantly non-mainstream (i.e. gay) work like *Parting Glance*, AIDS is a subject that movies have refused to deal with as anything but a side issue.

The word AIDS is never mentioned in *Sea of Love*, nor is the issue of condoms in sex scenes ever raised, but that doesn't stop the subject from resonating through the movie. The film looks like a mystery – a singularly under-populated mystery with a small cast that features far too few red herrings, and narrative holes that one could drive a small delivery van through. But the mystery – who is the personal ads killer? – is of less interest and importance than the film's love story and its subtext.

Director Harold Becker is nobody's *auteur*. A tame transcriber of the work of powerful writers, he is not as personality-free as, say, Arthur Hiller, but nor is he someone worth studying for revelations of a powerful personal vision. His breakthrough films were adaptations of Joseph Wambaugh's *The Onion Field* and *The Black Marble*. In *Sea of Love*, he works fruitfully with another novelist, Bronx-born Richard Price (*The Wanderers*, *The Color of Money*).

Price's gifts are not essentially narrative. *The Wanderers*, his best-known novel (and an under-rated film) is an impressionistic portrait of a moment in social history. The same thing can be said of *Sea of Love*. Price is a New Yorker to his bones, and he knows the costs of the last decade in emotional fear and suspicion.

The subtexts of sexual disease and emotional dis-ease are so closely intertwined that one senses the two might actually operate as cause and effect, the way that some researchers have suggested that the stress of thinking about cancer might actually cause cancer. If the theme song of New York's single life is Pat Benatar's 'Love Is a battlefield', then *Sea of Love* is a movie about the walking wounded.

Someone has killed two men who placed ads in the personal columns of a New York weekly. The men were shot in the back of the head at close range. Two detectives are assigned to the case – Al Pacino, giving his best film performance in a decade and his first since the disastrous *Revolution*, and the ever-reliable John Goodman as his drunken partner. Pacino is a divorced, burnt-out cop who makes drunken late-night calls to his ex-wife, now married to one of his co-workers.

Goodman and Pacino place their own ad in hopes of attracting the killer. They draw an assortment of women (nice portrait of Manhattan singles desperation) and then Ellen Barkin arrives, a vision of tight red leather and unbridled sexual aggression. After some minor preliminaries and against the advice of Goodman, Pacino takes her out, doesn't get her prints (well, he does, but not on any part of him that can be dusted by a police lab) and begins a relationship with her that is tainted by his suspicion and spiced by their mutual insatiability.

The key scene is their first night in his apartment. They are busy getting very sweaty when she asks him the way to the bathroom. He points her at it and, as she enters, he spots the handle of a gun in her purse. If *Sea of Love* is a film about AIDS, then this is the most powerful and precise symbol imaginable. The purse, with its feminine connotations and traditional vaginal symbolism, contains not merely a phallic symbol, but a lethal phallic symbol.

Then, when she comes out of the bathroom, Pacino's cop instincts take over and he frisks her – searching for death. The imagery could not be more exact if he had asked to see the results of her last blood test. As a practical image (Barkin carries it 'because there are lots of creeps out there') it functions as an emotional symbol of the absence of trust and the dangers of relationships in the present age.

Sea of Love takes its power from the universality of its subtext. Everyone who has not yet found the stability of the couple is out there, on edge, usually looking for love in all the wrong places and finding something else. Nobody ever told us that the sexual revolution was actually a game of musical chairs. The person you were with when the music stopped was the person you were with. Period.

What gives *Sea of Love* its flavour is the specificity of Richard Price's script. It's the element that elevates New York films above those pictures set in cities with less defined personalities – the way that New York writers and directors use the voices, the neighbourhood styles, the Balkanization that is New York's dominant feature.

Price has a vivid perspective on his fellow Gothamites, and he draws on that in developing the Pacino character. The best line of dialogue comes when the police are deciding whether victim number one knew his killer. (They only found the victim because the killer had left a song playing on the turntable – the eponymous 'Sea of Love' – that finally got on the nerves of the next-door neighbour.) 'Nobody whips out his old records on anything but the first or second date when they're doing the wonder-of-me thing, showing that you're sensitive because you kept your old singles – once you know'em, who gives a shit?' It's a line written by someone who's spent some time in the singles trenches and knows the nature of that war.

Sea of Love is a powerful evocation of a certain place and moment in the war between the sexes, depicting the shifting alliances and unreliable ground across which two distressed and shattered armies stare. In an age that sees numberless hordes rushing into the haven of coupledom, this is a movie that honours the casualties.

JOHN HARKNESS

SEX, LIES AND VIDEOTAPE

French critics missed the point when Steven Soderbergh made Cannes history by winning the festival at age 26 with his first film. The chauvinists preferred Bertrand Blier's *Trop belle pour toi!* – and took umbrage at Soderbergh's confession of wilder days: 'One night I was in a bar and within a radius of two feet, there were three women I was sleeping with.'

Normal for our directors, said Paris critics. As for Soderbergh's film, it's okay, but small, nothing to match previous winners. '*Merde alors*, only other film that received Cannes awards for best picture and best actors was *Wages of Fear* in 1953. Surely this is not as good as that?'

But *sex, lies and videotape* is the freshest, liveliest, by turn most erotic, caustic, sad, funny and honest American film about American sex since *Carnal Knowledge* in 1971. Soderbergh's win was good news for American independent cinema. And for Cannes – even though it was only dug out of the Directors' Fortnight section at the last minute and invited into the competition because Brando refused to tango on the Croisette with *A Dry White Season*.

It's not that Soderbergh changed the face of the seventh art, he simply refreshened it. Via four people in Baton Rouge. (To say four characters would imply the usual Hollywood cardboard cut-outs.) A married couple (Andie MacDowell, Peter Gallagher) with everything. Except sexual intimacy. He hasn't been allowed to touch her for months. And anyway, he's too busy screwing her sultry sister (Laura San Giacomo).

Enter his friend: Graham (James Spader) lives in his car, loves living with one key and is impotent with anyone else around. He gets his jollies by video-interviewing women about their sex lives. And proceeds to cause as much trouble as Terence Stamp in *Theorem*, while Soderbergh examines, often steamily, the quartet's bad, sad, funny, truthful sexuality.

'The success is odd,' says Soderbergh, 'because *sex, lies and videotape* was the most aggressively uncommercial film I've ever written. My other scripts are much more . . . normal! With a slight spin to them, I hope, just because I am who I am.' His film did not, of course, match *Indiana Jones* at the box-office but then when did Spielberg last make a $1.2 million movie? And he never won Cannes at his first try. 'It's all downhill from here on,' says Soderbergh.

Not so. Never had a Cannes triumph created so many waves in Hollywood. Some 500 calls reached the novice's agent within a month, as they checked on other Soderbergh scripts developed for his backers: an ex-studio executive and an ex-shrink who call their outfit Outlaw.

'I'm offered films that are about to start shooting . . . "This is a go-movie! We're shooting in four weeks. We need a director." It's strange that, after seeing *sex, lies* and videotape, they surmise I'd want to jump in at the last minute like that. I only want to make things I'm passionate about.'

By now, he's finished *Kafka*, in Paris with Isabelle Adjani and Jeremy Irons, before turning to an adaptation of William Brinkley's novel, *The Last Ship*, for the same Universal Pictures that passed on *sex, lies and videotape*. Sydney Pollack did the sales-pitching on that one and Pollack's pal, Robert Redford, is behind plans for another upcoming Soderbergh picture, *King of the Hill*.

My first encounter with Soderbergh – born in Georgia, raised in Texas, Pennsylvania, Virginia and Louisiana before sharpening his scripter's pencil in LA – was early on in Cannes. When his big prize had been meeting Spike Lee. A week later he received the Golden Palm.

Despite Lennon specs, Soderbergh looks not unlike a more polished Woody Allen. Except he has something Woody would give up Mia Farrow for – Swedish blood via his paternal grandfather. Inevitably he was hailed (like Spike Lee) as a new Woody. 'That, I don't buy! Frankly, I don't think he's willing to get this ugly, this primal, about sex. He's into intellectual exercises, sexual relationships in a drawing room. He's made some masterpieces. And, as everybody has, some films where I'd wanna burn the negatives.'

Apart from shorts, Soderbergh's previous movie was the Yes group's concert film, *9012 Live*. 'Never found anybody who's seen it – apart from Yes!' He shelved two other Outlaw scripts – including his US answer to OO7, *Revolver* – to write *sex, lies and videotape* as an act of self-catharsis. He didn't care if nobody read it.

'It sprang full-blown onto the page! Very autobiographical, yet nothing in the film actually occurred. I've certainly been or known all of those characters, the women included. I was once very much like the husband, leaving this trail of human wreckage behind me. Not nice! And frustrating to feel yourself becoming a person you don't like and being powerless to do anything about it. Took a lot of effort to make significant changes in my relationships.'

'Now I'm more in the mode of Graham's character. Not that extreme! But the idea of only having one key is very appealing. I've been somewhat successful in stripping things down in terms of material possessions. Part of the problem was wanting to believe I was unique. That everything happening to me was special when, as I later discovered, these are very common problems. That was disappointing!'

So was the reaction to the scenario. Soderbergh's specific ideas never matched those of his readers. Based on other movies about sex, they made assumptions. 'This is just pornography, I don't want to see this.' Or, 'I don't want to admit I want to see this.' Or, 'I'll see it but I won't make it.'

Soderbergh stuck by what he saw as the universality of his story. 'Movies reaching for large audiences try to cover everything. You should scale it down, get as specific as you can – with each character. The only position I took was: if you're gonna behave a certain way, understand that it has consequences, good and bad. I never set out to be judgemental, pointing a finger. I have my rules, but no desire to make you live by them.'

Universal read it all wrong. So did another member of the Hollywood Establishment – the wife of Soderbergh's Outlaw boss, who happens to be development director at Spielberg's Amblin. By page 25, she had thrown out the script. But her husband, Robert Newmyer, kept reading. 'When he wanted to be involved,' says Soderbergh, 'I was surprised. His tastes are more mainstream than mine.'

The first Cannes winner to publicly thank his publicists, Soderbergh also paid tribute to his cast. He had wanted at least two recognizable faces. He chose Andie MacDowell and Laura San Giacomo for the wife and sister in New York, while James Spader was fighting in LA to be Graham – and recommending Peter Gallagher as the husband.

Soderbergh believes in casting perfect people, letting them do their job by giving them room and guidance. 'The film is significantly better than the script, mostly due to their input. James wouldn't let me lie on the ending. Peter brought an awful lot to the husband – the least well-drawn character in the script. He made him more difficult to peg. Just as you thought, "Oh, I've got this guy," he kept finding ways to slither away.'

Soderbergh's main goal was to beat the trap of most American films containing sex rather than sexuality. 'Americans see sex differently to Europeans. They're deceptively open about it. At least up to a point. But they're afraid to get to the painful, uncomfortable parts, for fear of putting people off. Sex is a very complex and powerful force. It deserves more careful examination than flippancy.'

French critics moaned on about scant sex and nudity. 'It's not about the sexual act!' ripostes Soderbergh. 'When I see somebody take their clothes off, I'm out of the movie. I've immediately forgotten the character: "Oh, that's Greta Scaachi and she's taken her shirt off." I didn't want that to happen. Ultimately, it wasn't necessary. The film is so drenched in sexuality, I didn't feel the need to be explicit. Nothing would have been gained. If somebody's disappointed because nobody disrobes . . . it's an aspect of the lies in the title!"

Oh yes, the title – an improvement on Canadian TV's *Spies, Lies and Naked Thighs* (1988), and fastest into global headlines, helped by the breaking of the Rob Lowe video-affair during Cannes. 'I thought: How would Graham describe this movie? He's very blunt. So, that was it. We're sold sex, we're told lies and everybody has a VCR. All the bases are covered!'

Too many for US video marketing people. During 'insane conversations', they told him: 'Buyers of the video-cassettes think that the public will think that it was shot on videotape. So, sex, lies – we can keep that! But the third word . . . can we lose the third word?'

TONY CRAWLEY

SHE-DEVIL

Recipe for a success. Take America's top movie actress. Team her with America's top TV-sitcom star. Put them in a film adaptation of a best-selling novel. Bake the dish in the artistic oven. Then serve it to your guests garnished with a dead gerbil.

Garnished with what? Who put that dead gerbil in there? Director Susan Seidelman, step forth. And screenwriters Barry Strugatz and Mark R. Burns, you too. For the mark of the rodent is upon you all.

She-Devil is an amazing act of cinematic self-destruction. Fay Weldon's novel *The Life and Loves of a She-Devil* is almost idiot-proof as material for dramatization, as its acclaimed British TV serialization proves. It gives us a comically appalling anti-heroine in Ruth Patchett, riding the chariots of wrath and jealousy. It gives us a comically appealing victim in Mary Fisher, husband-stealing romantic novelist. And it gives us a plot that's like an urban-post-feminist variant on the seven plagues of Egypt. For frogs, locusts and rivers of blood, read arson, child-offloading and career destruction.

What goes wrong in the film? Almost everything. But misapplied feminism is the first and chief offender. Seeking to humanize her she-devil heroine and present her as a sex-warrior more sinned against than sinning, Susan Seidelman signs up America's most plangently loveable TV star. Token attempts are made to fit Roseanne Barr to the movie's title. Placing a black wart on her face and framing her twice behind hell-flames, the film thinks it's doing enough to honour Weldon's comic diabolism while keeping Ruth human and lovable. But all it achieves is the reek of compromise. This she-devil is so underpowered she's like a housewife essaying Medea at the village theatricals.

By contrast, La Streep seems to think she's Sarah Siddons essaying the rôle of an American Barbara Cartland. Dressed in Parnassian swathes of pink organdy, she behaves as if taxi-ing for celestial take-off in a Tiepolo painting. She sighs; she swoons. She crooks her extended arms in baroque languor. She speaks on in-takes of breath rather than out-takes. At best it's RADA gone rococo; at worst it is acting's answer to hyperventilation. 'Calm down, dear,' one wants to say, 'you've won your Oscars already. This is a comedy.'

The outcome of this high-concept twinning of stars is that an irresistible force (Streep) collides with an immovable object (Barr) and the result resembles a nasty traffic accident on Hollywood Boulevard.

In *Desperately Seeking Susan*, Seidelman hit on the magic formula for a comedy that combined down-home humanity with kooky surrealism. Airheaded waif Rosanna Arquette will-o'-the-wisped through a tale of love, mystery and newspaper appeals, while a pre-superstardom Madonna lent street-smart gravity and her hip-swinging earthiness.

In *She-Devil*, as in her last two films, *Making Mr Right* and *Cookie*, Seidelman has not just lost the magic formula; she shows all the desperation of a scientist down on his knees on the laboratory floor looking for the damn thing. Occasionally the film erupts with a hopeful 'Eureka!': as when Streep gets her airs and graces under control for a nicely judged parody of a TV interview, or when Barr reacts to her own gerbil-in-stew dinner accident with a deadpan, 'I'll go get a strainer.'

But these better moments are deceptive and short-lived. Having underdone her she-devil heroine, Seidelman feels obliged to overdo everything else in sight. Sylvia Miles hams it up berserkly as Streep's vulgarian mother, wheeled out of an old people's home to cause havoc in Casa Fisher. Linda Hunt, all pint-size malevolence, is whisked on and off as an imp of the nursing industry. And comic effects of editing and camerawork are poured on like paraffin on a reluctant fire. Speeded-up motion for a wall-decorating scene; or a jump-cut from Streep launching into fellatio with Barr's husband to Barr chopping up a cucumber in her kitchen. (Yeek!)

The feminist tub-thumping, overt or covert, seldom lets up. 'Men get away with murder,' intones Barr. 'It seems that if you're a woman in this world, there's just no justice.' Yet the effect of the movie's pantomimic casting is to load the scales of justice so that no one could give an accurate reading even if they tried. The first question the audience asks itself is the most deadly. How did the dumpy, plain Ruth Patchett ever get hitched to Adonis yuppie Bob (Ed Begley Jr.) in the first place?

This is a marriage made in high-concept Heaven. These two have been put together with the sole purpose of being snapped apart: or precipitating a farce about infidelity. Everything about She-Devil reeks of 'arrangements'. The Streep poodle is a spoiled horror that we know has been put on the payroll so it can be run over or thrown off a cliff. (The latter, it turns out.) Streep's Hispanic stud-manservant wears an invisible label reading 'Hell hath no fury like a toy boy scorned.' We know he'll be instrumental in the later revenge plan. Just look at all that macho nostril-work. And the crudely depicted squalor and paralysis of the early scenes in the old people's home is a sure set-up for the equally crude knockabout in which the revivified oldies play football.

Fay Weldon's novel is also pantomimic in its way, and it's certainly a feminist fable. But the contrivances and messages are sewn seamlessly into a story with its own energy, passion and conviction. She-Devil the movie, far from being seamless, is like an old mattress with all the springs and tickings exposed. Even the final shot is nakedly messagey. A vengeance-sated Miss Barr walks serenely towards us through the foreshortened shimmer of a telephoto-lensed sidewalk. The all-female crowd moving with her is composed of many races and colours. The image says 'Join hands and let us all be women strong and free.' It belongs in a Party Political Broadcast, which is the direction She-Devil has been moving in all along.

HARLAN KENNEDY

STRAPLESS

avid Hare may still be best known for his work in the theatre, but he has now made three feature films. The first, W*etherby*, was a signal achievement – a 'state of the nation' movie fashioned into an allusive narrative with the commentary embedded in the cinematic texture. P*aris by* N*ight* sought to amplify the thriller undertones of its predecessor into something like full-blown melodrama, to questionable effect. But at least its first half had the adroit observation which distinguished W*etherby* and, if the film as a whole seemed to lack trajectory, the broadening of its horizons intimated a readiness to escape from the sort of parochialism which is apt to beset British movie-making. And now Hare's third film, S*trapless*, appears to extend the process of reaching for a richer stylistic mix. The question, of course, remains: to what purpose is this stylistic elaboration being put?

While the credit sequence shows us images of statuary in a Mediterranean landscape, the soundtrack swells with an old pop standard, Nat King Cole singing 'When I Fall in Love'. The two figures to whom we are introduced – the woman on a solitary vacation, the enigmatic charmer who dispenses with convention in seeking to initiate a relationship with her – are played by actors respectively American (Blair Brown) and German (Bruno Ganz), with the latter describing himself in so many words as a citizen of the world. The atmosphere and the situation are languidly and consciously 'foreign', redolent of an 'international' art-house movie.

But as this ambiguous liaison apparently comes to nothing, we are suddenly thrust – and the transition is a striking one – back on to home ground and into the hurly-burly of a London NHS hospital that's being stretched by financial stringency. Here, we discover, the woman, Lillian, works as a doctor; but if the talk of cuts and of the need to fight them puts specific political realities on to the film's agenda, then the introduction of one of Lillian's patients, a 30-year-old building worker with inoperable cancer, evokes something more elemental.

Shortly we meet the film's third principal figure, Lillian's much younger sister Amy (Bridget Fonda), fecklessly 'now' in her manner of living; and political comment resurfaces after a fashion in the revelation that her current inamorato is a photographer seeking easy money with candid camera snaps of minor royalty. Soon the well-heeled Raymond (Ganz) reappears on the scene, and the apparent theme of the movie begins to come into focus.

The mainstay of American 'screwball' comedy has sometimes been termed its capacity to dramatize the lure of irresponsibility; and though S*trapless* could hardly be termed a comedy, the film, with its prologue that might even be seen as a variant on the 'meeting cute' convention of the screwball genre, does seem to adhere to that tradition.

Lillian may, initially, decline Raymond's impulsive offer of marriage, but she moves into his home. 'For once in my life,' she tells Amy, 'I want to go over the stages.' Gambling, and bad debts, form a *leitmotif* in the action and, after Lillian has clinched her jump into the unknown by actually becoming Raymond's wife, the financial chickens start to come home to roost and, as Raymond himself disappears from the scene, his creditors succeed in cleaning her out.

Meanwhile, though, as Lillian moves into deeper waters, a kind of transference is enacted, and Amy, pregnant by the now absent photographer, embraces the doctrine of self-reliance, devoting herself to preparation for motherhood and a career in fashion design. At work, Lillian suffers a breakdown, locking herself in a store room. 'The giving's great,' she tells a colleague, 'but when do I get something back?' Her boss arrives, bearing with judicious irony the English panacea of a cup of tea. 'It's good work,' he assures her. 'You bring comfort.'

Up to this point, *Strapless* has succeeded in weaving a tapestry of a rewardingly thought-provoking kind. The manner may be more literary than in Hare's previous films, but the movie is adroitly cast and played, and pieced together with an unobtrusive skill, which contrives to feed back its assorted components into something distinctively British – a mood, perhaps, of stoicism analogous with the wry epilogue to *Wetherby*. And imagistically, the illusoriness of the credit-line affluence which surrounds Raymond's lifestyle might be said to have its own implication for the recent political and economic management of Britain.

It is, disappointingly, in the resolution of this drama that *Strapless* seems unable to deliver the goods. Ostensibly the film becomes a sort of detective story, with Lillian tracking down Raymond's past. We visit the public school where he was effectively adopted by a house master and his wife, and the Cotswolds cottage where Raymond's first wife and their son now live. English enough settings, certainly, but the effect is somehow closer to the English Tou ist Board; evasiveness enters the film, and it stays there. By the conclusion, Amy s baby is born (to the strains of Mozart in a sort of water bed, presumably at great expense and certainly not on the NHS). Lillian reverses her previous unreadiness to be a leader in the hospital staff's anti-cuts campaign, and makes a ringing speech to her colleagues about preserving the quality of British life (but what about all the hard slog and spadework that such a campaign entails?). And finally she and others take part in a fashion show for the cause ('Save the NHS'), at which Amy's creation of a strapless evening dress ('They shouldn't stay up, but they do') makes its symbolic début. The symbolism, though, remains beside any very evident point, and the image of showbiz socialism on which the movie ends only contrives, alas, to open up the divide between 'them' and 'us'.

Ultimately, the comment on British life, or at least on British Left thinking, provided by *Strapless* seems a rather peculiar one.

TIM PULLEINE

SWEETIE

Since the bubble burst for the Australian Cinema Renaissance of the 1970s, carbon copies of Hollywood have proliferated. It's especially heartening then that 1989 should have seen the emergence of two distinctive first features, both by young women directors: Ann Turner's unexpectedly gothic *Celia*, in which the 1950s rabbit epidemic and virulent anti-communism are seen through a young girl's eyes; and Jane Campion's even more remarkable *Sweetie*, a quizzical, nightmarishly comic view of family politics, made in such an individual style that it seemingly could be set in any period.

Not that Jane Campion came from nowhere. Born in New Zealand, she made her name at the Australian Film and Television School with three shorts that were the toast of the Cannes Film Festival in 1986. *A Girl's Own Story* merged Beatlemania, the tyranny of the family and incest; *Passionless Moments* linked a variety of banal, suburban activities with unexpected, tangential thoughts; *Peel* (which won the Golden Palm for short films) found a family breaking up in a lay-by, the result of an argument over the disposal of orange peel. Thereafter Campion made a much admired television film called *Two Friends*, which followed the disintegration of the friendship of two schoolgirls, its particular feature being that events were seen in episodic form in reverse chronological order. Throughout Campion's work, in terms of budgets, small has proved to be beautiful – *Sweetie* was made for the equivalent of $1 million.

Sweetie, which, like most of her films, was written in collaboration with one-time lover Gerard Lee, is a summation of all these themes – the story of a family at odds with each other, but always bound by the inescapable tie of common blood. Kay, for whom depression seems the natural condition of life, is elder sister to Dawn, nicknamed 'Sweetie', and has never been able to tolerate the attention her father devoted to the apparently talented, more extrovert younger sibling. Kay embarks on her first live-in relationship with the earnestly casual Louis, on whose forehead the combination of greasy lock and small mole form the question mark a fortune-teller tells her will signify the man in her life.

Following a dispute over growing a little elm tree in their back yard, the couple descend into what they can only describe as 'a non-sex phase'. Retiring to separate rooms until Kay's self-imposed cold improves, the situation is made worse by the intrusion of the hopeless Sweetie into their home, together with an ineffectual degenerate named Bob who has been designated as 'producer' to her undefined artistic ambitions. In contrast to the dowdy Kay, Sweetie has the accoutrements of an overweight punk, and in her sexual appetite proves anything but unobtrusive. Louis attempts to show sympathy, but this only makes Kay more antagonistic ('She was just born. I don't have anything to do with her'). The house is further cluttered by Kay and Sweetie's father, abandoned by their mother for a month's trial separation. But whatever the other characters' personal problems, the focus always returns to the now monstrous and unstable

Sweetie, the relation who is both a burden and a dangerous catalyst.

And yet the importance of Sweetie – and what makes her the film's dramatic centre – is that for all her possible insanity and pathetic uselessness, she has an irrepressible vitality that eludes the other characters. Kay is lost mainly to her private world of superstition – a morbid fear of tree roots, for one – and physical repression. The ineffectual Louis is willing to acquiesce in Kay's moments of withdrawal, occasionally escaping cross-legged into deep meditation. Father is at sea without the attentions of his wife (before leaving him, she has to prepare an appropriate cold dish for each day of the week) or his object of devotion, Sweetie. Only mother has the strength to investigate a new way of life (as cook to a station of Jackaroos, Australian cowboys), but once home she shows more concern for the wider social order (what will the neighbours think?) than for her own flesh and blood. Campion herself has described Sweetie as being like 'a gorilla in a cage', a creature whose anarchic force cannot find a home in conventional society. And in a film filled with pleasingly offbeat performances, there's an especially brave one from Genevieve Lemon, who succeeds in making Sweetie never hateful even in her worst tirades.

Made with a fine eye for detail and the nuances of social embarrassment, *Sweetie* has been described as like an episode of *Neighbours* directed by David Lynch, but that only gives the Australian soap undeserved credit. There's no-one approaching the fake sweetness of a Kylie Minogue in Campion's gallery of characters. As for the Lynch comparison, it's true that Campion brings a special visual and aural quality to her work, but this was fully signalled in her student films. Apart from one track into the root of a tree that does echo the insects in the grass shot from the opening of *Blue Velvet*, Campion's individuality rests mainly on framing her characters in the far corners of the wide screen, using dramatic contrasts in perspective, lighting and colour, as well as a particular fondness for overhead shots (Campion has worked consistently with one director of photography, Sally Bongers, but the one short she shot herself displays exactly the same style). According to Campion, 'They are not conventional frames, they  play with the edges of the situation a lot. You put that together with very natural performances. Everything is about tone as far as I'm concerned, and how you shoot is just another way to create tone.'

These dynamic compositions are brilliantly in tune with the marginal nature of Campion's characters, as well as increasing the sense that they are entrapped in a scheme of things beyond their grasp. At the same time the film's imagery – the roots of a tree as an oblique symbol of how a family structure controls and threatens its members – is superbly integrated. Perhaps not surprisingly for a former art student, Campion's feeling for visual textures is also apparent, as in the image of a floral carpet beneath Kay's feet that seems to be a living organism, or the way Kay's drab manner of dress stifles what is evidently a beautiful body. Campion's use of spirituals on the soundtrack adds further to the sensation that the film is really dealing with interior feeling at odds with a clumsy, badly organized physical existence.

In case that makes *Sweetie* sound unapproachably abstract, it must be said that the film is often sublimely funny and touching. There are some deliciously deadpan moments, such as when the family (by a cruel ruse temporarily liberated from Sweetie) visits mom at her outback ranch, and cowboys and suburbanites waltz together in the moonlight. The movie's structure is pleasingly open to an edgy causality; Campion is not afraid to ditch orthodox dramatic form and simply unfold the film as if the viewer is a stranger meeting the characters on a casual basis, much as we do in real life. We discover Sweetie about 20 minutes in, just as Louis stumbles across her in ignorance that Kay even had a sister; the parents first appear as they split up after another 20 minutes. And right up to the film's tragic conclusion, Campion really does convey the difficulty of knowing people, as well as how comparatively easy it is to reject those umbilically attached to us.

Ultimately, the film's theme is love, but not the fictional sort of romantic entanglement. Rather it is the messy love that we experience from the day we are born into a family. Perhaps the fortune-teller is right for most of us when she comments that love is really nothing more than 'sex and courage'. But of Campion's deep passion for the medium of cinema, there can now be little doubt. As she herself says, 'The film is made for those people who really want some excitement or challenge in their cinema.' Australian suburban life will never look the same again.

DAVID THOMPSON

A TALE OF SPRINGTIME
(Conte de printemps)

Eric Rohmer launches into a new series entitled 'Four Seasons' with another beguiling drama of spoken conceits and unspoken desires. Jeanne, a young philosophy graduate with an absent lover, accepts the invitation of teenage Natacha to stay over at her father Igor's apartment. Their friendship established, Jeanne finds herself manipulated by Natacha towards replacing Igor's current unpopular choice of young lover. It's cooler and less overtly comic than his earlier tales, but at least he's raising the age limit on his characters, and the casual precision of his cast and the selfless direction are as satisfying as ever. **DT**
Director/script Eric Rohmer **producer** Margaret Ménégoz **camera** Luc Pagés **editor** Maria Luisa Garcia **cast** Anne Teyssèdre, Hugues Quester, Florence Darel, Eloise Bennett, Sophie Robin
Running time: 112 mins
UK release: Artificial Eye, Jun 15, 1990

TALES FROM THE DARKSIDE: THE MOVIE

More Creepshow than Dead of Night, this is 'Four Stories in Search of a Style', as John Harrison lays on flashy angles, chiaroscuro lighting and peculiar POV shots to little effect. Neither of the writers have produced their best material – a college student raises a mummy to wreak revenge, an old man hires an assassin to kill a cat, a man witnesses a monstrous murder then meets a mysterious woman – and the best of the stories (the last, with James Remar and Rae Dawn Chong) is also the most predictable. Best viewed with fast-forward button in hand. **JH**
Director John Harrison **producers** Richard P. Rubinstein, Mitchell Galin **script** Michael McDowell , George A. Romero **camera** Robert Draper **editor** Harry B. Miller **design** Ruth Ammon **music** Donald A. Rubinstein, Jim Manzie, Pat Regan, Chaz Jankel, Harrison **cast** Deborah Harry, Christian Slater, David Johansen, William Hickey, James Remar, Rae Dawn Chong, Robert Klein, Steve Buscemi, Matthew Lawrence, Robert Sedgwick, Julianne Moore, Michael Deak
Running time: 93 mins
US release: Paramount, May 4, 1990

▟ TALK RADIO

Eric Bogosian plays a loud-mouthed suit salesman who has risen through sheer tonguemanship to the heights of local radio stardom. He hosts a late-night phone-in-and-rant show during which he interacts with psychos, whackos, Nazis and scumbos with nothing else to do but call up Barry and be abused. As the show progresses, and the calls get weirder and wilder, Bogosian starts reaching deeper into the darkness and learns some unpleasant things about himself and his audience. Just because Talk Radio was squeezed into Oliver Stone's busy schedule between two big-budget movies, is no reason to think of it as a minor work. Bogosian gives a spellbinding performance, mostly solo in his cave-like studio, interacting with the frightening voices of his callers. And those anonymous callers, who represent an entire spectrum of human misery, complacency and monstrousness, finally come to dominate the movie as the camera circles round Barry or moves in on his spitting lips. It's screamingly funny, but also deeply upsetting as Barry fields questions, taunts and abuse from timid conservatives, self-hating rapists and a succession of Jew-hating, swastika-waving Texan fascists. **KN**
Director Oliver Stone **producers** Edward R. Pressman, Kitman Ho **execs** Greg Strangis, Sam Strangis **script** Eric Bogosian, Stone, from play by Bogosian, Ted Savinar **camera** Robert Richardson **editor** David Brenner **design** Bruno Rubeo **music** Stewart Copeland **cast** Eric Bogosian, Alec Baldwin, Ellen Greene, Leslie Hope, John C. McGinley, John Pankow, Michael Wincott, Zach Grenier, Anna Levine, Robert Trebor, Linda Atkinson, Allan Corduner
Running time: 110 mins
US release: Universal, Dec 21, 1988
UK release: Fox, Sep 15, 1989

TANGO AND CASH

Sylvester Stallone, sharing centre scene with fellow macho man Kurt Russell, here attempts a change of pace by abandoning the blue-collar machismo of his usual screen persona for a sharp suit, some rimless glasses and a spectacular mix of cop action and comedy very obviously patterned on Lethal Weapon. All pretense at gritty realism has been neglected, and the whole thing is constructed as a series of stunts and escapes, with the location changing every 20 minutes and a new piece of hardware brought on for each new set of explosions. Stallone and Russell constantly squabble, jockeying for position, exchanging macho boasts and yet falling more or less in love with one another during their breathless adventure. The vacuum at the centre of the film arises because neither star is really able to play off the other as required while Andrei Konchalovsky, slotting more than ever into the American commercial mainstream, is patently more comfortable with the comedy than the action. The film's biggest wink at the audience comes when an onlooker accuses Tango of thinking he is Rambo, whereupon Stallone grins and spits 'Rambo is a pussy'. **KN**
Director Andrei Konchalovsky **producers** Jon Peters, Peter Guber **exec** Peter MacDonald **script** Randy Feldman **camera** Donald E. Thorin **editor**

Stuart Baird **design** J. Michael Riva **music** Harold Faltermeyer **cast** Sylvester Stallone, Kurt Russell, Jack Palance, Teri Hatcher, Michael J. Pollard, Brion James, Geoffrey Lewis, James Hong
Running time: 98 mins
US release: Warner, Dec 22, 1989
UK release: Warner, Mar 23, 1990

✂ TANK MALLING

Despite some imaginative sleaze, this is a boring and confused thriller which mixes 1970s American paranoia with TV-style London gangsterism. While Peter Wyngarde is entertaining as a crazed Mary Whitehouse-cum-Oswald Mosley figure and Glen Lord makes something out of the rôle of the polite nipple-slitting thug who does the dirty work, Ray Winstone blunders about like an idiot, Amanda Donohoe gets hysterical without adding to the plot, and Jason Connery is laughable in the change-of-pace rôle of the evil, yuppie mastermind with slicked-back hair. There are clichés aplenty, embarrassing speeches, gory bits sure to be snipped from the video version and an ending at once depressing, predictable and bathetic. There should be more British films like *Tank Malling*. It might stop Richard Attenborough and David Puttnam being pompous about Britain's great and prestigious film industry. **KN**
Director James Marcus **producers** Glen Murphy, Jamie Foreman **exec** Terence Murphy **script** James Marcus, Mick Southworth **camera** Jason Lehel **editor** Brian Peachey **design** Geoffrey Sharpe **music** Rick Fenn, Nick Mason **cast** Ray Winstone, Jason Connery, Amanda Donohoe, Glen Murphy, Marsha Hunt, Peter Wyngarde, John Conteh, Terry Marsh, Nick Berry, John Bett, Paul Mari, P. J. Davidson
Running time: 109 mins
UK release: Cineplex/Parkfield, Nov 24, 1989

TEENAGE MUTANT NINJA TURTLES

HIT • HIT • HIT • HIT • HIT

Director Steve Barron **producers** Kim Dawson, Simon Fields, David Chan **exec** Raymond Chow **script** Todd W. Langen, Bobby Herbeck, from cartoon characters created by Kevin Eastman and Peter Laird **camera** John Fenner **design** Roy Forge Smith **music** John Du Prez **cast** Judith Hoag, Elias Koteas, Joch Pais, Michelan Sisti, Leif Tilden, David Forman, Michael Turney, Jay Patterson, Raymond Gerra, James Saito, Toshishiro Obata
Running time: 93 mins
US release: New Line, Mar 30, 1990

THREE FUGITIVES

An American remake, by the same writer-director, of a previous French success, this is an energetic comedy-thriller, with Nick Nolte in good grizzled form as a paroled robber who, within minutes of getting out of jail, is taken hostage in a bank hold-up executed by a bungling amateur (Short), and has to go on the run with him and his young daughter. Despite the latter's being autistic, sentimentality is mostly kept at bay, and there's a splendidly ridiculous set-piece in which Nolte gets medical treatment from a senile retired vet, who at first discouragingly suggests that the patient would be best put to sleep, but rewards him on recovery with a bowl of dog food. The overall craftsmanship is enhanced by the hard naturalistic lighting of the veteran Haskell Wexler, which does much to offset the incipient frenzy. **TP**
Director/exec/script Francis Veber **producer** Lauren Shuler-Donner **camera** Haskell Wexler **editor** Bruce Green **design** Rick Carter **music** David McHugh **cast** Nick Nolte, Martin Short, Sarah Rowland Doroff, James Earl Jones, Alan Ruck, Kenneth McMillan
Running time: 96 mins
US release: BV, Jan 27, 1989
UK release: Warner, Aug 25, 1989

THREE WOMEN IN LOVE (Der Philosoph)

The lanky, reclusive author of a philosophical tome on love buys himself a new suit to celebrate its publication. The three shop girls who attend him show an unexpected interest in his life and work, to the point of disrobing and seducing the gawky fellow. But are the frequently naked ladies in fact three goddesses teaching him valuable lessons in fleshly delights and shared love? Rudolf Thomé, a noted scholar, actually called his film 'The Philosopher'. But as his British distributor happily realized, this thin parlour game of a movie has less to do with Rohmer-like disquisitions on love than feeble wish-fulfilment and a bit of skin. **DT**
Director/producer/script Rudolf Thomé **camera** Reinhold Vorschneider **editor** Dörte Völz **Mammarell design** Eve Schaenen **music** Hanno Rihné **cast** Johannes Herrschmann, Adriana Altaras, Friederike Tiejenbacher, Claudia Matschulla, Jürgen Wink, Werner Gerber, Anton Rey
Running time: 90 mins
US release: Mainline, Jun 8, 1990

TIE ME UP! TIE ME DOWN! (¡Atame!)

A beautiful film star (Abril) falls in love with her abductor in this Pedro Almodóvar film that's guaranteed to offend almost everyone in sight.

It's *The Collector* with kitsch. Puritans will tut-tut at the candid sex scenes. Feminists will wince at the implication that male aggression wins female hearts. And Almodóvar fans will wonder if the Spanish director hasn't bitten off less than he can chew in this slimline tale teased out to feature length. Visually, though, it's the usual lollipop-coloured feast. And what other living director could have dreamed up the scene involving a bath, a nude lady and a clockwork toy frogman? HK
Director/script *Pedro Almodóvar* exec *Agustín Almodóvar* camera *José Luis Alcaine* editor *José Salcedo* design *Ferrán Sánchez* music *Ennio Morricone* cast *Victoria Abril, Antonio Banderas, Loles León, Francisco Rabal*
Running time: 101 mins
US release: Miramax, May 4, 1990
UK release: Enterprise, Jul 6, 1990

THE TIME OF THE GYPSIES (Dom za Vesanje)
Emir Kusturica improbably won the best director prize at Cannes for this slovenly, overlong and sentimental tale of gypsies in the modern world. While there are impressive moments, there are also too many landscape shots and too much accordion music on the soundtrack. Told from the point of view of Perhan, a gypsy boy on the brink of adolescence, this one has police raids, drunken husbands, mystical images, random brutality, 'everything but the bloodhounds snappin' at the rear end.' JH
Director *Emir Kusturica* producer *Mirza Pasic* exec *Milan Martinovic* script *Kusturica, Gordan Mihic* camera *Vilko Filac* editor *Andrija Zafranovic* design *Miljen Kljakovic* music *Goran Bregovic* cast *Davor Dujmovic, Bora Todorovic, Ljubica Adzovic, Husnija Hasmovic, Sinolicka Trpkova, Zabit Memedov*
Running time: 142 mins
US release: Columbia, Feb 9, 1990

⚑ TO KILL A PRIEST
As directed by Agnieszka Holland, the story of Poland's Father Popieluszko – his life and untimely death at the hands of secret police – comes on like a potboiler by Jerzy Le Carré or Andrzej Ambler. France's Christopher Lambert (priest) and America's Ed Harris (killer) hack their way through yards of banal plotting and B-movie dialogue, and the international enterprise is rendered yet more esperanto by the presence of Brits Joanne Whalley and Joss Ackland. Another instant write-off from David Puttnam's Columbia production slate. HK
Director *Agnieszka Holland* producer *Jean-Pierre Alessandri* script *Holland, Jean-Yves Pitoun* camera *Adam Holender* editor *Hervé de Luze*

design *Emile Ghigo* cast *Christopher Lambert, Ed Harris, Joss Ackland, Tim Roth, Timothy Spall, Peter Postlethwaite, Cherie Lunghi, Joanne Whalley, David Suchet, Charle Condou*
Running time: 117 mins
US release: Columbia, Oct 13, 1989
UK release: Col/Tri-Star, Nov 18, 1988

TOO BEAUTIFUL FOR YOU! See Trop belle pour toi!

TORRENTS OF SPRING (Acque di primavera)
Turgenev's short novel is fairly faithfully followed in Skolimowski's film, the director's first foray into a costume subject since his ill-fated *Adventures of Gerard* some 20 years ago. In the event, the period trappings sometimes weigh rather heavily, though the film works better when the tone is shifted more towards romantic melodrama. The casting of Timothy Hutton as a Russian landowner, and Nastassja Kinski as the voluptuary who lays low his chances of happiness with a German shopkeeper's daughter, strike a rather odd note. Skolimowski himself puts in a guest appearance as the drunken sybarite who engagingly provides a mock-choric presence, but elsewhere his personal touch seems only intermittently in evidence. TP
Director *Jerzy Skolimowski* producer *Angelo Rizzoli* exec *Mario Cotone* script *Skolimowski, Arcangelo Bonaccorso, from novel by Ivan Turgenev* camera *Dante Spinotti, Witold Sobocinski* editor *Cesare d'Amico* design *Francesco Bronzi* music *Stanley Myers* cast *Timothy Hutton, Nastassja Kinski, Valeria Golino, William Forsythe, Urbano Barberini, Francesca De Sapio, Jacques Herlin, Antonio Cantafora, Christopher Janczar, Christian Dottorini, Jerzy Skolimowski*
Running time: 101 mins
US release: Millimeter, Feb 9, 1990
UK release: Hobo, May 18, 1990

TOTAL RECALL
HIT • HIT • HIT • HIT • HIT
Director *Paul Verhoeven* producers *Buzz Feitshans, Ronald Shusett* execs *Mario Kassar, Andrew Vajna* script *Shusett, Dan O'Bannon, Gary Goldman from story* We Can Remember It For You Wholesale *by Philip K. Dick* camera *Jost Vacano* editor *Frank J. Urioste* design *William Sandell* sfx *Eric Brevig, Thomas L. Fisher, Dream Quest Images* music *Jerry Goldsmith* cast *Arnold Schwarzenegger, Rachel Ticotin, Sharon Stone, Ronny Cox, Michael Ironside, Marshall Bell, Mel Johnson Jr., Michael Champion, Priscilla Allen*
Running time: 109 mins
US release: Tri-Star, Jun 1, 1990
UK release: Guild, Jul 27, 1990

TREASURE ISLAND

Bearing in mind the dodgy cast and that this latest version of Stevenson's pirate tale was relegated to TV in the US, it's a surprisingly good kid's movie. With the exception of Richard Johnson's almost senile Squire Trelawney, it's played straight – even by Oliver Reed – and although Charlton Heston's Long John Silver isn't as terrifying as the makers would like to think, Fraser Heston has seen enough of his dad's films to make the proceedings look pretty exciting too. **TW**
Director/producer/script Fraser C. Heston **exec** Peter Snell **camera** Robert Steadman **editor** Eric Boyd-Perkins **design** Tony Woolard **music** Paddy Maloney **cast** Charlton Heston, Richard Johnson, Oliver Reed, Christian Bale, Julian Glover, Christopher Lee, Clive Wood, John Benfield, Isla Blair
Running time: 132 mins
UK release: Warner, Jun 15, 1990

TREMORS

Ron Underwood's first feature is an unfussy, cleverly-written pastiche of the 1950s monster movie. A folksy desert community is terrorized by man-eating, sand-burrowing worms that turn out to be merely the mouth-tentacles of larger creatures. Fred Ward and Kevin Bacon are dim-witted cowboy handymen who discover the monsters and proceed to spend more time arguing about what they ought to be called or trying to think of a way of turning the creatures into a profitable business, while heroine Finn Carter is a seismologist who gets irritated when the locals expect her to be an instant expert on the life-cycle of the inexplicable monsters just because she is a scientist. Broadly humorous in its opening stretches, the film becomes more suspenseful as a small group of the monsters surround the town, forcing the handful of survivors up onto the roofs to think of various home-made methods of seeing them off. The monsters, although essentially absurd, are cleverly-designed creations which make formidable villains, and the threads of humour make the whole B-movie feel fairly endearing. **KN**
Director Ron Underwood **producers** S. S. Wilson, Brent Maddock **exec** Gale Anne Hurd **script** Wilson, Maddock **camera** Alexander Gruszynski **editor** O. Nicholas Brown **design** Ivo Cristante **music** Ernest Troost **cast** Kevin Bacon, Fred Ward, Finn Carter, Michael Gross, Reba McEntire
Running time: 96 mins
US release: Universal, Jan 19, 1990
UK release: UIP, Jun 29, 1990

TRIUMPH OF THE SPIRIT

While avoiding the pitfalls that could have turned this into 'Rocky Goes to Auschwitz', Triumph of the Spirit is no triumph. Salomo Arouch was one of the few concentration camp inmates to interact with the Germans, through his continual success in their gladiatorial boxing matches. Instead of exploring his experiences, the film simply runs over the old familiar ground – the trains, the furnaces, the slave labour, etc. Brief moments stand out, as does Edward James Olmos's performance as a brutal gypsy, an uncompromising portrait of the depths men will sink to in order to survive, and the under-employed German cast catch some of the moral malaise of the camps. But the well-fed, well-tailored Americans play worthy and resilient to a man, giving a dignity to the inmates that robs the film of shock and real integrity. Once again the question is asked; how could people do this? By failing to even consider answering it, the film renders itself redundant. **TW**
Director Robert M. Young **producers** Arnold Kopelson, Shimon Arama **script** Andrzej Krakowski, Laurence Heath **camera** Curtis Clark **editor** Arthur Coburn **design** Jerzy Maslowska **music** Cliff Eidelman **cast** Willem Dafoe, Edward James Olmos, Robert Loggia, Wendy Gazelle, Kelly Wolf, Costas Mandylor, Kario Salem, Edward Zentara, Hartmut Becker, Burkhard Heyl
Running time: 120 mins
US release: Triumph, Dec 8, 1989
UK release: Guild, Jun 22, 1990

TROP BELLE POUR TOI! (Too Beautiful for You!)

Bertrand Blier longs to understand women but knows men too well. Here, Gérard Depardieu's car salesman rejects his perfect wife (Bouquet, the obscure object of desire herself) for his plump, rather plain secretary (Balasko). With its elaborate formal devices – interlocking fantasies and flashbacks, direct address, characters commenting on the soundtrack (all Schubert) – Trop belle pour toi! seems more complicated than it is. But it possesses enormous emotional integrity, anchored by its performers – especially Depardieu, who does some of his most daring work for Blier – and by Blier's commitment to his material. This is his best film since Get Out Your Handkerchiefs. **JH**
Director/script Bertrand Blier **producer** Bernard Marescot **camera** Philippe Rousselot **editor** Claudine Merlin **design** Theobald Meurisse **cast** Gérard Depardieu, Josiane Balasko, Carole Bouquet, Roland Blanche, François Cluzet, Didier Benureau, Philippe Loffredo, Sylvie Orcier, Myriam Boyer, Flavien Lebarbe, Juana Marques
Running time: 91 mins
US release: Orion Classics, Mar 2, 1990
UK release: Artificial Eye, Mar 2, 1990

TRUE BELIEVER

Wearing a curly grey ponytail, James Woods is a burned-out leftish lawyer reduced to getting drug dealers off on technicalities. Wide-eyed Robert Downey Jr. joins his practice and reawakens Woods' idealism. Woods takes on the DA, seeking to expose his plot to imprison an innocent man for the greater good of jailing drug dealers. Woods is his usual frayed-nerve self in Joseph Ruben's gripping, if somewhat predictable, courtroom drama. **BM**
Director *Joseph Ruben* **producers** *Walter F. Parkes, Lawrence Lasker* **exec** *Peter Rosten* **script** *Wesley Strick* **camera** *John W. Lindley* **editor** *George Bowers* **design** *Lawrence Miller* **music** *Brad Fiedel* **cast** *James Woods, Robert Downey Jr., Yuji Okumoto, Margaret Colin, Kurtwood Smith, Tom Bower, Miguel Fernandes, Charles Hallahan*
Running time: 103 mins
US release: Columbia, Feb 17, 1989
UK release: Col/Tri-Star, Sep 29, 1989

👍 TRUE LOVE

True Love's subject is a half-comic study of the wedding of two young Italian-Americans in an ethnic enclave of the Bronx. Where a Hollywood filmmaker might have gone for farce in the *Moonstruck* mould, début director Nancy Savoca never condescends to her characters or their milieu, depicting instead their anticipations and terrors, and the social pressures that form their responses, especially the way that the sexes develop as almost different species. With its dramatic delicacy, social insight and superbly deployed cast of young, largely unknown actors, *True Love* is one of the year's most promising first films. **JH**
Director *Nancy Savoca* **producers** *Richard Guay, Shelley Houis* **script** *Savoca, Guay* **camera** *Lisa Rinzler* **editor** *John Tintori* **design** *Lester W. Cohen* **cast** *Annabella Sciorra, Ron Eldard, Star Jasper, Aida Turturro, Roger Rignack, Michael J. Wolfe, Kelly Cinnante, Rick Shapiro, Suzanne Costallos, Vinny Pastore, Marianne Leone, John Nacco, Ann Tucker, Marie Michaels*
Running time: 104 mins
US release: UA, Oct 20, 1989

TURNER AND HOOCH

With a small-town detective having to take custody of an obstreperous dog which is the supposed 'key witness' to a gangland slaying, this is yet another variation on the 'odd couple' cop movie theme, albeit (see *K-9*) a not wholly original one. In the upshot, the statutory comic business that results from the burgeoning devotion between the slobbering Hooch and the initially ultra-fastidious Turner remains largely separate from the working out of the no less statutory cops-and-robbers narrative, since the generic context of small-town comedy is not allowed sufficient elbow room to let the disparate elements fuse together. Tom Hanks' bachelor charm comes off the peg, and it was surely a tactical error to have his canine cohort fatally wounded in the climactic affray, even though he has by this time sired the puppies which furnish the 'happy ever after' conclusion. **TP**
Director *Roger Spottiswoode* **producer** *Raymond Wagner* **exec** *Daniel Petrie Jr.* **script** *Dennis Shryack, Michael Blodgett, Petrie, Jim Cash, Jack Epps Jr.* **camera** *Adam Greenberg* **editor** *Garth Craven* **design** *John DeCuir Jr.* **music** *Charles Gross* **cast** *Tom Hanks, Mare Winningham, Craig T. Nelson, Reginald VelJohnson, Scott Paulin, J. C. Quinn, John McIntire, David Knell, Ebbe Roe Smith, Kevin Scannell*
Running time: 99 mins
US release: BV, Jul 28, 1989
UK release: Warner, Jan 12, 1990

🗡 TWO MOON JUNCTION

How could you get Kristy McNichol, Millie Perkins, Burl Ives, Louise Fletcher, Herve Villechaize, and Screamin' Jay Hawkins all into one film and still give 90 per cent of the screen time to total dead-losses like Sherilyn Fenn and Richard Tyson? Ask Zalman King who wrote and directed this slice of poseur's porno. Fenn is the daughter of an aristocratic Southern family which is building up to her big wedding while she smoulders with what is supposed to be sensuality and can't get any satisfaction from her rich-kid fiancé. And Tyson is a carnival attendant with a girlie haircut who turns up in her shower one day to persuade her to have steaming, smouldering, blazing, thirst-quenching sex with him. She falls for his macho-but-sensitive approach, being dragged off to motels and various other locales for more soft-focus humping. It's a slow, draggy, stately, downright tedious little movie. Fenn and Tyson are one-star acting talents trapped in five-star bodies, and their nipples are more expressive than their faces. **KN**
Director/script *Zalman King* **producer** *Donald P. Borchers* **execs** *Mel Pearl, Don Levin* **camera** *Mark Plummer* **editor** *Marc Grossman* **design** *Michelle Minch* **music** *Jonathan Elias* **cast** *Sherilyn Fenn, Richard Tyson, Louise Fletcher, Burl Ives, Kristy McNichol, Martin Hewitt, Juanita Moore, Don Galloway, Millie Perkins, Nicole Rosselle, Kerry Remsen, Herve Villechaize, Screamin' Jay Hawkins*
Running time: 105 mins
UK release: Oasis, Nov 3, 1989

TEENAGE MUTANT NINJA TURTLES

They sing, they dance, they eat pizzas. They wear Sam Brown belts and coloured 'blindfolds' with eyeholes in them. They combat crime wherever they meet it. And they have so far earned over $130 million from American movie-goers.

Meet the heroes on a half-shell. *Teenage Mutant Ninja Turtles* is the box-office phenomenon of 1990. Its success proves the old William Goldman adage that in the film business 'Nobody knows anything.' Taking a popular, off-the-wall comic-strip (with matching TV series), three producers from Britain and America turned it into a feature film.

Fully aware that it might be another *Howard the Duck*, they nonetheless liked the logistics. 'I looked at the comic strip and something snapped' says Golden Harvest CEO Thomas Gray. 'I thought, "We can do this. All you have to do is put stunt men in turtle suits and you could knock this off for a very low budget".' So they did. The budget came in at a piffling $10.4 million. And they hired a British director almost no one had heard of: Steve Barron. He's a pop promo director whose only previous feature, 1984's *Electric Dreams*, sank without trace.

By March 1990 the first weekend's turtle figures were in and even the movie's producers, Golden Harvest, and its distributor, New Line Cinema, didn't believe them. $25 million. Surely some mistake. But the film thundered on towards six figures, its appeal to new viewers matched only by a re-see factor obvious to anyone stumbling into an American cinema where it was playing. Lines of dialogue are noisily anticipated; fights are pre-choreographed ('Look out, he's going to hit him!' 'Watch out!'); and pre-emptive hankies come out before Wise Old Ratty, hanging from the torture-chamber wall, has started in on the sob stuff.

So much adulation; such a daft movie. So what went right for New Line and Golden Harvest? And what went wrong with the venerable Hollywood saw which says that you only win big money and big audiences if you put in big money and big ambitions? (Once-in-a-blue-moon exceptions like *Easy Rider* prove the rule.)

Wise old ratty, as moulded by the late, great Jim Henson, could no doubt tell us. Raising a mouldering snout and sepulchral rasp, he would pinpoint *Teenage Mutant Ninja Turtles'* greatest feat: its blend ing of seen-before comic-book elements with a judicious dash of sophisticated mockery.

Seen before: the trusty mentor-pupil relationship between Ratty and the turtles (*Rocky*, *The Karate Kid* and Luke-Yoda in *The Empire Strikes Back*); the cute metamorphic characters, giving another workout for the Henson workshop; the prevailing air of up-to-the-minute street smarts. This last commodity means that sub-human creatures not normally expected to show powers of locution can, in a movie, behave as if they have majored in Advanced Valleyspeak. 'Excellent!', 'Righteous!', 'Awesome!' These turtles have obviously seen and got high on *Bill and Ted's Excellent Adventure*.

But if the film is in part a mixture of well-tried youth-culture tropes, it also boasts a dash of sophistication. It assumes that the average film-going boy or girl is well enough educated to see the joke in our four heroes' names (Leonardo, Michelangelo, Raphael, Donatello). And it expects today's children to catch on to dry throwaway quips like that uttered by one turtle on watching a reunion embrace by two others (one of them just recovered from near-death): 'It's a Kodak moment.'

The film's success proves that young audiences today have a capacity to take an adventure story seriously and to see it sent up at the same time. Even the title, an adult joke on the idiocy of mix-and-shake genre cocktails, fails to deflate youngsters' enthusiasm with excess derision.

It all shows that the much-chastised age of the short attention span carries compensating virtues. Young film-goers take in audio-visual information more quickly than their forebears, and with speed comes agility. They can wrap their movie-going responses around conflicting tones and moods within the same film. *Teenage Mutant Ninja Turtles* challenges young viewers' powers of perceptual co-ordination. Like a video game, it's there not just to be enjoyed but to be taken on as a challenge and beaten.

Once beaten, of course, it's as disposable as any other junk software. Whenever *Teenage Mutant Ninja Turtles* slows down, one starts to see how decrepit some of the components are. If the good jokes are good, the bad jokes are pathetic. ('What do you apply to bruised turtle limbs?' 'Why, turtle wax!'). And a good kilo of sentimental clichés has been emptied into the sub-plot: in which a TV station director's delinquent son runs off to join the villains but – yes – sees the light in the final reel and helps save Ratty while routing the baddies.

So what? The film bounds on through the record books (highest-grossing independent film ever) and a turtle sequel is already in the pipeline.

Literally so. For by siting its hero-vigilantes in the New York sewer system, *Teenage Mutant Ninja Turtles* gives them kudos as, in all senses, 'underground' heroes. The turtles don't just span an age-appeal that ranges from child to adult, they span a comic-book spectrum extending from mainstream kids' adventure comics to the quasi-guerrilla 'commix' of Art Spiegelman. They are the goofy creations of a post-drugs culture trying to come down to earth. At the same time as performing heroic deeds, the turtles subscribe to a junk consumerism that feeds us all as surely as other kinds of effluent feed the other sewer-dwellers.

Takeaway pizzas, personal stereos, pulp magazines – the turtles, like the rest of us, go for the lot. And who can be surprised, in an age when value judgements have been rendered meaningless by a society where almost everything – depending on the day and the headline – is publicized as being bad for us? (Don't eat that egg; stay away from that beef; comics are bad for you.) *Teenage Mutant Ninja Turtles* combines the philosophy of the 1960s – do your own thing, cleave to your own values – with the super-hero action stuff of the 1980s. Perhaps that's what makes it the first popular pacemaker of the 1990s.

HARLAN KENNEDY

TOTAL RECALL

Action films deal in certainties. Like the Westerns of old, they brush aside shades of grey in favour of the argument that there is no problem that cannot be solved with a gun. You don't like apartheid? We'll get Mel Gibson and Danny Glover to blow away South Africa's diplomats in *Lethal Weapon 2*. The government won't do anything about the MIAs in Vietnam? Don't worry, boys, Sylvester Stallone will bring ya home in *Rambo II*. These days your hero can be suicidal, nihilistic, masochistic or even fascistic, but he never questions his actions, and thank God he's on our side.

The most notable aspect of contemporary cinema's contribution to myth is the hero without an Achilles heel who quips his way through mass slaughter with pre-kill one-liners. Even those heroes who started out caught between the light and the darkness have become sanitized. Mad Max started off near-psychotic but ended up a lovable tough guy, whereas Mel Gibson in *Lethal Weapon* took time out from chewing on the muzzle of his own gun for dinner with his partner's family. True, James Bond lost his temper last year, and we were given plenty of hints as to how much in need of psychiatric care was the man who dresses up as a bat to defeat demented clowns, but for the most part the genre is content to streamline its characters as a way of offsetting their violence. This year, however, has produced a new kind of hero.

Doug Quaid is as ordinary as a man with a body like Arnold Schwarzenegger's can be – good job, nice home, a loving wife. In just about any other movie such a character would be forced into violence by outside elements (such as the terrorist kidnappers of *Commando* or the mob in *Raw Deal*). But in *Total Recall* the action comes from Quaid's search to discover his real identity and his true nature, and the complex plot keeps us guessing not only as to whether he is hero or villain but whether what we are seeing is really reality. As soon as he and we think solid mental ground has been reached at last, the grounds for that assumption are pulled spectacularly away. Rather than being simply a series of set pieces strung together by a high-concept thread, this is intricate commercial cinema with a brain – and the most breathless and exhilarating ride of the year.

Quaid's identity crisis begins when, troubled by recurring dreams of Mars and unable to persuade the missus to go there with him for a holiday, he goes to Recall Inc. (First Class Memories Guaranteed) to have the memory implanted, with the optional extra of an 'ego trip' in which he becomes a rebel leader on the politically unstable colony.

Only one problem: it turns out that his 'real' memory was previously erased – he's already been to Mars, and his best friends are desperate to kill him.

Discovering a message from his previous self, Quaid journeys to Mars, only to discover that he could either be a government agent or simply the product of his own imagination in a Recall programme gone wrong. As the walls of reality come tumbling down – most impressively in a hotel room stand-off that may or may not be happening – Quaid (or whoever he is) finds that his identity is not so much a state of mind but a choice he has to make and, this being an Arnie film after all, he gets to kill an awful lot of people along the way (although there's less here of the kind of graphic violence that director Paul Verhoeven brought to *RoboCop*).

The film owes much of its texture to the best sci-fi literature, not surprisingly when you consider its origins in the Philip K. Dick story *We Can Remember It for You Wholesale*. The only previous film derived from Dick's prolific, often chemically inspired, output was *Blade Runner*, which captures the humanism of its source, *Do Androids Dream of Electric Sheep*, amid a designer-decayed future hell that the three-times more expensive *Total Recall* does not aspire to (opting instead for the Albert Speer-like Mexican architecture). *Total Recall* comes closer to cinematically mirroring Dick's style and obsessions – psychic mutants, discompassionate capitalism, the subversion of dissent through consumerism (in this case the villain sells air!) and different planes of mental and physical existence.

For all Verhoeven's skill with action, much of the credit for the film must go to Schwarzenegger who nursed the project through most of its protracted gestation. What distinguishes him from rivals like Stallone is not just his sense of humour (and one-liners are here kept to a minimum) or his tendency to veer away from Sly's monolithic typecasting – having already played stupid (*Twins*) and heartless evil (*The Terminator*) as well as heroic macho – but also his willingness to make films which subvert audience expectations.

In *Total Recall*, as previously in *Predator*, *Commando* and *The Terminator*, the clichés are turned on their heads just when you least expect it. For a time Sharon Stone plays a perfect Doris Day wife with a centrefold body, but it turns out she's married to Michael Ironside's relentless villain. The comic relief sidekick turns out to be a traitor, and the *real* villain of the piece comes as a big surprise. While most other stars are refining their screen persona, only Arnie seems interested in expanding his in new directions, while never failing to deliver what an increasingly loyal audience requires of him. With its intoxicating blend of high-octane thrills, satire and trips through alternative realities, *Total Recall* is, to adopt Quaid's vernacular, the best mind-fuck yet.

TREVOR WILLSMER

UHF

Musical parodist Weird Al Yankovic certainly lives up to his name in this wildly erratic send-up of local TV programming stateside. Under his guidance, Channel 62 makes everything else look like PBS, with programming that has Indiana Jones raiding the temple of doom to steal an Oscar, Rambo destroying the Coliseum, 'Conan the Librarian' and 'Gandhi II – the Revenge' ('this time he's not taking any shit') and a brilliant re-creation of the Geraldo Rivera incident featuring a Klansman and Jason from *Friday the 13th*. There are a few too many gross-out jokes and the bogey-picking competition is truly disgusting, but it's hard to resist a movie with lines like 'Lesbian nazi hookers abducted by UFOs and forced into weight-loss programmes – all this week on *Towntalk*.' **KN**
Director *Jay Levey* **producers** *Gene Kirkwood, John Hyde* **exec** *Gray Frederickson* **script** *Al Yankovic, Levey* **camera** *David Lewis* **editor** *Dennis O'Connor* **design** *Ward Preston* **music** *John Du Prez* **cast** *Weird Al Yankovic, Victoria Jackson, Kevin McCarthy, Michael Richards*
Running time: 96 mins
US release: Orion, Jul 21, 1989

👍 UNCLE BUCK

Just when you thought you had John Hughes pigeon-holed as the man who specializes in films about uproarious, free-spirited, anarchic teenagers terrorizing uptight, straight-laced, materialistic adults, he turns round and gives you *Uncle Buck*, which is about an uproarious, free-spirited, anarchic adult who terrorizes an uptight, straight-laced, materialistic teenager. Three kids are left in the care of their Uncle Buck (Candy), a 40-year-old disgrace with no family, career, prospects or sense of values. Soon, there's a war on between the teenage princess (Kelly), who has cultivated the world's most supercilious sneer, and Buck, who owns a car that rates as a major disaster area and uses the microwave to wash clothes. As always, the minor characters prop up the showy central performance, especially the three marvellously eccentric children. It sounds cutesy in synopsis, but this is a perfectly put-together movie. And it probably establishes Hughes as the best comedy director in Hollywood. **KN**
Director/script *John Hughes* **producers** *Hughes, Tom Jacobson* **camera** *Ralph Bode* **editors** *Lou Lombardo, Tony Lombardo, Peck Prior* **design** *John W. Corso* **music** *Ira Newborn* **cast** *John Candy, Jean Louisa Kelly, Gaby Hoffman, Macauley Culkin, Amy Madigan, Elaine Bromka, Garrett M. Brown, Laurie Metcalf, Jay Underwood*
Running time: 100 mins
US release: Universal, Aug 16, 1989
UK release: UIP, Apr 13, 1990

VALENTINO RETURNS

Director Peter Hoffman uses a small town setting in the 1950s to create a pleasant little film that works hard to keep the audience off-guard. Nothing happens quite the way we expect it to and, if the material is familiar in outline (sex, death, coming of age, pink Cadillacs), Hoffman's handling of Leonard (*Fat City*) Gardner's script is not. He is helped immeasurably by wily veterans Frederic Forrest and Veronica Cartwright as respectively the hero's wastrel father and a housewife sliding into a nervous breakdown. **JH**
Director *Peter Hoffman* **producers** *Hoffman, David Wisnievitz* **script** *Leonard Gardner, from his story* Christ Has Returned to Earth and Preaches Here Nightly **camera** *Jerzy Zielinski* **editor** *Denine Rowan* **design** *Woody Romine* **cast** *Barry Tubb, Frederic Forrest, Veronica Cartwright, Jenny Wright, David Parker, Seth Isler, Miguel Ferrer, Kit McDonough, Macon McCalman*
Running time: 88 mins
US release: Skouras, Jul 21, 1989

VALMONT

    T U R K E Y • T U R K E Y • T U R K E Y

Director *Milos Forman* **producers** *Paul Rassam, Michael Hausman* **script** *Jean-Claude Carrière, from* Les Liaisons Dangereuses *by Choderlos de Laclos* **camera** *Miroslav Ondricek* **editors** *Alan Heim, Nena Danevic* **design** *Pierre Guffroy* **music** *Christopher Palmer* **cast** *Colin Firth, Annette Bening, Meg Tilly, Fairuza Balk, Siân Phillips, Jeffrey Jones, Henry Thomas, Fabia Drake*
Running time: 137 mins
US release: Orion, Nov 17, 1990

◄▦ THE VANISHING (Spoorloos)

The Vanishing not only shows that it's possible to do creative things with the sort of multinational casting and cross-border locations that coproduction financing requires, but it also makes the argument for a European cinema that doesn't kow-tow to Hollywood values. With a script that breaks many of the supposed rules of thriller writing, but has enough character perception and insight into what keeps an audience watching to end up totally engrossing, the film divides its attentions between a frantic individual (Bervoets) whose wife disappears from a French petrol station, and the perverse obsessive (Donnadieu) who has grabbed her for his own mysterious purpose. The film nicely counterpoints Donnadieu's calculated, sometimes comic, preparations for his criminal act, and the hysteria with which Bervoets confronts the situation even three years after the event. Drawn out by Bervoets's persistence in the hunt, Donnadieu lures his secondary victim back to the scene of the crime for the shocking finale. **JP**

Director *George Sluizer* **producers** *Anne Lordon, Sluizer* **script** *Tim Krabbé, from his novel* The Golden Egg **camera** *Toni Kuhn* **editor** *Sluizer, Lin Friedman* **design** *Santiago Isidro Pin, Cor Spijk* **music** *Henny Vrienten* **cast** *Bernard-Pierre Donnadieu, Gene Bervoets, Johanna Ter Steege, Gwen Eckhaus, Bernadette Le Saché, Tania Latarjet, Lucille Glenn, Roger Souza, Pierre Forget, Didier Rousset, Caroline Appéré*
Running time: 106 mins
UK release: Metro, Jun 2, 1990

VENUS PETER

Venus Peter is so deep-frozen that it makes *Pelle the Conqueror* look like *Happy Days*. The title character (Strachan) is a young lad named after his grandfather's boat, who models knee-length shorts and a shaved neck as the misfit of a Scottish fishing village. 'The sea is everything,' people mumble from time to time, and we get a lot of opportunities to look at it. At his baptism, the holy water is frozen so he has to be doused in sea water. Later, a whale is beached and the preacher (Hayman) makes a speech about being nice to them. A new teacher (Cusack) encourages his interest in poetry. Grandad (McAnally) loses his ship to the bank and is depressed. Venus Peter's long-absent father drops in for a visit and has a row. Various old people die. It looks bloody chilly. Audiences pray for the end. The worst kind of British film. **KN**
Director *Ian Sellar* **producer** *Christopher Young* **exec** *Colin MacCabe* **script** *Sellar, Christopher Rush, based on novel* A Twelvemonth and a Day *by Rush* **camera** *Gabriel Beristain* **editor** *David Spiers* **design** *Andy Harris* **music** *Jonathan Dove* **cast** *Ray McAnally, David Hayman, Sinead Cusack, Gordon R. Strachan, Sam Hayman, Caroline Paterson, Alex McAvoy, Emma Dingwall, Peter Caffrey*
Running time: 94 mins
UK release: Oasis, Dec 1, 1989

VINCENT AND THEO

Robert Altman's two and a quarter hour feature version of a drama also destined (at four hours) for a TV miniseries slot. The plot about two Dutch brothers called Van Gogh – one an art dealer, the other an unsuccessful painter – sprawls voluptuously and untidily in its confrontation with genius, as a cat sprawls before a fire. Sometimes it purrs happily as in the Paris-set scenes with Paul Rhys's splendid Theo (a neurotic evangelist struggling to 'sell' his brother's genius). At other times it yawns and stretches, attacked by *déjà vu* as we trek with Vincent through corn fields, Paul Gauguin's visit and climactic ear surgery. A piebald biopic, more curate's egg than golden egg. **HK**

Director *Robert Altman* producer *Ludi Boeken*
exec *David Conroy* script *Julian Mitchell* camera
Jean Lepine editors *Françoise Coispeau, Geraldine
Peroni* design *Stephen Altman* music *Gabriel
Yared* cast *Tim Roth, Paul Rhys, Jip Wijngaarden,
Johanna Ter Steege, Jean-Pierre Cassel, Wladimir
Yordanoff, Bernadette Giraud, Adrian Brine, Jean-
François Perrier, Vincent Vallier, Hans Kesting,
Anne Canovas*
Running time: 138 mins
UK release: Blue Dolphin, Jun 22, 1990

VITAL SIGNS

Vital Signs is to medical school what *Top Gun*
was to mass murder – a false and effective
recruitment ad. While the cast (including *LA
Lawyer* Jimmy Smits) is good and the script
(about a group of third-year medical students
outdoing each other in the selfless department) is
sharp, Marisa Silver too often chooses to pump
up the emotional volume to deafening, rock video
levels. If you think you've seen this stuff before
under the title *Gross Anatomy*, you're right. **CB**
Director *Marisa Silver* producers *Laurie Perlman,
Cathleen Summers* script *Larry Ketron, Jeb Stuart*
camera *John Lindley* editors *Robert Brown,
Danford B. Greene* design *Todd Hallowell* music
Miles Goodman cast *Adrian Pasdar, Diane Lane,
Jimmy Smits, Norma Aleandro, Jack Gwaltney,
Laura San Giacomo, Jane Adams, Tim Ransom,
Bradley Whitford*
Running time: 103 mins
US release: Fox, Apr 13, 1990

VALMONT

Remakes were a little faster this year . . . Milos Forman's *Valmont* is the same story as Stephen Frears's *Dangerous Liaisons*. But not half as good. Nor is it, strictly speaking, a re-tread. Both films were shooting in various wondrous French chateaux during the summer of 1988.

Tales of rivalry between the two productions were legion, with Forman generally coming off worst. His production manager kept trying to book some of the eight castles already hired by Frears's unit. Forman then phoned John Malkovich to enquire about his father-in-law's château in the South. And when he met Glenn Close in a Paris restaurant one night, he apparently offered her the rôle of Valmont's aged aunt, even though she was already mid-way through the far juicier rôle of the wicked Marquise de Merteuil for Frears.

The general verdict among those on Frears's set who had read the rival French script was that there was nothing to beat. And they were right. *Valmont* is a very expensive chocolate-box movie. Beautiful to look at; some of Forman's castles make Frears's film look quite middle-class. Except that there's nothing inside the gilded box. Apart from remarkably soft and mouldy centres.

Forman, as is his wont, chose the teenage route. He likes young, inexperienced casts he can mould to glory. His glory. But not this time.

His chief problem with a *Valmont* that should be called 'Cécile' is . . . Cécile. She's played by Fairuza Balk – who also failed in trying on Judy's shoes in Walter Murch's *Return to Oz* flop five years ago. Even when having her bottom kissed by Valmont (that was the French poster), Balk is so McDonalds-plump, American looking, that she turns the whole enterprise into Gidget Does Europe.

Yet it's the entrapment of Cécile by Valmont and Merteuil that fascinates both Forman and his script-writer Jean-Claude Carrière. Writer and director were so entranced with the virgin convent girl turning on to the eighteenth century's sexual mores that they even insist on supplying her with a marriage more lush and ritzy than Di's or Fergie's. When, in truth, Cécile had been packed off back to a convent for her sins.

We know her fate, as both the Frears and the Forman films are based on *Les Liaisons dangereuses*, a French classic. *Valmont* is a French film, not a classic. And it just might have been better in French. At least that would have given the impression that these characters inhabited the same landfall.

Frears and his producer Norma Heyman were clever in their casting. Choosing aristocrats from New York: Glenn Close, John Malkovich, Uma Thurman, Swoosie Kurtz, Mildred Natwick. And the lone middle-class lady from LA: Michelle Pfeiffer. Result: the accents worked.

As he had done more successfully for *Amadeus*, Forman shopped all over, settling on players who supply a grating mix of London-English, theatrical-English, New York and LA 'English'. And then, almost at the end (of the budget?), young Danceny's seconds arrive to arrange his duel with Valmont, and speaka le broken-engleesh. Forman can only defend the resulting Babel by intoning Malkovich's much repeated line from the Hampton script. 'It's beyond my control!'

Apart from the fact that nobody sings in this near-opera version, Danceny was the main surprise as played by Henry Thomas. He's now ten years older and a few feet taller than he was when following the trail of sweets that led to E.T., but he's not yet old enough or a sufficiently solid actor to tackle a character of such complexity. When Valmont finds him (alone) in Merteuil's bed, one can imagine he's still searching for his missing alien friend.

Colin Firth is no better. He can't help it, of course, but he invariably and disconcertingly resembles Tim Robbins (aka Erik The Viking). Also, we don't see his demise. Somewhat bizarre for a title rôle character. Most actors in such mortal rôles relish the idea of watering a few eyes with their death scenes. Not here. Valmont *succumbs*, as *Variety* always phrases it, far from a camera. Difficult, you see, to put a bloody duel on a chocolate box.

Then we have Meg Tilly. Poor girl. She's utterly wasted in the Michelle Pfeiffer rôle, as the Présidente de Tourvel. Tourvel starts out as a most virtuous lady, who's faithful to her off-screen husband. Forman takes virtue too far and turns Tilly into a nun, inspired no doubt by her performance in *Agnes of God*. She appears devoid of make-up and is never once allowed to look like the kind of woman who would make Valmont fall in love for the first time in his rakehelly, promiscuous life.

Ironically, Forman wanted Michelle Pfeiffer to play the wicked, scheming Merteuil. He entrusted her, instead, to a Jennifer Jones lookalike from Broadway, Annette Bening. She is no match for Glenn Close. Or not yet. She must have something, though, since Frears has cast her in his much-awaited first Hollywood movie, *The Grifters*.

If having the wrong actress playing Cécile – Uma Thurman was perfect in the Frears version – does not help the film, Forman further compounds this error by selecting the wrong actress as her mother.

Cécile, of course, is 17. Yet her mother is played by Siân Phillips, rather older than Frears's Swoosie Kurtz at 55. Ladies just did not have babies around 40 in those days. And each time Phillips shares a scene with Bening, you can almost hear her teeth grinding in her eagerness to sink her choppers into the Merteuil part and show everyone how she should be played. With some fire.

In France, where this was producer Claude Berri's first flop after *Jean de Florette*, *Manon des sources* and *The Bear*, certain lofty critics attacked colleagues for comparing the two ventures. Impossible not to, of course.

Even Stephen Frears felt there was more than one way to tell this story. Milos Forman has proved him wrong. Only dangerous liaison in *Valmont* is between Forman and Choderlos de Laclos' novel. The result is a cross between an opera sans arias – and a waxworks commercial for Euro-Disneyland.

TONY CRAWLEY

THE WAR OF THE ROSES

HIT • HIT • HIT • HIT • HIT

Director Danny DeVito **producers** James L. Brooks, Arnon Milchan **execs** Polly Platt, Doug Claybourne **script** Michael Leeson, *from novel by* Warren Adler **camera** Stephen H. Burum **editor** Lynzee Klingman **design** Ida Random **music** David Newman **cast** Michael Douglas, Kathleen Turner, Danny DeVito, Marianne Sägebrecht, Sean Astin, Heather Fairfield, G. D. Spradlin, Peter Donat
Running time: 116 mins
US release: Fox, Dec 8, 1989
UK release: Fox, Mar 9, 1990

WAR PARTY

After a promising start that gives some indication of the discrimination still facing Native Americans today, Franc Roddam's film takes a sharp and effective turn into thriller territory, only to turn into *Tell Them Willie Boy Is Here* via *First Blood* as its innocents are mercilessly pursued by a posse of rednecked lawmen onto their home ground. There's a lot to admire but there's more to annoy, and ultimately the film fails to add anything new to its clichés. **TW**
Director Franc Roddam **producers** Jon Daly, Derek Gibson, Bernard Williams **execs** Chris Chesser, Roddam **script** Spencer Eastman **camera** Brian Tufano **editor** Sean Barton **design** Michael Bingham **cast** Billy Wirth, Kevin Dillon, Tim Sampson, Jimmy Ray Wales, Kevin M. Howard, M. Emmet Walsh, Cameron Thor, Jerry Hardin
Running time: 99 mins
US release: Hemdale, Apr 14, 1989

▼ WEEKEND AT BERNIE'S

This farce takes nearly half its running time to set up its central premise, that the two faceless young leads must try to pass off their deceased boss as a live swinger during a weekend at his beach residence. *Weekend at Bernie's* opts for all the cheap humour it can get from the concept, with the dead man's mistress noisily making out with him without noticing his condition, the geeky heroes making him seem alive by tying his shoelaces to theirs and walking him around, or by having the body 'ski' behind a speeding boat, with all the vacuous residents of Long Island blithely waving and chatting at the corpse. Ted Kotcheff and Robert Klane, who each have one decent comedy in their credits (*Fun With Dick and Jane*, *Where's Poppa?*) here make do with a clumsily-worked-out central idea, compounded by the charmlessness of the leads and the ugliness of the whole production. **KN**
Director Ted Kotcheff **producer** Victor Drai **execs** Robert Klane, Malcolm R. Harding **script** Klane **camera** François Protat **editor** Joan E. Chapman **design** Peter Jamison **music** Andy

Summers **cast** Andrew McCarthy, Jonathan Silverman, Catherine Mary Stewart, Terry Kiser, Don Calfa, Catherine Parks, Eloise Broady, Gregory Salata, Louis Giambalvo, Ted Kotcheff
Running time: 92 mins (99 mins in US)
US release: Fox, Jul 5, 1989
UK release: Rank, Mar 16, 1990

WELCOME HOME

Franklin Schaffner's final film is a poor epitaph, recalling his early TV work rather than his great screen successes. It's doubtful, however, that anyone could have made much of this material. Kristofferson comes home after seventeen years missing in Vietnam, to find his wife remarried and the son he never knew convinced he's a coward. Although there's some evidence in the direction of a struggle to find genuine emotion in the story, the script opts for clichés all the way, with only Brian Keith, Trey Wilson and, in particular, Sam Waterston (genuinely convincing as the confused second husband) keeping their heads above water. **TW**
Director Franklin J. Schaffner **producer** Martin Ransohoff **execs** Don Carmody **script** Maggie Kleinman **camera** Fred J. Koenekamp **editor** Robert E. Swink **design** Dan Yarhi **music** Henry Mancini **cast** Kris Kristofferson, JoBeth Williams, Sam Waterston, Trey Wilson, Ken Pogue, Brian Keith, Thomas Wilson Brown, J. J., Kieu Chinh, Matthew Beckett, Jessica Ramien
Running time: 92 mins
US release: Columbia, Sep 29, 1989
UK release: Rank, Jan 19, 1990

▼ WE'RE NO ANGELS

The budget apparently topped $30 million for this modest period 'comedy' about two inadvertently escaped convicts masquerading as priests in the hope of crossing the Canadian border. This is a movie made by people with no understanding of comedy but who thought it would be fun to try it. For anyone who saw Neil Jordan's previous attempt at pulling silly faces and running around shouting at the top of your voice – *High Spirits* – the results are all too predictable. **TW**
Director Neil Jordan **producer** Art Linson **exec** Robert De Niro **script** David Mamet, *from play* La Cuisine des anges *by* Albert Husson **camera** Philippe Rousselot **editors** Mick Audsley, Joke Van Wijk **design** Wolf Kroeger **music** George Fenton **cast** Robert De Niro, Sean Penn, Demi Moore, Hoyt Axton, Bruno Kirby, Ray McAnally, James Russo, Wallace Shawn, John C. Reilly, Jay Brazeau, Ken Buhay, Elizabeth Lawrence, Bill Murdoch
Running time: 106 mins
US release: Paramount, Dec 15, 1989
UK release: UIP, Jun 2, 1990

WE THINK THE WORLD OF YOU

Ill-matched gay couples are a new staple of the English cinema. Throw in a dog and you've got all the clichés covered. Yet Colin Gregg's film is a relatively fresh account of how love can dwindle into possessiveness and be deflected into indifference. It's the early 1950s and upper-middle-class Bates loves working-class Gary Oldman. But when Oldman goes to prison, Bates gradually transfers his love to Oldman's dog, battling Oldman's wife (Barber) and mother (Smith) for custody. It's all very funny-pathetic, anchored by Bates's sympathetic portrayal of frustration and repression. **BM**
Director Colin Gregg **producers** Tommaso Jandelli, Paul Cowan **script** Hugh Stoddart, from novel by Joseph R. Ackerley **camera** Mike Garfath **editor** Peter Delfgou **design** Jamie Leonard **music** Julian Jacobson **cast** Alan Bates, Gary Oldman, Max Wall, Liz Smith, Frances Barber, Sheila Ballantine
Running time: 94 mins
US release: Cinecom, Dec 22, 1988
UK release: Oasis, Sep 22, 1989

WHAT HAVE I DONE TO DESERVE THIS? (Que he hecho YO para merecer esto!!)

Delectable apprentice work (1984) by Pedro Almodóvar. In and around a Madrid apartment block, we meet love-hungry cleaning lady Gloria (Maura), her cabbie husband Antonio (who once co-forged some Hitler letters), prostitute Cristal, telekinetic youngster Vanessa and heaven knows who else. Sex, murder and play-school colour schemes abound, announcing the Almodóvar signature. At worst a soap opera with the added ingredient of 'derangement'. At best a piquant rehearsal for the finer excesses of Law of Desire and Women on the Verge of a Nervous Breakdown. **HK**
Director/script Pedro Almodóvar **producer** Tadeo Villalba **exec** Hervé Hachuel **camera** Angel Luis Fernandez **editor** José Solcedo **design** Pino Morales, Roman Arango **music** Bernardo Bonezzi **cast** Carmen Maura, Luis Hostalot, Angel De Andres-Lopéz, Gonzalo Suarez, Verönica Forqué, Juan Martinez, Miguel Angel Herranz
Running time: 101 mins
UK release: Metro, Aug 4, 1989

WHEN HARRY MET SALLY

Actresses have becomes stars by faking orgasms before, but never in a diner as Meg Ryan does to great effect here. There are a lot more trenchant blows to male sexual vanity dispensed along the way (usually in the form of one-liners); enough to make you overlook the sense that this is a pale imitation of Annie Hall ten years on. Boasting what has to be the longest meeting-cut in movie history – twelve years – When Harry Met Sally is little more than a very smart, classy and funny romantic comedy of manners and social ritual that breaks no new ground but provides an ideal dating movie. **TW**
Director Rob Reiner **producers** Reiner, Andrew Scheinman **script** Nora Ephron **camera** Barry Sonnenfeld **editor** Robert Leighton **design** Jane Musky **cast** Billy Crystal, Meg Ryan, Carrie Fisher, Bruno Kirby, Steven Ford, Lisa Jane Persky
Running time: 95 mins
US release: Columbia, Jul 12, 1989
UK release: Palace, Dec 1, 1989

WHEN I FALL IN LOVE (Everybody's All-American in US)

Strangely retitled for British consumption, this long-winded episodic saga, covering some 25 years in the declining fortunes of a self-centred one-time college football star (he sees the light in the final reel) has about as much style and texture as the average TV miniseries. The principals – Quaid as the footballer, Lange as his long-suffering wife, Hutton as a long-suffering relative (labouring under the nickname of 'Cake') – all look too old at the start and too young by the finish, while the passing years are marked by less than imaginative interpolation of pop songs and actuality footage. **TP**
Director Taylor Hackford **producers** Hackford, Laura Ziskin, Ian Sander **exec** Stuart Benjamin **script** Tom Rickman, from novel by Frank Deford **camera** Stephen Goldblatt **design** Don Zimmerman **design** Joe Alves **music** James Newton Howard **cast** Jessica Lange, Dennis Quaid, Timothy Hutton, John Goodman, Carl Lumbly, Ray Baker
Running time: 127 mins
US release: Warner, Nov 4, 1988
UK release: Warner, Feb 16, 1990

WHEN THE WHALES CAME

Considering that it is designed as family entertainment, there is a rather dark and dank air about this movie, set on Bryher in the Isles of Scilly in 1914. Two children in an impoverished fishing community strike up a friendship of sorts with the hermitic 'Birdman' (Paul Scofield, chuntering in Mummerset), who turns out in his childhood to have witnessed a slaughter of whales which brought calamity upon a nearby island. Eventually, of course, the children are the instruments of helping him prevent a repetition of the tragedy. Sympathetic as the preservationist message may be, the climax is less than plausible, and the poverty and superstition which compound the background consort none too easily with the film's picturesque, storybook aspects. **TP**

Director *Clive Rees* producer *Simon Channing Williams* exec *Geoffrey Wansell* script *Michael Morpurgo, from his novel* camera *Robert Paynter* editor *Andrew Boulton* design *Bruce Grimes* music *Christopher Gunning* cast *Helen Mirren, Paul Scofield, David Suchet, Barbara Jefford, David Threlfall, Barbara Ewing, John Hallam, Jeremy Kemp, Max Rennie, Helen Pearce*
Running time: 100 mins
US release: Fox, Oct 20, 1989
UK release: Fox, Sep 8, 1989

⚐ WHERE THE HEART IS

This is a repulsive 'comedy' about people who have no money made by people who don't know what that means. To toughen up his children (Amis, Thurman, Hewlett), Dabney Coleman throws them into an abandoned building that the city won't let him demolish. They take in boarders, none of whom have any money, and try to make a go of it, though they never really find jobs. (Thurman doesn't even consider modelling.) As time passes, it becomes increasingly difficult to credit *Point Blank* as anything but a happy accident in Boorman's career, and anybody who made *Zardoz* as a straight film really shouldn't attempt comedy. **JH**
Director/producer *John Boorman* exec *Edgar F. Gross* script *John Boorman, Telsche Boorman* camera *Peter Suschitzky* editor *Ian Crafford* design *Carol Spier* music *Peter Martin* cast *Dabney Coleman, Uma Thurman, Joanna Cassidy, Crispin Glover, Suzy Amis, Christopher Plummer, David Hewlett, Maury Chaykin, Dylan Walsh, Ken Pogue, Sheila Kelley*
Running time: 94 mins
US release: BV, Feb 23, 1990

WHO'S HARRY CRUMB?

Watching John Candy make a complete ass of himself may bring chortles to some; others it drives up the wall. Here he plays a private dick whose adoption of disguises – a punk with frizzy hair swinging in a windowcleaner's cabin outside the window of a copulating couple; a Hungarian visiting the beauty parlour from which a girl has been kidnapped; an Indian air-conditioning man – produces some reasonably funny moments. But the plot is just too predictable: Candy takes too long to recognize that his employer is the kidnapper, and marks down as the criminals those who wish to murder the kidnapped girl's father. One begins to wish he could get a few smarts together instead of rampaging around like the blind man in the glass shop – destroying model boats, prehistoric relics and tropical fish. **JP**
Director *Paul Flaherty* producer *Arnon Milchan* exec *John Candy* script *Robert Conte, Peter Martin Wortmann* camera *Stephen M. Katz* editor

Danford B. Greene design *Trevor Williams* music *Michel Colombier* cast *John Candy, Jeffrey Jones, Annie Potts, Tim Thomerson, Barry Corbin, Shawnee Smith, Valri Bromfield, Doug Steckler, Renee Coleman, Wesley Mann, Fiona Roeske*
Running time: 98 mins
US release: Tri-Star, Feb 3, 1989
UK release: Col/Tri-Star, Jul 7, 1989

⚐ WILD ORCHID

Suntanned and smirking, Mickey Rourke indulges his fantasies by copulating at length with Carrie Otis (the voluptuous naïf who melts his icy heart) after a meaningless saga of financial chicanery and sexual manipulation in Rio. Despite a good-humoured performance from Jacqueline Bisset as Otis's calm and beautiful boss, and a genuinely erotic cameo by the magnificent Assumpta Serna as a frustrated wife liberated on the back seat of a limo, there aren't 9½ minutes of fun or feeling to be had in this risible celebration of the star's untrammelled narcissism. **GF**
Director *Zalman King* producers *Mark Damon, Tony Anthony* execs *David Saunders, James Dyer* script *King, Patricia Louisianna Knop* camera *Gale Tattersall* music *Geoff MacCormack, Simon Goldenberg* cast *Mickey Rourke, Jacqueline Bisset, Carré Otis, Assumpta Serna*
Running time: 100 mins
US release: Triumph, Apr 27, 1990
UK release: Entertainment, Aug 3, 1990

WILT

There are elements of TV sitcom in this adaptation of Tom Sharpe's farcical novel about a polytechnic lecturer suspected of murdering his ghastly wife, manifested not simply in the casting of Griff Rhys Jones (the lecturer) and Mel Smith (his bumbling CID adversary) but also in some of the dialogue and characterization. On the other hand, the film benefits from both brisk, purposeful direction (a welcome contrast to Mel Smith's own fussy handling of *The Tall Guy*) and from a quite ingeniously shaped narrative, which elucidates the mock-mystery by a succession of bluffs and ambiguities so as pleasingly to send up – or even, given the polytechnic milieu, deconstruct – the protocols of detective fiction. **TP**
Director *Michael Tuchner* producer *Brian Eastman* execs *Nick Elliott, Peter Fincham* script *Andrew Marshall, David Renwick, from novel by Tom Sharpe* camera *Norman Langley* editor *Chris Blunden* design *Leo Austin* music *Anne Dudley* cast *Griff Rhys Jones, Mel Smith, Alison Steadman, Diana Quick, Jeremy Clyde, Roger Allam, David Ryall, Roger Lloyd Pack, Dermot Crowley*
Running time: 93 mins
UK release: Rank, Nov 3, 1989

WINTER PEOPLE

As in *Witness*, Kelly McGillis plays a single mother in an isolated community who shelters a fugitive from the city. In Appalachia, the clans are feudin', and McGillis has made the mistake of loving a man from the wrong clan. While her guest (Russell) constructs a fancy clock for the town, she must make a Sophie-like choice or see the feud erupt in murder. McGillis' face and stature make her a natural as the primitive madonna. The material is sometimes a little Lil' Abner-ish, and Lloyd Bridges seems out of place as a rural patriarch, but for the most part Ted Kotcheff casts a believable spell. **BM**
Director *Ted Kotcheff* **producer** *Robert H. Solo* **script** *Carol Sobieski, from novel by John Ehle* **camera** *François Protat* **editor** *Thom Noble* **design** *Ron Foreman* **music** *John Scott* **cast** *Kurt Russell, Kelly McGillis, Lloyd Bridges, Mitchell Ryan, Amelia Burnette, Eileen Ryan, Lanny Flaherty, Don Michael Paul, David Dwyer, Jeffrey Meek*
Running time: 110 mins
US release: Columbia, Apr 14, 1989
UK release: Rank, Feb 23, 1990

WIRED

If ever there was a doomed project, this is it – all the principals being threatened with ostracism in Hollywood for dredging up the embarrassingly sordid story of comic-cum-addict John Belushi. It's also in the traditional biopic no-win situation of having to recreate its hero's act without catching any of his flair. Michael Chiklis's Belushi impersonation is pretty good, but it's difficult to make a martyred genius out of a performer whose main comic skills were belching and rubbing his belly. With musical interludes alongside plenty of shooting-up, scoring, paranoia and generally unhealthy behaviour, the film flounders in its search for some meaning in Belushi's chaotic life. Ultimately it's just a celluloid freak, and rather than coming away with any insight into America you'll go along with the cop on the case who chides journalist Bob Woodward for being interested in 'just another dead fat junkie.' **KN**
Director *Larry Peerce* **producers** *Edward S. Feldman, Charles R. Meeker* **execs** *P. Michael Smith, Paul Carran* **script** *Earl Mac Rauch, from book by Bob Woodward* **camera** *Tony Imi* **editor** *Eric Sears* **design** *Brian Eatwell* **music** *Basil Poledouris* **cast** *Michael Chiklis, Patti D'Arbanville, J. T. Walsh, Lucinda Jenney, Gary Groomes, Ray Sharkey, Alex Rocco, Jerre Burns, Clyde Kusatsu*
Running time: 109 mins
US release: Taurus, Aug 25, 1989
UK release: Entertainment, Oct 6, 1989

 ## THE WITCHES

A misogynist horror film for children, this doesn't quite manage to make the transition from *Suspiria* to *Honey, I Shrunk the Kids*, although director Nic Roeg certainly brings an unusual sensibility to the film. Jasen Fisher, recently orphaned and in the care of his tale-telling Norwegian grandmother (Zetterling), is taken for a holiday break to a seafront hotel where a convention of the Royal Society for the Prevention of Cruelty to Children is a front for a gathering of all the witches in England. Bald and hideous beneath their wigs and masks, the witches, under the presidency of evil queen Anjelica Huston are planning to turn all the children in the country into mice. Fisher is so afflicted, but manages to adjust to rodenthood and, with the help of his superstitious granny, tries to thwart the evil scheme. Roald Dahl's slyly nasty humour is retained by Roeg, which makes for a less amiable film than *Willy Wonka and the Chocolate Factory* or *Danny the Champion of the World*, but there are also all the special effects expected of a muppet-style Hollywood movie, and several doses of television-style 'British' comedy, courtesy of Rowan Atkinson and Bill Paterson. The film's major achievement, perhaps, is its creation of a new set of myths about witches, elevating them to the horror movie pantheon along with vampires and werewolves, and providing an excuse for some startling make-up effects. **KN**
Director *Nic Roeg* **producer** *Mark Shivas* **exec** *Jim Henson* **script** *Allan Scott, from story by Roald Dahl* **camera** *Harvey Harrison* **editor** *Tony Lawson* **design** *Voytek, Andrew Sanders* **music** *Stanley Myers* **cast** *Anjelica Huston, Mai Zetterling, Bill Paterson, Brenda Blethyn, Rowan Atkinson, Jasen Fisher, Charlie Potter, Anne Lambton, Jane Horrocks, Sukie Smith, Rose English, Jenny Runacre, Annabel Brooks, Emma Relph, Nora Connolly, Rosamund Greenwood*
Running time: 91 mins
US release: Warner, Feb 16, 1990
UK release: Warner, May 25, 1990

WITHOUT YOU I'M NOTHING

Sandra Bernhard, comedienne, actress and media personality, uses this film to comment on her own naked desire for success, assuming a variety of rôles and poses to identify with black and gay culture – in 1990, who else would use Sylvester's late 1970s disco hit, 'Do You Wanna Funk', as a vehicle for political consciousness? *Without You I'm Nothing* is less a re-creation of Bernhard's hit one-woman show than a commentary on it, and those who savour her subversive and abrasive comedy will be surprised by the amount of singing – she's not as good a singer as she thinks she is. It's a strange and interesting portrait of post-Warhol culture. **JH**

Director John Boskovich producer Jonathan D. Krane exec Nicolas Roeg script Sandra Bernhard, Boskovich camera Joseph Yacoe editor Pamela Malouf-Cundy music Patrice Rushen cast Sandra Bernhard, Steve Antin, John Doe, Lu Leonard, Ken Foree, Cynthia Bailey, Robin Byrd
Running time: 90 mins
US release: MCEG, May 4, 1990

THE WIZARD

The Wizard is designed to whet the appetites of kids for the next generation of Nintendo games. It's a marketing tool, but an interesting one. Fred Savage plays a kid who frees his emotionally withdrawn brother from an institution and sets out on a cross-country trip with him. It turns out the kid is a video-game wizard, and they scam their way to a huge Nintendo championship in California. Yes, it's crass and derivative, but at least it's honest. CB
Director Todd Holland producers David Chisholm, Ken Topolsky exec Lindsley Parsons Jr. script Chisholm camera Robert Yeoman editor Tom Finan design Michael Mayer music J. Peter Robinson cast Fred Savage, Beau Bridges, Christian Slater, Jenny Lewis, Luke Edwards, Will Seltzer, Sam McMurray, Wendy Phillips
Running time: 99 mins
US release: Universal, Dec 15, 1989

THE WOLVES OF WILLOUGHBY CHASE

Remember when they used to make wonderful films for children? Films like The Railway Children and The Amazing Mr Blunden with period settings, comically overbearing villains, clean and virtuous junior heroes, a few slightly scary bits, plenty of sobbing and suffering, and a rosily ecstatic last five minutes? Well, here is an attempt to revive the genre. It puts one foot right with the production/costume design, as it creates an imaginary nineteenth-century Britain overrun by wolves, and another with the casting of Stephanie Beacham as Letitia Slighcarp, the wicked governess who takes over Willoughby Chase and makes things rotten for the precocious Bonnie (Hudson) and her timid cousin Sylvia (Darowska). However, the rest of the movie is disastrously somnolent, thanks to a predictable screenplay, uniformly dreadful performances and a story that never really gets going. The wolves, incidentally, are big dogs dressed up in ratty fur coats, and they look especially silly. KN
Director Stuart Orme producer Mark Forstater script William M. Akers, from novel by Joan Aiken camera Paul Beeson editor Martin Walsh design Christopher Hobbs music Colin Towns cast Stephanie Beacham, Mel Smith, Geraldine James, Richard O'Brien, Emily Hudson, Aleks Darowska,

Jane Horrocks, Eleanor David, Jonathan Coy, Lynton Dearden
Running time: 93 mins
UK release: Entertainment, Dec 15, 1989

WORTH WINNING

This is a depressingly familiar throwback to the misogynist sex comedies of the 1960s as Mark Harmon proposes to three women at the same time and finds himself racing from one bedroom to another as he tries to keep them apart before a videotape gives the game away. Built solely around Harmon's long-ago People Magazine selection as 'sexiest man alive', neither star nor film has enough presence or charm to stay afloat, with only Warren's even more depressingly stereotyped housewife-cum-bondage-nympho providing anything that resembles humour. TW
Director Will Mackenzie producers Gil Friesen, Dale Pollock exec Tom Joyner script Josanne McGibbon, Sara Parriott, from novel by Dan Lewandowski camera Adam Greenberg editor Sidney Wolinsky design Lilly Kilvert music Patrick Williams cast Mark Harmon, Madeleine Stowe, Lesley Ann Warren, Maria Holvöe, Mark Blum, Andrea Martin Tony Longo, Alan Blumenfeld, Devin Ratray, David Brenner
Running time: 102 mins
US release: Fox, Oct 27, 1989

THE WAR OF THE ROSES

Ever since they started making movies, you could bet your life that any couple who hated each other in reel one would be married by the fade-out. *The War of the Roses* takes a slightly different tack: in reel one Barbara and Oliver Rose are head over heels. By reel twelve they've killed each other. This is a love story anybody with any experience of the real world can relate to — so how come it took on a long line of big-budget whimsy and wish fulfilment at the Christmas box-office and won?

Taking the love story on beyond the happy ending is by no means a new approach, but it is something to be remarked upon when such a film goes on to become a hit. Scorsese's *New York, New York* was a colossal flop in the pre-Reagan years, whilst the tone of the teflon presidency was so relentlessly upbeat that films like *Twice in a Lifetime* never stood a chance. But here comes a comedy so black it makes Billy Wilder look like Walt Disney, which strikes lucky in Bush's kinder, gentler America? Perhaps that's because, with the gipper out of the way, the American public is willing to face a certain amount of reality again. Perhaps in a nation with the highest divorce rate in the world such a film has a built-in audience. Or perhaps it's simply that the old-fashioned theme of revenge is always going to be a winner.

Revenge is certainly what's at issue in *The War of the Roses*. Throughout the film both characters pursue an escalating tit-for-tat revenge on each other and the furniture. The most convincing malice comes from Barbara, driven nearly insane by her husband's desire to submerge her identity while he pursues his career. Watching the two stars play off against each other, it's hard to forget the bitter memory of his suing her into making *Jewel of the Nile*, or to wonder how much of her performance comes out of anger at seeing him get paid seven times her salary on this film. Even Danny De Vito, the director here, joked that he wanted to leave both stars hanging from the chandelier that dominates the picture's finale while he went to lunch, in revenge for what the two had put him through on *Romancing the Stone*. But satisfying as it is for the recently divorced to see two people going through a separation far bloodier than their own, the film's real financial ace is its moral: marriage is a good thing.

Indeed, most of the film is about the couple's fairy-tale marriage. The small cracks that gradually become giant crevices — he finishes

Of course I love you.

her jokes, puts on a phoney laugh for the boss and never takes her ambitions seriously — are highlighted by ominous reverse zooms and other such devices, not merely to set up the gags but to act as warning markers: it's not marriage that doesn't work, it's the couple's self-complacency that doesn't let it work. The film even ends with De Vito's occasionally incongruous narrator begging a client not to divorce his wife. Marriage, he suggests, is infinitely preferable to the alternative.

Unfortunately, the message doesn't quite fit the scenario. As in Warren Adler's considerably toned-down source novel, the conflict revolves around Douglas's reluctance to let Turner divorce him. Everything he does is aimed at that goal — not so much because he still loves her (although it is clearly implied he still does) but because she plays a crucial part in his dream of a perfect family life. That's why he insists on staying put in the family home which she has spent most of her life developing, and which is the only thing she insists upon retaining in the divorce settlement. When he pisses on the pâté at her dinner party, it is to destroy the business ambitions that have taken his place in her life, and it's his desire to hold on to her that she really wants to break.

The War of the Roses is a have-it-all-ways movie, and as such perfectly captures the mood of the Bush era. A film about a married couple trying to kill each other, which still contrives to be a film rooting for matrimony, is no more absurd than a president talking of leading a kinder, gentler America after one of the dirtiest and most racist election campaigns of recent years. Despite all the nastiness along the way, the film refuses to leave you with a bad taste in the mouth. Even if the argument doesn't quite make sense, there's enough truth in it to strike a nerve, but there's also enough slapstick to its nightmare to reassure the audience that it doesn't mean the things it says.

Taken just as a comedy, the film has the advantage of being really quite funny, with some exquisite lines — such as Oliver Rose's courteously psychotic apology to Marianne Sägebrecht after throwing furniture at her, 'I'm sorry, I thought you were my wife.' And the slapstick is also beautifully timed — including Douglas's shocked half-skip as a chandelier crashes to the ground an inch behind him. But at the end of the day, it's just another slick, high-concept comedy that managed to say the right thing in the right way at the right time.

TREVOR WILLSMER

▲ YAABA

Majestic second feature from Idrissa Ouedraogo of Burkina Faso. Building its story patiently, stone by stone, the film depicts the friendship between a village boy and an outcast old woman suspected of being a witch. But the true drama is in the interaction of people and place. In long shots, sand and sky squeeze the human presence into a tiny scribble on infinity. Closer, the characters are elementalized into the shapes of nature herself: gnarled like the trees, laconic as the desert emptiness. But the film is never merely decorative. Performing its quiet alchemy, it creates a living drama from a minimum of dialogue and the barest of plots and encompasses a warm and comic view of West African village life that can speak to all audiences in its emotional truth. **HK**
Director/script *Idrissa Ouedraogo* **producers** *Pierre Alain Meier, Freddy Denaës, Ouedraogo* **camera** *Matthias Kalin* **editor** *Loredana Cristelli* **music** *Francis Bebey* **cast** *Fatima Sanga, Noufou Ouedraogo, Barry Roukietou, Adama Ouedraogo, Amade Toure, Sibidou Ouedraogo, Adame Sidibe, Kinda Moumouni*
Running time: 90 mins
US release: New Yorker, Oct 9, 1989
UK release: Oasis, Jan 26, 1990

YOUNG EINSTEIN

Yahoo Serious is no Paul Hogan. This vehicle, which he wrote, directed, produced and stars in, did *Dundee*-like business from Perth to Hobart but seems less wonderful beyond the Antipodes. Serious plays Albert Einstein, the son of simple apple farmers in Tasmania who makes his family's fortune in 1905 by turning their beer fizzy through judicious use of a formula he invented, $E=mc^2$. Einstein meets Marie Curie on his way to Sydney to have his formula patented. But the formula is stolen, so the boy invents the electric guitar. This is 1906. Travesty upon travesty follows, in student film fashion. **BM**
Director/editor *Yahoo Serious* **producers** *Serious, Warwick Ross, David Roach* **execs** *Graham Burke, Ray Beattie* **script** *Roach, Serious* **camera** *Jeff Darling* **design** *Steve Marr, Laurie Faen, Colin Gibson, Ron Highfield* **cast** *Yahoo Serious, Odile Le Clezio, John Howard, Pee Wee Wilson, Su Cruickshank, Basil Clarke, Esben Storm, Lulu Pinkus, Kaarin Fairfax*
Running time: 89 mins
US release: Warner, Aug 4, 1989
UK release: Warner, Oct 13, 1989

A ZED AND TWO NOUGHTS

Greenaway's second feature is far less accessible than his first, *The Draughtsman's Contract*. But its typically quirky slice of intellectual game-playing offers ample scope for enjoyment. Twin brothers are widowed when the car carrying their wives is hit by a swan. In attempting to assuage their grief, they become obsessed with the surviving driver and with the problem of physical decay. Firing off ideas, questions and riddles in all directions, this sparkling bagatelle might seem precious and pretentious were it not for its formal rigour, sumptuous visuals (shot largely in and around Rotterdam Zoo) and dry, eccentric wit. Further proof from Greenaway that cod philosophy can be fun. **GA**
Director/script *Peter Greenaway* **producers** *Peter Sainsbury, Kees Kasander* **camera** *Sacha Vierny* **editor** *John Wilson* **design** *Ben Van Os, Jan Roelfs* **music** *Michael Nyman* **cast** *Andrea Ferréol, Brian Deacon, Eric Deacon, Frances Barber, Joss Ackland, Jim Davidson, Agnes Brulet, Guusje Van Tilborgh, Gerard Thoolen, Ken Campbell, Wolf Kahler, Geoffrey Palmer*
Running time: 115 mins
US release: Skouras, May 25, 1990
UK release: BFI, Dec 5, 1986

AWARDS

EVENT	CATEGORY	WINNER

THE ABYSS

Oscar	Visual Effects	John Bruno, Dennis Muren, Hoyt Yeatman, Dennis Skotak

THE ADVENTURES OF BARON MUNCHAUSEN

BAFTA	Production Design	Dante Ferretti
BAFTA	Costume Design	Gabriella Pescucci
BAFTA	Make-up	Maggie Westeon, Fabrizio Sforza, Pam Meager

AND THERE WAS LIGHT

Venice	Special Grand Prize	Otar Ioselliani

THE ASTHENIC SYNDROME

Berlin	Silver Bear	Kura Muratova

AUSTRALIA

Venice	Cinematography	Yorgos Arvanitis

BACK TO THE FUTURE, PART II

BAFTA	Special Effects	Ken Ralston, Michael Lantieri, John Bell, Steve Galwey

BATMAN

Oscar	Art Direction	Anton Furst, Peter Young

BLACK RAIN

Oscar	Sound	Donald O. Mitchell, Kevin O'Connell, Greg P. Russell, Keith A. Waster

BLACK SNOW

Berlin	Outstanding Single Achievement	Xie Pie

EVENT	CATEGORY	WINNER

BORN ON THE FOURTH OF JULY

Golden Globe	Drama	A. Kitman Ho, Oliver Stone
DGA	Director	Oliver Stone
Oscar	Director	Oliver Stone
Golden Globe	Director	Oliver Stone
Golden Globe	Screenplay	Ron Kovic, Oliver Stone
Golden Globe	Actor	Tom Cruise
Oscar	Editing	David Brenner, Joe Hutshing

BYE BYE BLUES

Genie	Actress	Anny Wheeler
Genie	Supporting Actress	Robyn Stevan

CINEMA PARADISO

Oscar	Foreign Film	Giuseppe Tornatore
Golden Globe	Foreign Film	Giuseppe Tornatore
European	Actor	Philippe Noiret
European	Special Jury Award	Giuseppe Tornatore

A CITY OF SADNESS

Venice	Golden Lion	Hou Hsiao-hsien

COLD COMFORT

Genie	Adapted Screenplay	Richard Beattie, L. Elliott Simms

COMING OUT

Berlin	Silver Bear	Heiner Carow

COMMON THREADS: STORIES FROM THE QUILT

Oscar	Documentary	Robert Epstein, Bill Couturie

CRIMES AND MISDEMEANORS

NY Critics	Supporting Actor	Alan Alda
Board of Review	Supporting Actor	Alan Alda

A CRY IN THE DARK

Australian	Film	Verity Lambert
Australian	Director	Fred Schepisi
Australian	Adapted Screenplay	Fred Schepisi, Robert Caswell
Australian	Actress	Meryl Streep
Australian	Actor	Sam Neill

EVENT	CATEGORY	WINNER

CYRANO DE BERGERAC

Cannes	Actor	Gérard Depardieu
Cannes	Technical Achievement	Pierre Lhomme (cinematographer)

DANGEROUS LIAISONS

César	Foreign Film	Stephen Frears
BAFTA	Adapted Screenplay	Christopher Hampton
BAFTA	Supporting Actress	Michelle Pfeiffer

DEAD CALM

Australian	Cinematography	Dean Semler

DEAD POETS SOCIETY

BAFTA	Film	Steven Haft, Paul Junger Witt, Tony Thomas, Peter Weir
Oscar	Screenplay	Tom Schulman
BAFTA	Score	Maurice Jarre

DEATH OF A TEA MASTER

Venice	Silver Lion	Ken Kumai

DISTANT VOICES, STILL LIVES

LA Critics	Foreign Film	Terence Davies

DO THE RIGHT THING

LA Critics	Film	Spike Lee
LA Critics	Director	Spike Lee
LA Critics	Supporting Actor	Danny Aiello
NY Critics	Cinematography	Ernest Dickerson
LA Critics	Score	Bill Lee

DRIVING MISS DAISY

Oscar	Film	Richard Zanuck, Lili Fini Zanuck
Board of Review	Film	Richard Zanuck, Lili Fini Zanuck
Golden Globe	Comedy	Richard Zanuck, Lili Fini Zanuck
Oscar	Adapted Screenplay	Alfred Uhry
WGA	Screenplay	Alfred Uhry
Berlin	Joint Performance	Jessica Tandy, Morgan Freeman
Board of Review	Actor	Morgan Freeman

EVENT	CATEGORY	WINNER
Golden Globe	Actor	Morgan Freeman
Oscar	Actress	Jessica Tandy
Golden Globe	Actress	Jessica Tandy
Oscar	Make-up	Manlio Rocchetti, Lynn Barber, Kevin Haney

DRUGSTORE COWBOY

National Critics	Film	Nick Wechsler, Karen Murphy
National Critics	Director	Gus Van Sant
LA Critics	Screenplay	Gus Van Sant, Daniel Yost
National Critics	Screenplay	Gus Van Sant, Daniel Yost
NY Critics	Screenplay	Gus Van Sant, Daniel Yost

A DRY WHITE SEASON

Tokyo	Actor	Marlon Brando

EL DORADO

European	Director	Geza Beremenyi

ENEMIES, A LOVE STORY

NY Critics	Director	Paul Mazursky
NY Critics	Supporting Actress	Lena Olin
National Critics	Supporting Actress	Anjelica Huston

THE FABULOUS BAKER BOYS

NY Critics	Actress	Michelle Pfeiffer
Board of Review	Actress	Michelle Pfeiffer
National Critics	Actress	Michelle Pfeiffer
LA Critics	Actress	Michelle Pfeiffer
Golden Globe	Actress	Michelle Pfeiffer
National Critics	Supporting Actor	Beau Bridges
National Critics	Cinematography	Michael Ballhaus
LA Critics	Cinematography	Michael Ballhaus

FLYING FOX IN A FREEDOM TREE

Tokyo	Screenplay	Martin Sanderson

GLORY

Oscar	Supporting Actor	Denzel Washington
Golden Globe	Supporting Actor	Denzel Washington
Oscar	Cinematography	Freddie Francis
Oscar	Sound	Donald O. Mitchell, Gregg C. Rudloff, Elliot Tyson, Russell Williams 2d

EVENT	CATEGORY	WINNER

HENRY V

Board of Review	Director	Kenneth Branagh
BAFTA	Director	Kenneth Branagh
NY Critics	First-time Director	Kenneth Branagh
Oscar	Costume Design	Phillis Dalton

HIDDEN AGENDA

| Cannes | Special Jury Prize | Ken Loach |

HIGH HOPES

European	Actress	Ruth Sheen
European	Supporting Rôle	Edna Dore
European	Score	Andrew Dickson

HIVER 54, L'ABBE PIERRE

| César | Supporting Actor | Robert Hirsch |

I WANT TO GO HOME

| Venice | Screenplay | Jules Feiffer |

IMMEDIATE FAMILY

| Board of Review | Supporting Actress | Mary Stuart Masterson |

INDIAN NOCTURNE

| César | Cinematograpy | Yves Angelo |

INDIANA JONES AND THE LAST CRUSADE

| Oscar | Sound Effects Editing | Ben Burtt, Richard Hyams |

INTERGIRL

| Tokyo | Special Jury Prize | Pyotr Todorovsky |
| Tokyo | Actress | Elena Yakovleva |

INTERROGATION

| Cannes | Actress | Krystyna Janda |

JESUS OF MONTREAL

Genie	Film	Roger Frappier, Pierre Gendron
Genie	Director	Denys Arcand
Genie	Script	Denys Arcand
Genie	Actor	Lothaire Bluteau
Genie	Supporting Actor	Remy Girard
Genie	Cinematography	Guy Dufaux

EVENT	CATEGORY	WINNER

LANDSCAPE IN THE MIST

| European | Film | Theo Angelopoulos |

LARKS ON A STRING

| Berlin | Golden Bear | Jiri Menzel |

LIFE AND NOTHING BUT

BAFTA	Foreign Film	Bertrand Tavernier
European	Special Jury Award	Bertrand Tavernier
European	Actor	Philippe Noiret
César	Actor	Philippe Noiret
Tokyo	Artistic Contribution	Bertrand Tavernier

THE LITTLE MERMAID

Oscar	Score	Alan Menken
Golden Globe	Score	Alan Menken
Oscar	Song	Alan Menken, Howard Ashman
Golden Globe	Song	Alan Menken, Howard Ashman

LITTLE VERA

| European | Screenplay | Maria Khmlik |

MISSISSIPPI BURNING

BAFTA	Cinematography	Peter Biziou
BAFTA	Editing	Gerry Hambling
BAFTA	Sound	Bill Phillips, Danny Michael, Robert Litt, Elliot Tyson, Richard C. Kline

MUSIC BOX

| Berlin | Golden Bear | Costa-Gavras |

MY LEFT FOOT

NY Critics	Film	Jim Sheridan
Oscar	Actor	Daniel Day Lewis
BAFTA	Actor	Daniel Day Lewis
NY Critics	Actor	Daniel Day Lewis
LA Critics	Actor	Daniel Day Lewis
National Critics	Actor	Daniel Day Lewis
Oscar	Supporting Actress	Brenda Fricker
LA Critics	Supporting Actress	Brenda Fricker
BAFTA	Supporting Actor	Ray McAnally

EVENT	CATEGORY	WINNER

THE NASTY GIRL
| Berlin | Best Director | Michael Verhoeven |

RECOLLECTIONS OF THE YELLOW HOUSE
| Venice | Silver Lion | Joao César Monteiro |

ROGER & ME
NY Critics	Documentary	Michael Moore
Board of Review	Documentary	Michael Moore
LA Critics	Documentary	Michael Moore
National Critics	Documentary	Michael Moore

SEX, LIES AND VIDEOTAPE
| LA Critics | Actress | Andie MacDowell |

SHE'S BEEN AWAY
| Venice | Actress | Peggy Ashcroft, Geraldine James |

SHIRLEY VALENTINE
| BAFTA | Actress | Pauline Collins |

SILENT SCREAM
| Berlin | Actor | Iain Glen |

STEEL MAGNOLIAS
| Golden Globe | Supporting Actress | Julia Roberts |

STING OF DEATH
| Cannes | Grand Prix | Kohei Oguri |
| Cannes | International Critics | Kohei Oguri |

STORY OF WOMEN
NY Critics	Foreign Film	Claude Chabrol
Board of Review	Foreign Film	Claude Chabrol
LA Critics	Foreign Film	Claude Chabrol

SWEETIE
| Australian | Screenplay | Jane Campion |

TAXI BLUES
| Cannes | Director | Pavel Lungin |

EVENT	CATEGORY	WINNER

THAT SUMMER OF WHITE ROSES

| Tokyo | Grand Prize | Rajko Grlic |
| Tokyo | Director | Rajko Grlic |

300 MILES TO HEAVEN

| European | Young Film | Maciej Dejczer |

TILAI

| Cannes | Grand Prix | Idrissa Ouedraogo |

TROP BELLE POUR TOI!

César	Film	Bernard Marescot
César	Director	Bertrand Blier
César	Screenplay	Bertrand Blier
César	Actress	Carole Bouquet

LA VOUIVRE

| César | Supporting Actress | Suzanne Flon |

WHAT TIME IS IT?

| Venice | Actor | Marcello Mastroianni, Massimo Troisi |

WHEN HARRY MET SALLY

| BAFTA | Screenplay | Nora Ephron |

WILD AT HEART

| Cannes | Golden Palm | David Lynch |

WOMEN ON THE ROOF

| European | Cinematography | Ulf Brantas, Jorgen Persson |

ALEC BALDWIN

In *Married to the Mob* 'Cucumber' Frank De Marco (Alec Baldwin) peers out from the bathtub steam at an intruder in a beige astrakhan coat. It's his friend and godfather, Don Dean Stockwell. What's he doing here? And is that a gun he's carrying or is he just excited to see me? It's a gun. And Dean is pointing it. Frank should get out of the bathroom, if he has any sense. He speaks. But conversation does not seem to interest the Don. Frank plays his last card:

'I loved you – like a father.' Pause.

'You disappointed the shit outa me.' Bang! Bang!

It's a movie sequence that has everything. Fear, humour, violence, character exposition, teasing visuals (all that steam) and a play-off between two top actors: one a veteran, the other a fast-rising newcomer.

Just like 'Cucumber' Frank de Marco, Alec Baldwin is emerging from the baptismal waters of movie initiation to face the blessings or bullets of stardom. In 1988, his apprentice year, he splashed around in no less than five feature films. In *Great Balls of Fire* he was preacher Jimmy Swaggart, roaring hell fire at Jerry Lee Lewis. In *Beetlejuice* he was a New England ghost battling invader-yuppies. In *Working Girl* he was Melanie Griffith's black lace-fancying boyfriend. ('Can't you buy me something I can wear outside the house?' she bleats poignantly). In *Talk Radio* he was a manic radio producer. In *Married to the Mob* he was – but that's where we came in.

Now, out of the font and into the firing-line, Baldwin is the star of *The Hunt for Red October* and *Miami Blues*. And more is on the way. He has even reached the Olympian stage of passing up leading rôles. After signing on to star in Philip Kaufman's forthcoming *Henry and June*, Baldwin decided 'No' to shaving his head and going to Paris as author Henry Miller. ('I wanted to play June, but they wouldn't let me,' he comments.)

Alec Baldwin is that rare thing, a preppie with fire. There are few enough of them around. Rob Lowe comes to mind and then goes away again. Ryan O'Neal has the ivy-league looks but lacks the ivy-league emotions to go with them. Baldwin looks as if he had stepped out of school and straight into a gangster training academy. His voice is a husky, charismatic growl that could grow up to become the true mafia laryngitis. His looks are dark and Italianate: though as the bespectacled husband in *Beetlejuice* he could have passed for a beardless Steven Spielberg. And he acts a lot with his neck and shoulders, just like his favourite star James Cagney.

What is mannerism and what is essence? *The Hunt for Red October* put Baldwin on that dangerous hero-rôle height, where an actor abandons the base-camp warmth and nourishment of character rôles and relies on himself. No tics, no tricks: just the naked personality confronting the audience across the icy wastes of the auditorium. Since Baldwin has been signed to play Jack Ryan again in a follow-up Tom Clancy thriller, we must assume that Paramount liked what they got. Since audiences paid over $100 million to see the film, we must assume they liked it too.

Baldwin as hero has a rangy, hungry energy: he's a predator with brain power. In *The Hunt for Red October* you *see* him thinking. Unlike the Californian action man Eastwood-style, where the thoughts lie deep behind the sun-squeezed eyes, Baldwin's New England edginess puts everything on the surface: and makes it volatile, mercurial. Spin this hero around so that he loses his moral bearings and he might bring the same munching, fidgety curiosity to villainy.

Which is what he does in *Miami Blues*. Anyone doubting Baldwin's star power should watch him chewing up the Art Deco scenery in his latest incarnation. In George Armitage's film of Charles Willeford's thriller novel, Baldwin is the breezy nutcase who brings crime, madness and one-liners to the Sunshine State. Whether robbing or running; whether wisecracking or wassailing (tequila a speciality); whether lying on bed doing shtik soliloquies in a Mexican accent or expounding his own brand of Marx Brothers existentialism ('My problem is I can have anything any time I want, but I don't know what I want'), Baldwin is riveting.

He makes this round-the-clock psychopath, who begins by killing a Hari Krishna donation-seeker and ends by losing his fingers to a machete in a botched robbery, seem not just believable but (we hate ourselves for it) lovable. His fast, flaky, frog-throated criminal plays off against the wooden-Indian rectitude of Fred Ward's detective. And please pass a handkerchief – we don't know whether to laugh affectionately or cry – at girlfriend Jennifer Jason Leigh's touching words over the dying Baldwin at movie's close. 'He had some good qualities,' she flutes. 'He always ate everything I cooked for him.'

And that's doubtless why he has grown up the way he has. Born in Massapequa, Long Island, in 1958, Baldwin is now the best prospect for hero-with-an-edge stardom since Harrison Ford. Like any good heroic actor, he has burned the bridges of bourgeois respectability. Born of Irish-Catholic parents, Baldwin planned to go to law school and once dreamed of being America's president. (Today he describes himself as being 'a total lefty, a Kennedy democrat.')

Other vital facts. Baldwin is allergic to cats. He claims to have had 60 jobs before acting, including selling shirts and being a waiter. He appeared on Broadway in Caryl Churchill's *Serious Money* and Joe Orton's *Loot*. He was paid $400 a week for his first regular acting job on TV, a soap called *The Doctors*. (He was later a fixture of *Knots Landing*.) Asked recently to pick a golden moment in his movie work to date, he said: 'Getting killed by Dean Stockwell was indeed the high point of my career.' Which, again, is where we came in.

HARLAN KENNEDY

PATRICK BERGIN

Patrick Bergin has proved himself to be an actor who learns from his mistakes. It's a quality that may have something to do with his background. Born in Dublin, but moving to London at the age of seventeen, he was described as one of the brightest boys in his school, although poor exam results kept him out of college. He then took his further education into his own hands, working in a library by day and studying by night, while also starting up a small theatre group as writer, producer, director and actor.

Within four years he had been accepted at the North London Polytechnic for a teaching course. Developing an intense dislike of conventional pedagogy, he devised his own methods with puppetry and video for regular truants before deciding to break into acting full time in 1980, only to find that the only work available consisted of bit parts on such TV shows as *Boon* and *Hard Cases*, in which even the most eagle-eyed star spotter would have to admit he made amazingly little impression.

His first major rôle came with *The Courier*, in which he plays Gabriel Byrne's sidekick to underwhelming effect; he fails to convey any real malevolence and seems to act with his head rather than his body. The only hint of future promise comes in an early scene when Bergin tries to convince an associate to get off drugs by extolling the virtues of armed robbery. Although he focuses too hard on internals, and seems oblivious of the camera, his performance does show a mind at work.

Along with many in the supporting cast of *The Courier*, Bergin went on to appear in Francis Megahy's toy-town thriller for the hard-of-thinking, *Taffin*. His rôle as the eponymous debt collector's brother is slightly more substantial than in the previous film but much less interesting. Although noticeably more competent than his two leads, Bergin's inability to flesh out the single dimension of the character ensures that he makes little impression. What he does bring to the part is more assurance with the camera, although too often in his reaction shots he appears to be responding to off-camera directions (as do most of the cast) than trying to establish any relation to normal human behaviour.

Against the odds he won the key rôle of an IRA informer trying to start a new life in Australia in the miniseries *Act of Betrayal*. He grabbed the part with both hands and made it considerably more than the sum of its parts. As well as garnering excellent reviews, the show demonstrated his ability to build upon his strengths. This is his most noticeable similarity to Sean Connery in his early days – a favourite comparison of critics since the release of *Mountains of the Moon*.

In Bob Rafelson's epic character-study, charting the friendship and betrayal of two very different explorers in their search for the source of the Nile, Iain Glenn's subtle portrayal of the repressed homosexual Speke has the edge on Bergin's exuberant but tortured Burton, but it is to the latter we are constantly drawn, and not simply because he is the more colourful of the two: he has real presence.

Glenn gives us a convincing portrait of a man whose psyche is out of key with his surroundings, but Bergin seems to be in his natural habitat with a quality as large as the man and the genre. Such is the charisma he brings to the part you could believe him leading an army on horseback into the jaws of hell itself, yet such is the emerging talent to back it up that he could show his (one suspects not wholly honourable) motives for doing so with but a single look. What makes his performance so cinematic is his ability to paint the many shades of the man by doing so little.

One of the best examples of this visual shorthand comes in his first meeting with Speke – one of the (too many) key scenes cut from the release prints (although curiously still to be found in the trailers). In the space of barely a second, his initial anger and indifference completely disappear as the younger man asks to accompany him on his quest. In Burton's eyes is the excitement of a mystery worth more to him than the prize of the Nile – why does this man want to join him, what drives him?

To Bergin's Burton, people are only of interest for as long as they have something to offer the development of his own soul. Whilst he is content to linger in the many villages *en route* to the mountains of the moon, once he has taken all he needs he moves on – until the realization that there are events beyond his control makes him lose interest even in his stated goal. At the court of the African tribal king Ngola his confidence is shattered when his innate authority is undermined. Imprisoned and drugged, he is unable to guarantee the safety of an escaped slave who had unwillingly joined his expedition. In the film's most challenging sequence, he kills the man in what he knows is a futile attempt to regain control of his own destiny; yet merely achieves physical salvation at the cost of spiritual destruction. From here on Bergin gives us a new Burton, struggling to cope with the obliteration of all his certainties – his friendship with Speke, his reputation as a geographer – willing and wanting to forgive in the hope of vindication and a return of his old self, but unwilling to confront Speke for fear of that hope being dashed. Bergin takes us on every stop of the journey with nary a wrong step.

Even if the film failed to conquer at the box-office, it has proved an impressive launch-pad for Bergin's career. With his performance as the devil in *Highway to Hell* already behind him, he has also recently played opposite Julia Roberts in *Sleeping With the Enemy* and Sean Young in another currently untitled film. According to Bergin, when he secured the rôle of Burton, the casting director phoned up his agent and said 'Shall we make Patrick a star?' Having completed his apprenticeship and delivered a magnetic performance as the kind of man every boy wants to be when he grows up, he just might make it.

TREVOR WILLSMER

MORGAN FREEMAN

Few actors have established themselves quite so firmly in the minds of cinema-goers over the past twelve months as Morgan Freeman. With major rôles in *Glory*, *Driving Miss Daisy* and *Johnny Handsome*, and *Clean and Sober* only just released in Britain, Freeman seems to have been in more movies in one year even than John Goodman. What makes this all the more surprising is that he's a middle-aged black actor who has avoided the usual rapist/pusher stereotypes and is developing a trademark integrity that stars like Eddie Murphy or Richard Pryor forfeited long ago. Even as a bad guy, his malice has nothing to do with typecasting shorthand – not that typecasting seems to have troubled him of late: professions he's been called upon to bring to life include those of pimp, teacher, cop, chauffeur, drug counsellor, soldier and judge.

If 1990 was the year in which audiences finally put a name to Freeman's face, he's been working his way into their consciousness for the best part of a decade, via lines here and there in *Brubaker*, *Harry and Son*, *Teachers*, *That Was Then, This Is Now* and *Marie*, not to mention equally minor rôles in tele-movies such as *Attica* and *The Atlanta Child Murders*.

For more satisfying parts Freeman had to turn to the theatre. Having landed his first professional job as a dancer for the 1964 New York World Fair, his acting career began with a small rôle in the touring production of *The Royal Hunt of the Sun*. During 1967, he made his Off-Broadway début opposite Stacy Keach and Viveca Lindfors in *The Nigger Lovers*, which led to a singing and dancing rôle in the Broadway production of *Hello Dolly!* His subsequent five-year stint as the Easy Rider on TV's *The Electric Show* (a sort of *Sesame Street* without puppets) probably had more to do with the demands of his landlord than anything else. And despite a Tony award nomination (for his wino in *The Mighty Gents*) and Obies for *Coriolanus* and *The Gospel at Colonus*, movies still didn't beckon – at the time they were more interested in blacks as manifestations of white society's urban paranoia than as human beings. It was only after he had played a pimp that Morgan Freeman started being offered scripts.

Fast Black, the vicious and manipulative pimp who makes the most of being mistakenly turned into a minor media celebrity in *Street Smart*, easily stole the film from Christopher Reeve's limited lead. Freeman's portrayal of that frightening figure went beyond the second-hand dialogue to create a multi-faceted and charismatic opportunist, and wowed the critics sufficiently to lead to the Supporting Actor award from the New York Film Critics, and a nomination for the Oscar. Suddenly casting directors started to take notice.

Freeman's first lead was the controversial high-school principal in *Lean on Me*, making some sense of a man whose teaching methods were evenly divided between the use of compassion and a baseball bat. That was quickly followed by a succession of different rôles in which he aged up and down, and cheerfully commuted not only between class, but also between different periods of American history.

His drug counsellor in *Clean and Sober* clearly demonstrated his ability to make something out of very little: despite bare dialogue and scant screen time, he displayed a quiet power that hinted at a man struggling to control himself with the strength he drew from addicts who looked to him to do the same for them. Then there was A. Z. Drones, the cynical police lieutenant wandering through *Johnny Handsome* like a Greek chorus waiting for the inevitable. Again it wasn't much of a part, but Freeman made audiences notice him and provided the film's best moment with his amazed reaction to the discovery that Johnny's girlfriend (Elizabeth McGovern) really is a nice girl.

Glory was something else again. According to Freeman, his part as the first NCO of the first coloured regiment in America's Civil War was left open, as were all the black parts, for the actor to create. Drawing on his four years in the Air Force (he had originally intended to be a fighter pilot), Freeman dominates his major scenes in the film with soft-spoken, paternalistic authority and warmth.

The film of *Driving Miss Daisy* provided less freedom for improvisation. But having originated the part on the stage (and secured himself another Obie in the process), it's doubtful if he was much troubled. The resulting second Oscar nomination confirmed his promotion to star status and renewed some of the controversy his previous nomination had aroused. First a pimp, now a chauffeur – wasn't he just playing the white man's nigger all over again? Freeman didn't see it that way, pointing out that some New York blacks were pimps just as some Southern blacks were chauffeurs; what was important was to show that they were also human beings. Indeed, while *Driving Miss Daisy*'s Hoke starts out playing the rôle both society and his employer expect of him, his humanity is allowed gradually to emerge alongside the social changes of the film's 20-year timescale, albeit a little too cosily. If he behaves like Uncle Tom at the beginning, that's because whites demanded that he behave that way.

More controversy followed when Freeman was cast in Brian De Palma's adaptation of *Bonfire of the Vanities*. Aware of local opposition to the picture's alleged racism, the producers ignominiously fired Alan Arkin and replaced him by Freeman in the hope that a black face in the judge's robes would dampen the flames. The response of the rest of the cast was to threaten a strike. Since completing his rôle on that picture, Freeman has returned to the stage, playing opposite Tracey Ullman in a Wild West version of *Taming of the Shrew*. He's waiting for the new cinema rôle to come along. But while he's content to play the same part five days a week on the stage, he's made it clear he won't do the same on the big screen. 'When I was younger I wanted to be a star,' he explains, 'but now I want to be a force!' With leads in two of the biggest surprise low-budget sleepers of recent years, he just might do it.

TREVOR WILLSMER

ANDY GARCIA

You can see from the way that Andy Garcia has come up the Hollywood ladder from bits parts to the brink of stardom that he must have had to endure a fair amount of bullshit in the early days of schlepping around agents and casting directors.

On the one hand, he's bound to have run into stereotyping – 'Oh, you Hispanic right? Sorry, we ain't got no drug-dealing rôles this week'. The typecasting followed – 'You played a drug-dealer right in that Hal Ashby film. You any good with knives? We might have something for you, this psycho right. Hey, where ya going?'

Add to this Cuban-born Garcia's empathy with the Method and you can see yet more crap descending on him. 'Hey, my man, this is Andy, the new Al Pacino. He's got the mumble down pat. Show them, Andy.'

While there are some elements in Garcia's performances that bring Pacino to mind, particularly the way he tends to rest his head on his hand, a finger propping up his forehead as he surveys his quarry, Garcia has proved himself to be his own man. With Mike Figgis's American début, *Internal Affairs*, he achieved a new intensity in performance that marks him out for great things in the 1990s.

Garcia's early credits are eclectic rather than a study in development. But he got the stereotyping to work for him by playing a psychopathic drug dealer in Hal Ashby's overwrought thriller, *Eight Million Ways to Die*. He made the part his own by imbuing the character with a mass of insightful and idiosyncratic mannerisms. The New York critics nominated him best supporting actor in 1986 for that film.

Ashby encouraged lead Jeff Bridges, an alcoholic ex-cop trying to finger cocaine dealer Garcia for the murder of a prostitute, to improvise with Garcia. Their scenes are the most electric in an otherwise rambling essay in redemption through love.

It's Garcia's pony-tailed control freak, with his gravel-cracked voice, constantly tugging on his jacket and seemingly always on the edge of an explosion of psychotic violence, that dominates the screen. But with dialogue such as 'the street light makes my pussy hair glow in the dark' it's hard to take the proceedings too seriously.

Garcia then turned up as the Italian marksman in Brian De Palma's operatic *The Untouchables* as part of Kevin Costner's crime-busting group. Slick, stocky and with a fiery mumble, his George Stone is a study in understatement, a wise choice against Sean Connery's grizzly-bear Irish beat cop.

Maurice Hatton's *American Roulette* brought him his first lead. Garcia plays a South American president exiled to London, trying to decide whether to be a poet or a politician, as the junta at home send an assassination squad to hunt him down. His performance is the only element of interest in an otherwise tired exercise in convoluted plotting and arcane dialogue about love and freedom.

Hatton's camera listlessly follows a slightly podgy Garcia as he meanders around London in every conceivable form of transport. Yet there are hints of performances to come, as Garcia tries to anchor the film around his sombre, brooding presence.

Garcia's next rôle, playing a doomed sidekick to Michael Douglas's maverick cop in Ridley Scott's culture-clash *policier, Black Rain*, showed him edging closer to star status. While Douglas's scruffy obsessive tends to push everyone else off the screen, Garcia's earnest cop generates enough sympathy for his dramatic exit – he's beheaded by bike-riding Japanese gangsters in an underground car-park in Osaka – to more than justify Douglas's hell-bent quest for revenge.

But it's *Internal Affairs* that really shows what Garcia can do. Rogue cop Richard Gere seeks to stop internal affairs cop Garcia investigating his crime-financed lifestyle. It becomes apparent that Figgis is essaying a contemporary *Othello* as Gere gets to Garcia's wife in order to manipulate his sexual fears.

Gere, a monstrous caricature of rampant heterosexuality, displays a racist hatred of Garcia and an ability to push the buttons that will send him into a frenzy of jealousy and emotional confusion.

Garcia is at his most riveting as he tries to shake out of his head the monochrome images Gere has fed into his mind of his wife being sodomized. When he confronts her over over an innocent lunch date, the intensity of the violent explosion that follows underscores the deep-rooted misogyny which Garcia shares with Gere.

The two protagonists are wrapped up in their own selfishness. When Gere justifies the numerous homicides he has carried out to protect the world he has created for his eight children, his image of himself as a distorted mother-earth figure is punctuated by him screaming 'selfish yuppie' at Garcia before he is killed. As funny as this is, it also strikes a note of recognition in the rôle Garcia has built up, of someone aspiring to promotion as part of a career-orientated and childless couple. When he tells Gere to get off his bed, before he kills him, it's because he recognizes the extent to which Gere has become part of his world. He is left standing in his bedroom with his wife, stranded in the huge cavern of uncertainty that Gere's malicious probings have so effectively uncovered.

Garcia's watchful, beady stare underscores the voyeurist nature of his profession and personal life, as he searches for indiscretions in the faces of others, old friends and new enemies. Having lost a little weight, his high cheek bones, sunken dark eyes and spiky-cut black hair suggest features being pressured by the bone structure underneath. Figgis was the first director to effectively channel the undercurrents of intensity that boil away behind Garcia's immobile features.

With Coppola struggling to finish *The Godfather III*, Garcia's rôle as nephew to Al Pacino will provide an interesting mirror with which to reassess his talents. *Internal Affairs* took Garcia ethnic away from stereotyping. With *The Godfather III* he has the chance to confirm his individuality alongside the one Method actor to whom he has so often been compared.

STEPHEN DARK

LAURA SAN GIACOMO

'It was not at all titillating!' Laura San Giacomo laughs when recalling her experience on *sex, lies and videotape*. 'Everyone was very protective on the set. No peeking around the corner to see what was going on. Even though we had to be very open with each other, there was so much tension. By the end, everyone was saying: "Oh my God, if we have to close the set once more ... if we have to talk about masturbation and sex one more time ... we'll go out of our minds".'

The perfect movie had the perfect players. And none of them ever had it this good before. Andie MacDowell had her Southern tones dubbed by Glenn Close in *Greystoke*. Peter Gallagher survived *High Spirits of Summer Lovers*. James Spader will no longer be *Pretty in Pink* or a *Wall Street* yuppy after his performance made him the Cannes Best Actor in its Best Film.

Only Laura San Giacomo was a new face for cinema-goers. She still carries a Cannes postcard in her luggage to prove it all happened. Devastatingly so ...! She's the sister Cynthia – hot, silky, sulky who keeps phoning the husband to order torrid quickies as if they were home-delivered pizzas, and thus revenging herself on her sister, the wife, always more beautiful, always more likely to succeed.

'Somewhere along the line, something happened and Cynthia started to resent the so-good, so-beautiful sister. But what could she be better at than Ann? Sexuality! And this is the ultimate – to be fucking John. In her sister's bed. It gives her a perverse thrill.'

Around the world, the quartet – in their mixed-up couplings – were the poster. In Britain, it was Laura, solo, perched on the edge of a bed. In black dress – and boots. Ready for anything.

This exotic Italian-American was born in New Jersey – Bruce Springsteen and John Sayles country. She trained in the Carnegie Mellon acting programme. Played Shakespeare in Pittsburgh, Philadelphia, and off-Broadway. As a struggling New York actress, she also stomped around as a waitress or bar-tender. Casting directors kept seeing her that way.

Before she became known, she made a medical student number, *Vital Signs*, playing 'a waitress, putting my guy through school'. Her next stage job: John Patrick Shanley's Italian-American *Reconciliation*. A waitress, again.

'Two years ago, I threw away all my waitressing clothes and said: I now affirm I will not be a waitress anymore ... And every rôle I'm a waitress. Better playing them than being them!'

Despite being Coppola-rejected for Michael Corleone's daughter in *Godfather III*, Laura has certainly done best from the Soderbergh experience. She swapped

Toms – leaving Cruise's *Days of Thunder* to Nicole Kidman in order to partner Selleck in *Quigley Down Under*. Then, rushing into Lasse Hallstrom's Hollywood début, *Once Around*, with the *Always* together Richard Dreyfuss and Holly Hunter.

A remarkable switch from what she terms her personal nightmare. 'I haven't told this story yet,' she confided at Cannes. 'I was cast in a two feature films at once and had to decide between them.' She hit the wrong button.

She does not like to name the films – or not both. She chose *Miles From Home*, in order to work with the Steppenwolf stage people. 'I have such respect for Gary Sinise, John Malkovich, Kevin Anderson and all those other guys. I love to watch them work.'

It was a small part in a bar. 'I had three scenes as this quirky prostitute, who does drugs and asks Kevin Anderson up to her room.' She rehearsed in Los Angeles, went to Iowa for the shoot . . . and they cut the entire rôle.

'Typical Hollywood story. I had these two very big feature films. Then, I had no feature films. That's okay. I learned real fast you can't count on anything. It doesn't happen until it happens. Even so, Iowa was a very good experience – Gary Sinise will not forget me.' (Richard Gere didn't – her first post-Soderbergh rôle was in *Pretty Woman* as Julia Roberts' professional accomplice and roommate).

She's sure her agent never actually read the *sex, lies and videotape* script, but Laura was instantly attracted. 'Everyone's interested in sex and everybody lies! It made me think about my own nightmares, about lying to people – and to myself. Also what hit me was the nightmare of each of these relationships.'

She devised 'a little essence of Cynthia' to win her audition: flinging a chair around and sitting bestride it, Dietrich-style. Like all the quartet, Laura added input and insight to Soderbergh's script.

'I looked at it from the angle of, why is she the way she is?' says Laura. 'Why is she different from Ann – and what's that relationship about? I believe that Ann is the reason why she created her overt sexuality. To be different from Ann. Imagine growing up in a small town where everyone knows you. "Oh, you're Ann's sister!" And she's so good, she gets such good grades, she's so pretty.'

She never viewed Cynthia as an easy lay or wet-dream male fantasy. 'She's someone who knew she could attract men just by her sheer being. I don't think she thinks she's so gorgeous or anything. She dresses to attract men. She knows she can interest men. She has that line: "You're just afraid he'll be irresistibly drawn to me".'

'Everything in the film is so very truthful. You can identify a little with each character. Scarey! Not *Jaws*-scarey, but relationship-scarey. It's compelling, watching these people act out the worst thing that you've done to someone and the worst thing that's been done to you. And you go: "Omigawd, I know this! I've done this! I was there!"'

'It was a great story to tell. And when you've worked that hard on something you believed in, and enjoyed working on it, and then it's hitting everybody the way it hit us, well that's incredible!

TONY CRAWLEY

JOHN GOODMAN

When they were looking for the male lead to play opposite Bette Midler in *Stella*, a reworking of the classic Barbara Stanwyck melodrama *Stella Dallas*, the latter-day movie's three producers came up with three different ideas about who would be right for the movie.

One of the producers apparently cast his vote in favour of the actor he'd recently seen playing Dennis Quaid's has-been footballing buddy in *Everybody's All-American* (aka *When I Fall in Love*). Another thought they should go for the guy who played Sally Field's insurance salesman husband in *Punchline*, while the third insisted some actor he'd seen called John Goodman was the only possible choice for the rôle.

As it turned out, the three producers were all talking about the same person, and offering Goodman the rôle of the drunken bar-owner Ed Munn in *Stella* proved to be an inspired piece of casting for a film which shows few other signs of inspiration.

Not many actors are capable of holding their own against Bette Midler, who has the brash, bright presence of a technicolor cartoon character. Fewer still, with the hyperactive Miss M beside them, can keep their nerve and still offer a thoughtful, carefully nuanced performance. To his credit, John Goodman manages to do both.

Were it not for the fact that *Stella* was so long in the making, its producers might also have prided themselves on discovering in John Goodman a movie-star-to-be. As it was, by the time the film reached American screens, the hefty actor, who weighs in at over sixteen stone, was regularly popping up in films – as Al Pacino's sidekick in *Sea of Love* and alongside Holly Hunter and Richard Dreyfuss in *Always* – and has, indeed, already become something of a national obsession.

No matter that his physique is more Michelin Man than he-man, Goodman suddenly found himself being touted as the sex symbol of the moment. Critics described him as 'a working-class heart-throb'; Sally Field called him 'a great big man with the soul of a puppy', and readers of a popular American weekly awarded him the title of The Sexiest Man Alive.

According to John Goodman, fame was unexpected enough – 'I never thought it would happen, so I never really prepared myself,' he's reported to have said – but being branded a pin-up was simply insupportable. 'People who write that sort of stuff have obviously got too much time on their hands,' he says. 'I mean people really go for big, fat, sweaty guys, don't they?'

Well, yes, as a matter of fact, it seems they do, although, for those who don't already know, the fuss John Goodman has generated hasn't been really caused by his so-far rather fleeting film appearances, but by his starring rôle in one of America's most popular sitcoms of recent years, *Roseanne*. Every week around 23 million American households tune in to see the cherubic-looking Goodman verbally outmanoeuvred by the sharp-tongued and, incidentally, heavier Roseanne Barr.

After a decade in which American television viewers had gloated themselves on the improbable glamour of *Dynasty* and the soft-focus cosiness of the Cosby clan, the unglamorized *Roseanne* was a hit show waiting to happen and John Goodman might have been born to play the archetypical blue-collar Dan Conner. Yet as Goodman, perhaps a fraction irritably, is fond of pointing out to his interviewers, he had 'a pretty healthy career going' long before *Roseanne* came along.

He may have been a new face to television audiences, and the casting directors of *Roseanne* may have spotted him in a stage production of *Anthony and Cleopatra* in Los Angeles, but plenty of film-goers remember John Goodman as the lovelorn bachelor in David Byrne's *True Stories*, as the crooked cop in *The Big Easy* and as a baby-besotted criminal in the Coen brothers' *Raising Arizona*.

Goodman, who was born in St Louis, Missouri, in 1953, claims he began clowning around as a way of attracting the attention of girls. 'I could certainly never talk to them normally, so I used to do things like stick a pencil up my nose,' he's since said. 'Getting up on stage and making a fool of myself was just an extension of that sort of behaviour I suppose.'

John Goodman didn't begin acting properly, however, until he was at university. He was studying on an athletics scholarship, but lost interest in football and soon afterwards became a member of Missouri University's drama department, where he was a contemporary of Kathleen Turner. Well and truly bitten by the acting bug, he moved to New York upon graduation with his life savings of $1000 in his pocket.

Goodman still maintains he never had any ambitions beyond making his living as an actor and, ironically, he might never have achieved his current celebrity had it not been for his final abandonment of the crash dieting which kept him looking relatively fit during his early years in New York. Once he reached his current weight, he soon found himself in demand for a succession of character rôles.

His first real break came when he was cast as Huckleberry Finn's father in the Broadway musical *Big River*. He took a call from David Byrne offering him top billing in *True Stories* soon after and the rest, as they say, is history.

Goodman's rare ability as a film actor, and it's arguably this which has propelled him on his way quite as forcefully as *Roseanne*, is to take character rôles and bit parts, and play them with such intelligence and sensitivity that he always commands attention. This is a matter of craftsmanship rather than of hogging the screen – those in doubt should take a look at Goodman's delightfully flustered cop in *Sea of Love* – and, of course, it will translate into precisely the above-the-title status he says he never expected.

Since *Sea of Love* and *Stella*, Goodman has completed work on a comedy entitled *King Ralph I*, in which he plays a distant American cousin of the Windsors who ends up in Buckingham Palace, and Steven Spielberg has signed him up to play Fred Flintstone. Meanwhile the scripts and the offers are said to be coming in, and fame, Goodman insists, is a nuisance.

'I can't walk down the street any more and I hate reading some of the stuff they write about me in the newspaper,' he complains. He openly wonders if he'll ever get used to it. He'd be well advised to try.

SIMON BANNER

JENNIFER JASON LEIGH

ennifer Jason Leigh may never be voted feminist of the year, but there is no moral surrender in her willingness to strip for the camera. As Tralala, the teenage prostitute in *Last Exit to Brooklyn* – a combustible adaptation of Hubert Selby Jr.'s dirge-like parable of proletarian squalor and spiritual malaise – she boastfully spills her breasts in a bar full of pawing louts and lets them carry her out to a vacant lot; so many of them stand in line to violate her that they have to light a brazier to keep warm. As the hotel hooker Susie in *Miami Blues*, Leigh flicks off her top and pats the patch of bed between her legs, summoning her latest john as if he were a dog she was about to take for a brisk walk. In *Sunshine*, performed off-Broadway last winter, Leigh was a peepshow performer, proud of her ability to make clients ejaculate against the one-way window of desire that divides them.

So much abandon, so little eroticism – has any other female star been so naked and remained so unexploited? Whereas lesser actresses might have callowly sought sexual glory in these rôles, Leigh knows that any hint of sexiness would be a collaboration with the men who abuse her, and with the men in the audience. 'Absolutely,' she answers when asked if her research into the sex industry for *Sunshine* had made her hate men a little. 'The girls in the booths do help men with sex, but it's strange that men should desire this kind of thing.' She undercuts her allure with a brittleness that is painful – and deeply moving – to behold, and emerges from brutalizing sex scenes not as a male fantasy figure but as a tragic victim of male abuse, an unhinged martyr, strangely ennobled even in her degradation.

The daughter of screenwriter Barbara Turner and the late Vic Morrow, Leigh is an extreme case – an actress who has accidentally found a niche in screen harlotry: she also played a hooker in the miserable *Men's Club* (1986), and a 'sexy' murder victim in the equally misogynistic *The Hitcher* (1986). She is, she knows, in danger of being typecast as a vice girl, but she's adamant that she would play another if it challenged her; she's also secure in the knowledge that she has never played the same character twice. If the naïve, kindly housewife she plays opposite Alec Baldwin's vicious conman in *Miami Blues* is a fresh variant on the whore with a heart of gold, in *Last Exit* she is the Whore of Babylon, a snarling hoyden with no heart at all.

Tralala is amoral rather than immoral; no-one has told her it's wrong to lure her clients to a place where their heads will be smashed and their money stolen. She invites the gang-bang to expunge the sour memory of a sailor who has left her with a love letter instead of cash. 'She is by far the most innocent woman I have played,' says Leigh, 'even though she is a dishonest whore who is incredibly abused and abusive. She is unaware that there is any other way to be – the word "love" isn't in her vocabulary. Her initial reaction when she first sees the sailor's letter is rage and humiliation – she gave this guy three days and he gave her a piece of paper! Yet somewhere in her psyche, she knows that she's touched someone and it terrifies her, so she goes on a binge – saying to herself, "If everyone in this bar fucks me, I know I will feel great again." Because being cut off from all feeling is what being alive is to her.'

Was it traumatic for her to play a young girl being gang-banged? How could it not be? 'Well, it wasn't really, because during shooting I felt Tralala's desperation for it to happen, although everybody on the set was very concerned for me. But when I saw the scene I felt like I'd been kicked in the stomach – because I'd never seen it happening to me. I had avoided looking in the mirror so that I could keep her reality alive for me – the reality of someone flying into a wall of glass.'

When Leigh plays Tralala, or Susie, she can bring out the male impulse to rescue fallen women. But the fact is she doesn't need any man – the power in Leigh's performance resides in her ultimate sublime isolation from men, her defiant exertion of her own right to survive or self-destruct. Men defile Leigh's Tralala routinely, but they only destroy her when she wills it and, unlike her counterpart in the novel, she is still able to feel some compassion. Susie turns away at the end of *Miami Blues* with a gulp of resignation, but one senses she will endure, eventually finding – if not a decent man – the Burger King franchise she also dreams of. But maybe that's just a dream, too.

Shy but self-possessed, a 28-year-old with baby skin and a brow as wide and pale as the moon, Leigh is a robust and concentrated performer, and she may be the first serious American actress since Marilyn Monroe to address sex consistently in her rôles without suffering from the comparison. She resembles Monroe both in *Last Exit* – the platinum blond Tralala, sweat-stained and pimpled, is a grotesque parody of female predatoriness – and *Heart of Midnight*, in which she plays a woman who was physically abused by her uncle as a child and is struggling to stave off schizophrenia. Her performance there was the first indication that Leigh's jittery energy could sustain an entire film. We may never pin Leigh up on our walls, but we may care more deeply for the vulnerable women she plays. Nor can we expect her to play it safe. 'I'm an actress,' she protests. 'I want the juiciest, meatiest, most difficult rôles I can find. I don't want to play somebody's girlfriend, who is pretty, and who wears nice clothes and who's there just to show the guy is straight. If I had to try and make safe rôles interesting, I'd give up.'

GRAHAM FULLER

LAURIE
METCALF

Laurie Metcalf doesn't look like a movie star. She's hardly a raging beauty and her dry, unsentimental looks would not make anyone abandon his family for a dirty weekend in Puerto Vallarta.

As faces go, she isn't even that new, having floated about in supporting rôles since leaving Chicago's Steppenwolf Theatre Company. Steppenwolf, it will be remembered, was home to John Malkovich, Glenne Headly and Gary Sinise, and it was in such distinguished company that Metcalf cut her teeth on rôles such as that of a naïve mid-western prostitute in Lanford Wilson's *Balm in Gilead* (which won her an Obie) and the mother in Sam Shepard's *True West*.

It isn't the face so much as what comes through the face. She's had suporting rôles in *Desperately Seeking Susan* (as Rosanna Arquette's supercilious, suburban sister-in-law), in *Making Mr Right* (as a Florida lab technician who gets the hots for Malkovich's android) and in *Stars and Bars* (as the hysterical lover of Daniel Day-Lewis's repressed Englishman). She's also a largely ignored member of the cast of *Roseanne*, the sitcom in which she plays Roseanne Barr's sister.

On that show, which pretends to subvert, while actually reaffirming, the happy-happy values of the family sitcom, Metcalf's plain discomfort and refusal to make nice mark her out as the one character who would not be out of place on American television's truly subversive sitcoms, such as *Married With Children* and *The Simpsons*. (There are also three or four characters in *Twin Peaks* she could easily have played.)

It's typical of her career – or perhaps her luck – that in the oceans of ink spilled over the film that represented her big movie break, Metcalf's performance was largely ignored. The reviewers of Mike Figgis's *Internal Affairs* raved about Richard Gere's return to the screen as corrupt street cop Dennis Peck. Obeisance was paid to the rising star of Andy Garcia as Detective Raymond Avila. Notice was taken of the creamily beautiful Nancy Travis and of Annabella Sciorra. (Sciorra, the unabashedly Italian-American star of *True Love* and possessor of an important supporting rôle in *Cadillac Man*, merits some notice herself as a new face.) But few paid attention to the woman playing Amy Wallace, Garcia's sidekick.

Henry Bean's script (or what we see of it) gives us no biographical information about Wallace, aside from the fact that both Dennis Peck and Raymond Avila refer to her as a dyke. The key to Metcalf's performance is the discrepancy between the information we are given about Wallace and what Metcalf actually shows us about the character.

It's only if you look carefully at the film that you'll see the clues which could justify Avila and Peck reaching a conclusion about Wallace's sexuality. She is sitting with Avilla in a car park waiting for a suspect. One of those spectacular, only-in-California, blondes walks by their car. Both of them look at her, and Wallace looks longer. There is about a milli-second of eye contact between Wallace and Avila, and he knows and she knows that he knows. Which makes her, I think, the first heroic lesbian in a Hollywood movie, and certainly the first where the character's sexuality is secondary to what she does outside the bedroom.

From the controlled walk Metcalf gives to Wallace, we can see that she has at some point been sexually harassed, and is doing everything within her power to avoid sending out any sort of sexuality. And in a media world where police officers are notorious two-finger typists, Metcalfe also lets us know that Wallace was once trapped in the world of clerk typists; for her fingers fly over the keyboard.

Most important, in a film that sets out to undermine the conventions of its genre, Metcalf's cool realism lets us know that she has seen more than she wants of infantilized men who reckon guns enhance their potency. She has had male partners who have screwed up royally. Look at the cold anger on Metcalf's face when Avilla offers a minor villain a deal that he has no right to offer. She refuses to back him up. 'Why don't you and Dennis Peck pull it out,' she asks, 'and I'll decide who's biggest.' It's a great laugh line that manages to reduce an entire genre to its most basic level of macho posturing. Metcalf doesn't play it as a laugh line.

Internal Affairs is out to subvert a whole genre, and it is Metcalf's cool intelligence that does it. She also manages to put the pain back into being shot. When she has been hit at the end of the film (and, in a weird loose end, we never discover whether or not she lives), her physical reaction is startling. She clenches into a foetal position on her side, but not into a curled, comfortable foetal position. Her legs are bent and locked at the knee and hip, but not together – it's as if an electric current were running through her and will only kill her if she brings her knees together. (I suspect that Metcalf went out and found someone who had been shot in the chest and asked them about their reaction. She did her homework and, as we all know, performance quality lies in the details.)

To see Laurie Metcalf's performance in *Internal Affairs* is to suddenly realize that we have been looking at a major acting talent without ever quite recognizing that it's there.

JOHN HARKNESS

JULIA ROBERTS

Julia Roberts is six personalities (at least) in search of an actress. 1990 has been her year of wonder. She won an Oscar nomination for playing a dying diabetic in *Steel Magnolias*. Then, after a quick change in the powder room, she propelled *Pretty Woman* to the top of the charts with her performance as a kooky hooker entangled – and entangled is the world for this long-legged brunette – with Richard Gere.

Before those movies, she made her début in Peter Masterson's thriller *Blood Red*, then moved on to Bobby Roth's *Baja Oklahoma* and played a New England waitress yearning for better things in *Mystic Pizza*. And since those movies, she's been hitting the sci-fi trail with Joel Schumacher's *Flatliners*, in which Harvard medical students experiment with the other-worldly state between life and death. An apt story for her, since 'other-worldly states' are exactly what viewers, or at least male viewers, get into when contemplating Julia Roberts.

Who is Julia? What is she? Is she a comedienne or tragedienne? A waif or a vamp? Is she the new Rita Hayworth or the old Audrey Hepburn? Let us put her under the microscope and see what we see.

The first thing to note is that she's beautifully uncoordinated. After seeing her in *Mystic Pizza*, we thought this might be an act: the teetering, angular gait, the tendency to walk as if on high heels even when not wearing them. These could be the gauche-but-gorgeous mannerisms appropriate to a Portuguese-American girl in a New England fishing village who's trying to hitch a ride up the social ladder.

But no, it couldn't have been a put-on because Roberts has done it in every film since. Her precarious legginess is an asset only great comediennes have, and it instantly wins her the Kay Kendall diploma for stork-like grace.

The second thing: her lips. Julia Roberts' pout has been known to slay grown men and leave whole movie auditoria devastated. 'Bee-stung' is an understatement. Goodness knows what creature would have to sting a girl's lips to leave them so voluptuously swollen. Probably a black mamba.

Teetering walk, mamba-stung lips. What next? Well, there is the cataract fall of her chestnut hair, her eyes like twin jungle pools and her voice that subtly lisps, as if the mamba, in biting our subject, had bequeathed her its susurrant vocal patterns.

The lisp is the clincher with Julia Roberts. It pushes her straight into superstar class. It derives in her case from the impossibility of co-ordinating in speech her teeth, tongue-tip and upper lip when the Gods have designed those features for voluptuous visual impact rather than sensible functioning.

Where did this actress come from? Literally she came from the Deep South. Julia Roberts is a native of Smyrna, Georgia. There's no record of when the thespian spark first struck her: possibly in the cradle, possibly in the classroom. But if we look at a map of Georgia, we see that in terms of town-names this is a state with an identity crisis. Smyrna, Rome, Dublin, Athens, Manchester, Cairo . . . If you grew up in such a state you too might wonder where and who you were, and whether identity were not something as volatile and fly-by-night as an asteroid. The perfect geo-psychological matrix, in short, for an actress.

As she grew up, Julia Roberts was influenced unconsciously by the sound of wind rustling the Spanish moss in the great Georgian oak trees. This helped to form her voice, just as certain native birds of Georgia, like the famous Long-Leggedy Stork-Like Thing (celebrated and discovered by Audubon), helped to form her physical mannerisms.

As a critic, one has a complex perspective on Roberts' movies. They are flawed films. *Mystic Pizza* is deep-pan schmaltz with inadequate comic topping. *Pretty Woman* is a re-run of *My Fair Lady* without the wit or songs. And *Steel Magnolias* is a film that could be used on torture subjects: two hours of showbiz Southern accents as an all-star female cast runs about an overdressed Louisiana location competing for overcasting awards.

Roberts comes out best from that film and won a Golden Globe award for her performance. As diabetic Shelby, dying three years after the motherhood that everyone warned her would be fatal ('Whaah, we warned you it would be fatal, Shel-bee', etc.), she is poignant without plaintiveness, sweet without being cloying.

But comedy still seems her stronger suit. She lifts the schmaltz-prone *Mystic Pizza* up by the ankles and shakes it till the comic change falls from its pockets. Roberts is irresistible, whether doing a Rita Hayworth number on the stairs at home – shimmying in shoulderless dress and hand-swept hair – or staying native as she drives a fish-truck to the Country Club to ogle the high life. Here she has the film's best scene. Emptying the writhing contents of the truck into her boyfriend's open Porsche (she has espied him dining with another girl), she is shocked to be told that the girl is his sister. 'I fucked up,' quavers Roberts. 'Yeah,' says the boyfriend, 'but you gave it a 100 per cent effort.'

Exactly. Likewise in *Pretty Woman*. Here we watch as Roberts, spilling champagne charm and sweetness all over the Beverly Wilshire furniture, locks acting egos with Richard Gere, who appears to have been novocained shortly before shooting. As the wild and the unwilling go to it in Garry Marshall's romantic comedy, Roberts steals every scene and piles up her swag-bags at the side of the screen. By movie's end, they are tottering dangerously and threatening to engulf the hotel suite.

Two special moments. The first when Roberts is caught in Gere's bathroom *in flagrante* with the dental floss: 'I had all those strawberry seeds and you shouldn't neglect your gums,' she pipes in self-justification like a school child. The second when Roberts enters the midnight bedroom, sees the dormant Gere and murmurs simply, softly: 'He sleeps.' It's the shortest soliloquy in movie history but, as delivered by this actress, it contains a whole love story.

HARLAN KENNEDY

JEAN-CLAUDE VAN DAMME

Action movie heroes are to current cinema what cowboy stars used to be to series Westerns. Just as it would take a connoisseur to tell a Rex Allen from a Tim Holt or a Hopalong Cassidy from a Roy Rogers, so today's fans can distinguish between the skills of Sylvester Stallone and Arnold Schwarzenegger, Chuck Norris and Sho Kosugi, Jackie Chan and Cynthia Rothrock, Robert Ginty and Michael Dudikoff.

Stallone and Schwarzenegger have graduated to the Big Time, like John Wayne among cowboy heroes of old, and can now make super-produced action movies, but the true fans of the genre shun these muscle-bound sell-outs as mere pretenders. The true action movie has to be the modern equivalent of a 'B' or double-feature picture, destined for the racks of the local video store, where a credit on *Avenging Angel* ranks higher than one on *Rain Man*. This is the area of cinema populated by ninja warriors, MIA guerrillas, urban vigilantes, karate-kicking grudge-holders, vengeance-seeking assassins, rogue cops, redneck bar bruisers and kung-fu executioners.

It has become customary among superior critics to sneer at the action man heroes – Schwarzenegger, Norris, Dudikoff – for their lack of acting talent. However, in a very real sense, they aren't in these movies to act. They're on screen to kick unrighteous ass any way they want to – with a sword, with their feet and hands, with a pump shotgun, with their teeth, with a flame thrower. Let's face it, nobody complained that Fred Astaire wasn't great in the scenes between the dances, or that W. C. Fields falls flat in the 'serious, heart-warming' stretches between the gags. And when was the last time you saw Laurence Olivier drop-kick a moving car in the windscreen and dislocate a villain's neck, as Chuck Norris is sometimes wont to do, or John Gielgud do the splits like our current hero, Jean-Claude Van Damme.

Van Damme, a Belgian kickboxing champ, came to Hollywood much as nice young men who could ride and sing a few songs did during the Roy Rogers–Gene Autry heyday. They knew they had all it took to be singing cowboys, and he knew he could be an action movie star. His first break didn't pan out, when a redesign of the suit meant that he lost his rôle inside the monster in *Predator*, appearing in only a few brief glimpses in the finished film, and failing to match muscle with Arnie for a mud-soaked battle of the titans. Then, he consoled himself with a few villain roles, his nondescript European accent fortuitously helping him land a few Evil Commie Russian Bastard parts during the final flare-up of the Cold War in the late 1980s. In the original *No Retreat, No Surrender*, he is Ivan Brezin, 'Eastern Europe's most feared martial artist', and enjoys himself prancing around the ring shouting 'I am best! I am best!' when he isn't crippling the hero's Dad in this strange mix of *Rocky IV, The Karate Kid* and *Play It Again Sam*.

Black Eagle, with Sho Kosugi as a CIA martial artist in Cyprus, promised a showdown between the two champions, but decided instead to have Van Damme get his in the whirring propellors of a passing ship, disappointing the Romans in the audience who paid their dollars to see Christians eaten by lions and don't take kindly to being cheated.

Realizing that he would have to get out of the villain racket because his sad eyes and perky grin weren't really convincing in baddie roles, Van Damme determined that he would have to make an impression on Menahem Golan, the man who had been guiding the careers of Kosugi, Norris, Dudikoff, Bronson and many other action greats. He happened to encounter Golan in a Hollywood restaurant and kicked just over his head, impressing the then-head of Cannon into giving him a break and an appointment. 'When I finally see Menahem I did everything to show him I wanted to be in the movies,' Van Damme has said. 'My eyes were almost crying. I took off my shirt. I did the splits and while I was in the split position I told him, "Look, I am very young and very hungry. I'm also very inexpensive." I only wanted a small part. He gave me a full script. It was *Bloodsport*.' This turned out to be Van Damme's big thick-ear break, a based-on-fact story about Frank Dux, the only American ever to win the Kumite, an illegal freestyle fighting competition held in the Far East. The film could charitably be described as a piece of crap, but it does feature non-stop thumping, kicking, gouging, sneering, killing, dying, shouting, bleeding, bone-breaking, sweating and stripping.

Since then, Jean-Claude Van Damme has been busy. He followed up *Bloodsport* with *Kickboxer*, a more-of-the-same item which has him go through the humbling process of being trained for the big fight at the end by a perky martial arts master who uses coconuts as gymnastic equipment. Then, he got into *Cyborg*, a quickie in which he is seeking revenge on some baddies who kill his family and make him feel rotten about it. It's a scrappy *Mad Max* imitation, but it does allow Jean-Claude to be crucified in the rôle of hero Gibson Rickenbacker, who is described as 'just one big walking wound.'

There's more coming up, including the long-announced *Wrong Bet*, and a projected move into the big time, perhaps with a weightier performer as co-star. In a sense, that would be a shame, because although Van Damme has yet to make a good or even an acceptable film, his amiability depends on the cheesiness of his surroundings. Like Chuck Norris, he is almost touching when his sheer lack of expression passes for numbed sensitivity, and the combination of his pretty-boy looks and graceful head-kicking makes him less threatening a screen presence than many spikier, thuggier action men. As long as there are bad guy heads to be kicked in, then the cinema should have a place for the likes of Jean-Claude Van Damme.

KIM NEWMAN

QUOTES

Compiled by Tony Crawley

If you make me eat shit, I'm going to make you eat shit.

Hollywood agent Mike Ovitz, quoted back to him in screenwriter Joe Eszterhas's Letter of the Year on leaving CAA for ICM

....

Wait till you see how big my Dick is.

Disney Studios chairman Jeffrey Katzenberg, clearly believing his own Dick Tracy *hype*

....

You see me travelling to Mars as a 300 pound, fat lady. Don't worry. The body is there. The strength is there.

Arnold Schwarzenegger on his rôle in Total Recall

....

Rambo IV will be the last one – and concerned with environmental issues. Rambo will be working for, like, Greenpeace.

Sylvester Stallone

....

You'll see Tom Cruise and Nicole Kidman in all their hormonal glory.

Days of Thunder *producer Don Simpson*

....

Very intense – at any moment he could blow up beyond belief. This is the behaviour of a genius kind of guy.

Arnold Schwarzenegger on director Paul Verhoeven

....

$11-million is what Jack Nicholson got for *Batman*. 11 million! He was in *Ironweeed*, if you recall. OK. All right. He was in *Heartburn*, if you remember. Okay. I was in

Out of fucking *Africa,* remember? *Kramer vs. Kramer!*
Deer Hunter! I'm saying it's a guy's game. If I asked for
$11 million, they would laugh. In my face.
Meryl Streep . . . in need of a better agent?

· ·

Bruce Willis was offered something like $7.5 million.
But they offered me less than for the first one. Less!
Why do they think actors want to do sequels anyway.
It's for the money!
Bonnie Bedelia, on her deal for Die Hard II.

· ·

A sequel is the last thing the world needs right now.
Yahoo Serious, refusing any Young Einstein II

· ·

To me, it's much bigger than a film – or an event. It's not
just America. It's the world. The world is in a great deal of
need of direction and help. Everyone's looking for the
answers. So this can be a great educator. It's a film very
much about good and evil and actually about two great
things on this earth. Love and fear. They are the only two
emotions there are. You choose which one to be – good or
evil. You choose love or fear. Everything else stems from
fear – anger, hatred, jealousy, greed, which causes war,
devastation, terrorism, everything that is happening in
the rain forests, the way the earth is now. And when
something like this happens, it's a real symbol from
someplace else that help is there – and it's in yourself. If
you love yourself, and give out love, then you get it back.
You can change the earth with that.
Kim Basinger, squeezing just about everything into Batman *but the Boat People, glasnost,
Salman Rushdie, hostages, condoms and AIDS*

I just put the success down to bats. They're primal creatures and pretty cool.

Tim Burton making Batman *more simple*

It's not easy filming a comic book. But they'll just smother this genre and move on to another.

Tim Burton

What he's trying to say is – some idiot will make *Spiderman.*

Kim Basinger

. . . .

I've never said this to anyone before in my life: if you give me this part, I'll let you fuck me!

Roseanne Barr begging Susan Seidelman for She-Devil

. . . .

Suddenly, some years back, they started to say I was a beauty. Now I'm revered — rather like some favourite old building!
I'm just an old potato.

Katharine Hepburn

. . . .

I'm a bit of an Irishman in France – the critics no longer speak about me.

I never make a film to have a hit or reach a wide audience. For me, it's the taste that counts. I prefer good cooking to fast food, no wine rather than bad wine.

Gérard Depardieu

. . . .

Sleeping well at night is all that really matters.

Virgin Records chief Richard Branson

. . . .

I'm personally not interested in money.
Disney chief Michael Eisner

....

I was raised thinking you were the enemy. You were raised thinking I was the enemy. We were both wrong. It's the French!
When Billy Crystal met Moscow.

....

I'd like to make Steven Spielberg my slave and have him make any movie I wanted.
Sean Young

....

I've never made a film that could remotely be considered a masterpiece. Not even remotely.
I see a definitive correlation between lack of box-office popularity and high quality.
Woody Allen

....

Rôles that get nominated sometimes are so self-important. There's a smell of the vanity piece, the acting exercise . . . Besides, you have to talk in a foreign accent.
Kathleen Turner on her Oscar losses

....

I'm going to tie you up with depositions and court dates so that you won't be able to spend any time at your typewriter.
Mike Ovitz, quoted in Joe Eszterhas's Letter of the Year

....

It's better to appear in a good commercial in Japan than a bad movie in America.
Valerie Kaprisky

....

I'm leaving St Tropez to the invaders, increasingly numerous, mediocre, dirty, badly behaved, shameless tourists leaving their condoms all over the place.
Brigitte Bardot

....

That's why I have a moustache – because Rhett Butler had a moustache. I'm just as cornball as anybody else.
CNN chief and Jane Fonda escort, Ted Turner.

....

I was taught to treat people well. I don't think you can get away with that star stuff. After a while, it just comes back and eats you.
Tom Cruise

....

I couldn't make a movie that was morally reprehensible just because it might make $100 million. I wouldn't touch *Top Gun*!
Ellen Barkin

....

He's a blue alien which is a step up from a bug.
Geena Davis on husband Jeff Goldblum moving from The Fly *to* Earth Girls Are Easy

....

I absolutely refuse to reveal my age. What am I – a car?
Cyndi Lauper

....

I want you to jump up and down and rock out! You're the wickedest children on earth!
John Waters directing Cry Baby

....

Like him? We're getting married?
John Waters on Pedro Almodóvar

....

You don't know real heat until you've spent several hours inside a giant condom.

Priscilla Presley on that scene in The Naked Gun

· ·

Elvis didn't have no movie made on him while he was still living, did he?

Jerry Lee Lewis on Great Balls of Fire

· ·

I'm not worried about the press. All those guys want is to write screenplays for Robert Redford.

Mike Ovitz, quoted in Joe Eszterhas's Letter of the Year

· ·

I'm Yugoslavian. They're passionate but not really ambitious. Life is eating and drinking and children.

Lolita Davidovich, the star of Blaze

· ·

I made the movie, they gave me the money – thank you! I never saw it, never heard of it and, you know, as far as I'm concerned, it never existed.

Christopher Walken on War Zone

· ·

I don't have a set pattern. I just lay back and wait for it to happen. And it usually does.

Liz Taylor

· ·

It's all in there. Flesh, milk, blood and sperm.

Gérard Depardieu on his upcoming Othello

· ·

The film uses many famous quotations – each one is repeated five times in case you don't understand them the first time.

Jean-Luc Godard on Nouvelle Vague

· ·

I think of ideas like a disease. If I talk too much about them, someone may come up with a vaccine.
John Waters

. . . .

Editing bores me – always feels like a rout, a retreat from your objective.
Oliver Stone

. . . .

I frighten myself sometimes.
Robert Englund, aka Freddy Krueger

. . . .

I've nothing against him. Except for spending an awful dinner with him in London . . . He was so rude that by the end of the night, we'd all moved to the far end of the table and left him speaking French on his own. He was so out of it, he must've thought he was in Paris.
Julien Temple on William Hurt

. . . .

Certain people are very offended by the language. When you have a sixteen-year-old blonde teen queen say: 'Fuck me gently with a chainsaw', alarms go off in a lot of people's heads, which I think is very funny. Hard for me to get upset about language, especially such beautifully written language.
Heathers *director Michael Lehmann*

. . . .

I got so thin I almost lost my Max Factor advertising contract.
Jane Seymour, on her concentration camp scenes in War and Remembrance

. . . .

There's too much emphasis on celebrity bullshit these days. Every time you turn around, there's another goddam TV talk show – what Connie Francis had for breakfast today. And people eat it up. That's kinda scary – like they don't have anything better to do than that?
John Goodman

....

The only shot I had was either to become a crook, a dope dealer – or an actor.
Hoboken-born actor Joe Pantoliano

....

It's easier to be depressed in comfort when you're wealthy.
Sarah Brightman, making ready to shoot The Phantom of the Opera

....

Writing about it? I have enough trouble talking about it. Because I never know what's true and what isn't.
Jane Fonda on Hollywood

....

If I wasn't happy, I'd be an idiot.
Arnold on Schwarzenegger

....

The part's okay, but the movie's the thing.
Morgan Freeman on Glory

....

She's got a ten-inch waist and nine-inch platform heels. To get her out of those heels, they'd have to be lanced.
Shirley MacLaine on Dolly Parton

....

I'm becoming fatalistic. Too much has happened in my life for me not to be fatalistic.
Liz Taylor

....

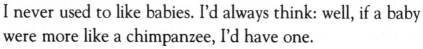

I never used to like babies. I'd always think: well, if a baby were more like a chimpanzee, I'd have one.
Candice Bergen (who did)

When I got through with the twin pregnancy, my abdominal skin was such that I had to fold it up and then stick it in my pants.
Cybill Shepherd

Typecast? I certainly hope so. I spent seven years without working, so if they're making cop movies, I'll play cops. I got two kids to bring up.
Andy Garcia

If somebody came . . . and took my Lichtenstein off the wall, I'd go after them. I'm going to go after you the same way. You're one of this agency's biggest assets.
Mike Ovitz, again in Joe Eszterhas's Letter.

I am not a painting hung on someone's wall . . . not a piece of meat to be traded for other pieces of meat . . . This isn't a game. It's my life.
Joe Eszterhas to Ovitz

Maybe it does go a bit too far.
Daniel Battsek, of Palace Pictures, on Peter Greenaway's The Cook the Thief his Wife and her Lover

I called up this guy who was quite attractive, connected, well educated and nice. And I said: about our evening tomorrow, let me tell you, if you think we're going to end up in bed, we're just not . . .! And he said: Oh, no, no, no.

And without fail, midnight, and I'm pushing him out the door. Men don't believe what you say.
Kathleen Turner

....

You can't be a movie star without it – and it's a big burden.
Jane Fonda on sexuality

....

When you give an interview and the feeling of being outrageous is present, please place this ball in your mouth and then tape your mouth shut. If you are still able to say oral sex after doing this, then you are hopeless.
Letter to Kim Basinger from her father

....

If you don't want someone to see your breasts, don't take your shirt off.
Ellen Barkin

....

I was gonna be nude in *She-Devil*. I would have done it. Someday, I'm gonna be nude in a film.
Roseanne Barr's four-minute warning

....

The moves were simple. We didn't want it looking like a choreographed dance. The dress had to be open enough so I could move in it. My only concern was not flashing my knickers.
Michelle Pfeiffer on Making Whoopee with The Fabulous Baker Boys

....

I like to be naked in movies. I've a reputation to uphold.
Alec Baldwin

....

Power is using whatever weapons you have at the time. The day after I won my second Academy Award, I went to see ABC-TV chief Tony Thomopolous about *The Dollmaker*. How was he going to say no to me?
Jane Fonda.

. . . .

I have a high feminine component. I grew up cutting out paper dolls and dressing Deanna Durbin cut-outs. Mia is the one who, at her farm, drives the tractor and knows how to repair the television set.
Woody Allen

. . . .

For fifteen years it was like writing on toilet paper.
Writer Ron Shusett on finally completing the twice abandoned Total Recall

. . . .

I've got a third of my life left. And it's mine. To act out those early family dynamics takes so much out of you.
Jane Fonda

. . . .

Schwarzenegger is the nicest star I've worked with since Barbara Stanwyck.
Hollywood production manager Elliot Schick

. . . .

I have marvellous memories of my second wedding day. Everyone was there. Unforgettable. Just a shame the marriage didn't last.
Jane Seymour

. . . .

I've been divorced four times. Every marriage started for bad reasons – and ended for good.
Producer Robert Evans

. . . .

Movies don't break a working marriage.
Jane Fonda after her second divorce

. . . .

Another marriage would be suicide for me.
And suicide is illegal, right?
Sylvester Stallone in France

. . . .

I know why I made the film, but I can't give instructions on how to view it.
Director Axel Corti on The King's Whore

. . . .

With Francis, a script is like a newspaper. You get a new one every day.
Dean Tavoularis, production designer on Godfather III

. . . .

I looked around and asked: why am I not being offered certain movies? And the hard answer was: you're not box-office, pal. You're fucked. The courageous think would be to get out of the business. Then I thought: no, the courageous thing is to stay in it.
Richard Gere on his comeback

. . . .

I'm not looking to be any more famous than I already am.
Jeff Bridges

. . . .

Baltimore has always inspired me. Anyway it suits me that everyone in my films has to stay in hotels and I get to sleep at home.
John Waters

. . . .

Hansel and Gretel on a bad acid trip.
Rupert Everett's description of The Comfort of Strangers

. . . .

I really can't complain . . . It was pretty relaxing.
A couple of times, I actually fell asleep.

American actress Maureen Mueller on being a corpse in Enid Is Sleeping

. . . .

I know I could do a great love story.

Arnold Schwarzenegger

. . . .

A strong director leaves you to your own devices.

Liz Taylor

. . . .

I feel sick.

Klaus Kinski's final words in his book, All I Need Is Love.

. . . .

Howard Hawks called me about *El Dorado*. 'Bob, what about doing a Western with Duke Wayne!' Sounds good – where? 'Let's shoot it down in old Tucson, Arizona.' Wonderful, great location, nice town – what's the story, Howard? 'No story, Bob, just characters. Stories bore people.'

Howard Hughes used to look right through you. When I was working for him and had all those midnight meetings in his office, he said one time: 'My God, Mitch, you're just like a pay-toilet. You don't give a shit for nothing.'

Robert Mitchum

. . . .

I fucking hate LA! People talk of LA as this mecca of enlightened thinking. I get out here and it's a filthy hole!

Alec Baldwin

. . . .

My foot soldiers who go up and down Wilshire Boulevard each day will blow your brains out.

Mike Ovitz, quoted in Joe Eszterhas's Letter of the Year.

Truly this appears to be one of those *Rashomon*
situations, and your letter simply makes little or no
sense to me.
Ovitz reply to Eszterhas

....

You can *Rashomon* it as much as you like, but words like
'my foot soldiers . . . will blow your brains out' and 'he'll
put you into the fucking ground' leave little room for
ambiguity.
Eszterhas to Ovitz

....

I believe Joe did have those things said to him. It was a
divorce! And often in a divorce people get angry, say
things they don't mean. CAA is a very powerful agency
with actors, but the best writers, the best directors, are
handled by ICM. Which sort of divests CAA of their
mythological image of totalitarian control of the
Hollywood community.
Steven Spielberg

....

How many rifles you got? 28, John.
Plenty of ammo? Yes, John. Then,
knock 'em dead, kid!
John Huston's final words

ELEPHANTS, DAISIES AND DINOSAURS

Hollywood has never been shy of hyperbole. But halfway through the 1980s, the hype began to sour. Haunting the industry was the spectre of *Heaven's Gate*, Michael Cimino's notorious super-flop – a $36 million fiasco that cost United Artists its independence. And while the movie moguls never really cut back on their profligate spending, they no longer publicly boasted of 'casts-of-thousands' and 'years-in-the-making' extravagance. Although the entertainment press refused to play along, tarring and feathering such big-budget turkeys as *Howard the Duck* and *Ishtar* with repeated reminders of their preposterous price-tags ($35 million and $45 million respectively), sanctimonious studio executives insisted that it was what was on screen that counted, not what it cost to get it there. Meanwhile, they tried to downplay their wanton ways.

Simultaneously, the burgeoning independent film movement, fed by investment-happy Wall Street speculators, began to seize the creative high ground. The 1985 Academy Awards were read as a rebuke to studio complacency, when William Hurt walked off with the Best Actor Oscar for his flaming queen in *The Kiss of the Spider Woman* and Geraldine Page captured the Best Actress statuette for her homeward-bound widow in *The Trip to Bountiful* – two films produced by feisty independents. The 1986 competition tilted even further in favour of iconoclastic outsiders: with Oliver Stone's *Platoon* leading the charge, 42 per cent of the nominations went to movies that hadn't been produced by the eight major studios. Suddenly, small seemed beautiful. The spendthrift studios, with their expensive overheads and lumbering bureaucracies, had reason to be embarrassed. Like the giant Detroit auto-makers, they briefly stood in danger of turning into clumsy dinosaurs.

Ironically, though, just as Wall Street's October 1987 dive signalled the beginning of the end of the roaring 1980s in America, mainstream Hollywood rallied. Private investment money dried up, pushing independent companies, which had expanded too quickly, up against the wall. By 1989, indies like the De

Laurentiis Entertainment Group, Cannon Films and Vestron Pictures were either bankrupt or up for sale. In contrast, the studios, with the exception of only a couple of laggards, were booming again. Having discovered new markets abroad – as well as new sources of foreign financing – Hollywood hyperbole was back in style. With a vengeance.

THE BATMAN EFFECT

Lingering memories of *Heaven's Gate* faded quickly, dwarfed by the phenomenal success of *Batman*, the movie that more than any other captured the prevailing hyperactivity. Its audience primed by six months of advance merchandising, the movie shattered all prevailing box-office records, selling an astonishing $40 million worth of tickets during just its first weekend of domestic release; and eventually grossing $250 million in the US and Canada, $450 million internationally. *Jaws*, in the summer of 1975, had established the tradition of the summer blockbuster, but *Batman* redefined industry expectations. Where studio executives had once been ecstatic to clear the $100 million mark, that figure suddenly began to look like small potatoes. With a summer haul of only $109 million, *Ghostbusters II* was judged a major disappointment.

. . . .

Having discovered new markets abroad – as well as new sources of foreign financing – Hollywood hyperbole is back in style. With a vengeance.

. . . .

Lusting after *Batman's* brass ring, the studios began spending money with abandon in their search for the next mega-blockbuster. Given its super-grosses, *Batman's* $45 million budget began to look almost reasonable. (And so what if Jack Nicholson, who shared in the movie's gross revenues for donning the Joker's bilious green greasepaint, raked as much as $50 million off the top?) By the time the summer 1990 sweepstakes kicked off, only high-rollers needed apply. Betting heavily on special-effects-laden action-adventure flicks, several of which were forced to pay pricey overtime charges as they rushed to make their release dates, budgets crept steadily upward: *Dick Tracy*, at $30 million, was a relative bargain. *Another 48 Hours*, at $45 million, was viewed as a guaranteed annuity. *Total Recall*, $50 million. *Days of Thunder*, $55 million. *Die Hard 2*, $60 million. Costs just kept escalating.

Even before the 1990 summer tab was figured in, the average price of producing a studio picture in 1989 had edged up to $23.5 million, a 40 per cent increase over the 1985 average. At the same time, the studios themselves cut back on the number of films in production, greenlighting just 112 movies in 1989, down sixteen per cent from the previous year's output of 134. In effect, the studios, having weathered the competition posed by the independents midway through the decade, entered the 1990s by spending more money on fewer films.

While the moguls all hoped to cash in at the domestic box-office, they knew that US ticket sales alone would not earn them back their wages. Although domestic ticket sales amounted to a record $5.02 billion in 1989, the *number* of tickets sold didn't increase appreciably, hovering around the one billion mark where it had been stalled for years. Moreover, ticket prices themselves may be hitting a ceiling. As first-run theatres in major American cities began charging $7.50 per admission, they ran the risk of discouraging the repeat business required to produce a true blockbuster.

Fortunately for the studio gamblers, other revenue sources are sweetening the pot. Video revenues, which rose to $2.9 billion in 1989, actually outpaced theatrical rentals. (Of the $5.02 billion worth of tickets sold, theatre owners turned $1.9 billion back to the studios.) Network, pay-TV and syndication added nearly another $2 billion to the kitty. And, like so much gravy, for every dollar the studios earned at home, they collected another 70 cents abroad. With the privatization of TV increasing the need for product in Western Europe, new markets waiting to be exploited in Eastern Europe and the overall growth of videocassette sales worldwide, the foreign returns for American movies are expected to increase yet further.

At the moment, the big bucks go to callow talents with a knack for noise.

In that light, the $60 million that Carolco Pictures spent to send Arnold Schwarzenegger to Mars in *Total Recall* looked like less of a risk. The muscle-bound star, even at a salary of $10 million plus a piece of the gross, is considered money in the bank thanks to proven international appeal. Of course, the fact that Schwarzenegger also exhibits an affinity for bone-crunching, adventure yarns doesn't hurt. Action not only speaks louder than words – action pictures also translate most easily into foreign cultures where American comedies and dramas, with their more specific cultural references, sometimes fall flat.

BONE-CRUNCHERS

The danger is that the expanding foreign market, however beneficial its contributions to the studio coffers, will have a damaging impact on American movies themselves. Although the wise-cracking Schwarzenegger has proven himself a much more ingratiating screen presence than the deadly earnest Sylvester Stallone, action movies as a genre are inherently self-limiting. There are only so many ways to crash a car or dispatch a drug lord. This was admitted by director Walter Hill as he put the finishing touches on the Eddie Murphy vehicle, *Another 48 Hours*; 'One of the hardest things about movies like this – not just sequels, but cop movies – is that you always know who's going to win.' Yet, when it comes to allocating their resources, the studios would much more willingly dish out $50 million for a by-the-numbers shoot-'em-up than ante up $10 million for an intimate character study.

While Hollywood's actresses routinely complain that nobody writes good parts for women any more, that's because there's more money to be made from a routine buddy-cop movie than from all but the most extraordinary 'woman's picture'. Though male stars, led by Schwarzenegger, Stallone, Eddie Murphy, Tom Cruise and Jack Nicholson, are currently demanding as much as $10 million upfront to step before the cameras, no American actress rates more than $5 million. It's not really a question of equal pay for equal work – when compensation hits such stratospheric marks, it's simply a reflection of perceived box-office value. As such, it's a vivid demonstration of where Hollywood places its priorities. And heading into the 1990s, the success of the international action movie has made Hollywood, more than ever, a man's industry.

. . . .

The danger is that the expanding foreign market, however beneficial its contributions to the studio coffers, will have a damaging impact on American movies themselves.

. . . .

SCRIPT WARS

Even screenwriters, traditionally the low-men on the industry totem pole, are feeling the effects. The spring of 1990 witnessed a frenzied escalation in the prices paid for original screenplays. Amid frenzied bidding, masterfully orchestrated by the talent agencies pitting studio against studio, producer against producer, Columbia Pictures inaugurated the script wars by shelling out $1.1 million to David Mickey Evans, a relative unknown, for his screenplay *Radio Flyer*, a fantasy told from the viewpoint of two abused kids. Rival studio executives professed themselves horrified at the sight of screenplays crashing the $1 million barrier, and then, just as quickly, they all jumped into the fray. In what may have been an unintended metaphor for the risky decisions involved, the NAMETK Agency delivered a ticking alarm clock to prospecting buyers by way of announcing that it was putting *The Ticking Man*, an action drama about a runaway, nuclear-armed robot by Laurence Dworet and Robert Roy Poole, on the block; by the end of a day-long auction they had eight major companies fighting for the rights. Lawrence Gordon's new Largo Entertainment walked off with the prize for a cool million. Writer Shane Black, the creator of *Lethal Weapon*, did even better with his latest effort, *The Last Boy Scout*, another buddy-cop pairing replete with tough-guy talk, violent explosions and general mayhem – it went to the Geffen Film Co., which will produce for Warner Bros, for a record-shattering $1.75 million. As a group, the newly rich writers all have one thing in common: they're guys, and fairly young guys at that. Senior members of the Writers Guild can only curse their bad lack for having followed in the footsteps of such revered wordsmiths as Ben Hecht and Preston Sturges. At the moment, the big bucks go to callow talents with a knack for noise.

BATMEN BOUGHT

The macho posturing that characterizes such projects – both on the page and in their selling – trickles down from the top. For while *Batman* was looting the

box-office, *Batman*'s producers Peter Guber and Jon Peters were holding up the Sony Corp. When Sony shelled out $3.4 billion to acquire Columbia Pictures in the fall of 1989, Hollywood barely blinked. After all, the acquisition had long been rumoured: in order to promote technologies like 8mm video and High Definition TV, Sony felt it needed a studio like Columbia. With its library of old movies and the promise of new hits, Columbia provides a way of luring entertainment consumers into buying Sony's new hardware. Following similar strategies, JVC, the Japanese VCR manufacturer, advanced producer Larry Gordon some $100 million to open a new production company, Largo Entertainment, and the Pioneer Electronic Corp., another big Japanese hardware maker, funnelled $60 million into Carolco Pictures.

. . . .

The success of the international action movie has made Hollywood, more than ever, a man's industry.

. . . .

Still, the film industry couldn't help but do a shocked double-take when Sony's conservative, corporate leadership chose Guber and Peters, two of the most notoriously freewheeling operatives in Hollywood, to run Columbia Pictures. Admittedly, Guber, a fast-talking attorney-turned-producer, and Peters, a former hairdresser who entered the film business via a liaison with Barbra Streisand, were on a *bona fide* roll. *Rain Man*, released in 1988, had performed the tricky task of winning over both critics and the public before copping a Best Picture Oscar as an extra bonus. *Batman*, following close on its heels, demonstrated the duo's marketing savvy – as much calculation went into the famous logo as was lavished on the film itself. Nevertheless, the certified odd couple did not enjoy universal respect.

Since joining forces in 1980, their hits ranged from *Flashdance* and *The Color Purple* to *The Witches of Eastwick* and *Gorillas in the Mist*. But not *everything* the two Midases touched turned to gold. Witness *Vision Quest*, their paean to high-school wrestling; *Clue*, a board game in search of a plot, or *The Clan of the Cave Bear*, which offered up Darryl Hannah as a shiksa-among-the neanderthals. If Guber has a particular talent, it is for spending lavishly to snap up best-selling novels and true-life stories rather than developing original screenplays, while Peters excels at promotion, first selling A-list stars and directors on the properties themselves, then selling the finished product to prospective audiences. But neither could be called true filmmakers since, once they hire the talent, they frequently step aside, particularly on their more prestigious projects. Steven Spielberg, for example, brought in his own producing partners to handle the day-to-day chores on *The Color Purple*, and director Barry Levinson shouldered the main responsibility, along with his producer partner Marc Johnson, for *Rain Man*. As studio heads, such a laissez-faire approach could serve Guber and Peters well – moguls aren't expected to stand around on the set of every picture they set in motion – but they also have yet to demonstrate the ability to orchestrate a slate of twelve to fifteen pictures annually that a studio's distribution apparatus requires.

Nevertheless, at the urging of Walter Yetnikoff, who runs CBS Records for Sony, the Japanese conglomerate was determined to sign up Guber and Peters. First, it bought their production company for $200 million – of which the two producers personally pocketed $55 million. Then, it signed the boys to five-year contracts, for which each would be paid $2.75 million annually, rising to $2.9 million over the life of the contract. And then, just to ensure they had an incentive to work real hard, Sony established a $50 million bonus pool for the two to share with other top executives. The only hitch was that Guber and Peters were, at the time, under a five-year contract with Warner Bros which, thanks to *Batman*, led all other studios in the 1989 box-office rankings. When informed of the pending deal, a furious Steve Ross, Warner's chairman, refused to let them go. With Warners threatening a $1 billion lawsuit against Sony, heated negotiations finally led to an unprecedented trade involving, among other provisions, Warners swapping its interests in the old MGM studio facility in Culver City for Columbia's share of the Burbank Studios, where Warners is headquartered. By the time the dust settled, it appeared that Sony had ponied up an additional $500 million to secure Guber and Peters' services.

Forced to leave their existing projects behind at Warner Bros – like the film adaptation of Tom Wolfe's *Bonfire of the Vanities* – as well as the rights to any *Batman* sequels, Guber and Peters arrived at Columbia with only their well-stuffed Rolodexes, their fine-honed competitive instincts and a proven flair for spending whatever money is needed to grab blue-chip properties. But, in a sense, the eventual outcome of their tenure is immaterial. They may have already scored the biggest coup of their careers simply by signing under such lucrative terms. The reverberations throughout Hollywood's executive suites were immediate. As Peter Dekom observed in the *New York Times*, 'Executive salaries will skyrocket, at least for those executives who are considered essential. I guarantee that every top executive is looking at his compensation package today and complaining to his board.' Shortly thereafter *Top Gun* producer Don Simpson and Jerry Bruckheimer signed a new contract with Paramount Pictures, which effectively handed over to them a $500 million blank cheque to make whatever movies they want, free of any studio approvals. As if to underline the fact that such cushy arrangements are as much about ego displays as anything else, Paramount announced the signing with full-page newspaper advertisements that treated Simpson and Bruckheimer like box-office stars.

ESZTERHAS vs OVITZ

In a year characterized by such flagrant self-aggrandizement, Michael Ovitz, the president of the Creative Artists Agency (CAA), was one of the few to duck the limelight – even if the light cast his way was hardly flattering. Since its creation fifteen years ago by five young agents defecting from the venerable William Morris Agency, CAA had grown into a fearsome giant, controlling many of the industry's major players, from actors like Tom Cruise, Robert Redford and Barbra Streisand, to such directors as Sydney Pollock, Ivan Reitman and David Lynch and writers of the stature of Gore Vidal, John Hughes and Stephen King. And, as the ringmaster who orchestrates CAA's moves by combining its writers, directors and stars into saleable 'packages', the agency has a huge influence on what movies the studios make – Ovitz himself has earned the unofficial title of most powerful man in Hollywood.

With a deep aversion to personal publicity, no doubt sensing that insecure stars don't like being upstaged in the press by their agents, Ovitz had always maintained a resolutely low profile. But as CAA's influence has increased, so has media interest in the agency's power-brokering. And so when writer Joe Eszterhas, with credits including *Flashdance* and *Jagged Edge* and an asking price of $1.25 million per script, fired Ovitz in a blistering letter, it made for one of the season's juicier scandals. Ostensibly, Eszterhas decided to move from CAA to the rival International Creative Management Agency (ICM) not out of any unhappiness with CAA, but out of long-standing loyalty to an old champion who had joined ICM. But when the writer informed Ovitz of his decision, Ovitz, Eszterhas claimed, retaliated with 'morally repugnant' threats.

The American movie-going public is growing older and, as it matures, is looking for entertainment that offers more than just gun battles and expletives.

Eszterhas made the charge in a private letter to Ovitz that was somehow fed to fax machines all over Hollywood and then on to the press. Detailing an emotionally-charged meeting, Eszterhas recounted how Ovitz had allegedly promised that if the writer left CAA, 'my foot soldiers who go up and down Wilshire Boulevard each day will blow your brains out.' Understandably embarrassed, Ovitz responded with a conciliatory missive, also leaked to the press, in which he claimed to be 'totally shocked since my recollection of our conversation bore no relationship to your recollection.'

Ovitz's defence failed to convince, if only because the whole controversy underscored the widespread perception that, given his undeniable clout, Ovitz is capable of stage-managing the industry at will. Indeed, when reports subsequently appeared to the effect that Ovitz had turned down Sony's invitation to run Columbia, cynics joked that Ovitz didn't need the Columbia job, since he already ran all the studios in town anyway. In any event, the whole affair, though providing a colourful view of clashing temperaments, hardly damaged the principals involved. Though CAA currently faces increased competition from several, new upstart agencies, it remains the dominant player. And Eszterhas, casting himself as the principled little guy fighting the big bosses, may have written one of the most dramatic scenes of his career. 'You might very well be able to hurt me,' he signed off to Ovitz, 'but I will risk all that ... I have my family and I have my old manual, imperfect typewriter and they have always been the things I've treasured most.' Apparently, Ovitz's foot soldiers aren't as dangerous as the writer feared. For, less than a year later, Eszterhas became the highest-paid screenwriter in Hollywood by selling his sexual suspense thriller *Basic Instinct* to Carolco Pictures, for an incredible $3 million.

LITTLE DAISY

Amid all of the clashing egos, noisy hype and financial extravagance, one of the few grace notes in an otherwise crass year was the selection of *Driving Miss Daisy* as Best Picture at this year's Oscars. Though hardly a great movie, the modest, racial drama recounting a 20-year-long friendship between an elderly Jewish widow, played by Jessica Tandy, and her loyal chauffeur, acted by Morgan Freeman, made a virtue out of its own modesty. Produced by Warner Bros, for a bare-boned $7.5 million, after most of the competition had rejected it as resoundingly uncommercial, the unexpected hit went on to gross more than $100 million domestically – a sure sign that, as studies have indicated, the American movie-going public is growing older and, as it matures, is looking for entertainment that offers more than just gun battles and expletives. Hollywood, as it chases worldwide riches, isn't yet ready to take that lesson to heart, but at least *Miss Daisy*'s success stands as a valiant rebuke to the big-is-best mentality that permeates a film industry suffering from a bad case of elephantitis.

GREGG KILDAY

PRIME MINISTER SEEKS OSCAR

Various British film luminaries went to Downing Street in June to tell the prime minister that their industry was going under. Only 27 feature films, they told her, had gone before the cameras during 1989, as against almost twice that number the previous year. Cinema admissions were steadily rising, but British producers couldn't benefit from this improved situation because, without access to tax incentives, they had no chance of enticing risk capital, and without subsidies, they couldn't tap into European coproduction finance. In short, the government had put them in a position where they just couldn't compete.

A TIGHT HOLE

It's certainly true that eleven years of a Tory government applying its free-market dogma to the film industry have left the nation's filmmakers in a very tight hole from which to engineer another revival. But if the economics of the British film industry are shaky, the creative health of the nation's cinema is no less so – and that can't be blamed exclusively on the shortage of funds. Can a film industry that produces such a flat comedy as *Nuns on the Run*, such a muddled gangster picture as *The Krays*, such a forlorn slice of World War 2 nostalgia as *Chicago Joe and the Showgirl* or the desperately old-fashioned *Diamond Skulls*, really argue for its right to survival?

'I was fed up with English filmmakers who seemed to think that they were automatically entitled to have a film industry,' recalled the late Michael Powell in his autobiography and it's difficult not to feel some of the same impatience with those now putting forward a case for increased government intervention. It's one of the tragedies of the British film industry that the only thing which can draw its 'members' together is the pitch for public funds. What's really needed is a working party to investigate the question of what brought down the hopes and dreams of the past ten years, and what the conditions would be for building a British cinema with genuine popular appeal. Suggesting that tax breaks and government cash would solve the deeper malaise shows a blindness to the wasted opportunities of recent years.

At the beginning of the decade, filmmakers briefly found a way to make films that critics wanted to see, and just occasionally they produced pictures that attracted audiences worldwide. In an effort to increase the number of such hits, producers spent steadily larger amounts of money on films that steadily fewer people wanted to see, until the industry reached its current sorry state. The money was there for a while but filmmakers never found what's been missing from British cinema for most of the past 40 years; an understanding of the aesthetics of popular cinema, and of the institutional mechanisms required to foster it.

If the economics of the British film industry are shaky, the creative health of the nation's cinema is no less so – and that can't be blamed exclusively on the shortage of funds

David Puttnam, Richard Attenborough and all the others who trotted off to see the prime minister considered it something of a breakthrough to have secured four hours of her time and several jugs of her coffee. They might have reflected on what normally happens following a meeting with a minister responsible for the film industry – they're generally out of that particular office within hours of saying farewell to the film people. Mrs Thatcher may last a few more months, even another year or so, but her willingness to see the film people was reasonably interpreted as a desperate pitch for approval from the chattering classes, almost a recognition that she may soon be headed for the retirement home.

A PROBLEM SHARED

Had they accepted there was precious little chance of securing an increase in government funding for the film industry before a new prime minister enters Downing Street, the filmmakers might have dedicated the time to discussing a problem they share with Margaret Thatcher. For an industry whose senior members largely claim allegiance to the other political party, it's uncanny how its fortunes have mirrored those of the Conservative Party. Was it not the resurgence of national pride coinciding with the Tory accession which fed the success of *Chariots of Fire*, and inspired such vigorous counterblasts as *The Ploughman's Lunch* and *My Beautiful Laundrette*? And has not the political confusion about British policy towards a wider, stronger Europe, caused as much dismay among filmmakers as among those Hope and Glory English nationalists who have traditionally found their home within the Conservative Party.

British filmmakers felt happy when they could confidently trumpet, or rail against, the nationalist cause, just as Thatcher's premiership had its high point when war against the Argentine bred nationalistic jingoism. At the time it seemed there was an expanding market for British films in America, leading to the easy assumption that there was something 'special' about British filmmaking. But just as the 'special relationship' between Britain and America has wilted now Ronald Reagan is no longer in the White House, so recent pictures from Spain (*Women on the Verge of a Nervous Breakdown*) and Italy (*Cinema Paradiso*) have made at least as much impact as anything to come out of the UK in the same period. Could Mrs

Thatcher have been hoping that helping David Puttnam and Richard Attenborough to win Oscars would mean another term for her?

She might hope for it, but she isn't going to get it unless these producers and others find a set of new ideas to fuel their filmmaking. David Puttnam's public agonizing about the fact that his financiers wouldn't let him make a film about a British bomber crew, rather than the Americans featured in *Memphis Belle*, and Richard Attenborough's emphasis on the status of Charlie Chaplin, the subject of his planned next film and one of the great figures of American cinema, as a very English genius, suggest these two producers still want to bang the nationalist drum that now sounds as hollow as the Conservative preoccupation with sovereignty.

POOR EUROPEANS

Some of those luminaries in Downing Street sought to present themselves as Good Europeans, appealing for funds to 'level the pitch' with their counterparts in France, Germany, Italy and Spain. But the appeal was bred of desperation, and for the most part British filmmakers carry on like Little Englanders in thrall to the United States. Britain, they claim, has it within its grasp to be the centre of the European film industry – even though climate, if nothing else, would argue for Spain. We have the studios, they point out, and might even have The Studio if only MCA could be persuaded to come and drive the birds off Rainham Marshes, making way for a theme park celebrating *Jaws* and other slices of Americana. What with our relative proximity to the US, a shared language, and the fact that Americans have traditionally liked working in London, how can we not become the conduit for Europe's ambitions on the international cinema audience?

. . . .

Long years of submission to the Hollywood mandate may have crushed British filmmakers' self-esteem to the point where they no longer have the confidence to embrace the new European direction

. . . .

Much of what British producers say on the subject of Europe and cinema contradicts all the principles that have been argued for by the continental counterparts over the past decade. At issue is the sort of strategy that's required to develop a film industry both more 'European' and more 'international' than the current fragmented mess. Yes, take on Hollywood at its own game. Yes, learn from Hollywood about ways to make films that can draw audiences from many cultures and many lands. But that doesn't mean playing by all the Hollywood rules. Don't try to crush the diversity of European cultures into one mono-culture. And recognize the need to raise significant capital for production, and set up mechanisms for distributing pictures across borders, while also acknowledging that bigness can be inimical to creation.

If the Conservatives understood the way other European filmmakers talk about the evolving film industry they might put aside some of their own fears about loss of national identity. But it's when people feel their identity is under threat that they're most keen to define it, and the long years of submission to the Hollywood mandate may have crushed British filmmakers' self-esteem to the point where they no longer have the confidence to embrace the new European direction. That may be an element in the difficulties facing British filmmakers of much more significance than the absence of subsidies to put on the negotiating table.

EYES ON THE US

Securing an American deal still remains the primary desideratum for British filmmakers. Despite producers' complaints about their paucity, there were a number of distributors still ready to do business with Brits. BBC TV's expanding film ambitions got a kick-up from liaisons with HBO on *Fellow Traveller* and Avenue Pictures on *The Object of Beauty*, the latter starring John Malkovich and Andie MacDowell in a story of two American tourists trapped in London without any cash. Eric Fellner's Initial Pictures secured backing from Universal for James Dearden's thriller *A Kiss Before Dying* and from Hemdale for Ken Loach's *Hidden Agenda*, another thriller this time set against the backdrop of contemporary Northern Ireland. And Miramax came in with Palace on David Leland's boxing saga, *The Big Man*, Neil Jordan's *The Miracle* and the US-located *Rage in Harlem*.

Despite some lamentation about directors like Mick Jackson and Stephen Frears going off to make Hollywood pictures, respectively *Chattahoochee* and *The Grifters*, the willingness of David Leland and Neil Jordan to return to home turf suggested that emigration need not be permanent – although the unenthusiastic response to the latter two's US films, *Checking Out* and *We're No Angels*, also argued that a return to base could be a sensible career move. But what British film producers really have to work out, however, is how it was that director Mike Figgis could follow his home-base dud *Stormy Monday* with a superb movie like *Internal Affairs*; or how Steve Barron could hit the big time with *Teenage Mutant Ninja Turtles* six years after his abysmal feature début, *Electric Dreams*.

THE AMERICANS COME AGAIN

Still, British talent that stays at home now has more opportunity to establish connections with the US studios. Encouraged by the prospect of a consolidated European market, the Americans are looking to build a foothold in this territory. Twentieth Century-Fox is backing John Goldstone to provide new comedies out of the UK, and has also established a separate office to pick up projects, while Paramount's Ileen Maisel is looking for films to follow such European successes for the company as Stephen Frears's *Dangerous Liaisons* and Lewis Gilbert's *Shirley Valentine*. Meanwhile New Line is making *Delta of Venus* in Paris with director Michael Radford, and John Daly's Hemdale, a British company in origin, has announced plans to back local pictures. These developments were greeted by hungry local filmmakers with enthusiasm amounting to hysteria, but those who remember the Americans coming and rapidly going in the 1960s, might ask what the Yanks will do to improve the creative infrastructure of British filmmaking. Paramount's Sydney Ganis apparently sees Europe as a way out of the bind in which American cinema seems to find itself in, offering an alternative to sequels with 'new story ideas, new directors and fresh, unencumbered personalities', but he will find that even in Europe ideas don't grow on trees; they have to be carefully nurtured.

DEFICIENT EXPERTISE

What closer links to the Americans offer is much the same as what European collaboration is intended to provide – access to international distribution, a substantial source of ongoing production funds, and continuity of production. But what British and many other filmmakers need is expertise in making films that distributors will want to distribute, and audiences will want to see. And that can only happen if filmmakers learn to organize their creative endeavours around some new ideas about cinema.

It's because European film industries are so fragmented that filmmakers find it so difficult to fertilize ideas, and nurture them into entertaining films. Everyone talks about training schemes and film schools, and about the need for a group of production companies working with talented writers and directors on a regular basis, but some extra sort of effort is going to be required before filmmakers will start to respond imaginatively to contemporary realities, contemporary movies and the mish-mash of ideas percolating through the contemporary cultural scene.

COURSE OF LEAST RESISTANCE

It's generally agreed that there's no market anymore for the sort of low-budget films that fuelled the British Film Renaissance, but there's a problem moving on to bigger, riskier projects before filmmakers have worked out what it is they're about. Having failed to justify their approach to cinema at the box-office, all they can do is take the course of least resistance. Which is what British filmmakers are doing when they make films out of the scandals and *causes célèbres* of recent British history – *Chicago Joe and the Showgirl, Scandal, Buster, The Krays* and various other projects now in the works. There's little sign here of imaginations working at full throttle, of filmmakers driven by strong visions and reaching out to touch contemporary fears and aspirations.

The luminaries came away from their meeting with Mrs Thatcher, seemingly pleased to have secured a £5 million fund for coproductions, as well as ministerial agreement to listen to proposals for tax writeoffs and increased funding through TV and video levies. If anything worthwhile is to come from these offers and proposals, then the industry will have to use the opportunities provided much more creatively and adventurously than they did last time, and achieving that is going to take an awful lot of thought and discussion.

JAMES PARK

BOOKS

by Andrew Kelly, Phil Hardy, Timothy Gee and James Park

STAR LIVES

LOUISE BROOKS
Barry Paris (*Hamish Hamilton*)

It was impossible for Louise Brooks to write her memoirs because she could not tell the truth about her sexual activities. But the definitive story can now be told, and the resulting book provides a candid portrayal of one of the greatest personalities in film history. Its 550 pages trace the Brooks legend from early, unhappy years with her mother, through her dancing days, the reluctant entry into motion pictures, the heyday marked by her work with G. W. Pabst and *Pandora's Box*, and on to her downfall. Too independent for Hollywood and near breaking point with the studios, Brooks refused the chance to star with James Cagney in *The Public Enemy*, preferring to go to New York for one of her many affairs. The years that followed were barren, with a succession of jobs (including gossip columnist and radio commentator) and a long period of alcoholism. The final part of the book outlines the revival of interest in her career and her later rôle as a historian of the classical Hollywood she despised. The sexual truth pervades the pages: abused at the age of nine, her affairs with some of the leading actors and directors of the day are fully documented, along with two marriages, one quite bizarre. Taking Brooks beyond the cult of *Pandora's Box*, Paris offers a full assessment of all her films that shows how, even in minor rôles, she tended to act other performers off the screen. His eye for detail is sometimes overwhelming, but overall he has produced a comprehensive, readable and engrossing biography.

NORMA SHEARER
Gavin Lambert
(*Knopf/Hodder & Stoughton*)

Florenz Ziegfeld said she'd never make it – with her thick thighs, poor figure and a cast in one eye. D. W. Griffith confirmed that judgement, pointing out that her blue eyes would look blank in close-up. And her first test at MGM was a washout. But a New York astrologer had promised 'success and happiness somewhere far away', and she was right. As an actress who would lose herself in whatever character she was playing on the screen, Norma Shearer might seem a rather unpromising biographical subject, but her marriage to Irving Thalberg, and subsequent impact on MGM's internal politics, gives Gavin Lambert his subject. After she had overcome the obstacles to success through hard work and ruthless ambition, it was Thalberg who nurtured Shearer's career, transforming her into Hollywood's answer to Broadway. Although she successfully rebuilt that career after her husband's death, won several battles against Louis B. Mayer and found new outlets for sexual energies that had been dammed up in marriage – including an unlikely liaison with the sixteen-year-old Mickey Rooney – she went out gracefully in 1943, almost fulfilling Thalberg's wish that her career should end with his demise. A handsomely produced and elegantly written book.

ONCE A WICKED LADY: A Biograpy of Margaret Lockwood
Hilton Tims (*Virgin*)

Within its fan-book parameters, this is a quite detailed run-through of Margaret Lockwood's working and private life. Melodrama seems to have characterized the latter as well as the former, at least as regards Lockwood's relationship with her cold, domineering mother (a rôle fit for Gladys Cooper), who at the 1951 custody hearing that followed her daughter's divorce, amazingly testified on behalf of her former son-in-law to the effect that Margaret was an unfit parent: 'Margaret and her mother never spoke to or saw each other again'. There are a few interesting professional asides (Lockwood unwisely turned down the rôle of the wife in *The Browning Version*), and some bizarre reminders of bygone mores: Jympson Harman's review of *The White Unicorn* observed, 'I do wish Margaret would do something about her lipstick . . .' The epilogue finds the retired star solitary in Kingston: 'She watches television, rarely missing one of her own films' but seldom ventures from the house 'unless it is down to the local parade of shops to replenish her stock of cigarettes.'

ROBERT DE NIRO: The Man, the Myth and the Movies
Patrick Agan (*Robert Hale*)

Robert De Niro is a frustrating, if enticing, subject for the biographer. Patrick Agan thought he could get 'behind the mask of Hollywood's most powerful actor' by talking with friends and colleagues. But, of course, anyone who wants to remain in the latter category isn't going to pour out indiscretions. The result is a biography that never gets very close to De Niro. One sees where he goes, what he does and the films in which he makes an appearance, but the inner core is never revealed. Agan wraps with a mention of *Stanley and Iris* as an upcoming film, and doesn't anticipate the latest stage in De Niro's career – as restaurant owner, property developer and producer. A conscientious book, but not very revealing.

COOPER'S WOMEN
Jane Ellen Wayne (*Robert Hale*)

The key text for Jane Ellen Wayne's follow-up to *Crawford's Men* and *Gable's Women* is the nymphomaniac Clara Bow's declaration that 'Gary's hung like a horse and can go all night.' So important is this statement to the book's argument – that Gary Cooper was a great lover, bringing sexual joy to the likes of Carole Lombard, Grace Kelly, Merle Oberon, Ingrid Bergman, Tallulah Bankhead and scores of others – that it appears twice in the book's first sixteen pages. Unfortunately, no source is given, nor is there any sort of statistical back-up. The trouble with the book is that its preoccupation with one aspect of its subject's persona – the one most difficult to research – ends up implying there's nothing more interesting to say about Gary Cooper than that he had a big cock and used it to full effect. This is a man who almost got bumped off by a former lover, the tempestuous Mexican, Lupe Velez, because his mother had dissuaded him from marrying her – now there's an interesting Oedipal relationship!

ROBERT REDFORD
Minty Clinch (*NEL*)

By the end of this biography it is still impossible to be sure how the author feels about Robert Redford. By turns his arm's length attitude to the Hollywood Establishment is seen as sound business practice and arrogance; his involvement with ecological issues as a rich man's hobby and a mark of genuine concern for the environment; his success as an actor as natural talent or a limited ability which he takes much too seriously. The resulting book does little to separate private man from publicity department myth. Minty Clinch has read widely to research this life, but there are questions which no hunt through press clippings can ever answer.

MIA FARROW
Sam Rubin, Richard Taylor (*Robson*)

An intriguing departure from the standard star biography formula has been adopted here. The life and career are examined in the first ten chapters, followed by 25 pages aiming to provide a 'comprehensive discussion of her films'. The two parts of the book could hardly be more different. Farrow had a strict Roman Catholic upbringing, and considered taking vows as a nun. But she has now been married three times (to Frank Sinatra, André Previn and Woody Allen), and taken on nine children. This is promising material for a life story. Sadly, the approach is one of downmarket popular journalism of the most sloppy kind. But in the final chapter, the writing is trenchant, the opinions clearly formulated and pithily argued. It's simply impossible to believe that the author of this chapter had anything to do with the previous ten. But which of the two authors on the title page should take the credit?

DIANE KEATON: The Story of the Real Annie Hall
Jonathan Moor (*Robson*)

Jonathan Moor here offers a sympathetic, if conventional, appraisal of Diane Keaton's life and career. His respect for the actress and her work is evident. The problem is that there are few newsworthy episodes for him to report. Although there have been liaisons with Woody Allen and Warren Beatty, neither marriage, children nor divorce have ensued. Moor turns his attention instead to the films, which he reads as successive revelations of her personality. This does not particularly over-value her contribution to the films in which she has appeared, but her performances in *Reds*, which Beatty directed, and in Woody Allen's films, do seem to stand apart from the rest of her work.

HOLLYWOOD'S FALLEN IDOLS
Roy Pickard (*Batsford*)

Although the connection between the ten essays in this book is extremely tenuous, there is much of interest in individual pieces. Little new can be said about Judy Garland, Montgomery Clift, Marilyn Monroe, Charlie Chaplin or Errol Flynn, but the less familiar names yield richer rewards. George Sanders was an Englishman in Hollywood who never really belonged in the 'English colony', and it's good to be reminded of his ability to hold his own with the right material. Pickard also has some valuable points to make about Erich Von Stroheim, Bela Lugosi, Sterling Hayden and even Orson Welles. The pictures, which show the effect of passing years on the faces of Pickard's subjects, almost make the words superfluous.

THE TRIAL OF ROCK HUDSON
John Parker (*Sidgwick & Jackson*)
Rock Hudson was told that he was suffering from AIDS in May 1984. He informed his secretary of the diagnosis, but not his sexual partner, Marc Christian, who only learned what was wrong from a public statement made in July 1985, two months before the star's death. Christian sued the Hudson estate on the grounds that his life had been unreasonably endangered. This book is a record of the case that came to trial in the Los Angeles Superior Court in January 1989. Along the way it provides some insights into the way in which the gay actor's sexual preferences were concealed during the period of his studio contracts, and also underlines the material benefits that an extended period of success in the American film industry can still confer.

MARILYN ON LOCATION
Bart Mills (*Sidgwick & Jackson*)
The stream of books on Marilyn Monroe shows little sign of abating. First there were books about her life and death; these were followed by books about the books. Bart Mills here provides a life without any serious examination of the major uncertainties. 'She couldn't be sure who her father was' he writes, and leaves it at that. In a way it's refreshing to read the familiar story without a slant of any kind.

JAMES DEAN IN HIS OWN WORDS
(*Omnibus*)
The title is misleading insofar as this book contains about as many words by other people on James Dean as it does apothegms from the star himself. But since Dean was never loquacious, this is probably no bad thing. Where talking about acting or fast cars, he tended to be pithy and opinionated. The book is stylishly produced, with photographs that capture several lighter moments alongside the familiar brooding mood.

THE MAN WHO SHOT GARBO: The Hollywood Photographs of Clarence Sinclair Bull
Terence Pepper, John Kobal
(*Simon & Schuster*)
The exhibition of Clarence Bull's photographs at London's National Portrait Gallery only months before Garbo's death provided a worthy epitaph for the supreme star of Hollywood's golden years, and this accompanying volume offers a unique opportunity to study her face at leisure. Although there are pictures of Jean Harlow, Joan Crawford, Clark Gable, Gary Cooper, the Marx Brothers and Lassie, these other MGM artists are eclipsed by the star of stars. On the evidence of the pictures presented here, Garbo's was a face that offered no 'bad' angles.

MOVIE MAKERS

GOLDWYN
A. Scott Berg (*Hamish Hamilton*)
Ten years in the making, with research so extensive it makes the search for Charles Foster Kane resemble an easter-egg hunt, the definitive biography of the great mogul arrives. At sixteen, facing anti-semitism, poverty and a difficult mother, Schmuel Gelbfisz left Warsaw. Walking virtually all the way to Britain, he caught a ship to the US where, following his rapid rise in the glove business, he realized the potential of motion pictures after seeing a 'Bronco Billy' Western. With Jesse Lasky and C. B. De Mille he made *The Squaw Man* and what followed proved to be one of the most remarkable careers in film history. Despite being an independent for much of his career, he survived the ravages of two world wars, the Depression, HUAC, television and the collapse of the studio system by making literate and generally successful movies, including *Stella Dallas*, *Withering* (as he called it) *Heights*, *The Little Foxes* and *The Best Years of Our Lives*. He discovered and nurtured a number of stars – Ronald Colman, David Niven and Gary Cooper – but failed to find his Garbo. His relationship with directors and writers was often fraught, but even

those like William Wyler who resented his constant disruptions kept coming back for more. Goldwyn the man is covered in candid detail: the alienation from his mother, two loveless marriages (his second wife's life-long real love being the homosexual George Cukor), and terrible relationships with his two children. Inevitably, the book covers the Goldwynisms; the best being 'That H-Bomb; that's dynamite'. Scott Fitzgerald said 'You always knew where you stood with Goldwyn – Nowhere'; and Berg's biography pulls no punches in its depiction of its egocentric and sometimes monstrous subject. The result is a great book which makes an important contribution to film history.

THE HUSTONS
Lawrence Grobel (*Bloomsbury*)
If a criterion of genius were an infinite capacity for securing risqué reminiscences from elderly (or, in some cases, not so elderly) ladies, then Lawrence Grobel would have earned a place in the front rank. *The Hustons* clearly establishes John Huston as a twentieth-century Don Juan, and a man of extraordinary energy. Alongside its accounts of boozing, practical jokes and every

form of gambling, the book also encompasses big-game hunting, smuggling and riding to hounds. John Huston was one of the first directors to break out of the studio, travelling to South America, Europe, Africa and Asia as the subjects of his films dictated. But where he is, others, even other Hustons, tend to fade into insignificance, and this provides an obstacle to the book fulfilling its declared purpose. Those few who remember Walter Huston can only have known him towards the end of his career; he never wrote his memoirs and most of his screen rôles did not showcase his full talent. And the careers of Huston's children are only just beginning to develop. The Paiute chief who named John Huston 'Long Shadow' was a man of acute observation. Whatever other intentions Grobel may have had, *The Hustons* emerges as a biography of John.

CITIZEN WELLES:
A Biography of Orson Welles
Frank Brady (*Hodder & Stoughton*)

With biographies from Barbara Leaming and Charles Higham already on the shelves, and a weighty volume from Peter Bogdanovich on the way, this new biography doesn't aim to be the last word on Orson Welles. Frank Brady is fascinated by the way in which Welles spanned the media – theatre, radio, cinema, TV – and, as his title suggests, he sees *Citizen Kane* as the dazzling pinnacle of that career – a film that inaugurated 'the death of classical cinema', 'disturbed all preconceptions of what America was capable of producing and what cinema was about', and seemingly influenced everybody from Andrzej Wajda to Gabriel García Marquez. As a result, the second half of his book ends up being somewhat anti-climactic. But while Brady ignores much of the tittle-tattle about Welles's amours and later (disgusting) personal habits, he brings a host of new anecdotes to his account of Welles' creative achievements. Sometimes over-sympathetic to his subject, he doesn't give full weight to Welles's self-destructive urges, but he's sufficiently aware of the magician's talent for fabricating his own life to produce a persuasive biography.

SOME FREAKS
David Mamet (*Faber & Faber*)

Amidst some sharp pieces on his childhood, Jewishness, Ronald Reagan, Central American refugees, guns and opinion polls, David Mamet offers a revealing and amusing account of directing his first feature film, *House of Games*. Acknowledging that, while he could deal with actors and scripts, he knew nothing about the visual aspects of filmmaking, he describes the process of storyboarding the film as 'like taking a visual intelligence test for several hours every day, with the questions written in a foreign language'. But he has cause to be grateful for that work when shooting starts, and he finds that 'I could barely remember what the movie was about, let alone try to think where to put the camera.' Having suffered the sort of demoralizing experiences that seem regrettably to be the lot of screenwriters working for hire, he finds it exhilarating to be for once at the top of the chain of command. Directing films, he realizes, is 'gruelling, exhilarating, sobering and addictive.'

SCORSESE ON SCORSESE
ed. David Thompson, Ian Christie
(*Faber & Faber*)

Although collaged from a series of interviews carried out at different times by a diverse group of people, *Scorsese on Scorsese* is a highly readable account of the career of America's most interesting film director, and it's especially useful in bringing out the way films such as *Mean Streets* and *Taxi Driver* draw on his own experiences of living in New York, and his omnivorous film viewing. In its down-to-earth approach to filmmaking, the volume sometimes brings to mind Hitchcock's book-length interview with François Truffaut, with the most precious moments being the most apparently personal and honest, as when Scorsese says of *New York, New York*, 'I still don't really like it, yet in a way I love it'; describes *Raging Bull* as 'a kamikaze way of making movies: pour everything in, then forget all about it and go find another way of life,' and acknowledges his acceptance of the fact that since the 'industry is now run by businessmen . . . if I want to continue to make personal films, I have to show them I have some sort of respect for money.' What's missing are the questions being answered, which makes one wonder at times whether what's being discussed are Scorsese's obsessions or those of his interviewees.

DOUBLE VISION: My Life in Film
Andrzej Wajda (*Faber & Faber*)

Proceeding by a series of brief, perceptive chapters, Wajda presents what he describes as a letter to the young, ignorant filmmaker he once was. Every page contains some drop of distilled wisdom. Wajda points out the way powerful films use anecdote to illuminate big happenings and great issues, argues that the development of the film idea and key casting decisions are the most important aspects of a director's job and declares that a director must believe in an actor completely. While emphasizing the team aspects of the filmmaking process, he sees the director's function as being to provide a symbol of 'solidity, a fixed point of reference' and a 'source of energy and inspiration to everyone, actors and crew.' He also reveals that he knows a scene will hit an emotional chord when the duodenal ulcer he developed on his first picture produces an acute pain. Wajda sadly recognizes that the dream of an Eastern European cinema that could communicate to the West has come to little, to which one could add that the values of emotional intensity to which he bears witness seem a world away from contemporary Hollywood.

EMOTION PICTURES: Reflections on the Cinema
Wim Wenders (Faber & Faber)

Most of the articles in this book were written in the late 1960s, before Wenders had started making films, and it's interesting to see how the writing style anticipates his later filmmaking; he is more concerned to *describe* what he has seen than comment upon it. As a result he pronounces himself too much in love with films to be a critic and professes his distaste for those film writers to whom writing about films is an exercise of power. He closes with a poem arguing that cinema (as he understands it) and America have become incompatible terms. The culprit is television, which has so far taken over the eyes and ears of Americans that they can no longer see what is happening around them, or feel authentic emotions: 'Sham depiction of feeling – sham feeling.'

SATYAJIT RAY: The Inner Eye
Andrew Robinson (Deutsch)

As he explores the Indian director's life and career, from his early years surrounded by printing presses, and his breakthrough to European attention with his first film, *Pather Panchali*, through the projects he's made and those he hasn't – the latter including an Indian version of *Anna Karenina* proposed by David Selznick, to feature Jennifer Jones in the title rôle – Andrew Robinson reveals himself to be a writer somewhat in awe of his subject. His reluctance to engage critically with Ray's films sometimes leads to dull reading, but the book does fulfil magnificently purpose of presenting the films from both a Western and an Indian perspective. Ray is a director rooted in Bengali culture, who feels that filmmakers should only deal with cultures to which they sufficiently belong to ensure that they can offer some real insight into them. He can be grateful to have as sympathetic a biographer as Robinson.

TARKOVSKY: Cinema as Poetry
Maya Turovskaya (Faber & Faber)

Western critics have had difficulty coming to terms with the seven films of André Tarkovsky, the visionary Russian director who died four years ago. In the introduction to this collection, Ian Christie rather stupidly takes Tarkovksy to task for wishing to disassociate himself from cinema's status as popular entertainment.

Fortunately, Maya Turovskaya is more sensitive to the tension between Tarkovsky's élitist statements and desire to reach a broad audience. She writes without the hesitations and uncertainties that muddy analyses by non-Soviet critics, and provides illuminating information on the development of Tarkovsky's film scripts.

LETTERS
François Truffaut (Faber & Faber)

The frustrating thing about this collection of letters is that there aren't more of them. Covering the period from Truffaut's miscreant teenager years until shortly before his death, they offer glancing insights into his career rather than a continuous commentary. The most interesting letters illustrate the vitality of the Paris film scene during the late 1950s and early 1960s – where young cinéastes hunted down films in seedy viewing theatres, argued over the merits of directors without having their brains dunned by publicists' propaganda, talked about each other's scripts and helped each other get their films made. Truffaut's later letters offer unique testimony to a filmmaker's ongoing struggle to work through the conflict between the demands of financiers and a filmmaker's desire to address an audience, between the truth of a story and the need to structure a suspenseful narrative.

FILM DIRECTORS ON DIRECTING
John Andrew Gallagher (Praeger)

What do film directors talk about. Well when they're on the stump, hyping their latest release, it's usually the creative synergy that surrounded their production. When they're retired, their place in film history assured, they gamely accept, albeit with an air of puzzlement, the interpretations of their earnest interviewers even though they're much happier talking about the gallery of actors, studio heads and writers that they worked with. But what do they talk about when they're still working? If *Film Directors on Directing* is anything to go by, the answer is The Deal and its aftermath. How a film (finally) came about, how that one fell though and this one took its place, how it did at the box-office and how it was better received in Europe than America. Which is just as well because, when they get on to the films themselves, a lot of them talk tommy rot. Few attempt general reflections on cinema – a notable exception being François Truffaut, whose comments on the French New Wave, *auteur* theory and Howard Hawks are as illuminating as they are incisive.

MAJOR FILM DIRECTORS OF THE AMERICAN AND BRITISH CINEMA
Gene D. Phillips
(*Lehigh University Press*)

In this book Gene Phillips offers his assessment of a peculiar assortment of directors: Bryan Forbes is in but not Michael Powell; George Stevens is in but not John Ford. The brief accounts – each of his fourteen subjects gets a fifteen-page chapter – are rudimentary at best and lean heavily on quotes from the obvious sources. Seemingly its only function is to add to Phillips' list of publications and ensure his university tenure. Since its publication has done that, it seems unnecessary to read it.

A BRITISH PICTURE: AN AUTOBIOGRAPHY
Ken Russell (*Heinemann*)

Ken Russell's autobiography is like many of his films: iconoclastic, challenging and enjoyable. He eschews chronological narrative for a wide-ranging exploration, where each thought or action sparks off many others. The story shifts from the making of *Valentino* to a television contract for a film on his childhood, travelling to Southampton, the making of *Delius*, back to Southampton, early love of cinema, first sexual experiences, meetings with his mother (now ill), father and other members of his family. That's just the first chapter. His early life at home, nautical college, the army and attempts at ballet dancing are well covered and there are candid accounts of his two marriages. Three amateur films helped him to a job with the BBC and *Monitor*, setting him on the road to feature-filmmaking. But, despite accounts of the making of *Altered States* and *The Rainbow*, this is a portrait more of the man than of his films. There are a few other shortcomings. It would have been nice to have had some photographs, and there's no index. However, even those who hate his films could not fail to be captivated by this revealing, witty, honest and very readable account, which belies Russell's reputation as the *enfant terrible* of British cinema.

DAVID LEAN
Stephen M. Silverman (*Deutsch*)

'The best movie director in the world,' asserts Katharine Hepburn of David Lean in her introduction, but the succeeding text does nothing to substantiate or analyze such a claim. It comprises, rather, a chronological ramble through Lean's career, with conversational input from sundry collaborators and from the great man himself. There is no necessary reason to be snooty about a project as rigorously unacademic as this, since gossip can be revealing as well as diverting. But while some of the anecdotage casts residual light on Lean's personality and working methods, and on the oddities of filmmaking in general, a good deal of it, unfortunately, is inconsequential to an embarrassing degree. But the visual side of this coffee table publication is strong, with a strikingly well-chosen and deployed range of production stills.

THE HOLLYWOOD SYSTEM

THE GENIUS OF THE SYSTEM: HOLLYWOOD FILMMAKING IN THE STUDIO ERA
Thomas Schatz (*Simon & Schuster*)

For Thomas Schatz the canonization of the director has gone too far. The producer and the studio executive, whom he labels 'the most misunderstood and undervalued figures in Hollywood film history,' were much more important in the Hollywood studio system between the 1920s and 1950s. Through a close study of four studios and their films – Universal, Warner Bros, MGM, Selznick International Pictures – Schatz emphasizes motion picture production as a collaborative art. The importance of the director – along with many other members of the studio staff – is not denied, though even those favoured by the *auteur* theorists (Hitchcock, Capra, Ford and Hawks) are seen as dependent on producers and the system for the success of their films. This is particularly exemplified in the rôles of the *wunderkind* Irving Thalberg at MGM and David Selznick's relationship with Hitchcock. But Schatz also shows where the system failed as well as succeeded. Universal was only saved from bankruptcy by Deanna Durbin and Selznick's preoccupation with blockbusters after *Gone With the Wind* caused serious problems, even though most of his films continued to make a profit. The book is not free of errors: Junior Laemmle's rôle in *All Quiet on the Western Front* is overstated and its famous final scene was shot by Karl Freund, not Arthur Edeson. Additionally, given film's espousal of fascism, it's difficult to see how MGM's *Gabriel Over the White House* can be described as a left-wing fable. Nevertheless, Schatz's book is an important contribution to film theory and history with some valuable detailed information on production budgets. Academic in tone, it's nonetheless very readable, although a poor notes section does not help in justifying some of the author's arguments.

WRITERS IN HOLLYWOOD 1915–1951
Ian Hamilton (*Heinemann*)

Lured by handsome remuneration but disgruntled at prostituting their talent for little credit or respect, the screenwriters of Hollywood's Golden Age had an ambivalent relationship to their craft. Needing good writers to bring increasing sophistication to silent films, the studios attracted prominent authors. The advent of the talkies led to a less distinguished influx – over 800 came to Hollywood by 1931, the majority being 'struggling playwrights, ill-paid newspapermen and magazine writers.' Most were unsuccessful. This readable, but limited, study traces the trials of the writers and their films. Disappointingly, the book retells the familiar Fitzgerald, Faulkner, West and Hecht stories, with the lesser documented and, therefore, more interesting writers, such as Donald Ogden Stewart and Jules Furthman, again being sidelined. And, classic that it is, did the writing of *Citizen Kane* really have to be recounted in such detail? Inevitably, much of the talkies section examines the political lives of the writers, trotting out again the histories of the Screenwriters Guild and the HUAC hearings. Although it makes good use of Hays Office material, the book relies on already exhausted secondary sources, and most of the anecdotes are really rather stale. There are also a number of factual errors. A useful starter, perhaps, but Ian Hamilton's use of mainly standard sources and some irritating unreferenced quotations do not provide much assistance for further study.

GONE WITH THE WIND: The Definitive Illustrated History of the Book, the Movie and the Legend
Herb Bridges (*Simon & Schuster*)

THE ART OF GONE WITH THE WIND: The Making of a Legend
Judy Cameron, Paul J. Christman (*W. H. Allen*)

A CELEBRATION OF GONE WITH THE WIND
Adrian Turner (*Dragon's World*)

The writers of these books are, for the most part, people totally in thrall to *Gone With the Wind*. So obsessed is Herb Bridges with the film, on which he claims to be 'the world's leading authority', that this is now his fourth book on the subject; both Judy Cameron and Paul Christman claim 'a life-long interest'. Unsurprisingly, both of their books take it for granted that *GWTW* is a definitive masterpiece, and make no attempt to persuade those who would argue it's just another ponderous movie featuring some overblown performances. Adrian Turner, by contrast,

acknowledges that the film was 'old-fashioned on the day of its release and remains so', and makes an attempt to understand the sort of nostalgia (for another cinema and another time) that feeds the attitude to the film all too evident from the rival volumes. And whereas the focus of the others is on memorabilia (with Bridges providing the largest selection of production stills, Cameron and Christman the more striking presentation), Turner's book runs colour frame enlargements and quotes from the soundtrack alongside text about the making of the film. In thus focusing attention on the film itself, rather than the paraphernalia of its production and distribution, Turner provides much the more stimulating tome.

THE MAKING OF THE WIZARD OF OZ
Aljean Harmetz (*Pavilion*)

THE WIZARD OF OZ: The Official 50th Anniversary Pictorial History
John Fricke, Jay Scarfone, William Stillman (*Hodder & Stoughton*)

As might be expected from its title, Fricke, Scarfone and Stillman's book is angled very much at diehard *Wizard of Oz* fans, with half its pages devoted to the film's production, and the rest to its after-life – including reproductions of the publicity campaigns and merchandising materials. It even finds space for a picture that shows cast members from the Long Beach Civic Light Opera performance of 1988 posing with statues of the film characters. More interesting are the production stills from scenes that were not included in the final film – like the two weeks of footage turned in by Richard Thorpe before he was replaced by George Cukor (for three days) and then Victor Fleming. With many fewer illustrations, Aljean Harmetz provides a more considered examination of the film's production in this revised edition of her 1977 book, now published for the first time in the UK. Taking the reader through the various studio departments, she gives her account an edge through recognizing the flaws of the film and the MGM production system. Harmetz claims that the film has only acquired its present cultural status through repeated showings on TV, pointing out how little entranced were some of its early critics. The members of the Wizard of Oz Club led by John Fricke won't have any of this, and reproduce seven pages of enthusiastic reviews by way of retort. Contemporary moguls might usefully reflect upon the fact that MGM didn't show a profit on the picture for almost 20 years, even though it's been bringing in substantial money to corporate coffers ever since.

HOLLYWOOD: 50 Great Years
Jack Lodge, John Russell Taylor, Adrian Turner, Douglas Jarvis, David Castell (*Prion*)

Nostalgia blurs the edges of this foray on the history of Hollywood, which inevitably starts with the 'golden age', when cinema was 'a universal, popular art'. Although each writer argues the merits of their assigned ten-year period, the book as a whole gives the impression of continuous decline. That's because any volume that concerns itself with 'Hollywood' is bound to favour the earlier periods when the studios functioned as coherent entities, and before they became just the centre of multiple different production initiatives. The authors are so preoccupied with getting everything in that they have no space to develop a broader perspective, and the book, as a result, reads more like a list of movies than a real history.

RASPUTIN IN HOLLYWOOD
David Napley (*Weidenfeld & Nicolson*)

An engaging oddity, *Rasputin in Hollywood* tells the story of the libel case brought in 1934 by Prince Youssopouf, a leading member of the group who murdered Rasputin, against MGM, who, in the film *Rasputin the Mad Monk*, suggested that one of the reasons for the murder was that the Prince's wife had been ravaged by Rasputin. In the opening section Napley sets out the facts (as far as they can be ascertained) about the events surrounding the murder, and then moves on to an account of the film in which, though Youssoupoff and his wife are not named, they (as would later be established in court) are clearly identified. Napley is no lover of Hollywood pulp and clearly has little appreciation of the vagaries of film production. As a result his comments on *Rasputin the Mad Monk* are of little interest. But he does know about the law and his account of the trial is fun. It reads rather like those annotated reports of chess games in which the commentator, usually rather acidly, queries certain moves. That said, the game under examination is only of margical significance in either film or legal history. An enjoyable read, but no more.

MISOGYNY IN THE MOVIES: The De Palma Question
Kenneth MacKinnon
(*University of Delaware Press*)

This is an earnest book. Written with the best of intentions, it attempts to rescue Brian De Palma from the onslaughts of (mostly feminist) critics who have denounced his films for their depiction of women. Along the way Kenneth MacKinnon offers detailed and illuminating descriptions of key De Palma movies (notably *Dressed to Kill* and *Body Double*) and (more usefully) an account of recent developments within film criticism as a result of the growing influence of feminism. Finally, however, MacKinnon fails to convince, in large part because his book lacks a sense of history.

MONSTERS AND MAD SCIENTISTS: A Cultural History of the Horror Movie
Andrew Tudor (*Blackwell*)

Few books come with a more superficially offputting presentation than this history of the horror film. The graphs, charts and evolutionary trees with which Andrew Tudor peppers the text – the result of feeding some 1,000 film plots through his word processor – suggest a dry-as-dust approach that seems inappropriate to analyzing such a visceral genre. And instead of providing a continuous account of horror's development, Tudor goes through the whole thing three times – trying first for a basic typological breakdown, then looking at the principal narrative conventions, and finally breaking things down by three major sub-genres. But what Tudor gains by this process is much more than what he loses, and the book is ultimately a fascinating account of the twentieth-century's developing phobias. It's a journey from conviction that all dangers can be overcome to the contemporary condition of paranoia, where we see ourselves as 'either isolated victims of human psychosis, or doomed members of untrustworthy social institutions.' If you want to find out why Tudor thinks this may not be such a bad thing, you'll have to read the book.

CAPTURED ON FILM: The Prison Movie
Bruce Crowther (*Batsford*)

Even though their books are aimed at quite different slices of the film-buff market, some of Tudor's rigour would certainly have helped Bruce Crowther find his way through the 3,000 prison-themed American movies of the past 90 years. The chapter headings are sensible – Women in Prison, Reform School Movies, Prisoners of War in Europe, etc. – but since he doesn't do much more than provide accounts of various films, Crowther never extracts much significance from his groupings. He recognizes that what makes prison films interesting is the way they evoke our sympathy with the criminal, but he doesn't really approve, and makes only muddled attempts to link the changes in prison films to shifts in social attitudes and the prison system itself.

FILM AND THE WORKING CLASS: The Feature Film in British and American Society
Peter Stead (*Routledge*)

The title and the cover blurb, which promises a look at 'films specifically concerned with working-class conditions and struggle', are somewhat misleading. This is really a book about the intellectuals' desire for films that deal with the realities of working-class life and convey socially-progressive messages. As such, it revives the old lament that the showmen and the movie moguls have corrupted the movies with romance, fantasy, adventure and entertainment. But while some of Stead's basic assumptions may be irritating, he does provide insights into why some 'realist' films did reach a large working-class audience, focusing particularly on the rôle of such stars as Charlie Chaplin, James Cagney and Marlon Brando. And the decision to focus on both British as well as American cinema throws some useful light on the way UK filmmakers reacted to Hollywood movies.

THAT'S ALL FOLKS: The Art of Warner Bros Animation
Steve Schneider (*Henry Holt/Aurum*)

This is a book both for youngsters who discovered the magic of adventurous animation from *Who Framed Roger Rabbit*, and for oldies who chuckled through the *Merry Melodies* and *Looney Tunes* one-reelers in the cinemas. Steve Schneider lovingly traces the development of Warner Bros cartoon factory, both as a collaborative institution and as a group of creative individuals who were responsible for

some of the company's wildest and most subversive inventions – people like Tex Avery, Bob Clampett and Chuck Jones, described in an introduction by Ray Bradbury as 'gatekeepers and inmates of the grandest penal nuthouse in the world'. The book concludes with 'biographies' of Bugs Bunny, Daffy Duck, Porky Pig, Wile E. Coyote, Yosemite Sam, Speedy Gonzales and many others.

THE DAME IN THE KIMONO: Hollywood, Censorship and the Production Code from the 1920s to the 1960s
Leonard J. Leff, Jerome L. Simmons (*Weidenfeld & Nicolson*)

This is a readable and informative treatment of its subject. The first section of the book covers the years 1922-34, and the longer second section takes us from 1934, when the Production Code Administration was established under the formidable Joseph Breen, until 1966, time of 'New Hollywood' and the introduction of the ratings system. This second part is structured in the form of case histories of significant individual films, from *Dead End* to *Who's Afraid of Virginia Woolf?* There are sundry farcical asides, such as the endless wrangling over whether the word 'damn' could be uttered in *Gone With the Wind*. But the main brunt is to reflect the manner in which industrial imperatives alternately boosted and thwarted the impulse to censorship (for example, the audience downturn of the early 1950s made exhibitors reluctant to cold-shoulder the 'saucy' *The Moon Is Blue*).

VIDEO GUIDANCE

THE TIME OUT FILM GUIDE
ed. Tom Milne (*Longman*)

The size of this fat entry in the increasingly competitive film guide stakes is explained by the length of the entries, rather than their number. In fact, *The Time Out Film Guide*, covering only 9,000 films, seems something of a minnow when set beside Halliwell's 15,000 or Leonard Maltin's 18,500. It's also bested by Halliwell on credits, as it provides only the director's name and leading cast. Compensating is its inclusion of nearly all the films you'd ever want to see – giving weight to the whole range of world cinema – and entries that are mostly far more informative, zestful and interesting than you'd find anywhere outside the 2000-entry *Bloomsbury Foreign Film Guide*. The book is, in short, an invaluable volume for film buffs everywhere. It does seem dishonest, however, to claim that the pieces were written by critics 'as they emerged blinking from the preview cinema', and then to have entries rewritten

where critical judgement has changed. A description of *Chariots of Fire* as 'an overblown piece of self-congratulatory emotional manipulation' is clearly 1989 vintage, not 1982. We should have been told.

SCIENCE FICTION: The Complete Film Source Book
THE ENCYCLOPEDIA OF WESTERN MOVIES
ed. Phil Hardy (*Aurum*)

The joy of having edited a successful encyclopedia is that you'll probably get a chance to correct those irritating, but inevitable, mistakes that creep into any major undertaking. Phil Hardy has done just that for these new editions of his invaluable tomes, so that no longer does Marion Davies stand erroneously as Randolph Hearst's wife, and the place of *Reptilicus* (1962) as the first Danish science-fiction film after *Himmelskibet* (1917) is given due acknowledgement. Nevertheless, the number of corrections sent in by readers is sufficiently few to vindicate the original research. Despite the publication of various omnibus film encyclopedias since the first editions of these books, these are volumes worth having – both because of the length of the entries, and the opportunities they provide for cross-referencing across the genre. Those who have previous volumes probably won't find enough material in the Western book to justify a new purchase – even through definitions are stretched sufficiently to take in films such as *Revolution*, *Glory* and *Old Gringo* – but there are over 140 new science-fiction films to read about. Both books should attract new followers.

THE FILM HANDBOOK
Geoff Andrew (*Longman*)

With so much attention now being paid to studios, screenwriters and producers, *The Film Handbook* is a title that suggests something more all-encompassing than Geoff Andrew offers – a critical guide to some 200 directors, from D. W. Griffith to Terence Davies. That said, Andrew makes a good case for seeing most of those he includes as *auteurs*, and his apportionment of critical venom or praise has all the more force because he is so conscientious in laying out the facts about each director's work, and their place in film history. There are inevitably figures who really don't seem to belong, like Richard Attenborough; others whose entry seems premature, such as James L. Brooks, and one or two whom one feels should have been forced out because of the amount of dross they've produced since making their initial contribution to cinema history, like John Frankenheimer. The book might also have benefited from Andrew giving a clearer upfront indication of his critical position, but in general it provides a useful guide for those looking to put their film viewing in some sort of context.

THE MOVING IMAGE:
An International History of Film, Television & Video
John Wyver (*Blackwell/BFI*)

Commissioned as a read-more resource for visitors to the Museum of the Moving Image on London's South Bank, *The Moving Image* hovers smoothly over an enormous range of material and provides an invaluable primer for anyone who wants to grasp the history of image-making from its earliest days to contemporary techno-wizardry. The first chapter spans the years from the Panoramas of the 1880s to today's Imax screens, and the rest of the book, organized thematically but with some eye to chronology, has the same tendency to run away with itself – so that

television makes its appearance just after the arrival of sound in the cinema, and the film avant-garde is described just before the Hollywood studio era. John Wyver throws up interesting insights simply by showing the development of the two media in parallel. He could usefully return to the subject in a later volume, pursuing a more opinionated approach, and developing some more confident speculations on the future shape of the audiovisual world.

CALMAN AT THE MOVIES
Mel Calman (*Bodley Head*)

Cinema lover since the age of five, Mel Calman realized the movies 'were a madness and a business as well as entertainment and art' when he overheard two studio executives inflating their grosses over croissants at Cannes. This book attempts to understand the movies by interweaving short pieces from interviews with leading film personalities, commentators (and Steven Spielberg's mother) with linked cartoons. There are some insights: Frederic Raphael is told that Hollywood needs 'no brainers'; Verity Lambert on women producers at the BBC in the 1960s; Betsy Blair speaking warmly of the studios, despite having been blacklisted; Saul Bass on film titles and directing part of *Psycho*. But these are few and far between. Described as 'affectionate and funny', it is mostly the former.

HOW TO GO TO THE MOVIES:
A Guide for the Perplexed
Quentin Crisp (*Hamish Hamilton*)

Quentin Crisp loves the movies. From his childhood, when he 'saw the silent movies with silent eyes', through to the present, cinema-going has been his 'forgetting chamber', a place of fantasy where everyday life can be abandoned. The book is part meditation on movie-going (the viewer needs to go seriously, incessantly, reverently but always critically), part discussion of stardom – with some lovingly-crafted biographies of favourite actresses – part travel-writing on Hollywood and Los Angeles and, the bulk of the book, a collection of reviews first published in *Christopher Street* magazine. The wide-ranging critical pieces, focusing mainly, though not totally, on gay themes, provide incisive, witty and erudite descriptions of recent world cinema. Although Crisp finds good movies increasingly difficult to find, even the worst films have redeeming factors. There are a few total dislikes: *My Dinner with André* is 'as boring as being alive', and he finds little of merit in *The Big Chill* or *Big Top Pee Wee*. Crisp's solution to attracting movie-goers back to the cinema is not new: crushing the unions, reducing seat prices, returning to low-budget filmmaking and the double feature. Some comments may irritate but, generally, this is a pleasant, easy and, in some places, provocative read.

OUTSIDE HOLLYWOOD

BRITISH CINEMA:
The Lights That Failed
James Park (*Batsford*)

The general mediocrity of British cinema has been attributed to low budgets, poor production and national character. James Park adds a new dimension: the dismal quality of British screenwriters. A good screenplay is always important, but it is crucial for low-budget productions where script deficiencies cannot be masked with special effects, locations and stars. Goldcrest's downfall is attributed mostly to poor screenplays for *Revolution*, *The Mission* (ironically two of the most expensive films ever made by a British production company) and *Absolute Beginners*, whilst the relative success of the low-budget *Dance With a Stranger* lies in the assiduous development of the script. In a previous book, *Learning to Dream*, Park looked with a little optimism at the future of the British film. Six years later that emerging talent has either failed to materialize or been diverted into disappointing big-budget Hollywood product, and the domestic conditions for feature film production have worsened. Park proposes a new emphasis on the screenplay and the formation of script factories – salaried screenwriters working together to ensure a better production basis. A useful book, though over-ambitious in its scope, its final sections covering the last five sad years are the most valuable, and include an excellent essay on the writing of *Dance With a Stranger*.

MY INDECISION IS FINAL: The Rise and Fall of Goldcrest Films
Terry Ilott, Jake Eberts (*Faber & Faber*)

Terry Ilott opens this book by describing Goldcrest as having been for ten years a 'creative powerhouse' at the heart of the British film industry. The remaining 680 pages, written by Ilott and Jake Eberts, the company's two-time chief executive, disprove that proposition. Goldcrest put money into the script of *Chariots of Fire* and also backed such hits as *Gandhi* and *The Killing Fields*, but the creative power always came from outside: Goldcrest's expertise lay in spotting projects with potential. Eberts' departure from the company in 1983 led to internal dissensions which made it increasingly difficult for anyone at the company to make sensible decisions, let alone turn promising scripts into exciting films, and the result was a string of duds. Although the book's detailed quotations from office minutes and memoranda sometimes make for heavy reading, its ruthless inquest on a company tearing itself to pieces stands as a salutary warning for anyone else who ever thinks that good intentions will substitute for an understanding of cinema when trying to put the British film industry back together again.

THE ASIAN FILM INDUSTRY
John A. Lent (*Christopher Helm*)

This is a useful book. Moreover, coming as it does when the Asian cinema is inching its way on to the world stage, its appearance is timely. A source book, rather than a critical companion or guide, John Lent's survey is simply structured. For each of the ten areas covered, from China to Pakistan, Lent and his collaborators offer a brief historical background and (very up-to-date) notes on the contemporary scene. Some of the surveys are better (The Philippines) than others (Japan), but each contains the basic information about production, distribution, directors and local themes.

WARHOL: Film Factory
ed. Michael O'Pray (*BFI*)

It's a peculiarity of Andy Warhol's oeuvre, and much other 'conceptual' art, that people feel quite happy talking about films they haven't seen. And even those who have seen them either 'got' what he was on about, or didn't – illustrated by the fact that when Stan Brakhage viewed *Sleep* at the wrong speed he told Warhol's associates that they were working with a phoney but, after screening it at a correct 16 f.p.s. he decided that he'd seen an entirely new vision of the world. Until it's possible to make a full appraisal of Warhol's films, this will be a useful guide, with its compilation of classic pieces from the likes of Jonas Mekas, Parker Tyler and Gregory Battcock alongside recent analytical texts by Peter Wollen (on Warhol's place in the cultural ferment of 1960s New York) and Tony Rayns (on why Paul Morrissey's very different creative outlook was adopted by Warhol, resulting in such films as *Flesh*, *Trash* and *Heat*) and others.

OBITUARIES

Compiled by Trevor Willsmer

JIM BACKUS

Despite a varied career encompassing stage, radio, TV and film, it was as the voice of the mind-bogglingly short-sighted Mr Magoo that Backus will go down in screen history. The animated character, whose blustering voice was loosely based on Backus's father, made its début in UPA's 1949 short *Ragtime Bear* and proved a constant money-spinner throughout the ten-year life of the series. Backus also appeared in such films as *The Great Lover* (1949), *Pat and Mike* (1952), *Don't Bother to Knock* (1952), *Androcles and the Lion* (1952) and, most memorably, as James Dean's weak-willed father in *Rebel Without a Cause* (1955). In later years he appeared in *The Wonderful World of the Brothers Grimm* (1962), *It's a Mad Mad Mad Mad World* (1963), *Hurry Sundown* (1967) and *Myra Breckinridge* (1970) as well as the notoriously low-brow TV comedy *Gilligan's Island* (1964-6).
Died Santa Monica, 3 July 1989, aged 76

LYNN BARI (Marjorie Fisher/Bitzer)

Bari, who gave her date of birth as 1920 (although it was probably 1913) and her real name alternatively as Fisher or Bitzer, was the perennial other woman in a career dominated by B-movies. After early rôles in *Dancing Lady* (1933) and *Stand Up and Cheer* (1934), she moved to Twentieth Century-Fox, where her career received a push from parts in two Glenn Miller musicals, *Sun Valley Serenade* (1941) and *Orchestra Wives* (1942), as well as *The Bridge of San Luis Rey* (1944). The public didn't enthuse, although she continued to work on the likes of *Home Sweet Homicide* (1946), *Has Anybody Seen My Gal* (1952), *Francis Joins the WACS* (1954) and *Abbott and Costello Meet the Keystone Cops* (1955) until her retirement after *The Young Runaways* (1968).
Died Goleta, CA, 20 November 1989, in her 70s

ERIC BARKER

A successful comedy performer on radio (where he starred in one of the first radio series to dispense with the studio audience), Barker became a familiar figure to post-war British cinema-goers through his portraits of bespectacled and frequently indignant figures of bureaucracy, including C.O.s, barristers and men from the ministry, in such comedies as *Brothers in Law* (1956), *Blue Murder at St Trinians* (1958), *Carry On Sergeant* (1959) and *Heavens Above* (1963).
Died Faversham, England, 1 June 1990, aged 78

BEN BARZMAN

Canadian-born Barzman was a journalist, novelist and author of musical revues such as *Labour Pains*, *Horrorscope* and *Meet the People* before he moved to Hollywood in 1942. It was not long before the likes of *The Boy With Green Hair* (1948), written for Joseph Losey, infuriated the House Committee on UnAmerican Activities (HUAC). Whilst in London to visit Edward Dmytryk, he was summoned to the American embassy, where his passport was taken away and his citizenship revoked. He found that British producers were only too happy to take advantage of his talent and his misfortune – provided he took low fees and used a pseudonym – and he found himself working alongside such fellow exiles as Jules Dassin and Losey. For the latter he wrote such minor gems as *Blind Date* (1959) and *The Damned* (1960). These brought him to the attention of producer Samuel Bronston and director Anthony Mann, for whom he revised *El Cid* (1961) to satisfy both Charlton Heston (who demanded regular rewrites) and General Franco (who offered the Spanish Army for free if he liked the script!). By 1963 it was possible for Mann to insist that Barzman be billed under his own name for his work on *The Fall of the Roman Empire*. The film was a remarkable attempt to show the roots of the empire's collapse, with Barzman injecting notes of warm humour and humanity usually absent from the genre. Although a spectacular flop, it restored Barzman's reputation sufficiently to facilitate the return of his passport that year – upon his return to the US he was presented with a bill for nine years' back taxes. He collaborated again with Mann on *The Heroes of Telemark* (1965) and also worked on *The Blue Max* (1966). Although that film confirmed his return to the Hollywood mainstream, he retired shortly after its release.
Died Santa Monica, CA, 15 December 1989, aged 79

MADGE BELLAMY

A star of silent movies and early talkies, Bellamy made her stage début at the age of five before going on to make her first film, *Riddle Woman*, in 1920. She appeared in such prestigious pictures as *The Iron Horse* (1924) and the early talkie *White Zombie* (1931). But her career in pictures came to an abrupt end when her love life started to attract more attention than her movies: she tried to 'scare the gizards' out of a boyfriend by shooting at him, which led to a six-month suspended sentence and convinced Hollywood there were more amenable fish in the sea.
Died Upland, CA, 24 January 1990, in her 90s

IRVING BERLIN (Israel Baline)

The greatest mystery about the life of Irving Berlin is that no-one ever turned it into a movie. Like so many who eventually had a significant influence on America's musical heritage, he was born in Tsarist Russia and moved to the US as a child. There he supported his family after his father's death by singing on street corners and playing the piano by ear (he never learned to read music). His first song earned him a mere 37 cents but later efforts were to prove increasingly lucrative, and he finally hit the big time with 'Alexander's Ragtime Band' in 1911. Although many of his songs found their way into early movie musicals, it wasn't until *Top Hat* (1935) that he started to write directly for the screen, spawning a series of hits – 'Let's Face the Music and Dance' for *Follow the Fleet* (1936), 'White Christmas' for *Holiday Inn* (1942), 'A Couple of Swells' for *Easter Parade* (1948) and 'There's No Business Like Showbusiness' for *Annie Get Your Gun* (1950). So firmly entrenched in American culture did his work become that films were built around the songs themselves, leading to *Alexander's Ragtime Band* (1938), *White Christmas* (1954) and *There's No Business Like Show Business* (1954). In later years he featured in the trade press because of his refusal to sell 'Always' to Steven Spielberg for his film; even though over 100 years old, he still had 'big plans for that song.'
Died New York, 22 September 1989, aged 101

JULIET BERTO

Most commonly associated with the films of Jean-Luc Godard, Berto's upbringing as the daughter of left-wing French factory workers led to her eschewing mainstream cinema, where her looks would have guaranteed success, to work with more experimental directors. A small rôle in *Two or Three Things I Know About Her* led to more substantial work on *La Chinoise* and as an urban guerrilla in *Weekend* (all 1967). She turned in probably her best performance in *Céline and Julie Go Boating* (1974) but, after *Mr Klein* (1977) and a couple of Alain Tanner films, *Retour d'Afrique*

(1973) and *Le milieu du monde* (1974), she turned her attention to directing, with most conspicuous success on her first film, *Neige*, set among the drug traffickers of the Pigalle.
Died Paris, 10 January 1990, aged 42

MEL BLANC (Melvin Jerome Blank)

If Lon Chaney was the man of a thousand faces, Blanc could beat him double for voices – Bugs Bunny, Porky Pig, Daffy Duck, Tweetie Pie, Foghorn Leghorn, Speedy Gonzalez, Pepe Le Pew, Barney Rubble and even the engine of Jack Benny's car were just part of his repertoire. A musician and a vocalist, his talent for mimicry came into its own when the cast of a radio show was unable to reach the snow-bound studio: Blanc played all their parts perfectly and was immediately offered his own show. His vocal cords (compared by one specialist to Caruso's) were in much demand when he moved to Warner Bros in 1937, where his talent and influence soon led to an exclusive contract. It was Blanc who suggested that 'the happy rabbit' should change his 'What's cookin'?' catchphrase to 'Eh, what's up, doc?' and his name to Bugs Bunny (ironically, Blanc was allergic to carrots, so all the carrot crunching had to be left to last when recording). He played an important rôle in refining the more psychotic aspects of Bugs, Duffy and Elmer Fudd from the earlier Tex Avery cartoons – such was his dedication that he studied at a pig farm to find a more sympathetic voice for Porky. He was the first voice-over artist ever to receive a screen credit, and his 1950 song 'I Tawt I Taw a Putty Cat' became a worldwide hit. Away from Warners, he worked extensively with Jack Benny on radio and TV, voiced Woody Woodpecker for Walter Lantz (the laugh came from a noise Blanc used to make in the echoing corridors of his High School), Barney Rubble in *The Flintstones* (1960-5) and, in later years, the robot Twikki in *Buck Rogers in the 25th Century* (1978). He returned to his old ground for many TV specials, commercials and *Who Framed Roger Rabbit* (1988).
Died Los Angeles, 10 July 1989, aged 81

HENRY BRANDON

Berlin-born Brandon was one of the few German character actors not to be typecast as a Nazi on his entry to American films; instead he was typecast as an Indian, most memorably as Scar in *The Searchers* (1956). He slowly graduated from the likes of *Harem Girl* (1952) to small rôles in more prestigious efforts such as *Pony Express* (1953), *Vera Cruz* (1954), *War of the Worlds* (1953) and *Knock on Wood* (1954). He carried on working until shortly before his death, but mostly on voice-overs for commercials.
Died Hollywood, 15 February 1990, aged 77

JOHN BRIGHT

One of the many Hollywood screenwriters who got into Joe McCarthy's bad books, Bright put his early experience as a Chicago journalist during prohibition to good use when he adapted his novel *Blood and Beer* into *The Public Enemy* (1931), the film that made James Cagney one of Warner Bros' biggest stars. This led to Bright writing again for Cagney with *Taxi* (1932), *Blonde Crazy* (1931) and *The Crowd Roars* (1932). He moved on to Paramount, where he adapted *She Done Him Wrong* (1933) for Mae West. A flamboyant character, he was in thrall to fast cars, hard liquor and dangerous living. A co-founder of the Screenwriter's Guild, he was fired from MGM in 1945 for refusing to cross a picket line. Rather than help the HUAC with their enquiries, he emigrated to Mexico and became a key figure in that country's emerging film industry. When he finally returned to the US in the 1960s it was to a very different country than the one he had fled. With his style of punchy writing no longer in demand, he returned to journalism.
Died Panorama City, CA, 14 September 1989, aged 61

KARL BROWN

Brown was a lab assistant and stills photographer before a bit part in *Home Sweet Home* (1914) led to his becoming assistant to cinematographer Billy Blitzer on D. W. Griffith's films, including *Intolerance* (1917). He graduated to the post of cinematographer, and his stunning and unusual plays with light on *The Covered Wagon* (1923) gave birth to many of the Western genre's visual clichés. Brown went on to write a series of classic silent movies – *One Glorious Day*, *Ruggles of Red Gap* (1923), *Merton of the Movies* (1924) and *Pony Express*. He continued as a B-movie screenwriter well into the 1940s.
Died Woodland Hills, CA, 25 March 1990, aged 93

CAPUCINE (Germaine Lefebvre)

While working as a model in Paris, Capucine's cool, elegant looks attracted the attention of American producer Charles K. Feldman, who flew her to Hollywood for a small rôle in *Song Without End* (1960). Although initially unable to speak English, her career soon blossomed thanks to her performance as a prostitute in *Walk on the Wild Side* (1962). Most of her dramatic rôles, as in *The Seventh Dawn* (1964), were one-dimensional, and she was at her best parodying her poised screen persona in comedies, most notably in *The Pink Panther* (1963), where she played Inspector Clouseau's neurotic and unfaithful wife, and *What's New, Pussycat?* (1965). Despite appearing in *Fellini Satyricon* (1969), her career soon ran out of steam and, not long after being relegated to the romantic interest in the bizarre samurai-spaghetti Western *Red Sun* (1971), she retired. She briefly returned to the screen for *The Trial of the Pink Panther* (1983) and, like many of the film's cast, met an untimely end. She threw herself from the window of her Lausanne apartment, following a bout of depression.
Died Lausanne, 7 March 1990 aged 57

JAMES CARRERAS

Carreras revitalized his father's Exclusive Films distribution company after World War 2 and turned it, as Hammer Films, into probably the most successful British film company of all time. Originally specializing in low-budget programme fillers featuring imported Americans stars such as Robert Preston, Richard Carson, Zachary Scott and Brian Donlevy, Hammer hit a public nerve with two films based on the *Quatermass* TV series and then launched an ongoing series of gothic horrors with titles such as *The Curse of Frankenstein* (1957), *Dracula* (1958), *The Hound of the Baskervilles* (1959) and *The Mummy* (1959). In addition to a plethora of profitable sequels, the company tried out various other horror lines, diversifying into a truly bizarre series of caveman movies such as *One Million Years BC* (1966), and producing almost by accident such minor classics as *The Damned* (1960), *The Devil Rides Out* (1967) and *Blood from the Mummy's Tomb* (1972).
Died Henley-on-Thames, England, 9 June 1990, aged 81

GRAHAM CHAPMAN

Despite having one of the longest film credit lists of any member of the Monty Python team, it was generally on television that Chapman excelled. Coming from Cambridge, where he studied medicine, he worked on *At Last the 1948 Show*, *Marty* and *The Frost Report* before forming a writing partnership with John Cleese that led to *Monty Python's Flying Circus* – where he became familiar as the army officer who stopped the more bizarre sketches on the grounds that they were getting far too silly. Despite working on screenplays for *The Magic Christian*, *The Rise and Rise of Michael Rimmer*, *Doctor in Trouble* (all 1970) and the execrable *Rentadick* (1972), his only screen successes were in association with the rest of the Python team – he was co-director with Terry Gilliam of *Monty Python and the Holy Grail* (1974) and appears as the non-saviour himself in *Life of Brian* (1979). He returned to directing with the pirate spoof *Yellowbeard* (1983), but the film was a disaster of such a scale that later solo film projects had no chance of reaching fruition.
Died Maidstone, England, 4 October 1989, aged 48

IAN CHARLESON

After amassing an impressive array of theatrical credits, and making his film début in Derek Jarman's caustic *Jubilee* (1978), Charleson's mainstream screen career got off to a flying start when he played Eric Liddell, the devout Scots missionary, in *Chariots of Fire* (1981). Managing to capture the elusive essence of spiritual faith without seeming priggish, he said modestly that he only secured the part because 'there were not too many young Scottish actors who could run very fast.' The colossal success of the film seemed to promise bigger and better things; yet apart from the disappointing *Ascendancy* (1983), a portrait of one of the early followers of *Gandhi* (1983) and a cameo as a sadistic expatriate in *Greystoke* (1984), Charleson seems to have been regarded as too risky a proposition for big-screen stardom – his rôle in the homoerotic *Jubilee* being scrupulously scrubbed from his c.v. As a result, his later work was confined to TV and the stage, where his final performances as Hamlet at the National Theatre gained poignancy from the knowledge that he was dying of septicemia and AIDS.
Died London, 6 January 1990, aged 40

BETTE DAVIS
(Marion Cecilia Douras)

Few contract players can have given a studio as much trouble as Bette Davis gave Warner Bros, for whom, after a three-year false start that was only checked by an Oscar for *Dangerous* (1935) and her performance in *The Petrified Forest* (1936), she gave a string of classic performances in such melodramas as *Jezebel* (1938), *Dark Victory* (1939), *The Little Foxes* (1941) and *Now Voyager* (1942). She was suspended and sued by the studio for breaking her contract when she attempted to make a film in the UK and, on being welcomed back, gave the studio hell about any aspect of her films that met with her disapproval. She left the company in 1949 and, despite giving one of the classic displays of screen bitchery in *All About Eve* (1951), she made little of merit during the following decade. Her career received an unexpected boost from *Whatever Happened to Baby Jane?* (1962), although her on-screen conflict with co-star Joan Crawford was apparently a walk in the park compared to that which took place on the set. A series of *grand guignol* rôles followed, in films such as *Hush, Hush Sweet Charlotte* (1964), *The Nanny* (1965) and *The Anniversary* (1967). In her later years she took small parts in some unlikely films and some of her most interesting work appeared on television, although she turned in a strong character performance alongside Lilian Gish in *The Whales of August* (1987). Bizarrely, Davis was replaced by Barbara Carrera after walking off the set of her final film, *Wicked Stepmother*, by which

time the notorious chain-smoker was already battling against cancer.
Died Neuilly-sur-Seine, France, 6 October 1989, aged 81

SAMMY DAVIS JR.

When asked by a golfer for information on his handicap, Sammy Davis replied, 'I'm a short one-eyed Jewish negro, what more do you want?' Encountering extreme racism from the beginning of his career as 'silent Sam, the dancing midget' at the age of three, he had his nose broken by his fellow soldiers in the army, went on to perform as a song-and-dance man in clubs that wouldn't serve him a drink and was threatened with the loss of his second eye (he lost the first in a car crash in 1954) when he stepped out with Kim Novak. It was his stage success in *Mr Wonderful* (1956) that launched his career, winning the admiration of Frank Sinatra who secured him the lead in Otto Preminger's *Porgy and Bess* (1959). He spent much of his screen career as a member of the Rat Pack with the likes of Sinatra, Dean Martin and Peter Lawford in *Ocean's Eleven* (1960), *Sergeants Three* (1962), *Robin and the Seven Hoods* (1964) and *Cannonball Run II* (1983), as well as appearing in *Sweet Charity* (1969), *Salt and Pepper* (1968) and the deeply embarrassing *Sammy Stops the World* (1978). More of an all-round entertainer than a great actor, Davis was haunted by fears of ending up like his hero Bill 'Bojangles' Robinson, who died forgotten and in poverty. An over-generous, inveterate gambler, Davis was broke when he died of cancer; Sinatra had to pay for the funeral.
Died Beverly Hills, CA, 16 May 1990, aged 64

ANTON DIFFRING

This tall, Aryan aristocratic German was the film industry's favourite Nazi, effortlessly commuting between honourable men on the wrong side (*Reach for the Sky*, 1956) and sadistic creatures of intellect (*Operation Daybreak*, 1976). Born into one of Europe's most respected theatrical families, he became a refugee from Hitler's Germany. Following wartime internment in Canada, he worked extensively in theatre before being offered a small part in *State Secret* when he visited England in 1950. Rôles followed in *Hotel Sahara* (1951), *Albert R. N.* (1953), *I Am a Camera* (1955) and *The Man Who Could Cheat Death* (1959), as did a rare lead in *Circus of Horrors* (1960). Eventually he tired of playing Nazis and nutters (about the only sort of rôles British cinema was prepared to offer him) and, following a strong performance as one of the 'firemen' in *Fahrenheit 451* (1967), he moved to Rome in order to escape typecasting. Despite being a charismatic supporting actor with a constantly surprising range, he did undistinguished work on *Zeppelin* (1971),

Dead Pigeon on Beethoven Street (1972), *The Beat Must Die* (1974) and *Valentino* (1977). His last major performances were as the sports commentator in *Escape to Victory* (1981) and yet another military man in *The Winds of War* (1984). Needless to say, both were Nazis.
Died Chateauneuf-de-Grasse, France, 20 May 1990, aged 70

ALDO FABRIZZI

Fabrizzi's memorable performance as the martyred priest of Roberto Rossellini's *Rome, Open City* (1945) was to set the style for much of this comic actor's later work, with films such as *Vivere en pace* and *Mio figlio professore* (both 1946), and he went on to direct a neo-realist film of his own, *Emigrantes* (1949). He was cast well against type as the pompous nobleman in the following year's *Francesco, giullare di dio*, and his best rôle was to be as the policeman tracking a con-man in *Guardie e ladri* (1951). In later years he divided his time between small parts in · international films and writing cookbooks in verse.
Died Rome, 2 April 1990, aged 85

CHARLES FARRELL

Becoming manager of a vaudeville act because his father disapproved of his acting ambitions, Farrell worked his way up from extra work to small rôles in *The Cheat* and De Mille's original *The Ten Commandments* in 1923, leading to his first romantic lead opposite Madge Bellamy in *Wings of Youth* (1925). *Old Ironsides* (1926) made him a box-office star and resulted in eleven films with Janet Gaynor – notably *Seventh Heaven* (1927) – that led to their becoming America's favourite lovebirds, and the most famous couple of the 1920s. But Farrell's Boston accent hurt his career, since it seemed incompatible with his athletic good looks and, although he went on to play various character rôles, he retired in 1941, going into partnership with Ralph Bellamy to form the famous Charles Farrell Racquet Club (which was later to serve as the title and backdrop to a 1950s TV series in which he starred). In addition to serving as mayor of Palm Springs for seven years, he was instrumental in developing the land from worthless desert, and he became a multi-millionaire in the process.
Died Palm Springs, CA, 14 May 1990, aged 89

GRETA GARBO
(Greta Louisa Gustafsson)

One of the greatest Hollywood stars, both in the silent and the sound eras, Garbo's name and face are known to many who have never seen her films. She had the rare gift of seemingly doing nothing, yet expressing everything, the moment the camera was turned upon her face. A former fashion model, it was her appearance in *The Saga of Gosta Berglin* (1924) that brought her to the attention of Louis B. Mayer. Signed to MGM along with her director Mauritz Stiller, she went on to become one of the studio's leading ladies through films such as *Flesh and the Devil* (1927) and *A Woman of Affairs* (1928). She caused a sensation with her first talkie *Anna Christie* (1930), in which her husky voice perfectly matched the fatal beauty of her character, and she consolidated her reputation with *Mata Hari*, *Grand Hotel* (both 1932), *Queen Christina* (1933), *Anna Karenina* (1935), *Camille* (1936) and *Ninotchka* (1939), going on to earn the highest salary of any star on the studio lot. But the outbreak of World War 2 had a disastrous effect on her career since her movies were dependent on the now-closed European market for profitability, and the studio made a forlorn effort to turn her into an American screwball comedienne in *Two-Faced Woman* (1941). Despite frequent rumours of a comeback, she became a recluse, which only served to enhance her legend. Unlike other stars who faded or faltered in their attempts to turn back the clock, Garbo left behind a perfect image of beauty and sophistication that could not be tarnished even by the constant attention of paparazzi vying for pictures of the ageing star, or rumours that she cackled through the *Benny Hill Show* on TV while in a state of intoxication.
Died New York, 15 April 1990, aged 84

AVA GARDNER

Gardner secured an MGM contract at the age of seventeen, but the studio never quite knew what to make of her. Only after she had been lent out in 1946 for *The Killers* did she start to secure real parts. A small rôle in *The Hucksters* (1947) led to a succession of big pictures, including *One Touch of Venus* (1950), *Showboat* (1951, one of the few pictures in which she was allowed to use her southern accent) and *Mogambo* (1953), although she was possibly better employed in more outlandish films like *Pandora and the Flying Dutchman* (1951). Her strong performance in *The Barefoot Contessa* (1954) encouraged her to leave Hollywood for Spain, where it was inevitable that Samuel Bronston would rope her into an epic. Stories of her misbehaviour on the set of *55 Days in Peking* (1962) did substantial damage to her career and, following a lead rôle in *Night of the Iguana* (1964), Gardner found herself doing cameos in films such as *Mayerling* (1968) and *The Life and Times of Judge Roy Bean* (1972) and then doing time in such 1970s disaster movies as *Earthquake* (1974), *The Cassandra Crossing* (1977) and *City on Fire* (1979). When she retired to live in London, she seemed philosophical about the petering out of her career.
Died Kensington, London, 25 January 1990, aged 67

JACK GILFORD (Jacob Gellmann)

'Do you believe in the overthrow of the United States government by force and violence?' 'No, just gently.' This 1956 exchange with the HUAC earned comic actor Jack Gilford one of the last places on the blacklist. Best remembered as an elderly Jewish character player, he had been discovered by Milton Berle, who insisted he change his name to something less Jewish, and enjoyed considerable early success in the original stage productions of *The Diary of Anne Frank*, *A Funny Thing Happened on the Way to the Forum* and *Cabaret* as well as Phil Silvers' *Arrow* TV series. It was not until 1966, and the film of *A Funny Thing Happened to Me on the Way to the Forum* that his screen career got into its stride. With his comic timing and the bemused air of someone who knows the world just doesn't make any sense, he livened up *Who's Minding the Mint* (1967), explained *Catch 22* (1970) to Alan Arkin, envied George C. Scott's delusions in *The Might Be Giants* (1971) and turned down eternal life in the *Cocoon* films. His most acclaimed rôle was as Jack Lemmon's dismayed business partner in *Save the Tiger* (1973), trying to balance his sense of morality with the desperate state of the books.
Died New York, 2 June 1990, aged 81

PAULETTE GODARD
(Pauline Marion Goddard Levy)

A former child model who went on to appear in a Ziegfeld show and land every chorus girl's dream with a wealthy marriage (that quickly ended in divorce), Godard played small parts in *The Kid from Spain* (1933) and various Hal Roach films that caught the eye of Charlie Chaplin, who cast her in both *Modern Times* (1936) and *The Great Dictator* (1940), going on to become her second husband. Following her rôle in *The Women* (1939), she won a lucrative Paramount contract that made her a major star with films such as *The Cat and the Canary* (1939), *The Ghost Breakers* (1940) and a string of Cecil B. de Mille films – *Northwest Mounted Police* (1940), *Reap the Wild Wind* (1942) and *Unconquered* (1948). She also earned an Academy Award nomination for her supporting rôle in *So Proudly We Hail* (1943). After *The Diary of a Chambermaid* (1946), in which she co-starred with third husband Burgess Meredith, her career stuttered to a halt in a series of mediocre movies that reached their nadir with *Babes in Bagdad* (1952), and she gave up the screen for a final happy marriage with author Erich Maria Remarque, in whose name she posthumously donated $20 million to an American university.
Died Switzerland, 23 April 1990, aged 84

DEXTER GORDON

A famous jazz saxophonist, Gordon found the rôle of a lifetime in Bertrand Tavernier's *'Round Midnight* (1986), for which he earned a surprise Oscar nomination. Although the part of a bluesman riddled with booze and drugs was modelled on Bud Powell and Lester Young, it acted as a mirror for much of Gordon's own life. His only previous screen rôle had been as an extra in *Unchained* (1955), set in Chino Penitentiary where he was serving a sentence on a drugs charge.
Died Philadelphia, 25 April 1990, aged 67

DIMITRI DE GRUNWALD

The son of a Russian diplomat who had fled to Paris and then London after the 1917 Revolution, De Grunwald worked for a while with his more famous brother Anatole before becoming the independent producer responsible for bringing together Peter Sellers and Sophia Loren on *The Millionairess* (1960). He went on to produce a series of films, such as *Mr Topaze* (1961) and *Shalako* (1968), whose interest lay almost exclusively in the way they were financed. De Grunwald was always looking for new ways of structuring deals, most innovatively when he formed a consortium of merchant banks to distribute films – only to see it crumble three years later in the wake of the soaring budget and indifferent box-office of *Murphy's War* (1971). He tried again in 1972, forming Script Developments with Robert Bolt, Anthony Harvey and John Hopkins, which was intended to give creative talents more control over their films; it failed with its first venture, *Lady Caroline Lamb* (1972). The final straw came when his pet project, *Carnival*, about an exiled Russian musician returning to his roots, was cancelled only days before shooting was to begin. De Grunwald returned to a successful career in pharmaceuticals.
Died Hove, England, 26 May 1990, aged 76

REX HARRISON
(Reginald Carey Harrison)

Lancashire-born Harrison joined the Liverpool Repertory Company at the age of sixteen before making his London stage début six years later in 1930. It was another eight years before his success in *Heroes Don't Care* on the stage led to a film contract from Alexander Korda and *Storm in a Teacup* (1937). Harrison continued to perform on the stage while creating rôles in *The Citadel* (1938), *Night Train to Munich* (1940) and *Major Barbara* (1941) that established his persona as an aloof, arrogant and debonair character with an acid charm that was perfect for the screen but would have been intolerable in real life. His impeccable comic timing was best demonstrated in *Blithe Spirit* (1945), which secured from its author Noël Coward the compliment that 'After me, you're the best light comedian in the world.' Harrison's films declined steadily in quality during

the 1950s until his success in the Broadway show and later the film of *My Fair Lady* (1956 and 1960) helped to revive his career. This led to his participation in a series of glossy, over-priced epics where his performance was often the only reason to keep one watching. Following the death of his somewhat Shavian Julius Caesar in *Cleopatra* (1963), that film had nowhere to go, while his impatient warrior Pope in *The Agony and the Ecstasy* (1965) easily upstaged Charlton Heston's melancholy Michelangelo. But Harrison's off-screen behaviour was generally outrageous, and he added millions to the budget of *Dr Dolittle* (1967) by insisting Lerner and Lowe be hired to rewrite the score, walking out before shooting and then returning after Christopher Plummer had been paid to take his place. Apart from *My Fair Lady* (1964), which brought him his only Oscar, Harrison's 1960s films lost millions and later film rôles were not memorable – *The Prince and the Pauper* (1976), *Shalimar* (1977) and *Ashanti* (1978). On being awarded a knighthood in 1989 he was customarily ungracious, commenting: 'It's about time.'
Died New York, 16 May 1990, aged 82

JIM HENSON

Henson did more than anyone else to popularize puppetry and animatronics through his Muppet characters. Making their first appearance on the 1960s educational series *Sesame Street*, they came into their own when Henson moved to England in 1976 and received backing from Lew Grade for *The Muppet Show*, which had failed to interest a US network. The show quickly became one of the most successful in TV history, watched by an estimated 285 million viewers throughout the world. There followed three feature-film spinoffs – *The Muppet Movie* (1979), *The Great Muppet Caper* (1981) and *The Muppets Take Manhattan* (1983) – in which the mixture of guest stars and corny jokes proved only marginally less successful. Henson also developed, through his Creature Shop, such creations as Jaaba the Hut for *Return of the Jedi* (1983), the Mad Hatter in *Dreamchild* (1984) and the Teenage Mutant Ninja Turtles. He was responsible for the fantasy *The Dark Crystal* (1983), which created a completely non-human world, *Labyrinth* (1986), which he also directed, and *The Witches* (1990), which boasted a group of talking mice. He died of a bacteriological condition shortly after selling his Henson Organization to Walt Disney for an estimated $100 million.
Died New York, 16 May 1990, aged 53

JILL IRELAND

Ireland trained as a ballet dancer and it was her appearance in Powell and Presburger's *Oh Rosalinda!* (1955) which so impressed J. Arthur Rank that he signed her to a three-year contract.

Once there, he was never quite sure what to do with her, giving her sweater-girl rôles in *Hell Drivers* and *The Big Money* (both 1956). After bit parts in *Carry on Nurse* (1959) and the like, her career took a major turn in 1967, when she married Charles Bronson, and she went on to become his regular co-star 'because no other actress will work with him.' Whilst *The Streetfighter* (1975) and *From Noon Till Three* (1976) offered interesting rôles, for the most part she just stood on the sidelines as the body count rose in films such as *Violent City* (1970), *Breakheart Pass* (1976) and *Love and Bullets* (1979). She also coproduced three of Bronson's films – *Death Wish II* (1982), *The Evil That Men Do* (1984) and *Assassination* (1986). She penned two best-sellers on her fight against cancer, but the disease eventually proved terminal.
Died Malibu, CA, 18 May 1990, aged 53

GORDON JACKSON

A familiar face from British films and television, Jackson regarded acting as something of an ordeal. His professional career began more or less by accident: he was working as an engineer for Rolls Royce during the war when the BBC (for whom he had done some acting on radio) recommended him for a part in *The Foreman Went to France* (1942), which led to a series of further films – *Millions Like Us* (1943), *Pink String and Sealing Wax* (1945) and *Whisky Galore* (1949). He became a fixture in war movies as varied as *The Great Escape* (1963) and *Operation Crossbow* (1965), even playing a Nazi in *Night of the Generals* (1967). When not in uniform, the jobbing actor could be found in scores of classic movies – *Mutiny on the Bounty* (1962), *The Ipcress File*, *Those Magnificent Men in Their Flying Machines* (both 1965), *The Prime of Miss Jean Brodie* (1969) and *Scrooge* (1970). TV work in *Upstairs, Downstairs* (1970–5), as the butler Hudson, and *The Professionals* (1978) kept him in the public eye when the film rôles became more mundane – although he gave a solid performance as the gamekeeper in *The Shooting Party* (1984).
Died London, 15 January 1990, aged 66

ARTHUR KENNEDY

Despite five Oscar nominations – for *Champion* (1949), *Bright Victory* (1951), *Peyton Place* (1957) and *Some Came Running* (1958) – and a c.v. most actors would kill for, Arthur Kennedy never achieved above-the-title fame. Discovered by James Cagney and signed to a Warner Bros contract that led to rôles in *High Sierra* and *They Died With Their Boots On* (both 1941), he went on to make a huge impact on stage in *All My Sons* (1947) and *Death of a Salesman* (1948). After making the most of an underwritten part in *The Window* (1949), he moved towards charismatically cynical or violently neurotic parts,

exploiting to the full the moral ambiguity in Anthony Mann's *Bend of the River* (1952) and *The Man from Laramie* (1955), then taking strong supporting parts in *The Desperate Hours* (1955), *Elmer Gantry* (1960) and *Barabbas* (1962). His best known-rôle was probably as the cynical reporter chronicling the career of *Lawrence of Arabia* (1962), whom he describes in the film as 'a poet, a scholar and a mighty warrior . . . and also the most shameless exhibitionist since Barnum and Bayley.' Throughout the 1960s he alternated small rôles in films such as *Cheyenne Autumn* (1964) and *Nevada Smith* (1966) with more satisfying stage work. After completing *The Humanoid* in 1979 he retired to fight off cancer, briefly returning to the screen in 1989 to make *Granpa*.
Died Branford, Connecticut, 5 January 1990, aged 75

MICHAEL KLINGER

Klinger produced an erratic roster of English movies including *Get Carter* (1972), *Gold* (1974), *Shout at the Devil* (1976) and *Tomorrow Never Comes* (1978) – for the latter he audaciously took out adverts quoting the bad reviews and inviting cinema-goers to make up their own minds. 1980s projects were scuttled by the political climate (he announced a slate of Wilbur Smith adaptations to be filmed in South Africa shortly after the second Sharpeville massacre) and the precarious financial situation of his prospective backers, Cannon Productions.
Died Watford, England, 15 September 1989, aged 68

JOSEPH LaSHELLE

From early days in the Paramount laboratory, LaShelle worked his way up to assistant cameraman and then operator for Twentieth Century-Fox, before getting his first big break when Rouben Mamoulian was replaced by Otto Preminger on *Laura* (1944) and took original cinematographer Lucien Ballard away with him. Reshooting Ballard's footage, LaShelle won an Oscar for best black-and-white cinematography, marking the start of a distinguished career that led to *A Bell for Adano* (1945), *River of No Return* (1954), *Marty* (1955), *The Apartment* (1969), *Irma La Douce* (1963), *Kiss Me Stupid* (1964) and *The Fortune Cookie* (1966) as well as twelve further Oscar nominations. He managed to master the cumbersome three-camera Cinerama system for John Ford's episode of *How the West Was Won* (1962) and was to prove an adept exponent of both colour and black-and-white Cinemascope, particularly through his long association with Billy Wilder.
Died La Jolla, CA, 20 August 1989, aged 80

NAT LEVINE

Going into business as the distributor of numerous 1920s films that had been turned down by all the other studios, Levine formed Mascot Studios in 1927, taking over the old Mack Sennett lot. There he produced what was reputedly the first talkie adventure short, *King of the Congo*. As his output increased, he went into partnership with Herbert Yates, who owned the labs that printed all his films. As Republic Pictures, the company turned out a popular series of black and white quickies featuring Gene Autry and John Wayne. He retired in 1937 before rising costs and unionization drove the company into hard times.
Died Woodland Hills, CA, 6 August 1989, aged 90

GINA MANES

Best known for playing Josephine in Abel Gance's *Napoleon* (1927), Manes worked with many of the major French directors of her day, including Jean Epstein, Jacques Feyder and Germaine Dulac. A music hall, theatre and circus artiste, she came to public notice with Epstein's close-up work on *Coeur fidèle* (1923). Her most moving performance is said to have been in *Thérèse Raquin* (1928), of which no prints remain. Early talkie leads in films such as *Salto Mortale* (1931) gave way to smaller rôles before she somewhat bizarrely returned to the circus, only for an accident to keep her from all but sporadic film work until her retirement in the 1960s.
Died Toulouse, 6 September 1989, aged 96

SILVANO MANGANO

The 'pneumatic and primitive' star of *Bitter Rice* (1949), Mangano turned turn down Hollywood contracts in favour of becoming a sex goddess in Italian films and the wife of Dino De Laurentiis, with whom she spawned a veritable dynasty of Italian producers (Aurelia, Rafaella, Luigi). She was born to an Italian mother and an English father, trained as a dancer under Zhia Ruskaya before work as a model led to her winning the Miss Rome contest in 1946 and securing a series of bit parts in movies. Following her success as a rice picker interested in men, money and boogie-woogie, she worked mainly in arthouse films: the closest she came to the Hollywood mainstream was as the martyred Rachel in her husband's epic *Barabbas* (1962). She gave strong performances in films by Pasolini – including *Oedipus Rex* (1967), *Theorem* (1968) and *The Decameron* (1970) – and Visconti – she played the boy's mother in *Death in Venice* (1971) and one half of the *nouveau riche* couple in *Conversation Piece* (1975). Following the death of one of her sons she drifted away from Dino, and the couple separated in 1983. Her last major credit was *Dark Eyes* (1987).
Died Madrid, 16 December 1989, aged 59

JANE NOVAK

Between her 1915 début and her retirement in 1957, Jane Novak made some 110 films, most notably in the silent era alongside most of the great stars of the day – William S. Hart, Wallace Beery, Tom Mix, William Desmond Taylor and Richard Dix.
Died Woodland Hills, CA, 6 February 1990, aged 94

LAURENCE OLIVIER

Olivier's film work would never have won him the mantle of the greatest actor of his generation. He made his début in Germany with *The Temporary Widow* (1929), but it was not until 1935 and his romantic leads in *Fire Over England* and *The Divorce of Lady X* that he attracted attention. Following *Q Planes* (1939), he went to Hollywood, where he made an impressive Heathcliff in *Wuthering Heights* (1939) and struck just the right note of sinister superiority in *Rebecca* (1940). Returning to England to join the Fleet Air Arm, he was lent out for a small rôle in *49th Parallel* (1941) and, three years later, to direct and star in what was to be his main claim to cinematic posterity – *Henry V* (1944). Stylistically innovative and surprisingly cinematic, the film emphasized entertainment over culture and it still stands as one of the few successful attempts to bring Shakespeare to the screen. But his stilted *Hamlet* (1948) and *Richard III* (1956) failed to emulate its success and, during the 1950s, he was mostly involved in interesting failures, such as *The Prince and the Showgirl* (1957) and *The Beggar's Opera* (1953), although he did turn in a nice character study in William Wyler's *Carrie* (1952). The 1960s offered few lead rôles – although he gave skilfully underplayed performances in *Term of Trial* (1962) and *Bunny Lake Is Missing* (1965) – and he was introduced into several epic movies. He was superb as the calculating Crassus in *Spartacus* (1960) and utterly convincing as Air Marshal Dowding in *Battle of Britain* (1969), but his Mahdi in *Khartoum* (1966) owed more to Al Jolson than Islam. Soon he was playing cameos to dignify the credits of *The Shoes of the Fisherman* (1968), *Oh! What a Lovely War* (1969) and *Lady Caroline Lamb* (1974) while some of his performances veered towards ham: the subtle menace of his Nazi doctor in *Marathon Man* (1976) soon gave way to the silly voices and waving around of *Dracula* (1979), *The Jazz Singer* (1981) and *Inchon* (1982). By then he was working purely for the money, while his directors were far too much in awe of his reputation to give him direction. His final appearance was in Derek Jarman's *War Requiem* (1989) as a World War I veteran.
Died West Sussex, England, 11 July 1989, aged 82

JOHN PAYNE

A regular co-star with Alice Faye and Betty Grable, and a B-movie cowboy, John Payne's best-known rôle was as the young lawyer defending Santa Claus in *Miracle on 34th Street* (1947). After a run of musicals at Fox such as *Tin Pan Alley* (1940), *Sun Valley Serenade* (1941), *Hello Frisco Hello* (1943) and *The Dolly Sisters* (1945), he left the studio and became a movie cowboy in such low-budget gems as *Silver Lode* and *Rails into Laramie* (both 1954). He went on to star in his own Western TV series, *The Restless Gun*, from 1958–9. A car accident in 1961 put paid to his acting career, but he occasionally wrote for TV while working as a property developer.
Died Malibu, CA, 6 December 1989, aged 77

MICHAEL POWELL

A visionary British filmmaker, Canterbury-born Powell escaped a career in banking to work with Rex Ingram in Nice as stills photographer, cameraman, editor, actor, writer and assistant director. He came back to England at the beginning of the sound era and started directing quota quickies, then broke through to the mainstream with *The Edge of the World* (1937). He was signed to work for Alexander Korda, which led to his meeting with screenwriter Emeric Pressburger, and the start of a long collaboration. Having made something special out of such routine assignments as *The Spy in Black* (1938) and *Contraband* (1940), they began to find their distinctive voice with *49th Parallel* (1941), an exercise in subtle propaganda aimed at bolstering US support for Britain's war effort. Under the banner of their Archers company, Powell and Pressburger shared credits as writers-producers-directors on a whole string of subsequent classics – *One of Our Aircraft Is Missing* (1942), *The Life and Death of Colonel Blimp* (1943), *A Canterbury Tale* (1944), *I Know Where I'm Going*, *A Matter of Life and Death* (both 1945), *Black Narcissus* (1947), *The Red Shoes* (1948) – that were everything British cinema had failed to be until they came along: cinematically dazzling, thematically rich with dark, pagan undertones and an absurdist sense of humour. But stagnation set in during the 1950s with the disappointing *Gone to Earth* (1950) leading to the banal *Ill Met by Moonlight* (1957). The team split up, and Powell went on to produce his most disturbing and controversial film, *Peeping Tom* (1959). Since hailed as a classic study of the voyeuristic nature of cinema, it was savaged by the critics, barred from many cinemas and did irreparable damage to his career. Subsequent films – *The Queen's Guard* (1960), *Bluebeard's Castle* (1964), *They're a Weird Mob* (1966) and *Age of Consent* (1968) – were workmanlike and disappointing. His career underwent a critical revival during the 1970s, partly due to the enthusiasm of directors such as Martin Scorsese and Francis Ford Coppola, and the latter hired him as a technical adviser to his Zoetrope Studios, but this was not enough to enable him to direct again, although he nurtured such intriguing projects as A Wizard of Earthsea, The Tempest and The Fall of the House of Usher. In later years he worked on his memoirs and basked in critical approbation with an air of gentle bemusement.

Died Avening, Gloucestershire, 19 February 1990, aged 84

ANTHONY QUAYLE

Quayle began his career as the straight half of a music-hall act before going on to the legitimate stage in the 1930s, and it was not until after the war – during which he fought with partisans in Albania – that his screen career was launched. Small rôles in Saraband for Dead Lovers (1948) and Oh Rosalinda! (1955) led to more substantial parts in Battle of the River Plate (1956) and Ice Cold in Alex (1958), as well as prominent character rôles in The Guns of Navarone (1960), HMS Defiant (1962), Lawrence of Arabia (1962), The Fall of the Roman Empire (1964) and Operation Crossbow (1965), although few were as impressive as the sympathetic defence lawyer he played in Hitchcock's The Wrong Man (1957). He earned an Oscar nomination for his Cardinal Wolsey in Anne of the Thousand Days (1969) and began to alternate his later film work – in films such as The Eagle Has Landed (1976) and Murder by Decree (1979) – with prestigious TV miniseries such as QBVII (1974), Moses (1976) and Masada (1980). His last screen appearance was in Ermanno Olmi's The Legend of the Holy Drinker (1989).

Died London, 20 October 1989, aged 76

DAVID RAPPAPORT

The son of a Jewish taxi driver in Hackney, Rappaport stopped growing at the age of seven. He secured a PhD in psychology, but was determined to become an actor, only to find that the parts available for little people were generally grotesques or robots. Some good TV work, mainly on children's television, led to his playing the leader of the Time Bandits in 1981, but very little else. Apart from being one of the few good things in The Bride (1985), he spent most of his career on TV in a constantly frustrating career – Robin of Sherwood was cancelled after three series, Small World was pulled off because tall people patronizingly complained about it exploiting its large cast of little people, while his own US series, The Wizard, was cancelled due to low ratings. Despite an occasional rôle as the brilliant lawyer 'Mighty Mouse' on LA Law, one of the few rôles to allow him to play a human being and highlight

the problems of restricted growth in society, he frequently succumbed to depression. He died after the second of two suicide attempts.

Died LA, 2 May 1990, aged 38

BRUNELLO RONDI

Assistant director on Rossellini's Francesco, Giullare di Dio (1950) and co-writer of the same director's Europa 51 (1952), Rondi went on to become a director in his own right with films such as Il demonio (1963), Domani non siamo piu qui (1966) and Le tue mani sul mio corpo (1970) as well as co-writing Boccacio 70 (19621), Giuletta degli spiriti (1965) and Fellini Satyricon (1969). During the 1960s he taught at Rome's Centro Sperimentale and wrote a book on neo-realist cinema.

Died Rome, 7 November 1989, aged 64

FRANK ROSS

Entering the industry from the construction business as an actor in 1929, a succession of small parts led to his meeting and marrying actress Jean Arthur, and his moving into production at Hal Roach Studios, where he was associate producer of Of Mice and Men (1939). Turning independent, he produced The Devil and Miss Jones (1941) and won a special Oscar for the 1945 racial tolerance short The House I Live In (which starred a very gangly Frank Sinatra). His greatest success came with his long-cherished pet project The Robe (1953), the first CinemaScope film. Its colossal success led to an immediate sequel, Demetrius and the Gladiators (1954), as well as other prestigious, but generally dull, pictures such as The Rains of Ranchipur (1955).

Died LA, 18 February 1990, aged 85

FRANKLIN J. SCHAFFNER

Born to US missionaries in Tokyo, Schaffner graduated from television to become one of the best epic directors of the 1960s. After law studies, he found himself working as an assistant director on the March of Time series and was signed up by CBS to cover everything from baseball games to elections. Throughout the 1950s he was one of the best-known live TV drama directors with original productions of Twelve Angry Men (1954), The Caine Mutiny Court Martial (1955) and his award-winning The Defenders (1961). After a false start with the never-completed A Summer World, he broke into movies with The Stripper (1963, aka Woman of Summer), then really hit his stride with The Best Man (1964), Gore Vidal's satirical look at US politics. This led to Schaffner being chosen by Charlton Heston to direct the unusual mediaeval drama The Warlord (1965). Its box-office failure kept him out of work until The Double Man (1967) and Planet of the Apes (1968). The latter was a surprisingly successful combination of action, satire and philosophy in which his major achievement was to humanize the actors buried under complex simian make-up. Schaffner spent over a year directing his next film, *Patton* (1970), for which he won an Oscar. A less happy experience was *Nicholas and Alexandra* (1971) where Schaffner spent most of the shoot arguing with producer Sam Spiegel. That was followed by *Papillon* (1973), a relentlessly grim and cynical, yet often moving, drama about prisoners in the notorious French penal colonies. The failure of his pet project, *Islands in the Stream* (1976), was a signpost for worse times to come. His stylish direction failed to overcome the banal dialogue that ruined *The Boys from Brazil* (1978) and he suddenly found himself demoted to journeyman status with *Sphinx* (1981) and the execrable *Yes, Giorgio* (1982). *Lionheart* (1987) brought together many of those responsible for the success of *Patton*, but serious miscasting and heavy cutting rendered the film simplistic. By the time Schaffner came to direct *Welcome Home* (1989), he seemed to have become disillusioned with the whole process.

Died Santa Monica, 2 July, 1989, aged 69

BARBARA STANWYCK
(Ruby Stevens)

Her performance as the *femme fatale* of *Double Indemnity* (1944) established Barbara Stanwyck as the most callous of screen sirens, but there was much more to her than that. Holding down simultaneous contracts with Warners and Columbia during the early phase of her career, she worked for both William Wellman and Frank Capra, alternating evil, suffering and outright comic rôles. Early films such as *Baby Face* (1933), in which she sleeps her way to the top of the corporate ladder, and *The Bitter Tea of General Yen* (1932), in which she falls in love with a cruel Oriental warlord, ran into censorship problems, but performances in *The Plough and the Stars* (1936), *Stella Dallas* (1937), *Union Pacific* (1939), *Golden Boy* (both 1939), *The Lady Eve*, *Meet John Doe* and *Ball of Fire* (all 1942) contributed to her position in 1944 as the highest-paid woman in the US. Her career nosedived in the 1950s and she found herself playing alongside Ronald Reagan in the would-be classic *Cattle Queen of Montana* (1954). A five-year retirement following *Forty Guns* (1957) was ended with a small rôle as the leather-clad, lesbian bordello owner in *Walk on the Wild Side* (1962). *The Night Walker*, her final film, was made in 1965 with ex-husband Robert Taylor, but she did go on to work in television on *The Big Valley* and *The Colbys*.

Died Santa Monica, CA, 20 January 1990, aged 82

VIC TAYBACK

Best known as Mel, the cook in *Alice Doesn't Live Here Anymore* (1974) and its long-running TV spinoff, *Alice* (1976-85), for which he won two Golden Globe awards, Tayback learned his craft by taking a succession of part-time jobs to pay for acting classes, and going on to form a small theatre group, the Company of Angels, with Richard Chamberlain and Sally Kellerman. Alongside numerous stage and TV appearances, he became a familiar figure from supporting rôles in *Bullitt* (1968), *Papillon* (1974), *The Choirboys* (1977), *The Cheap Detective* (1978) and many more. More recently he provided the voice for the villainous Carface in Don Bluth's *All Dogs Go to Heaven* (1989).

Died Glendale, CA, 25 May 1990, aged 60

TERRY-THOMAS
(Thomas Terry Hoar Stevens)

Terry-Thomas was one of the first British film stars to come from television, via the successful series *How Do You View?* His stance of conspiratorial, utterly rotten but inevitably doomed self-interest was quickly put to good use in a string of British classics – *Private's Progress* (1956), *Blue Murder at St Trinians*, *Lucky Jim* (both 1957), *I'm Alright Jack* (1959) and *School for Scoundrels* (1960). He caught the eye of American and European producers, which led to his playing assorted bounders in *The Wonderful World of the Brothers Grimm* (1962), *It's a Mad Mad Mad World* (1963) and *Those Magnificent Men in Their Flying Machines* (1965). Despite being cast well against type as Jack Lemmon's butler in *How to Murder Your Wife* (1964), he generally stayed on the wrong side of fair play. Thomas was frequently troubled by illness in the 1970s and any money he made on *The Last Remake of Beau Geste* (1976) and the ghastly *Hound of the Baskervilles* (1978) was swallowed up by medical bills. Along with extreme generosity to friends, this contributed to his fortunes declining to the extent that by 1988 he was a pauper living in a south-west London flat that had been paid for by a church charity. A benefit show was put on at Drury Lane to raise money for treatment, although by then his Parkinson's disease was too far advanced for him to attend.

Died Godalming, England, 8 January 1990, aged 78

TOMMY TRINDER

Boasting the widest grin in British cinema, Trinder was one of the last music-hall stars. He first trod the boards in 1921, and regularly returned to the stage for variety shows and pantomimes. His relentless optimism and catchphrase, 'You lucky people!', became a regular feature of films produced at Ealing Studios in the 1930s and 1940s, including such comedies as *Fiddlers Three* (1944) and *Sailors Three* (1940), and also impressive wartime dramas, such as *The Bells Go Down* (1943) and *The Foreman Went to France* (1942). After playing the titular George

Leybourne in *Champagne Charlie* (1944), which invoked his music-hall persona, he appeared irregularly on the screen, generally in cameo rôles as in *Make Mine a Million* (1959) and *The Beauty Jungle* (1964). Despite enjoying considerable success with TV's *Saturday Night at the Palladium*, his later screen rôles became increasingly nondescript until he bowed out with *Barry McKenzie Holds His Own* (1974).
Died London, 10 July 1989, aged 80

ARMAND D'USSEAU

Born into a theatrical family, d'Usseau spent his early years in the business penning quickies such as *The Man Who Wouldn't Die* (1941) at RKO. However it was plays such as *Deep Are the Roots* (1945), a plea for racial tolerance with a controversial love scene, that were to bring him to the attention of HUAC in 1952. His fiery exchanges with Joe McCarthy the following year were among the most famous of the day, with d'Usseau angrily stating that he would answer any changes on neutral ground, 'but not where you have everything stacked.' The blacklist inevitably followed, although he went on working for the same studios as before, only for much less money and under someone else's name. During the 1980s he taught writing at New York University.
Died New York, 19 January 1990, aged 73

LEE VAN CLEEF

The skeletal-faced star of Italian Westerns had notched up literally scores of bit parts in films such as *High Noon* (1952), *The Beast from 20,000 Fathoms* (1954), *The Big Combo* (1955), *Gunfight at the OK Corrall* (1957) and *The Young Lions* (1958) before leaping to spaghetti stardom as the colonel in *For a Few Dollars More* (1966) and the villain of *The Good, The Bad and the Ugly* (1967). By then well into gaunt middle age, Van Cleef's cruel looks and demonic smile soon became a regular feature of late 1960s and 1970s Westerns, including lead rôles in *Sabata* (1970), *Captain Apache* (1972) and *The Magnificent Seven Ride* (both 1972). Most of his films were undistinguished, and they appeared less and less frequently in British or American cinemas.
He carried on working, however, until shortly before his death from a heart attack.
Died Oxnard, CA, 20 December 1989, aged 64

JIMMY VAN HEUSEN
(Edward Chester Babcock)

The man who took his name from a shirt label and whose music was popularized by Sinatra and Crosby was expelled from school for his first musical effort – singing an amended version of 'My Canary Has Rings Under His Eyes'. Landing a job playing the cornet on radio for $15 a week, his first break came when he offered a song to

the Dorsey brothers. This led to a series of notable collaborations with Jimmy Burke (the pair became known as the Gold Dust Twins), Johnny Mercer and Sammy Cahn, and Oscar-winning songs such as 'Moonlight Becomes You' (*The Road to Morocco*, 1942), 'All the Way' (*The Joker Is Wild*, 1957), 'My Kind of Town' (*Robin and the Seven Hoods*, 1964), and 'High Hopes', which was written for *A Hole in the Head* (1959) but went on to do service as John Kennedy's election campaign song.
Died Rancho, Mirage, CA, 6 February 1990, aged 77

MAX WALL

One of the last stars to graduate from music hall and the inventor of the original (and particularly grotesque) silly walk, Max Wall's ability to make people in the business dislike him, as well as a highly publicized private life, led to more than sixteen years of virtual unemployment after his breakthrough success as the time-and-motion man in the original London stage production of *The Pajama Game*. It was not until the 1970s that he re-emerged in the public eye, generally taking small rôles in such movies as *Jabberwocky* (1976), *The Hound of the Baskervilles* (1978) and *Hanover Street* (1979).
Died London, 22 May 1990, aged 82

JEAN WALLACE

Wife, co-star, business partner and general all-round accomplice to Cornel Wilde, Wallace had appeared in nightclubs before the start of an interesting, but not always distinguished, screen career that included *The Man on the Eiffel Tower* (1949), *Native Son* (1950) and a series of films with Wilde such as *Star of India* (1954), *Storm Fear* (1955), the amazing gangster movie *The Big Combo* (1955) and *Lancelot and Guinevere* (1963). She and Wilde were divorced in 1980.
Died Beverly Hills, CA, 14 February 1990, aged 61

LYLE WHEELER

One of Hollywood's most esteemed production designers, Wheeler was to win five Oscars as well as to receive another 24 nominations between *The Prisoner of Zenda* (1937) and *The Cardinal* (1963). Making his bow with *The Garden of Allah* (1936), he designed *A Star Is Born*, *Nothing Sacred* (both 1937), *The Adventures of Tom Sawyer* (1938) and *Intermezzo* (1939) for David O. Selznick before winning his first Academy Award for *Gone With the Wind* (1939). After *Rebecca* (1940), he moved to Fox where he was appointed supervising art director on all their films and earned four more statuettes, for *Ann and the King of Siam* (1946), *The Robe* (1953), *The King and I* (1956) and *The Diary of Anne Frank* (1959). Amongst other classics, he worked

on *My Darling Clementine* (1946), *All About Eve* (1950), *The Day the Earth Stood Still* (1951) and *Journey to the Centre of the Earth* (1959). He became a freelance in the 1960s, adapting his almost exclusively studio-shot style to outdoor work on a number of Otto Preminger pictures, such as *Advise and Consent* (1962) and *In Harm's Way* (1965) as well as *The Best Man* (1969) and *Marooned* (1969). In later years he fell on hard times and lost most of his Oscars when he couldn't pay for their storage.
Died Woodland Hills, CA, 10 January 1990, aged 84

CORNEL WILDE

Despite initially setting out to become a surgeon, Wilde became increasingly drawn to acting. When the 1940 Olympics, in which he was to have competed in the fencing team, were cancelled, his skill with a sword led to his playing the rôle of Tybalt in Olivier's disastrous Broadway production of *Romeo and Juliet* in the same year. After a performance in *The Lady With Red Hair* (1940) and a small part in *High Sierra* (1941), he found himself swashing buckles in a series of cheap and cheerful adventures, such as *A Thousand and One Nights* (1945), before an Oscar nomination for his portrayal of Chopin in *A Song to Remember* that same year made him a star. Nevertheless, his films were of variable quality, with only *The Greatest Show on Earth* (1951) and the below-the-belt thriller *The Big Combo* (1955) being at all significant. He decided to form his own production company, for which he directed an erratic slate of films, including his low-budget *Lancelot and Guinevere* (1963), the superb minimalist adventure *The Naked Prey* (1965), as well as the less interesting *Beach Red* (1967) and *No Blade of Grass* (1970).
Died LA, 15 October 1989, aged 74

CESARE ZAVATTINI

A key figure of Italian neo-realism, Zavattini was responsible for the scripts of *Shoeshine* (1946), *The Bicycle Thieves* (1948) and *Umberto D* (1951), and he went on to write over 40 other movies for such directors as René Clement, Luchino Visconti and Roberto Rossellini. A journalist and novelist, he moved into cinema in 1935 through a collaboration on the script for *Daro un milione*. He began to concentrate on film work and, in 1942, started a collaboration with Vittorio De Sica that was to span his whole career, resulting in scripts for *Miracle in Milan* (1951), *Two Women* (1961), *After the Fox* (1965), *The Garden of the Finzi-Continis* (1970) and *A Brief Vacation* (1973).
Died Rome, 13 October 1989, aged 87